The
African American
Encyclopedia

Second Edition

The

African American

Encyclopedia

Second Edition

Volume 9
Sui-Wil

Editor, First Edition
Michael W. Williams

Consulting Editor, Supplement to First Edition
Kibibi Voloria Mack

Advisory Board, Second Edition

Barbara Bair
Duke University

Carl L. Bankston III
Tulane University

David Bradley
City University of New York

Shelley Fisher Fishkin
University of Texas, Austin

Wendy Sacket
Coast College

Managing Editor, Second Edition
R. Kent Rasmussen

Marshall Cavendish
New York • London • Toronto • Sydney

Project Editor: McCrea Adams
Production Editor: Cindy Beres
Assistant Editor: Andrea Miller
Research Supervisor: Jeffry Jensen
Photograph Editor: Philip Bader
Page Layout: William Zimmerman

Marshall Cavendish Corporation
99 White Plains Road
Tarrytown, New York 10591-9001

Library of Congress Cataloging-in-Publication Data

The African American encyclopedia.—2nd ed. / managing editor, R. Kent Rasmussen.
        p. cm.
Includes bibliographical references and index.
1. Afro-Americans—Encyclopedias. I. Rasmussen, R. Kent.
E185 .A253   2001
973′.0496073′003—dc21
ISBN 0-7614-7208-8 (set)   00-031526
ISBN 0-7614-7217-7 (volume 9)   CIP

∞ This paper meets the requirements of ANSI/NISO Z39.48-1992 (R1997)
Permanence of Paper for Publications and Documents in Libraries and Archives

Contents

CONTENTS

The
African American
Encyclopedia

Second Edition

Suicide: Since the federal government began keeping statistics on suicide in 1900, the rate for African Americans consistently averaged about one-half that for whites through the early 1990's. In 1990 white suicides numbered 28,086, while black suicides totaled 2,111. Those figures represent a suicide rate of 12.7 per 100,000 white Americans, as compared with 6.6 per 100,000 African Americans. One disturbing trend is that the rate for all groups has been steadily increasing since 1945, when it was 10.5 for all Americans.

Since 1945 the suicide rate in the United States has grown steadily for all groups regardless of age, social class, or marital status, except African American WOMEN. African American women have the lowest suicide rate among all groups in American society. More than five thousand teens between the ages of thirteen and eighteen kill themselves each year in the United States, usually because of self-hate and severe depression. The most dramatic growth in the suicide rate has been in the category of individuals between the ages of twenty-five and thirty-four.

The increase in suicides among young black MEN in this age bracket has been especially high: The rate rose to 21.3 per 100,000 in 1989, almost double the level ten years before. Whites in the same age bracket still were more likely to kill themselves; their rate increased to

26.4 per 100,000. Nonetheless, suicide was the third leading cause of death for African Americans in this age group, exceeded only by murder and accidents. The same was true in the white community, but the white suicide rate continues to climb with increasing age, which is not true among blacks. Researchers have tried to discover what has led to the increase in suicide among young black men. They are also interested in learning why the suicide rate among blacks in general is so much lower than that for whites.

Causes of Suicide

A number of early theorists produced work suggesting that black suicide rates should be higher than white rates. Writing in the 1920's, for example, Lewis Wirth, a sociologist at the University of Chicago, developed what he called "anomie theory." Modeled on the work of Émile Durkheim, the great French social scientist, Wirth's idea suggested that deviant acts, such as drug addiction, murder, and suicide, resulted from the mental breakdown and rootlessness of life found in disorganized slum communities. Blacks, therefore, should have had an extremely high suicide rate. Wirth's theory, however, did not match the actual records for black suicides.

A few years after Wirth, social theorist Robert Merton developed the "strain theory" to explain behavior among disadvantaged groups. Merton traced deviant behavior to the stress, or strain, that developed among lower-class individuals who were denied equal opportunity by the majority group. These victims of prejudice, Merton theorized, turned to crime and delinquency out of frustration and anger, believing that they would never achieve success in the dominant culture. According to this theory, prevented from living full lives by the effects of discrimination, many members of minorities became drug addicts or victims of ALCOHOLISM. Some became thieves and murderers. Others directed their

Suicide Deaths per 100,000 People, 1995

Race and Sex	Age			
	5-14	*15-24*	*25-44*	*45-64*
Black males	1.1	20.6	18.9	NA
White males	1.3	24.1	26.1	23.8
Black females	NS	2.7	NA	NA
White females	0.5	3.8	6.5	7.0

Source: U.S. National Center for Health Statistics.
Note: NS = Figure too small for accurate calculation.
NA = Not available.

anger and rage outward against the cause of their distress—the white majority. Merton suggested that communities with high HOMI-CIDE rates would have low suicide rates because their people blamed someone other than themselves for their problems. Severely unhappy members of the majority, on the other hand, had no one else to blame for their failures, so they killed themselves.

Émile Durkheim's *Suicide* (1897) described four major types of suicide and suggested that rates of self-murder varied according to the strength of the family and the closeness of the community. Every society was "predisposed to contribute a definite number of voluntary deaths," he believed. Durkheim's types included the egoistic, or suicides caused by horrible conditions within families and neighborhoods.

According to Durkheim's model, life becomes absolutely meaningless in these cases, and death seems preferable to continuing the struggle. Is this a reason for the increase in young black male suicides? Durkheim's second suicide type, the altruistic, resulted from an excessive sense of self-sacrifice. For example, a person might give up his or her own life to ensure the welfare of comrades by falling on a hand grenade to absorb the full blast. This type of suicide is rare in all societies, including the African American community. A third type of suicide, the anomic, has been described by Wirth and includes individuals who do not want to live anymore because they can find no good reason for continuing. The fourth type of suicide, the fatalistic, occurs among people who feel constantly repressed and constrained by society, the police, parents, or a combination of other factors. It is the suicide of slaves and tortured individuals who believe the whole world is against them and there is no way out other than death. Death frees them from this world of enemies.

Sigmund Freud suggested that an impulse toward self-destruction is found in every human being. This death instinct makes constant war against its opposite, the life instinct, or the impulse toward survival. Suicide results from the victory of death over life. For Freud, suicide was murder in reverse. People killed themselves because they hated the world and everything in it, but they turned that loathing inward against themselves. Murderers, on the other hand, kill others because they blame others for all their troubles. According to Freud, the urge to take one's own life begins quite early and results from parental hostility and mental torture. Children are afraid to blame their mother or father for their unhappiness, so they start blaming themselves. In Freud's view, self-hatred can easily turn to extreme depression and self-murder.

Many psychologists since Freud have commented on the connection between depression and suicide. Some people cannot abide the continuing suffering that goes with a depression and free themselves from their troubles by taking their own lives. In his massive study *Black Suicide* (1968), New York City psychiatrist Herbert Hendin found depression to be a growing factor for suicide among young African Americans. Yet he also attributed the growing suicide rate among young blacks to the absence or loss of a sensitive, strong, loving, and masculine father. Fatherless households caused tremendous psychological damage, especially to boys, and that feeling of aloneness and abandonment led directly to suicide or at least contemplation of the act.

Rates of attempted suicides are virtually impossible to calculate, although most experts agree that there are at least ten attempts for every successful act of self-destruction. Among young people the ratio is much higher, possibly as many as fifty failures to one success. Hendin concluded that suicide among older African Americans, on the other hand, resulted from their failure to achieve the American Dream. The frustration and anxiety resulting from discrimination caused many to take their own lives. The high crime and POVERTY found in ghetto neighborhoods added to a sense of purposelessness and limited horizons and pushed many sensitive teenagers toward self-murder. Nevertheless, Hendin could not explain why the black suicide rate remained at half the rate for whites, and he did not speculate on the reasons for that difference. Was life twice as worthless for white people?

Reasons for the Disparity

The following theories have been offered to explain why fewer blacks commit suicide. According to one explanation, there is more community support found within black neighborhoods. Everyone is disadvantaged, so few reasons exist to be envious of one's neighbors. Unlike families in white middle-class suburbs, families in poor black neighborhoods have relatively similar incomes and amounts of property, so there is little anxiety concerning one's social status. Banding together to survive in a brutal environment may create a more intense sense of group membership among African Americans, and that feeling of solidarity reduces suicide levels.

Geography may also play a role in keeping the suicide rate at a lower level. Statistics show that for all categories, except young African American men, suicide is much more common in rural communities and suburbs than in cities. This situation may help explain the general low rate of suicide within the black population, since more African Americans live in urban areas than in the outlying suburbs or rural communities. Several reasons have been offered to explain this phenomenon. First, people are more lonely and isolated in rural areas than in city neighborhoods. On the whole, young people suffer far more from depression and boredom on farms and in small towns; they simply have fewer opportunities for human contact because people live farther away from each other. These individuals have more time to feel depressed and fewer chances

to distract themselves. As Durkheim observed, these factors increase suicide rates. Cities, on the other hand, can provide many diversions from the thought of self-destruction.

In his work *Understanding Deviance and Control* (1984), sociologist Charles Little provided a more chilling explanation of the low suicide rate in African American communities. According to Little, the high death rate for blacks as the result of murder, SUBSTANCE ABUSE and addiction, and ALCOHOLISM prevented a high suicide rate from developing. In this model, by the time blacks reached middle age, those who were most likely to turn to suicide had already been murdered or killed by their addictions.

Kevin Early, an African American sociologist, offers a less brutal answer to the question in his work *Religion and Suicide in the African-American Community* (1992). Exploring the question of why blacks have a low rate of suicide in the face of a very high level of social disorganization, Early attributes the low suicide rate to the influence of strong religious beliefs held by many African Americans and to the influence of an extended, rather than nuclear, family. White families have a mother and a father and children in the home, but often have little in the way of close ties with an EXTENDED FAMILY. Even in the most desolate neighborhoods, however, most African Americans have grandmothers, aunts, uncles, cousins, nephews, nieces, in-laws, great aunts, great-grandmothers, and many other more distant relations usually living in the immediate vicinity. There is always someone to call upon for help, and, according to Early, that assistance reduces suicide rates significantly.

RELIGION and ministers play another key role in reducing the level of suicides. Many black ministers and pastors who were interviewed by Early commented that suicide was a "white thing." Black churches have taught that struggle and pain enhance the quality of people's lives by building character. The terrible treatment suffered by blacks throughout American history showed that they could endure more hardships than whites and retain their self-respect. Life was a struggle in the ghetto, but the determination to survive the horrors of prejudice and hate offered the best means of hope for the future and for one's children. The church also gave individuals strength, a sense of identity, and a reason for living. To kill oneself was the worst crime imaginable, since it indicated that all the suffering endured by one's forebears and one's community had been for nothing.

Interestingly, Early asked the ministers why they thought churches had been less successful in the fight against drugs, crime, alcohol, and homicide than they were in their denunciation of suicide. All the ministers agreed that alcohol abuse and drug use were terrible sins, yet these acts of deviance were somewhat understandable, given the conditions of ghetto life. Given the sad state of public education in inner-city neighborhoods, a black unemployment rate twice as high as the rate in white communities, and the lack of long-term solutions for improving one's economic condition, the movement to crime, drugs, and violence was hardly surprising. The lives of drug addicts, alcoholics, and murderers were still salvageable, the ministers asserted. These individuals could learn to defeat their addictions, but only if they remained alive. Suicide ended all such hope. It represented the complete denial of African American history and culture. Self-murder rendered meaningless the tremendous suffering of all the slaves, all the victims of KU KLUX KLAN violence, and of lynch mobs, race killings, mutilations, tortures, and other humiliations suffered by blacks at the hands of whites.

Prevention

Many experts on suicide believe that the rise in the suicide rate for young black men will continue as long as life seems meaningless and without hope in inner-city ghettos. Young black men are especially at risk because many have lost their connection to their churches and families. African American women, because they have generally remained committed to their churches and believe that improved life possibilities for their children make their own suffering worthwhile, will probably continue to have a very low suicide rate. Reducing the suicide rate for young black men depends on many factors: making them feel less isolated and alone, fighting their growing dependence on alcohol and drugs, and giving them a chance for a meaningful life. Isolation and drug dependency are typical signs of depression, and studies have shown that depressed individuals are fifty times as likely to take their own lives than are other members of the general population. Many suicides can be prevented, but only by restoring hope.

—*Leslie V. Tischauser*

Suggested Readings:

Clark, Kenneth. *Dark Ghetto*. New York: Harper & Row, 1965.

Douglas, Jack D. *The Social Meanings of Suicide*. Princeton, N.J.: Princeton University Press, 1967.

Early, Kevin E. *Religion and Suicide in the African-American Community*. Westport, Conn.: Greenwood Press, 1992.

Farberow, Norman L., ed. *Suicide in Different Cultures*. Baltimore: University Park Press, 1975.

Hendin, Herbert. *Black Suicide*. New York: Basic Books, 1969.

Holinger, Paul C. *Violent Deaths in the United States: An Epidemiologic Study of Suicide, Homicide, and Accidents*. New York: Guilford Press, 1987.

Kushner, Howard I. *Self-Destruction in the Promised Land: A Psychocultural Biology of American Suicide*. New Brunswick, N.J.: Rutgers University Press, 1989.

Lester, David. *Suicide in African Americans*.

Commack, N.Y.: Nova Science Publishers, 1998.

_____. *Why People Kill Themselves: A 1990's Summary of Research Findings on Suicidal Behavior.* 3d ed. Springfield, Ill.: Charles C Thomas, 1992.

Molock, Sherry D., et al. "Suicidal Behavior Among African American College Students: A Preliminary Study." *Journal of Black Psychology* 20 (May, 1994): 234-251.

Sullivan, Leon Howard (b. October 16, 1922, Charleston, West Virginia): Religious leader and community organizer. Sullivan was educated at West Virginia State College, from which he received the B.A. degree in 1943. He attended Union Theological Seminary in 1945 and received an M.A. degree from Columbia University in 1947. Virginia Union University also granted him an honorary doctorate of divinity. Ordained a BAPTIST minister in 1941, Sullivan gained prominence as pastor of Zion Baptist Church in PHILADELPHIA, PENNSYLVANIA (1950-1988), as a community organizer, and as founder (1964) and director of the Opportunities Industrialization Centers of America, Incorporated (OIC), which became a national institution operating in one hundred cities in the United States.

Leon Howard Sullivan and Coretta Scott King address fellow passengers before beginning a flight to Ghana to attend the May, 1999, African-African American Summit. *(AP/Wide World Photos)*

Having been a part of A. Philip RAN-DOLPH's threatened march on Washington program to obtain jobs for African Americans, and having served as an aide to Adam Clayton POWELL, Jr., in his campaign for Congress, Sullivan was well prepared for the role he would play in the Philadelphia community movement which he initiated. He was the major figure behind the Philadelphia Four Hundred, an alliance of African American ministers who led a successful selective buying campaign in the early 1960's. The campaign spurned local businesses that discriminated in employment. The technique was so successful that it spread to other cities, such as ATLANTA, DETROIT, and NEW YORK. Sullivan then organized the OIC as a means of providing African Americans with the skills and training needed to fill the jobs that opened up.

Sullivan's prestige led to his selection as a member of the board of directors of General Motors in 1971. He was the first African American to participate in the direction of a U.S. automobile company at that high a level. In 1976 the Leon Howard Sullivan Chair was established in the school of social welfare at the University of Wisconsin. Sullivan received the Franklin D. Roosevelt Four Freedoms Medal in 1987. The Leon Howard Sullivan Scholarship Fund was established at Bentley College in Massachusetts in 1988.

Sullivan, Louis Wade (b. November 3, 1933, Atlanta, Georgia): Educator and government official. Shortly after he won the 1988 election, President-elect George Bush named Sullivan as U.S. secretary of health and human services, thus making him the highest-ranking African American in the BUSH ADMINISTRATION and the only African American in the cabinet. Sullivan served in the post throughout the Bush administration, from 1989 to January, 1993.

Sullivan was the younger of two sons of political activist and undertaker Walter Wade Sullivan and schoolteacher Lubirda Elizabeth Sullivan, who cofounded the NATIONAL ASSOCIATION FOR THE ADVANCEMENT OF COLORED PEOPLE. Sullivan distinguished himself at Morehouse College and graduated magna cum laude in 1954. He won a scholarship to Boston University Medical School and graduated cum laude as the only African American in the class of 1958. On completing residency at New York Hospital-Cornell Medical Center, he won a fellowship in pathology to Massachusetts General Hospital in Boston in 1960. In 1961 he obtained a research fellowship to Thorndike Memorial Laboratory at Harvard Medical School, and two years later he began an academic career as an instructor of medicine at Harvard.

From 1964 to 1966, Sullivan was assistant professor of medicine at New Jersey College of Medicine. He returned to Boston University as assistant professor and codirector of hematology at the university's medical center. He became associate professor in 1968 and full professor of medicine and physiology in 1974. He cofounded the Morehouse-affiliated medical school, which trained physicians for the rural South and urban America, where doctors were in scarce supply. As dean, he steered the program to a fully accredited four-year institution under the name of the MOREHOUSE SCHOOL OF MEDICINE, one of the only three black medical schools in the country. He led the school in researching health problems to which African Americans are especially at risk, such as SICKLE-CELL ANEMIA, HYPERTENSION, and some forms of CANCER. He also founded the National Association of Minority Medical Educators.

As secretary of health and human services, Sullivan was known as a hands-on administrator. He showed great sagacity in handling controversial issues related to abortion and the right to life, antitobacco laws, funding for the arts, and other government-funded programs.

Maxine Sullivan in 1973. *(AP/Wide World Photos)*

Sullivan, Maxine (Marietta Williams; May 13, 1911, Homestead, Pennsylvania—April 7, 1987, New York, New York): Singer. Sullivan began her musical career as a vocalist with the big band of Claude Thornhill in 1937. Her recording of the Scottish folk song "Loch Lomond" (1937) appealed to popular taste for sweet, folk music. An immediate success, it unfortunately typecast her as a singer of folk or semiclassical music.

Sullivan appeared in two Hollywood film musicals, *Going Places* (1938), in which she introduced the song "Jeepers Creepers" with Louis Armstrong, and *St. Louis Blues* (1939). She was also in the Broadway show *Swingin' the Dream* (1939), with Louis Armstrong and Benny Goodman. Sullivan performed in small jazz ensembles, most notably with saxophonist John Kirby and his combo, which specialized in low-key, quiet jazz, what has been called "chamber jazz." She married Kirby in 1938, and they starred in a radio program, *Flow Gently, Sweet Rhythm*, beginning in 1940. She eventually settled upon a solo career, singing at jazz clubs and occasionally performing on valve trombone and fluegelhorn. She was divorced from Kirby, then married Cliff Jackson in 1950.

During the 1950's, Sullivan embarked on another career, training as a nurse. She shifted her appearances to community-oriented activities, most notably services among the urban deprived. She concentrated on community service and performance in her later life but occasionally appeared at jazz clubs and jazz festivals, performing with the World's Greatest Jazz Band of Bob Haggart and Yank Lawson. She also toured the United Kingdom and was recorded by the British Broadcasting Corporation.

Summer, Donna (LaDonna Gaines; b. December 31, 1948, Boston, Massachusetts): Singer and composer. After launching a singing career from Germany, Summer became the biggest star of the 1970's disco trend in the United States. Known for long compositions with a beat-driven melody, she managed to appeal to disco, rock, and pop music fans.

Born into a family of five sisters and one brother, Summer sang in churches as a child and made her professional debut at Boston's Psychedelic Supermarket in 1967. At the age of eighteen, she landed a singing role in a production of the rock musical *Hair* in Munich, Germany. While in Europe, she also sang in the Vienna Folk Opera's version of *Porgy and Bess*, worked as a backup singer at Munich's Musicland Studios, and recorded several hit records.

Summer earned acclaim in the United States with the 1975 release of a controversial tune, "Love to Love You Baby," a seventeen-minute erotic single full of moans and heavy breathing. It became a major disco hit, ranking high on both the pop music and rhythm-and-

Donna Summer in 1980. *(AP/Wide World Photos)*

In the 1980's, Summer entered a new phase of her musical career. She abandoned her sexy, fantasy-like disco image for a devoutly Christian approach. Her first song with a born-again Christian message appeared on her 1980 album entitled *The Wanderer*. Similarly, her music moved away from the sound of disco and began to resemble more traditional forms of African American soul and pop music.

Summers, Edna White (b. September 4, 1919, Evanston, Illinois): Supervisor of Evanston, ILLINOIS. White attended Roosevelt University and the University of Wisconsin-Milwaukee before returning to settle in her hometown of Evanston. She was elected as alderman on the Evanston city council in 1968 and served until 1981. In 1974 she was employed as a social services worker for

blues charts. Soon after, Summer abandoned her high-pitched, breathy vocal style and recorded a series of top-selling hits including "I Feel Love" (1977), "MacArthur Park" (1978), "Bad Girls" (1979), and "Hot Stuff" (1979).

In 1978 Summer appeared in the disco film *Thank God It's Friday* and won a Grammy Award for her recording of "Last Dance" from the film's sound track. In the late 1970's, her duet "No More Tears (Enough Is Enough)" with singer Barbra Streisand reached number one on the pop charts. By 1982 Summer had received eight gold and two platinum albums in addition to ten gold and two platinum singles.

the state of Illinois, and she continued in this position until 1985. She became supervisor for Evanston Township in 1985, a position equivalent to MAYOR, and was the first African American woman to attain this post in the state of Illinois.

Supreme Court, U.S.: The U.S. Constitution established the Supreme Court as the highest court in the land and gave it the power of judicial review: the power to declare enactments of its coequal legislative and executive branches unconstitutional. This situation made the Supreme Court a deliberately antimajoritarian institution in the American constitutional democracy. As such, one of the Court's roles is to defend minorities against majority tyranny. Despite its countermajority character, however, the Court did not protect the rights of African Americans through most of American history. It was during the tenure of Chief Justice Earl Warren (1953-1969) that the Court played its largest role in protecting and advancing the interests of African Americans.

Until the American CIVIL WAR (1861-1865), the Supreme Court interpreted the Constitution strictly in line with its provisions allowing many states to perpetuate SLAVERY. In 1833, in *Barron v. Baltimore*, the Court upheld the common understanding that the U.S. Bill of Rights protected citizens only from the federal government and would not protect citizens, let alone African American slaves, from the actions of state governments.

The AMISTAD SLAVE REVOLT of 1839 led to an 1841 Supreme Court decision that proved to be a rare exception to the Court's prevailing tendency. The Court protected the rights of a small group of captured Africans who had risen up and commandeered the ship taking them to a life of slavery. The factual record in this case, however, was so unusual that the result offered small comfort to most African Americans.

In the infamous DRED SCOTT DECISION (*Scott v. Sandford*, 1857), the Supreme Court ruled that Dred Scott was still a slave even though he had once lived in a free state and at the time of the decision lived in a state that had a "once free, always free" legal doctrine. To reach this conclusion, the Court invalidated the 1820 MISSOURI COMPROMISE and set off widespread protests that were among the many causes of the Civil War. Chief Justice Roger Taney thought that through this decision he could end the controversy over slavery in the territories by having the Court come

down decisively on the side of slavery, but he seriously misjudged the character of opinion in the North.

Post-Civil War Rulings

In the wake of the Civil War, the U.S. Constitution was modified by three amendments that attempted to change the document so that African Americans would be protected in the future. Slavery was abolished by the THIRTEENTH AMENDMENT, equal citizenship status was promoted by the FOURTEENTH AMENDMENT, and the right to vote was protected by the FIFTEENTH AMENDMENT. Unfortunately, many parts of these three amendments were interpreted so narrowly by the Supreme Court that their promise of fair treatment for African Americans was largely not upheld.

On the face of the Fourteenth Amendment, adopted in 1868, all persons born or naturalized in the United States were citizens of the United States and of the state in which they

Chief Justice Roger Taney, author of the notorious Dred Scott decision. *(Library of Congress)*

lived. The amendment thereby created a simultaneous citizenship for all African Americans born in the United States. African Americans were granted the "privileges and immunities" given to all American citizens, and they were guaranteed due process of law and equal protection of law by state governments.

Yet despite this seemingly clear assertion of the equal citizenship of African Americans throughout the United States, the Supreme Court rendered several decisions emasculating the Fourteenth Amendment and denying African Americans significant equal rights.

In the *Slaughterhouse Cases* (1873), the Supreme Court interpreted the Fourteenth Amendment in such a way that it provided little protection for individuals from adverse actions by their state and local governments. The *Slaughterhouse Cases* ruled that white citizens could not seek protection under the Fourteenth Amendment, since the amendment had been passed to advance the interests of African Americans. While this ruling might be thought to be superficially favorable to African Americans, the Court made the Fourteenth Amendment much less important throughout America, at least until the mid-twentieth century.

In the case of PLESSY V. FERGUSON (1896), the Supreme Court further diminished the impact of the Fourteenth Amendment by ruling that states were in compliance with the amendment's equal protection clause if they provided SEPARATE BUT EQUAL facilities for African Americans. In reality, the separate facilities provided by southern states were never truly equal. The Supreme Court, reflecting the white consensus of the day, refused to take any significant steps to guarantee equality for African Americans. The long period of segregation that was legally upheld by *Plessy v. Ferguson* was most severe in southern states but occurred in various forms even in northern states where slavery had never existed.

As for the Fifteenth Amendment's protection of voting rights, the effects of litigation were similarly adverse to African American interests. Blacks were virtually shut out of political participation in the South, both as candidates and as VOTERS. The Supreme Court essentially accepted the southern states' arguments that primary elections were private, nongovernmental institutions that could restrict participation to whites. African Americans were thus shut out of the nomination process. Since the white-only primaries were used in areas in which the DEMOCRATIC PARTY was so dominant that nomination was tantamount to election, African Americans could not even get their names on the ballot. Upon election, the southern white victors passed a broad series of laws restricting African American civil and political rights, further worsening the legal and political situation of African Americans.

Twentieth-Century Developments

The long period of segregation and JIM CROW LAWS ended only as a result of the CIVIL RIGHTS struggle in the middle of the twentieth century. The Civil Rights movement did not emerge full-blown in the 1960's; a gradual, tentative movement in the direction of protecting African American rights had begun before then. The process of restoring the Fourteenth Amendment began with the concept of selective incorporation. This is the notion that certain values in U.S. Constitution's Bill of Rights are so fundamental to the due process clause of the Fourteenth Amendment that states are legally bound to make these provisions available to all their citizens, including African Americans.

Not all elements of the U.S. Bill of Rights qualified, but gradually—from the 1890's through the 1960's—an increasing number of values in the Bill of Rights were found to be so fundamental that they were incorporated by way of the due process and equal protection causes and applied to the states. By the end of the 1960's, a substantial portion of the Bill of Rights had been incorporated via the Fourteenth Amendment and applied to the states. This broad trend benefited all citizens as individuals and helped African Americans along with everyone else.

Regarding the Fifteenth Amendment, in SMITH V. ALLWRIGHT (1944), the Supreme Court ruled against the all-white primary. This decision finally ended the specious idea that primary elections are merely the nongovernment activities of private groups.

RESTRICTIVE COVENANTS, agreements that fostered segregated housing patterns, were declared constitutional but judicially unenforceable in SHELLEY V. KRAEMER (1948), and the separate but equal principle was used to attack the provisions of segregated law schools and other professional schools in various states before 1954.

Most significant for African Americans were a series of decisions up to and including the 1954 BROWN V. BOARD OF EDUCATION decision that gradually restored the meaning of the Fourteenth Amendment and protected African Americans from actions of their state governments. The critical role of *Brown* was in overturning the "separate but equal" doctrine of *Plessy v. Ferguson*. The *Brown* holding that separate facilities were inherently unequal for psychological reasons was a major blow to segregation and a major step forward for African Americans. Yet it is possible to overstate the impact of the Supreme Court on education. For example, for a full decade following the *Brown* decision against segregated school systems, only about 1 percent of African Americans were in integrated public schools, while the remaining 99 percent were still in segregated facilities.

Even when Supreme Court decisions favored African American civil rights, the passive character and limited power of the Court meant that the Court in and of itself was inade-

Earl Warren, the chief justice of the United States, pushed the Court to rule unanimously in *Brown v. Board of Education*. (*Supreme Court Historical Society*)

quate to the task of ending segregation. The Supreme Court has little direct power to enforce its decisions and must depend on the executive and legislative branches to do so. In 1957 the Court depended on President Dwight D. Eisenhower to enforce its decree with federal troops when a Little Rock, Arkansas, high school was integrated during the LITTLE ROCK CRISIS. Only with the passage of major legislation such as the Civil Rights Act of 1964 and the VOTING RIGHTS ACT OF 1965 could major gains for African Americans be achieved.

The Supreme Court also must depend on its ability to lead public opinion. Once public opinion moved Congress to pass the 1960's civil rights legislation, then the Court could support integration more fully. In the 1960's and early 1970's, the Court attempted to promote integration, going so far as to require mandatory school BUSING to integrate some formerly segregated school districts. The

When Thurgood Marshall (standing at right) joined the Warren court in 1967, he became its first nonwhite justice. *(Collection of the Supreme Court of the United States)*

Court ordered the redrawing of district lines and compulsory busing of African American minority students into majority white schools and vice versa. This approach proved unpopular, sometimes even among African Americans. Eventually, public opinion soured on such forcible approaches to integration. Moreover, new appointments to the Supreme Court led to ideological changes in the Court's composition, and the Court was unwilling to mandate further busing.

Under Chief Justices Warren Burger (1969-1987) and William Rehnquist (1987-   ) the Court resisted making further advances for African American and even rolled back some earlier rulings. In GRIGGS V. DUKE POWER COMPANY (1971), the Court had strengthened AFFIRMATIVE ACTION by requiring business to stop policies as discrimination if the effect, not merely the intent, of the policy led to a harmful result. In *Wards Cove Packing Company v. Atonio* (1989), the Rehnquist Court reversed *Griggs v. Duke Power Company*, and in *Patterson v. McLean Credit Union* (1989) the Court limited suits alleging discrimination by declaring that discrimination considered illegal in hiring was not necessarily illegal within employ-

ment. The Court did not carry public opinion with it regarding these issues, and Congress passed the 1991 amendments to the Civil Rights Act to overturn the *Wards Cove* and *Patterson* decisions.

The Impact of Reapportionment

The Supreme Court's decision in BAKER V. CARR (1962) had unintended positive consequences for African Americans. Here the Court declared that legislative redistricting was no longer to be considered a "political question" and so could be the subject of judicial determination.

Following *Baker v. Carr*, the Court decided a series of cases in such a way that legislatures were virtually compelled to use single-member, single-election districts for all legislative districts. Such districts significantly improve the chances for many otherwise unelectable minority individuals to succeed better than they could under most other election systems. These decisions helped a growing number of African Americans to enter the arena of electoral politics directly.

Following the passage of the Voting Rights Act of 1965, which took strong measures to promote voting by African Americans in southern states, African Americans began to win election to a wide range of federal, state, and local government positions. While the percentage of African Americans holding public office still lags behind their percentage in the population generally, the percentage elected is growing closer with the passage of time. The number of African Americans holding public office was about forty in 1960 but more than eight thousand by the mid-1990's. In the 1990's, the Supreme Court affected the growth of potential African American office-holders by expressing reservations over the practice of drawing House of Representative and state legislative district lines to carve out extremely contorted districts with significant African American populations specifically to increase the number of African Americans who are elected.

—*Richard L. Wilson*

See also: Civil rights and congressional legislation; Constitution, U.S.; Marshall, Thurgood; Politics and government; Segregation and integration; Thomas, Clarence.

Suggested Readings:

Abraham, Henry J., and Barbara A. Perry. *Freedom and the Court.* 6th ed. New York: Oxford University Press, 1994.

Berger, Raoul. *The Fourteenth Amendment and the Bill of Rights.* Norman: University of Oklahoma Press, 1989.

Fiscus, Ronald J. *The Constitutional Logic of Affirmative Action.* Durham, N.C.: Duke University Press, 1992.

Ginger, Ann F. *The Law, the Supreme Court and the People's Rights.* Rev. ed. Woodbury, N.Y.: Barron's, 1977.

Horowitz, Morton. *The Transformation of American Law.* 2 vols. New York: Oxford University Press, 1992.

Howard, John R. *The Shifting Wind: The Supreme Court and Civil Rights from Reconstruction to Brown.* Albany: State University of New York Press, 1999.

Kluger, Richard. *Simple Justice: The History of Brown v. Board of Education and Black America's Struggle for Equality.* New York: Vintage, 1976.

Schwartz, Bernard, and Alan M. Dershowitz.

The Rehnquist court in 1994: Seated, left to right: Antonin Scalia, John Paul Stevens, Chief Justice William H. Rehnquist, Sandra Day O'Connor, Anthony Kennedy; standing: Ruth Bader Ginsburg, David Souter, Clarence Thomas, Stephen Breyer.

Behind Bakke: Affirmative Action and the Supreme Court. Rev. ed. New York: Notable Trials Library, 1995.

Thomas, Brook, ed. *Plessy v. Ferguson: A Brief History with Documents.* Boston: Bedford Books, 1997.

Tushnet, Mark V. *Making Civil Rights Law: Thurgood Marshall and the Supreme Court, 1936-1961.* New York: Oxford University Press, 1994.

Supremes: Most successful of the "girl groups" in soul/rhythm-and-blues music in the 1960's and 1970's. The DETROIT teenagers from the Brewster-Douglass housing project first sang as the Primettes, taking their name from the Primes, who evolved into the Temptations. The girls signed with MOTOWN Records in 1961. Florence Ballard, Diana Ross, and Mary Wilson then changed the name of their group to the Supremes.

The Supremes' recording career started slowly, and none of the early records was a real hit. In 1963 Motown paired the group with the writing and producing team of Holland-Dozier-Holland. The Supremes' career took off with the release of "When the Lovelight Starts Shining Through His Eyes" in 1963. In 1964 and 1965, the group established itself at the top of American popular music with five straight number-one hits: "Where Did Our Love Go," "Baby Love," "Come See About Me," "Stop! In the Name of Love," and "Back in My Arms Again." Three more number-one releases followed in 1966 and 1967: "You Can't Hurry Love," "You Keep me Hangin' On," and "Love Is Here and Now You're Gone." In 1967 Ballard left the group and was replaced by Cindy Birdsong. Number-one songs continued, including "The Happening" (1967), "Love Child" (1968), and "Someday We'll Be Together" (1969).

Lead singer Diana Ross attracted increased attention, and in 1967 the trio was renamed Diana Ross and the Supremes. In 1970 Ross left the group for good to pursue a successful singing and acting career. She was replaced by Jean Terrell. The Supremes continued to record with some success into the late 1970's.

At their peak, the Supremes were the most successful American singing group of their day. Their success could be attributed to Holland-Dozier-Holland's producing style, which provided

The Supremes: Diana Ross (left), Cindy Birdsong (right rear), and Mary Wilson (right front). *(Motown Records)*

lush instrumental backgrounds, and the compatibility of the group with Ross's high lead voice. Usually sheathed in long gowns, the Supremes were less choreographed than other Motown groups, depending on coordinated hand and arm motions for visual effect. Efforts by the group to cross over into other areas of music were not very successful. The 1981 Broadway show *Dreamgirls* is based on the Supremes' story. After numerous personnel changes, the group dissolved in 1976.

Sutton, Percy Ellis (b. November 24, 1920, San Antonio, Texas): New York politician. Sutton became a major participant in NEW YORK CITY politics when he was elected president of the borough of Manhattan in 1966. As borough president (until 1977), Sutton had two votes on the city's Board of Estimate, which allocates funds for municipal departments and services. This position made Sutton one of the most influential black people in the United States. Sutton, an attorney, also served in the New York State Assembly.

Sutton, as a practicing attorney following his release from the U.S. Air Force, was involved actively in civil rights cases. Much of this was done in collaboration with the NATIONAL ASSOCIATION FOR THE ADVANCEMENT OF COLORED PEOPLE (NAACP). Sutton was director of the New York branch of the NAACP in 1961 and 1962. He received some of his experience with United States laws in the area of civil rights through his position as a trial advo-

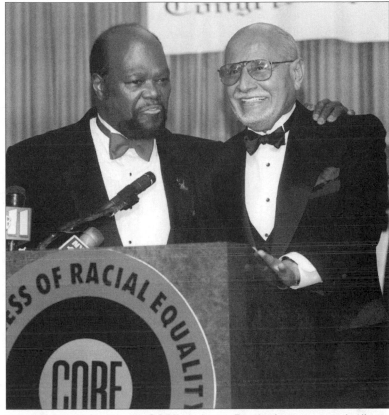

Percy E. Sutton (right) with CORE chairman Roy Innis at an awards dinner in early 1999. *(AP/Wide World Photos)*

cate judge in the U.S. Air Force.

During his brief tenure as a state assemblyman (1964-1966), Sutton organized other African American representatives into a bloc that won them membership on major committees. His organizational abilities and political knowledge served Sutton well in his capacity as borough president. As borough president, Sutton drew attention to urban problems and directed efforts to solve them. He also increased citizen participation in government. Sutton was a believer in citizens using the system to advance their interests. For example, in 1963 he formed, along with Charles Rangel, the Harlem Democratic Club (later the Martin Luther King, Jr., Club), which has hundreds of volunteer workers.

Following his tenure as borough president, Sutton devoted his energies to the media business. Sutton understood the power of media to advance the interests and well-being of African Americans. Sutton formed groups that purchased the AMSTERDAM NEWS, an African American newspaper. In 1977 Sutton became owner and chairman of the board of the Inner-City Broadcasting Company, which owns radio stations throughout the country.

Swain v. Alabama: U.S. SUPREME COURT discrimination case in 1964. Robert Swain, accused of rape in Talladega County, ALABAMA, argued that he was denied the rights granted him by the equal protection clause of the FOURTEENTH AMENDMENT because he had been tried by an all-white jury. He further claimed that the unrestricted power of attorneys to reject potential jurors was unfairly used to strike names of African Americans from the jury list. Although African Americans comprised 26 percent of those eligible for jury duty, none had served in recent years.

The state argued that the attorneys were not acting as officers of the state so they could not be prosecuted for discrimination by a federal court. The right of attorneys to reject whomever they wish for jury duty, even on the basis of race, was upheld by the Court, with two justices dissenting. However, in 1986, the decision was reversed in *Batson v. Kentucky*.

—*Rose Secrest*

See also: Jury selection.

Swann v. Charlotte-Mecklenburg Board of Education: U.S. SUPREME COURT school desegregation case in 1971. This case was filed in 1965 on behalf of James Swann, a six-year-old child who was denied admission to a predominantly white school located near his North Carolina home, and several other families. At the time the case began, fewer than 3 percent of the black children in the Charlotte-Mecklenburg school district were attending school with white children. Though the school district was operating under a "freedom of choice" plan, neighborhood segregation resulted in school segregation. The goal of the lawsuit was to have the court dictate that the school board end segregation in the district.

Swann v. Charlotte-Mecklenburg Board of Education spent several years in lower courts before reaching the Supreme Court. The results of the earlier cases were mixed. The plaintiffs' claims were denied until 1969, when a federal district judge decided that the school district was not meeting the requirements of a recently decided Supreme Court case, GREEN V. COUNTY SCHOOL BOARD OF NEW KENT COUNTY (1968), which stated that school boards must take whatever steps were necessary to end segregation immediately. The judge ordered that the attendance zones for secondary schools in the Charlotte-Mecklenburg district be redrawn and that elementary schools be grouped together for the exchange of students. The order called for the use of BUSING (busing children to schools other than their neighborhood schools) to accomplish the latter. This decision was appealed by the school board to the U.S. Court of Appeals for the Fourth Circuit, which affirmed the order for secondary schools but vacated the order for elementary schools.

In 1970 the U.S. Supreme Court agreed to hear the case, and it found in favor of the plaintiffs. The Court stated that school boards were to make every effort to desegregate schools to the highest degree possible. Busing was deemed to be a satisfactory solution. This case set the stage for future desegregation cases. School systems could be asked to take affirmative steps to end segregation regardless of whether the segregation was intentional. School segregation that was the result of neighborhood segregation would no longer be permitted, and busing students away from their neighborhood schools was viewed as an acceptable method of ending segregation.

By the end of the 1990's, many school systems in the country had ended their busing programs. Among them was the Charlotte-Mecklenburg district; in 1999 a federal judge ordered an end to the district's forced busing program, deciding that it had served its purpose and was no longer appropriate.

—Amy J. Orr

See also: Segregation and integration.

Sweatt v. Painter: U.S. SUPREME COURT discrimination case decided in 1950. Herman Sweatt was denied admission to the state-supported University of Texas Law School solely on the basis of race. He was offered, but refused, enrollment in a separate law school es-

Herman Sweatt, whose struggle to gain admittance to the University of Texas Law School led to a Supreme Court decision that struck another blow against segregation. *(Library of Congress)*

tablished for African Americans. A Texas court found that the separate law school was "substantially equivalent." The U.S. Supreme Court disagreed and reversed the state court's decision. Chief Justice Fred M. Vinson said the Supreme Court could not find "substantial equality" between the two schools. In both tangible and intangible factors, he wrote, the University of Texas Law School was superior. Unlike the black school, the whites-only school possessed "those qualities which are incapable of objective measurement but which make for greatness in a law school." The Court concluded that the equal protection clause of the FOURTEENTH AMENDMENT required that Sweatt be admitted.

Although this case did not overturn the "SEPARATE BUT EQUAL" provision of PLESSY V. FERGUSON (1896), it helped pave the way for the historic BROWN V. BOARD OF EDUCATION case four years later, which did.

—Raymond Frey

Syphilis: A sexually transmitted disease caused by a spiral-shaped organism called *Treponema pallidum*. Most medical historians contend that syphilis was not introduced to Europe until the fifteenth century, when Columbus's men returned with it from the New World. Some diagnoses of leprosy prior to that time, however, may have been misdiagnoses of syphilis. Whatever its origins, this disease has been a source of morbidity and mortality for many Americans. According to some authorities, African Americans have been at greater risk for the disease than other ethnic groups.

From the 1860's to the 1890's, physicians often attributed poor health among blacks to syphilis, although no studies were undertaken to determine the actual rate. Most agreed that through education, African Americans could reduce the incidence of the disease and more could lead healthy lives. By the beginning of the twentieth century, however, as race relations deteriorated throughout the United States, members of the medical community were more likely to believe that black people were more susceptible to syphilis than others as a result of their supposed immorality. Syphilis became perceived as an African American disease that the race had brought upon itself.

As with many serious diseases, medicine eventually gave physicians the means to control syphilis. In 1905 scientists identified the organism that causes the disease. Later, laboratory tests were developed to diagnose the disorder, and an array of drugs was used to combat it. All segments of the population benefited.

In 1932 the U.S. Public Health Service undertook an infamous and inhumane study of the effects of untreated syphilis. Using approximately three hundred black male residents of Macon County, Alabama, as human guinea pigs, researchers studied morbidity and mortality among untreated syphilis victims. During the course of the TUSKEGEE EXPERIMENTS, or the Tuskegee study, as they came to be known, the subjects who were in the later stages of the disease received no drug therapies. As one historian of medicine stated, the study was nontherapeutic and simply examined the course of untreated syphilis among black men.

By the 1980's, the incidence of syphilis had declined among all segments of the American population, an indication that the disease could be controlled successfully among all ethnic groups. According to some data, a resurgence of syphilis appeared to be under way in the United States around 1987. This apparent increase, however, might well be attributable to better reporting and a raised consciousness level regarding all sexually transmitted diseases during the era of the ACQUIRED IMMUNODEFICIENCY SYNDROME (AIDS) epidemic.

T

Talented Tenth: Concept articulated in the early twentieth century by W. E. B. Du Bois that the most capable one-tenth of African Americans should be given higher education and leadership training and accept responsibility for the economic and cultural elevation of all African Americans. Du Bois feared an overemphasis on the industrial education advocated by Booker T. Washington, believing that African Americans should be trained as teachers and professionals rather than solely as industrial workers. The phrase "Talented Tenth" was first used in print in 1903.

Advocates of the concept of the "talented tenth" argued that more African Americans should be trained as teachers. *(Martha McBride/Unicorn Stock Photos)*

Tampa Red (Hudson Woodbridge; December 25, 1900, Smithville, Georgia—March 19, 1981, Chicago, Illinois): BLUES guitarist. Still in his youth when orphaned, Woodbridge moved to Tampa, FLORIDA, to live with his maternal grandmother. He also took his mother's family name, Whittaker, but would soon be dubbed "Tampa Red" for his red hair and for the city where he spent his younger years. A self-taught slide guitarist, Tampa Red began to play in juke joints and honky-tonks up and down the Florida Gulf Coast in the early 1920's.

Around 1925, Tampa Red moved to CHICAGO, ILLINOIS, where he would spend the rest of his life. In his early days in Chicago, Tampa Red sang and played on the streets when he could not secure club work. By 1928 he had made his first recordings, on the Paramount label. He did some solo recording but also played as part of the Hokum Boys (with Thomas A. "Georgia Tom" DORSEY) and with Ma RAINEY, Madlyn Davis, Victoria Spivey, and others. One recording with Dorsey for the Vocalion label, "Tight Like That," was a major hit. Over the next four years, Tampa Red and Georgia Tom worked together, playing all manner of small engagements in the Chicago area, including work at juke joints, dance halls, rent parties, and vaudeville theaters.

By the early 1930's, Tampa Red was fronting his own band, the Chicago Five, and had moved to the Bluebird label after having made numerous recordings with Paramount and the Vocalion/ARC label group. Throughout the rest of the decade and into the early 1940's, Tampa Red worked at various Chicago nightclubs (especially the C & T Club) solo, and with Big Bill BROONZY, Big Maceo, and others. The popularity of Tampa Red's brand of music—

acoustic slide guitar—had begun to decline, however, with the discovery of the electric guitar by Chicago bluesmen. Following a stint in Gary, Indiana, working local clubs with Sunnyland Slim, Tampa Red returned to his usual round of club dates in Chicago, working places such as the Zanzibar, Sylvio's, the 708 Club, and the Peacock Lounge, while continuing to record, now with the Victor label.

After the death of his wife, Francis, in 1953, Tampa Red's involvement with music withered as he struggled with alcoholism. He was hospitalized frequently for treatment of the disease in the latter half of the 1950's. Tampa Red did, however, record on the Prestige-Bluesville label in 1960 and worked sporadically through the 1960's. He finally retired to a Chicago nursing home in 1974, having won a secure place in the annals of blues music.

Tanner, Henry Ossawa (June 21, 1859, Pittsburgh, Pennsylvania—May 25, 1937, Etaples, France): Painter. Tanner is one of the most important and renowned modern African American artists. His paintings include landscapes, seascapes, biblical figures, and studies of African Americans. His works have been acclaimed for their experimentations with light and color and for the fresh, nonstereotypical representations of African Americans. He was the first African American in the National Academy of Design.

Tanner's father, Benjamin Tucker Tanner, was made a bishop of the AFRICAN METHODIST EPISCOPAL CHURCH in 1888; his mother was a former slave who conducted a school in the family's home in Pittsburgh. One of the most important developments in Tanner's early life was his family's move to PHILADELPHIA in 1866. It was there that Tanner became interested in becoming an artist, after watching a landscape painter at work in Fairmont Park. His interest was deepened after he read an article about America's need for painters of

The paintings of Henry Ossawa Tanner are noted for their nonstereotypical representations of African Americans. *(Associated Publishers, Inc.)*

seascapes. He became less interested in this genre and by age thirteen turned his talents to painting animals. This wide-ranging interest in different genres later would be reflected by various phases of Tanner's adult career.

Although Tanner's parents discouraged him from pursuing a career as a painter—his father wanted him to be a minister—in 1880 he began one of the most important episodes of his life, studying at the Pennsylvania Academy of the Fine Arts, where he was the only African American student and where his teacher was the important American artist Thomas Eakins. After leaving the academy in 1882, Tanner struggled to make his career, exhibiting his works and infrequently selling them.

The next major event in Tanner's life came in 1891, when he went to France to study painting. Tanner would spend most of the rest of his life in France. The period of the early to mid-1890's was marked by some of Tanner's most renowned paintings, studies of African Americans which include *The Banjo Lesson*, *Old Couple Looking at a Portrait of Lincoln*, and *The Thankful Poor*. Some art critics have emphasized the greatness of Tanner's subtle yet complex renderings of African Americans in contrast to the patronizing or racist stereotypes produced by many white artists of the era.

In the mid-1890's, Tanner became interested in painting biblical subjects, an interest which lasted the rest of his life. Some of the acclaimed paintings of this genre include *Daniel in the Lion's Den* and *Christ and Nicodemus on a Rooftop*. Toward the beginning of the twentieth century, Tanner's paintings began to express the influences of Impressionism and of Symbolism. *Salome* is one such painting.

Tanner, Jack Edward (b. November, 1919): Federal JUDGE. Tanner attended the University of Puget Sound Law School, where he received his law degree. After passing the Washington State bar examination, Tanner was an attorney in private practice in Tacoma, WASHINGTON, from 1955 to 1978. He served on the board of visitors of the University of Puget Sound Law School and was a member of the school's national board of directors from 1962 to 1968. In 1978 President Jimmy Carter appointed Tanner to serve on the federal bench as U.S. district judge for the Western District of Washington State.

Tarrant, Caesar (1755?-1796?): Sailor. Tarrant was a VIRGINIA slave who was put to service by the American Navy in the AMERICAN REVOLUTION because of his experience as a pilot on the Chesapeake Bay. He probably was at the wheel of the *Patriot* when it and its crew were captured by the British. The Virginia legislature set him free in 1789 as a reward for his service.

Tarry, Ellen (b. September 26, 1906, Birmington, Alabama): Author. As a journalist in NEW YORK CITY, she was executive secretary of the Negro Author's Guild and a member of a writers' group organized in 1937 by Claude McKay, a poet associated with the HARLEM RENAISSANCE. During World War II, she was a staff member of the National Catholic Community Service. She published *The Runaway Elephant* (1950), illustrated by Oliver Harrington, who created "Bootsie," a cartoon character renowned in the African American press. Her other books include her autobiography, *The Third Door* (1955), and *The Other Toussaint* (1981), a biography of Pierre Toussaint.

Tatum, Art, Jr. (October 13, 1909, Toledo, Ohio—November 5, 1956, Los Angeles, California): JAZZ pianist. Tatum suffered severely impaired vision from a very early age. He was completely blind in one eye and possessed

Art Tatum, Jr., in 1957. *(AP/Wide World Photos)*

only limited sight in the other. As a teenager in OHIO, he attended the Toledo School of Music, but he was largely self-taught at the piano, relying on the "teachings" of piano rolls, recordings, and the radio. His commitment led to his memorization of many Fats Waller compositions and performances. By 1936 he was playing professionally in Toledo and Cleveland. By 1932 he had made his way to NEW YORK CITY, and in 1933 he made his first recordings. Increasingly, over the remainder of the decade and into the 1940's, Tatum became known as jazz's virtuoso performer on the piano. His performances on radio, and in clubs in Chicago, New York, and Los Angeles, brought him to a wide audience.

The critical appreciation Tatum received from writers and musicians, however, always seemed to be greater than the development of a true popular following. In 1943 Tatum formed a trio similar to Nat "King" COLE's, signing on with bassist Slam Stewart and guitarist Tiny Grimes, hoping to attract the popular following that so far had eluded him. The experiment had mixed success, but Tatum's continued brilliance at the piano was clear. His solo recordings made for producer Norman Granz in the early 1950's were seminal in jazz history.

Tatum's work has influenced pianists as diverse as Herbie HANCOCK and Oscar PETERSON, and artists on other instruments, such as saxophonist Charlie PARKER, were also affected positively. Tatum's improvisations were usually alterations of popular standards, but he remained close to the tradition of the BLUES. He is also known for his playful parodies of many classical works.

Taylor, Gardner Calvin (b. June 18, 1918, Baton Rouge, Louisiana): BAPTIST clergyman. Taylor earned his A.B. from Leland College and his Bachelor of Divinity from OBERLIN COLLEGE. He was ordained in 1939. Between

Gardner Taylor was the first African American to head the Protestant Council.

1938 and 1947, he served as pastor in Elyria, Ohio, New Orleans, Louisiana, and Baton Rouge, Louisiana. In 1948 he served as dean and professor at the Colgate-Rochester Divinity School.

Taylor was pastor of the Concord Baptist Church in Brooklyn for more than thirty years, beginning in 1948. He delivered the Lyman Beecher lectures at Yale Divinity School in the 1975-1976 academic year. Active in the New York State Democratic Committee, he was also the first Baptist and first African American to head the Protestant Council. Among his books are *How Shall They Preach* (1977), *The Scarlet Threat: Nineteen Sermons* (1981), and *Chariots Aflame* (1988).

Taylor, Hobart, Jr. (b. December 17, 1920, Texarkana, Texas): Political appointee. Taylor was on a number of important governmental commissions as well as serving as a member of the board of directors or as counsel to various businesses. He received his B.A. degree from Prairie View College, an M.A. from Howard University, and an LL.M. from the University of Michigan. He was appointed as executive vice chairman of the Committee on Equal Employment Opportunity by President Lyndon Johnson, who also named him to the board of Export-Import Bank. Besides being a partner in a law firm in Detroit, Michigan, he became a board member of Eastern Airlines, Aetna Life and Casualty Company, Standard Oil, and Westinghouse Electric Corporation.

Taylor, Koko (Cora Walton; b. September 28, 1935, Memphis, Tennessee): BLUES singer. In 1953 Taylor began to travel along the club circuit. Her gravelly voice and wry sensuality earned her nearly every award available to a blues singer, including a 1985 W. C. HANDY Award as entertainer of the year. She also accumulated a number of best-selling songs, beginning with "Wang Dang Doodle," a 1965 gold record. Taylor continued to record and perform into the 1990's, releasing *Force of Nature* in 1994 and performing at the 1999 Long Beach Blues Festival.

Blues singer Koko Taylor. (© Roy Lewis Archives)

Taylor, Kristen Clark (b. 1959?, Detroit, Michigan): Political appointee. Taylor grew up in Detroit as the youngest of seven children and graduated from Michigan State University. At the age of twenty-three, she served as the only African American woman on the start-up staff at *USA Today*. In 1986 she became senior writer for the vice presidential press office of George Bush. While in Washington, D.C., Taylor met and married Lonny Taylor, Sr., who worked as chief of staff for a Republican congressman.

Upon winning the presidency, Bush appointed Taylor to serve as White House director of media relations. Although press secretary Marlin Fitzwater had primary responsibility for the president's interviews with the Washington press corps, Taylor arranged for presidential interviews by other members of the print and broadcast media and was responsible for briefing Bush on issues that came up at press meetings and luncheons. She coordinated a White House luncheon with African American publishers to help foster better relations between Bush and the black-owned media. After the BUSH ADMINISTRATION, beginning in 1994, she served as vice president of external affairs for the Student Loan Marketing Association ("Sallie Mae").

Taylor, Lawrence (b. February 4, 1959, Williamsburg, Virginia): FOOTBALL player. Growing up on the outskirts of the restored historic colonial village of Williamsburg, VIRGINIA, Taylor began his sports career in Little League baseball before turning to football at the age of fifteen. An indifferent student, he was not heavily recruited by colleges. Taylor chose to attend the University of North Carolina, where he played as a nose guard for two years before being given a starting position as outside linebacker. During his senior year, Taylor's team won the Bluebonnet Bowl, and he was named Atlantic Coast Conference player of the year.

Taylor began his professional football career after being selected by the New York Giants as the second pick overall in the National Football League (NFL) draft in 1981. As a rookie, Taylor was named defensive player of the year by the Associated Press and was also voted NFL rookie of the year. In 1982 he won an unprecedented second consecutive award from the Associated Press. Taylor's defensive play enabled the Giants to gain berths in the

Lawrence Taylor during his early playing days. *(New York Football Giants, Inc.)*

playoffs for several years in a row, culminating in the Giants' 39-20 victory over the Denver Broncos in Super Bowl XXI. He returned with the Giants to Super Bowl XXV, helping the team to a narrow victory over the Buffalo Bills in January of 1991.

During his first ten years in the NFL, Taylor was named to the Pro Bowl team every year. He received numerous honors as all-NFL player and NFL defensive player of the year and was named NFL player of the year in 1986. That year marked the high point of his career, when he recorded 20.5 quarterback sacks—only 1.5 off the NFL record.

Taylor was touted as one of the game's premier players. By redefining the position of linebacker to take advantage of his skill at rushing the quarterback, Taylor set a new standard by which pass rushers are evaluated. He also received his share of criticism, particularly in the wake of testing positive for cocaine use in NFL-sponsored random drug tests in 1985 and again in 1988. In each case, Taylor agreed to participate in drug rehabilitation programs before undergoing follow-up tests in order to play football again. Taylor retired from the Giants at the end of the 1993-1994 season.

In 1995 Taylor formed his own company, called All-Pro Products, which, among other endeavors, marketed a computer game. He also continued to have problems with drugs in the 1990's, being arrested in 1996 and 1998 for possession of crack cocaine. Nevertheless, Taylor was inducted into the Pro Football Hall of Fame in 1999, as voters chose to reward his performance on the field and not to punish him for his failings in his personal life.

—*John Jacob*

Taylor, Major (November 26, 1878, Indianapolis, Indiana—June 21, 1932, Chicago, Illinois): Bicycle racer. The first widely known U.S. black athlete, Marshall W. "Major" Taylor overcame constant discrimination by cycling officials to win the world one-mile title in Montreal, Canada, in 1899. In 1900 he was recognized as the best sprinter in the nation, having won consecutive U.S. professional sprint championships and the 1899 world professional sprint championship. He retired in 1910 and wrote poetry and an autobiography, *The Fastest Bicycle Rider in the World* (1928).

Susan L. Taylor (left) with Dorothy Height and Maya Angelou in 1997. *(AP/Wide World Photos)*

Taylor, Mildred D. (b. 1943, Jackson, Mississippi): Author of children's novels. She received her bachelor's degree from the University of Toledo and attended graduate school at the University of Colorado. Inspired by her father's stories of African American slaves who retained their dignity despite their servitude, Taylor wrote a trilogy chronicling African Americans' attempts to establish themselves after SLAVERY. The first novel, *Song of the Trees* (1975), was named the outstanding book of the year by *The New York Times*; the second, *Roll of Thunder, Hear My Cry* (1976), received the Newbery Medal. In 1981 Taylor published *Let the Circle Be Unbroken*, the final novel of the trilogy. Her work also includes *The Road to Memphis* (1990) and *The Well: David's Story* (1995)

Taylor, Susan L. (b. January 23, 1946, New York, New York): Journalist. Taylor began her working life as an actor and licensed cosmetologist. She then became involved in freelance beauty and FASHION writing. She was a freelance beauty writer for ESSENCE magazine in 1970 and became its beauty editor in 1971. That department was broadened to include fashion. Taylor became editor-in-chief of *Essence* in 1981 and vice president of Essence

Communications in 1986, acting as host of its television program. In 1993 she published *In the Spirit: The Inspirational Writings of Susan L. Taylor*, a collection of her writings; the title was taken from her wide-ranging *Essence* column "In the Spirit." In the 1980's and 1990's Taylor also lectured and traveled widely.

Teague, Bob (b. January 2, 1929, Milwaukee, Wisconsin): Newscaster. Author of the autobiography *Live and Off-Color: News Biz* (1982), Robert "Bob" Teague had a diverse career, including time as a Big Ten halfback during his college years for the University of Wisconsin and writing the stage work *Soul Yesterday and Today*, based on Langston HUGHES's work. He was a newspaper reporter before he went to work for the National Broadcasting Company in 1963. Teague also appeared on several late-night news programs.

Teenage pregnancy: Although the pregnancy rate for teenagers declined between 1960 and 1999, by the latter year the United States still led most industrialized countries in teenage pregnancies, abortions, and childbearing. Approximately 10 percent of American teenage girls were still becoming pregnant each year. American teens do not engage in sexual activity more often than their peers in other countries—sexual patterns are similar in most developed countries. However, American teens are much more likely to become pregnant when they have sex. The United States also surpasses most other developed countries in the rate of abortions for this age group. These trends have held true for each racial group in the United States.

Pregnancy, Abortion, and Birthrates

Teenage pregnancy rates declined for both whites and blacks between the 1970's and early 1990's, both in actual numbers and in rates per 1,000 women. In 1976 more than 1.1 million teenagers became pregnant; by 1991, the number had dropped to less than 1 million. Even between 1990 and 1991, both groups showed a notable decrease. During these same two years, pregnancies for Hispanics increased by more than 10,000. (It should be noted that figures for Hispanic teen mothers may include Latinas of African descent.)

From 1980 through 1988, the rate of live births for adolescents remained relatively stable, but beginning in 1989 that rate began to increase. More than half the pregnancies for blacks and Hispanics ended in a live birth. Between 1990 and 1991, however, the number of births for both blacks and whites declined, as did the number of abortions. Hispanic birth and abortion rates, on the other hand, rose substantially, accounting for one-fifth of all teen births in 1992. Although there was a decline for blacks, their pregnancy rate in 1991 was still two and a half times as high as the rate for whites. In 1996 11.3 percent of births to white women, 22.9 percent of births to black women, and 17.4 percent of births to Hispanic women were to teenage mothers.

Single Mothers

Although the rates of pregnancies and live births dropped for white and African American teenagers in the 1990's, the number of teenagers who have babies is still a significant societal concern because the majority of these children are born out of wedlock. In the past, unmarried teens accounted for almost half of all out-of-wedlock births; by the 1990's, they accounted for less than one-third of such births. This figure may be misleading, however, because a number of women above the age of twenty have begun choosing to be single mothers. The number of unwed mothers is growing faster among whites than African Americans, but the percentage of African American teenage mothers who are unmarried is exceedingly high, standing at more than 90 percent.

Possible Causes

Ideas and arguments abound about why teenagers in the United States have such a high rate of pregnancy when compared with teens in other countries. Numerous theories have also been advanced to explain why African American girls have a substantially higher pregnancy rate than white girls. Two basic questions about teenage pregnancy in general need to be answered: why the pregnancy rate is so high, and why so many births occur out of wedlock. There are two general sides in the debate over how to decrease teen pregnancies: one that believes in educating teenagers more about sex and granting easier access to contraceptives, and another that stresses moral values and promotes abstinence.

Four key factors appear to determine the prevalence of teen pregnancy among African Americans. First, most African American teens have their first sexual experience at a younger age and marry at a later age. Second, they are less likely to use contraceptives and are more likely to become pregnant through incorrect use of contraception. Third, compared with their white peers, black teenagers generally earn lower wages and have a higher rate of unemployment. Finally, there are fewer marriageable men in the African American population as a whole, primarily as a result of a high rate of imprisonment and several other interrelated socioeconomic factors.

Early Sexual Experience and Late First Marriage
Statistically, African American teens, on average, begin sexual activity a full year earlier than white teens. Male African Americans, on average, begin having intercourse at the age of fourteen, while male white teenagers begin a year later. In surveys, more than half of African American women say that they began having intercourse before they were seventeen years old. On average, almost one-fourth of all teenage mothers will become pregnant again within two years of the birth of their first child. Because African American women tend to marry at a later age (twenty-six) than their white counterparts, they experience a longer period of sexual activity outside marriage. The earlier intercourse begins, and the more frequently it occurs, the greater the risk of pregnancy.

Contraceptive Use
According to 1990's statistics, about 75 percent of African American teenagers regularly used a contraceptive method, compared with approximately 80 percent of whites. Teens who live in low-income families often cannot afford to pay for even the most inexpensive forms of contraception. African American youths are also less likely than white youths to be well informed about contraceptive methods. African American teens not only are less likely to use contraception but also experience a higher rate of con-traceptive failure when they do use some form of contraception. Many teenage girls have trouble asking their partners to use contraception. In order to reduce the high rate of teen pregnancy among students during the 1990's, school districts in BALTIMORE, MARYLAND, and a number of other cities instituted programs to establish on-site clinics that would provide counseling and contraceptives to students.

Low Wages and High Unemployment
African American men and women have a higher unemployment rate than whites and, on the average, earn less than their counterparts. Some critics point to these inequities as a way to explain not only the high birthrate but also the rise in the number of out-of-wedlock births. When wages are low, there are no significant incentives to delay childbearing. Teenagers who have babies are more likely to be from a poor or low-income family. Women must have educational and career aspirations to discourage them from having children at a young age. If there is no significant reward to remaining in high school, and unemployment is high while wages remain low, there is little reason to delay childbearing. Under these conditions, it may also appear that there are few

Young mothers at Brooklyn's Project Teen-Aid day care center in 1993. *(Hazel Hankin)*

Births to Teenage and Unmarried Mothers as Percentages of All Births

	1985	1990	1991	1992	1993	1994	1995	1996
Percent of Births to Teenage Mothers								
White	10.8	10.9	11.0	10.9	11.0	11.3	11.5	11.3
Black	23.0	23.1	23.1	22.7	22.7	23.2	23.1	22.9
American Indian, Eskimo, Aleut	19.1	19.5	20.3	20.0	20.3	21.0	21.4	(NA)
Asian and Pacific Islander	5.5	5.7	5.8	5.6	5.7	5.7	5.6	(NA)
Hispanic origin	16.5	16.8	17.2	17.1	17.4	17.8	17.9	17.4
Percent of Births to Unmarried Mothers								
White	14.5	16.9	18.0	22.6	23.6	25.4	25.3	25.7
Black	60.1	66.7	68.2	68.1	68.7	70.4	69.9	69.8
American Indian, Eskimo, Aleut	40.7	53.6	55.3	55.3	55.8	57.0	57.2	(NA)
Asian and Pacific Islander	10.1	(NA)	(NA)	14.7	15.7	16.2	16.3	(NA)
Hispanic origin	29.5	36.7	38.5	39.1	40.0	43.1	40.8	40.9

Source: U.S. National Center for Health Statistics
Note: Percentages represent registered live births. Hispanic persons may be of any race.

reasons to marry the father of the child. Many fathers cannot contribute financially to the support of their children, and most women are unwilling to marry without that security. As an African American man's income rises, so does his chance of getting married.

Lack of Marriageable Men

There is a significant decrease in the ratio of African American men to African American women by the age of fourteen. The death rate of African American men after the age of fifteen is also three times as high as that of white men. A significant number of African American men are in prison or in the military stationed away from home. Also, more African American men than women marry outside their race, and there are also the previously mentioned problems of low wages and high unemployment. All these facts help explain why three-fourths of young African American children live with a single parent.

Although the rate of teenage pregnancy has slowed for African American adolescents, it remains high. An estimated one in four African American women becomes a mother before her twentieth birthday. The children of these young mothers are more likely to be low-birth-weight babies and to have health problems than are children of older mothers. Women who give birth in their teens remain in poverty longer than women who wait to have their first child later. Teenage mothers are also less likely to finish high school or go to college and are more likely to have to depend on public assistance. Finally, studies indicate a strong link between a mother's age at first sexual experience and the age when her daughter first has intercourse.

—*Nancy Hatch Woodward*

Suggested Readings:

Berlfein, Judy. *Teen Pregnancy*. San Diego: Lucent Books, 1992.

Bode, Janet. *Kids Still Having Kids: People Talk About Teen Pregnancy*. New York: Franklin Watts, 1992.

Dash, Leon. *When Children Want Children: The Urban Crisis of Teenage Childbearing*. New York: William Morrow, 1989.

Hendricks, Leo E., and Teresa A. Montgomery. *Teenage Pregnancy from a Black Perspective: Some Reflections on Its Prevention*. Washington, D.C.: Institute for Urban Affairs and Research, Howard University, 1986.

Kaplan, Elaine B. *Not Our Kind of Girl: Unraveling the Myths of Black Teenage Mother-*

hood. Berkeley: University of California Press, 1997.

Lerman, Robert I., and Theodora Ooms, eds. *Young Unwed Fathers: Changing Roles and Emerging Policies*. Philadelphia: Temple University Press, 1993.

Luker, Kristin. *Dubious Conceptions: The Politics of Teenage Pregnancy*. Cambridge, Mass.: Harvard University Press, 1996.

McCuen, Gary E., ed. *Children Having Children: Global Perspectives on Teenage Pregnancy*. Hudson, Wis.: Gary E. McCuen, 1988.

Meier, Gisela. *Teenage Pregnancy*. North Bellmore, N.Y.: Marshall Cavendish, 1994.

Williams, Constance W. *Black Teenage Mothers: Pregnancy and Child Rearing from Their Perspective*. Lexington, Mass.: Lexington Books, 1991.

Television industry: For most Americans, television is the primary source of daily entertainment, news, and information. It is also a public forum for debating ideas. Drawing on the popular arts of film, radio, theater, and literature, television has emerged as the dominant medium in American popular culture.

Television programmers have attempted both to mirror and to help shape popular moods and opinions by providing a variety of programs: daily news, dramas, comedies, feature documentaries, dramas, sports events, talk shows, and variety programs. In the midst of this television fare lie the industry's portrayals of African Americans. Through the years, network—and later, cable—television's portrayals of African Americans have provoked much discussion and been met with broad-based criticism.

The Formative First Decade
By 1948, when the mechanics of television broadcasting had been ironed out and the medium was becoming available to a wide cross section of American viewers, public discussions in print and broadcast media had already raised questions of how African Americans would be portrayed on television.

The popular mood of post-WORLD WAR II America (an era in which the fight against fascism was fresh in the minds of the public) led many to hope that television portrayals of minorities might be free of the bias that typically characterized depictions in popular literature, radio, theater, and film. CIVIL RIGHTS organizations, literary magazines, and entertainment personalities called for television to avoid negative stereotyping and to combat racial discrimination through the presentation of positive images and factual information.

Television broadcasting, however, was a business, and it depended upon the financing of advertisers and sponsors. Postwar reform sentiments were superseded by advertisers' desires not to alienate the widest cross section of consumers. Despite protests by many inside and outside the television industry, television programmers found it simplest and most profitable to continue the stereotypical images of African Americans that had gained popularity in other profit-based media.

Most of these stereotyped characters found a home in situation comedies such as *Beulah* (produced from 1950 to 1953 on ABC) and AMOS 'N' ANDY (shown from 1951 to 1953 on CBS), in which African American characters exhibiting unflattering qualities maintained enough popular support to keep such programs on the air for several seasons. Notable exceptions to these portrayals were rare. These nonstereotyped portrayals were primarily found in variety shows, sports programs, a few failed features, occasional documentary shorts, and a limited number of local productions.

The Civil Rights Era
Perhaps the most significant and unwitting challenge to television's portrayals of stereotyped African Americans came as a result of

the sheer impact of televised images of the Civil Rights movement that gained national attention in the 1960's. Images of African Americans being physically and verbally attacked while they protested against racial discrimination proved fortuitous for those who wanted progressive change both inside and outside the television industry. In addition to nightly news coverage, there were a number of documentaries, usually produced for feature news programs, which provided comprehensive analysis of topical issues affecting African Americans as well as in-depth interviews with CIVIL RIGHTS leaders.

These timely news features, coupled with the insistent protests that began in television's formative years, gave television programmers the go-ahead for using African Americans in increasing numbers of nonstereotyped roles. Initially meeting with some localized resistance, networks cautiously included occasional roles for African Americans in feature programs and drama specials. Eventually, by the early 1970's, network television featured African Americans starring or costarring in some nineteen series. A similar number of TELEVISION SERIES featured African Americans as significant supporting-cast members. Programs that focused on conscientious professionals and socially agreeable characters, were typical of television's new commitment to African American portrayals that were devoid of the minstrel-type characterizations of the previous decade.

While the new portrayals were applauded for their avoidance of stereotypes, they were also criticized for a refusal to deal with specific African American social, economic, and cultural themes. Many viewers, civil rights advocates, and media organizations were troubled by portrayals which seemed to indicate that social and economic equality was not to be gained through changes in public policy and practice but rather through compliance and individual achievement.

A combination of public advocacy and individual achievement compelled the television industry to make significant inroads in the employment of African American professionals in front of and behind the cameras in the civil rights era. More and more African Americans appeared as reporters, correspondents, news anchors, and camera operators. Additionally, small but groundbreaking steps were being made as African Americans joined the ranks of television writers, directors, producers, and executives, increasing hopes for a new era of bias-free, issue-oriented, and culturally concerned programming.

Exploring Ethnicity
Television programmers in the 1970's and early 1980's did attempt to present more African Americans in programs that revolved around relevant social, economic, and racial themes. However, most of these depictions were presented in the television comedy format—a format long criticized for its tendency to rely on superficial humor rather than to explore problems honestly. While some supported these comedies because the humor was drawn from elements of African American culture, others felt that their portrayals ridiculed rather than satirized the culture, revived jokes based solely on race, and even recalled the minstrel-type portrayals of 1950's television and earlier forms of entertainment. Nevertheless, such comedies as *Sanford and Son* (1971-1977), *The Jeffersons* (1975-1985), and *Good Times* (1974-1979) were extremely popular, frequently placing among the nation's top-rated programs during their runs.

In the less-common dramatic specials, African American portrayals depicted fact-based, historical, and often heroic stories and characterizations. Perhaps the most memorable of these dramas was *Roots*, an eight-part ABC miniseries broadcast in 1977 that explored the story of an African American family from slav-

(continued on page 2434)

Broadcasters and Executives

Bradley, Ed. *See main text entry*

Brown, Tony. *See main text entry*

Clayton, Xernona (b. Aug. 30, 1930, Muskogee, Okla.). Executive and talk show host. A former teacher, fashion model, and community activist, Clayton hosted *The Xernona Clayton Show* in ATLANTA, GEORGIA, on WAGA-TV. She founded the Atlanta chapter of Media Women and from 1972 to 1976 served on the Motion Picture and Television Commission. She was executive producer for BLACK HISTORY MONTH programs for the Turner Broadcasting System (TBS) and served as corporate vice president for urban affairs for TBS.

Turner Broadcasting System, Inc.

Cornelius, Don (b. Sept. 27, 1936, Chicago, Ill.). Host and producer. Cornelius created, produced, and hosted the television show *Soul Train*, featuring young adults who danced while records played and guest stars performed their hit songs. *Soul Train* began in 1970 as a local show in CHICAGO and later moved to Hollywood. In addition to providing a venue for black performers, Cornelius paid tribute to their musical talent by producing the *Soul Train Music Awards*. His Don Cornelius Productions company produced and syndicated the first *Soul Train Lady of Soul Awards* show in 1995 and the *Soul Train Twenty-fifth Anniversary Hall of Fame Special*, a retrospective of the program's twenty-five years on television.

Daniels, Randy (b. Nov. 30, 1949, Chicago, Ill.). Television reporter. Daniels began working as a correspondent for CBS in 1972. He covered the political conventions of both major parties.

Graham, Gordon (b. 1936, Coshocton, Ohio). Broadcaster. Graham began covering the House of Representatives for NBC news in January, 1971. Graham began his news career with radio station KGFJ in Los ANGELES, CALIFORNIA, in 1962 and had several other writing and reporting jobs prior to the NBC position.

Hunter-Gault, Charlayne. *See main text entry*

Jackson, Eugene (b. Sept. 5, 1943, Waukomis, Okla.). Broadcast executive. Jackson served as president of Unity Broadcasting Network.

Jenkins, Carol Ann (b. Nov. 30, 1944, Montgomery, Ala.). Broadcaster. An Emmy-nominated news correspondent, Jenkins worked with ABC-TV from 1972 to 1973, when she moved to WNBC-TV in NEW YORK CITY. She was promoted to anchor in 1990 and received that year's Lifetime Achievement Award from the New York Association of Black Journalists.

Johnson, John (b. June 20, 1938, New York, N.Y.). Broadcaster. Johnson began working with WABC-TV in 1968 and served as a correspondent, producer, writer, and director. In 1977 he received a Christopher Award for directing *To All the World's Children*.

Noble, Gilbert E. "Gil" (b. Feb. 22, 1932, New York, N.Y.). Noble is best known for hosting and producing the television show *Like It Is*, which first aired in 1968. It focused on black political figures and historical accomplishments and featured interviews with black cultural and political leaders from around the world. *Like It Is* and various specials had earned Noble six Emmy Awards by 1980.

Roberts, Deborah A. *See main text entry*

Robinson, Max C. *See main text entry*

Shaw, Bernard. *See main text entry*

Simpson, Carole. *See main text entry*

Sutton, Pierre (b. Feb. 1, 1947, New York, N.Y.). Broadcasting executive. Sutton became chairman of Inner City Broadcasting Corporation (ICBC) in 1990. WBLS-FM, its flagship radio station, set the standard for African American RADIO in the

Inner City Broadcasting Corp.

(continued)

United States and became the premier black station. It had been founded in 1972 by Sutton's father, Percy, and others when they purchased a single AM radio station in HARLEM. Percy Sutton guided the company through the acquisition of nine radio stations, the 1982 purchase and partial renovation of the legendary APOLLO THEATER in Harlem, and a $70 million cable television deal. Pierre Sutton was named president of the corporation in 1977. When his father retired in 1990, he became its chairman.

Watts, Rolanda. *See main text entry*

Williams, Montel B. (b. July 3, 1956, Baltimore, Md.). Talk show host and actor. Williams began hosting his television talk show, *The Montel Williams Show*, in 1991. Through his low-key and sympathetic approach, he inspired audiences to seek rational explanations and solutions to problems in the world. A former military officer—who rose to the rank of lieutenant commander—and motivational speaker, his ambition to reach out to people also led to a variety of acting roles. In the late 1990's, William's popularity suffered as a result of sexual harassment charges brought against him by former female employees. He was vindicated in court, however, and his talk show continued into the year 2000.

Winfrey, Oprah. *See main text entry*

---

ery to emancipation. *Roots* became the most-watched drama in American television history. Meanwhile, the Public Broadcasting Service (PBS) gained national attention, and from its noncommercial focus came a number of news journals and feature-length documentaries that were often written, directed, and produced by African Americans. Commercial networks' nonfiction coverage was much more infrequent.

It was children's television that would introduce some of the most marked changes in television's portrayals of African Americans in this era. Series such as PBS's *Sesame Street* and CBS's *Fat Albert and the Cosby Kids* made substantial use of African American actors and characters while providing educational information, teaching personal and social responsibility, and portraying harmonious racial environments. Many of these programs set new standards for children's television while simultaneously acting as supplements to formal education. Finally, the industry began to improve its record on the hiring of African Americans in nonperformance "behind-the-camera" roles.

Characterization Versus Caricature
By the mid-1980's, the television industry had begun to move toward more complex charac-terizations of African Americans in all genres. Such programs as THE COSBY SHOW, a 1984-1992 NBC series, proved that even situation comedies could be based on complex characterization and could provide sophisticated humor while maintaining a popular audience (*The Cosby Show* was number one in the ratings for its first five seasons.) Alongside comedic characterizations, more dramatic series and specials such as the 1989 miniseries *The Women of Brewster Place* featured African American lead characters and dealt sensitively with a wide variety of social, economic, and culturally specific issues. In addition, an increasing number of documentaries, of which the 1986 six-part PBS series *Eyes on the Prize: America's Civil Rights Years* was exemplary, provided comprehensive explorations of African American history and culture.

Mid-1980's and early 1990's television was also characterized by an influx of African Americans into genres in which they had not previously played a significant role. This was illustrated by such talk and variety shows as *The Oprah Winfrey Show* and *Arsenio*, both of which were hosted by African Americans and consistently ranked number one in their categories, and the 1989 debut of the first African American soap opera, *Generations*.

Criticism of mid-1980's and early 1990's television tended to be somewhat narrowly targeted. Individual documentaries, dramas, and comedy episodes were criticized for overlooking the historical development of problems, for not presenting a wide enough range of African American perspectives, or, in the case of some comedy skits on feature programs, for insensitive and caricature-like portrayals.

Nevertheless, by the 1990's many television portrayals of African Americans were meeting with great support from a wide cross section of American viewers. Programs featuring African Americans as leads, costars, hosts, anchors, writers, directors, and producers ranked as some of the most popular on television.

The success of the cable network BLACK ENTERTAINMENT TELEVISION (BET), as well as the Fox Network, the Warner Bros. Network (WB), and the United Paramount Network (UPN), all notable for their edgier approach to ethnically diverse programming, helped foster changes in the industry. Children's television shows, in particular, often gave positive and natural reflection to the country's growing ethnic diversity.

However, as the 1990's progressed, increasingly fewer African Americans appeared on major network shows. A number of protests concerning the situation were registered by black organizations until, in the spring of 1999, the NATIONAL ASSOCIATION FOR THE ADVANCEMENT OF COLORED PEOPLE (NAACP) attacked the four major television networks (ABC, CBS, NBC, and Fox) for the lack of minorities cast in major roles in their 1999 fall season shows. This criticism—coupled with threats of lawsuits and boycotts by NAACP president Kweisi MFUME—led industry executives to reevaluate their position on diversity in casting. Many scrambled to add or recast minority characters before the fall season shows premiered.

The NAACP cautiously approved this change in direction, but Mfume noted that continuing focus would be placed on the executive boardrooms where the decisions are made. The NAACP set a December, 1999, deadline for network leaders to offer proposals regarding increasing black roles, and that month the group stated that it was satisfied by the response of the networks and would not be sponsoring a boycott.

—Monique S. Simón
—Updated by Cynthia Beres
See also: Broadcast licensing; Radio broadcasting; Winfrey, Oprah.

Suggested Readings:
Barnouw, Erik. Tube of Plenty: The Evolution of American Television. 2d rev. ed. New York: Oxford University Press, 1990.

Bogle, Donald. Blacks in American Films and Television: An Illustrated Encyclopedia. New York: Garland, 1988.

Cosby, Camille O. Television's Imageable Influences: The Self-Perceptions of Young African Americans. Lanham, Md.: University Press of America, 1994.

Gray, Herman. Watching Race: Television and the Struggle for "Blackness." Minneapolis: University of Minnesota Press, 1995.

MacDonald, J. Fred. Blacks and White TV: Afro-Americans in Television Since 1948. Chicago: Nelson-Hall, 1983.

McKissack, Fred. "Television's Black Humor." The Progressive (April, 1999): 39.

McNeil, Alex. Total Television: A Comprehensive Guide to Programming from 1948 to the Present. 3d ed. New York: Penguin Books, 1991.

Means Coleman, Robin R. African American Viewers and the Black Situation Comedy: Situating Racial Humor. New York: Garland, 1998.

Torres, Sasha, ed. Living Color: Race and Television in the United States. Durham, N.C.: Duke University Press, 1998.

Zook, Kristal B. Color by Fox: The Fox Network and the Revolution in Black Television. New York: Oxford University Press, 1999.

Television series: During more than fifty years of television programming, television series that have featured African Americans in significant roles have largely reflected what television producers interpret to be the popular taste or mood of the masses.

In television's formative years, this popular taste was predicated largely on the portraits of African Americans that flourished in other popular media, such as radio and film. Given the racist bias of the popular media that preceded television, early television portraits of African American life were generally unflattering, antisocial, minstrel-like stereotypes. Among the early shows with central black characters were AMOS 'N' ANDY (1951-1953) and *Beulah* (1950-1953).

Over time, protests inside and outside the TELEVISION INDUSTRY called for change. Television was called upon to be a leader, rather than a follower, in helping to shape the popular conceptions of African Americans. By the 1970's, when virtually every home in the United States possessed a television set, the industry was uniquely positioned to shape public perception. During the mid- to late 1960's, television began seriously to examine how to portray African Americans as individuals rather than caricatured stereotypes. Television series began to feature African Americans as professionals within an integrated society that made little distinction between them and their white colleagues.

Among the groundbreaking shows were the often-noted *I Spy* and *Julia*, both NBC programs. *I Spy* (1965-1968) was a globe-trotting adventure drama about two undercover agents, one black (Bill COSBY) and one white (Robert Culp). The situation comedy *Julia* (1968-1971) was the first program to feature an female African American lead character, a nurse and widowed mother played by Diahann

CARROLL. Among the early programs to include blacks in ensemble casts were *Mission Impossible* (1966-1973, with Greg Morris), *Star Trek* (1966-1969, with Nichelle Nichols), *Hogan's Heroes* (1965-1971, with Ivan Dixon), *The Mod Squad* (1968-1973, with Clarence Williams III), and *N.Y.P.D.* (1967-1969, with Robert Hooks).

By the 1970's, more series began to examine the unique cultural background of and expressions within the black community. From the mid-1980's onward, the television industry seemed to have figured out how to blend these two approaches, striking a balance in portraying African Americans as socially integrated individuals and as complex characters with a unique cultural heritage. This trend continued as African American characters began to proliferate in all television genres, including comedy, drama, and documentary.

Julia, starring Diahann Carroll, was the first television series built entirely around an African American character. *(AP/ Wide World Photos)*

Comedy Series

Historically, more African American characters were included in situation comedy programs than in any other television genre. On one hand, this inclusion had the positive effect of exposing viewers to a wide variety of black characters and themes. On the other hand, comedy's tendency to avoid exploring social issues—or to deal with them superficially—perpetuated certain stereotypes about the black community. Television comedies generally raise an issue in order to satirize it rather than deal with it openly and directly.

Among the most popular situation comedies of the 1970's were *Sanford and Son* (1972-1977, with Redd Foxx and Demond Wilson), *Good Times* (1974-1979, with Jimmie Walker, Esther Rolle, and John Amos), and *The Jeffersons* (1975-1985, with Sherman Hemsley and Isabel Sanford). *The Jeffersons* was a spin-off from *All in the Family* (1971-1983), on which the Jefferson family had moved in next door to white bigot Archie Bunker. Later in the decade came *Diff'rent Strokes* (1978-1985, with Gary Coleman and Todd Bridges) and *Benson* (1979-1986, with Robert Guillaume).

A major shift occurred in the 1980's with the premiere of the NBC situation comedy THE COSBY SHOW, which starred Bill Cosby and aired from 1984 to 1992. Ranked as the nation's most-watched show during its first five seasons, *The Cosby Show* depicted the fictional Huxtables, an upper-middle-class African American family with a father who worked as a physician, a mother who worked as an attorney, and five generally well-behaved children living in a Manhattan brownstone. The show's humor was sophisticated, and its characterizations were complex. The Huxtables were portrayed as the archetypical all-American family who happened also to be black. Many

One of the most popular television shows of all time, *The Cosby Show* even achieved high ratings in South Africa when that country was under white rule. *(NBC Photo)*

of the issues that accompany racism and socio-economic deprivation were sidestepped because the Huxtable family was so well adapted.

Building on the success of *The Cosby Show*, many television networks began to release more comedies with all-black casts. Although many of these shows did not have successful runs, their rate of failure was no greater than that of most other television series, regardless of genre. In fact, since there were so many shows with African American casts for viewers to choose from, it was often the competition from similar all-black shows that caused other all-black shows to be canceled. Popular survivors were series such as ABC's *Family Matters* (1989-1998), which focused on a lov-

(continued on page 2442)

Notable Female Television and Film Actors

Allen, Debbie. *See main text entry.*

Bailey, Pearl. *See main text entry.*

Bassett, Angela (b. Aug. 16, 1958, New York, N.Y.). Bassett has appeared in plays such as *Ma Rainey's Black Bottom* and *Joe Turner's Come and Gone* (1988). She launched her film career with an appearance in *F/X* (1986); she went on to appear in *Kindergarten Cop* (1990), *Boyz 'N the Hood* (1991), *City of Hope* (1991), *Malcolm X* (1992), *What's Love Got to Do with It* (1993), *Strange Days* (1995), *Vampire in Brooklyn* (1995), *Waiting to Exhale* (1995), *How Stella Got Her Groove Back* (1998), and *Supernova* (2000).

Twentieth Century Fox

Beals, Jennifer (b. Dec. 19, 1963, Chicago, Ill.). While she was a first-year student at Yale, Beals made her film debut as a welder who dreams of becoming a ballet dancer in *Flashdance* (1983). She later starred in *The Bride* (1985), *The Vampire's Kiss* (1989), *Devil in a Blue Dress* (1995), *Wishful Thinking* (1997), and *The Last Days of Disco* (1998).

Beavers, Louise. *See main text entry.*

Belafonte-Harper, Shari (b. Sept. 22, 1954, New York, N.Y.). The daughter of actor and singer Harry BELAFONTE, Belafonte-Harper, has appeared in films and on television, including a major role in the popular series *Hotel* from 1983 to 1988. She had guest roles in television series and films throughout the 1990's.

Berry, Halle. *See main text entry.*

Carroll, Diahann. *See main text entry.*

Dandridge, Dorothy. *See main text entry.*

Fisher, Gail (b. Aug. 18, 1935, Orange, N.J.). Fisher played Peggy Fair on the *Mannix* television series from 1968 to 1974, winning an Emmy Award in 1969 for her performances. She was the first female African American actor to win an Emmy. In 1961 she became the first black performer to speak lines in a national television commercial. She continued to appear in television roles into the early 1990's.

Fox, Vivica A. (b. July 30, 1964, Indianapolis, Ind.). Fox has appeared in a number of television programs such as *Arsenio* (1997), *Getting Personal* (1998), and *City of Angels* (2000). Her film roles include *Independence Day* (1996), *Set It Off* (1996), *Booty Call* (1997), *Soul Food* (1997), and *Why Do Fools Fall In Love* (1998).

Givens, Robin (b. Nov. 27, 1965, New York, N.Y.). Givens appeared in the television series *Head of the Class* (1986-1991). She also appeared in the television movie *The Women of Brewster Place* (1989). Givens appeared in the films *A Rage in Harlem* (1991), *Boomerang* (1992), and *Blankman* (1994). In the late 1990's Givens continued to star in television and film roles.

Goldberg, Whoopi. *See main text entry.*

Graves, Teresa (b. 1949, Houston, Tex.). Graves came to public attention as a regular on the television comic review *Rowan and Martin's Laugh-In* 1969 and 1970. She appeared in black action films such as *That Man Bolt* (1973) and *Black Eye* (1974) before receiving her own short-lived ABC police series, *Get Christie Love!* (1974-1975).

Grier, Pam. *See main text entry.*

Horne, Lena. *See main text entry.*

Horsford, Anna Maria (b. Mar. 6, 1947, New York, N.Y.). Horsford is best known for her role as Thelma Frye on the hit television show *Amen*, which debuted in 1986. Her theater credits include *for colored girls who have considered suicide/ when the rainbow is enuf* in 1976. She has also produced for television, working with National Education Television from 1970 to 1981. She served as president of Black Women in

Theater from 1983 to 1984. Horsford continued to act into the 1990's appearing in television and film roles such as *Set It Off* (1996) and *One Fine Day* (1996).

Houston, Whitney. *See main text entry.*

Jackée (Jackée Harry; b. Aug. 14, 1957, Winston-Salem, N.C.). Jackée is most widely known for her role as flashy, man-crazy Sandra Clark on the television show *227*, which netted her an Emmy Award in 1987. In addition to her numerous theater performances, she appeared in such films as *Moscow on the Hudson* and *The Cotton Club* (1984). She also played a lead role in the 1990's television series *Sister, Sister*.

Johnson, Anne-Marie (b. 1961?, Los Angeles, Calif.). A costar of the NBC television drama series *In the Heat of the Night*, Johnson has appeared in various television shows, including *What's Happening Now!!* from 1985 to 1986. She starred in the hit film *Hollywood Shuffle* (1987) and appeared in the 1989 television film *Dream Date*. In the 1990's she frequently appeared on television and in films, such as *The Five Heartbeats* (1991) and *Down in the Delta* (1998).

Jones, Grace (b. May 19, 1952, Spanishtown, Jamaica). Jones's career choices have included modeling and singing. She appeared in the film *Gordon's War* (1973). Her numerous other film roles include the successful comedy *Boomerang* (1992). Jones continued her acting career well into the late 1990's.

Kelly, Paula (b. Oct. 21, 1943, Jacksonville, Fla.). Kelly's film career includes the screen version of *Sweet Charity* (1969), *The Andromeda Strain* (1971), *Trouble Man* (1972), and *Uptown Saturday Night* (1974). Other film credits include *Once Upon a Time . . . When We Were Colored* (1996) and *Run for the Dream: The Gail Devers Story* (1996). Her acting honors include England's Variety Award for best supporting actress in a musical for her role in *Sweet Charity* (1968).

King, Regina (b. Jan. 15, 1971, Los Angeles, Ca.). King appeared on several television shows, including *227*. She has appeared in numerous films including *Boyz 'N the Hood* (1991), *Poetic Justice* (1993), *Higher Learning* (1995), *A Thin Line Between Love and Hate* (1996), *Jerry Maguire* (1996), *How Stella Got Her Groove Back* (1998), and *Enemy of the State* (1998).

Kitt, Eartha. *See main text entry.*

Kotero, Patricia "Apollonia" (b. 1959, Mexico City, Mexico). In 1984 Kotero won the role as the female lead in the film *Purple Rain* (1984). Kotero has also worked as a singer. She returned to acting, appearing regularly in television's nighttime serial *Falcon Crest* in 1985 and 1986. In the 1990's Kotero continued to sing and act.

Lee, Joie (1962?, Brooklyn, N.Y.). Lee has been featured in her brother Spike LEE's films, including *She's Gotta Have It* (1986), *School Daze* (1988), *Do the Right Thing* (1989), and *Mo' Better Blues* (1990). She also appeared in the 1990 thriller, *A Kiss Before Dying*, and on the television programs *The Cosby Show* and *Saturday Night Live*. With Spike and their brother Cinque, she co-wrote *Crooklyn* (1994). Lee's other films include *Losing Isaiah* (1995), *Get on the Bus* (1996), *Personals* (1998), and *Summer of Sam* (1999).

Long, Nia (b. Oct. 30, 1970, Brooklyn, N.Y.). Long's first screen appearances were on television. Her film roles include *Boyz 'N the Hood* (1991), *Made in America* (1993), *love jones* (1997), *Soul Food* (1997), *In Too Deep* (1999), and *The Best Man* (1999).

Twentieth Century Fox

McGee, Vonetta (b. Jan. 14, 1950?, San Francisco, Calif.). She appeared in such films as *Blacula* (1972), *Hammer* (1972), *Shaft in Africa* (1973), and *The Big Bust Out* (1973). By the end of the 1970's, McGee had turned to television acting. She appeared in the short-lived series *Hell Town* (1985) and in such series as *Diff'rent Strokes* (1980), *The Yellow Rose* (1984), and *Cagney and Lacey* (1986). In 1994 she appeared in *Cagney and Lacey: The Return*, a television movie.

McKee, Lonette (b. July 21, 1956, Detroit, Mich.). The turning point in McKee's career occurred when she was cast in the film *Sparkle* (1976). She also appeared in two Richard PRYOR films, *Which Way Is Up?* (1977) and *Brewster's Millions* (1985). Her screen credits also include *Cuba* (1979), *The Cotton Club* (1984), *'Round Midnight* (1986), *Jungle Fever* (1991), and *Malcolm X* (1992). McKee is also known for her stage work. The first woman of true African descent to play the octoroon Julie in *Show Boat*, she received a

(continued)

Tony nomination for her performance in a 1983 production of the musical on Broadway. McKee has continued to act well into the late 1990's appearing in television movies and films such as *He Got Game* (1998).

McNair, Barbara (b. Mar. 4, 1939, Racine, Wis.). McNair appeared on such television series as *Hogan's Heroes*, *Dr. Kildare*, and *I Spy* in the mid-1960's. An album, *I Enjoy Being a Girl*, was released in 1964, followed by *Here I Am* in 1967 and *The Real Barbara McNair* in 1970. She starred in her own weekly musical variety television show, *The Barbara McNair Show*, from 1969 to 1971. McNair made appearances in several other films, notably *A Change of Habit* (1969) and *They Call Me Mister Tibbs* (1970). McNair made sporadic appearances in television and film during the 1990's.

Merkerson, S. Epatha (b. 1953?). Merkerson began gaining attention for her appearances on various television dramas during the late 1980's. She appeared in the plays *The Piano Lesson* (1990) and *I'm Not Stupid* (1991). During the 1993-1994 television season, Merkerson landed a role on the drama series *Law & Order*. Merkerson also acted in numerous television programs and a few films during the late 1990's.

AP/Wide World Photos

Nicholas, Denise (b. July 12, 1944, Detroit, Mich.). Nicholas perhaps is best known for her work on the television series *Room 222*, (1969-1974), earning her three Emmy nominations. Her television and film credits are numerous. Her feature film appearances include roles in *Blacula* (1972), *The Soul of Nigger Charley* (1973), *Let's Do It Again* (1975), *A Piece of the Action* (1977), *Capricorn One* (1978), *Marvin and Tige* (1983), and *Ghost Dad* (1990). In the late 1990's Nicholas continued to appear in television with occasional appearances in film.

Nichols, Nichelle (b. Dec. 28, 1936, Robbins, Ill.). Nichols began her theatrical career singing with Duke ELLINGTON and dancing with Sammy DAVIS, Jr. She is primarily known for her role as Lt. Uhura

on the *Star Trek* television series. She also lent her voice to the animated *Star Trek* series (1973-1974) and appeared in the six motion pictures (1979-1991) based on the original television series. Into the late 1990's Nichols continued to appear in television programs related to the *Star Trek* series.

Pace, Judy (b. 1946, Los Angeles, Calif.). Acting in more than two dozen television programs during her career, Pace's credits include series roles in *Peyton Place* and *The Young Lawyers* in the late 1960's and early 1970's as well as appearances in *The Mod Squad* (1968) and *Sanford and Son* (1982). Her film appearances include *The Thomas Crown Affair* (1968) and *Getting Straight* (1970). She won an Image Award in 1970. In the 1999 film *Looking for Oscar* she appeared as herself.

Pinkett Smith, Jada (b. September 18, 1971, Baltimore, Md.). Pinkett Smith began appearing in the television series *A Different World* in 1991. She went on to appear in such films as *Menace II Society* (1993), *The Inkwell* (1994), *Jason's Lyric* (1994), *Set It Off* (1996), and *Woo* (1998).

Pryor, Rain (b. June, 1969). The daughter of comedian Richard PRYOR, Rain Pryor began playing the character of T. J. on television's *Head of the Class* sitcom in 1989. She went on to appear in the short film *Blackbird Fly* (1990) and the television series *Rude Awakening* (1998).

Rashad, Phylicia (b. June 10, 1948, Houston, Tex.). Rashad is best known for her leading role as Claire Huxtable on the enormously successful television series *The Cosby Show* (1984-1992). Her theater work includes performances on and off Broadway in *The Wiz*, *Into the Woods*, *Dreamgirls*, and *Ain't Supposed to Die a Natural Death*. She has appeared in several films, including *Uncle Tom's Cabin* (1987), *False Witness* (1989), *Polly* (1989), *Polly Once Again* (1990), and *Jailbirds* (1991). In 1991 she received an outstanding achievement award from Women in Film. In 1996 she returned to series television in *Cosby*.

Reid, Daphne Maxwell (b. July 13, 1948, New York, N.Y.). Educated at Northwestern University, Reid's successful career in television has included roles on the series *WKRP in Cincinnati* and *Simon and Simon* and in the film *The Long Journey Home* (1987). She played the role of Hannah on the series *Frank's Place* and also appeared on the *Fresh Prince of Bel Air*. She appeared in the films *Once Upon a Time . . . When We Were Colored* (1996) and *Asunder* (1998).

Richards, Beah. *See entry in Theater essay's stage actor table.*

Rochon, Lela (Lela Rochon Staples; b. April 17, 1966, Los Angeles, Ca.). Rochon has appeared on numerous television shows such as *The Cosby Show, The Fresh Prince of Bel-Air*, and *Hangin' with Mr. Cooper*. Her film roles include appearances in *Boomerang* (1992), *Waiting to Exhale* (1995), *Why Do Fools Fall in Love* (1998), and *Any Given Sunday* (1999).

Rolle, Esther (b. Nov. 8, 1922, Pompano Beach, Fla.—Nov. 17, 1998, Los Angeles, Calif.). Best known for her roles on *Maude* (1972-1974) and *Good Times* (1974-1979), Rolle began her career on the stage. Her credits include *The Blacks* (1962), *Blues for Mister Charlie* (1964), *The Amen Corner* (1965), *MacBeth* (1977), *The River Niger* (1983), *A Raisin in the Sun* (1984), and the one-woman show *Ain't I a Woman*. Her film work includes *Cleopatra Jones* in 1973. She was inducted into the black Filmmakers Hall of Fame in 1991.

Sanford, Isabel (b. Aug. 29, 1917, New York, N.Y.). Sanford gained fame for her Emmy-winning (1981) television role as Louise Jefferson of the black situation comedy *The Jeffersons* (1974-1985). She developed her signature character on *All in the Family* (1971-1975). She also achieved recognition on stage and film and played a maid in *Guess Who's Coming to Dinner?* (1967).

Simms, Hilda. *See entry in Theater essay's stage actor table.*

Sinclair, Madge (Madge Walters; b. Apr. 28, 1940, Kingston, Jamaica-Dec. 20, 1995, Los Angeles, Calif.). Sinclair's numerous film, theater, and television credits include the films *Conrack* (1974)—for which she won an Image Award–*Star Trek IV: The Voyage Home* (1986), and *Coming to America* (1988). From 1980 to 1986 she had a regular role in the television series *Trapper John, M.D.* She won an Emmy Award as best supporting actress in the television series *Gabriel's Fire* in 1991.

Summer, Cree (b. July 7, 1970). Summer had a successful career as an actor in film, theater, and on tele-

vision in Canada before appearing on the television series *A Different World* in 1989. After the show went off the air, Summer joined Cicely Tyson on the cast of *Sweet Justice* (1994-1995). In the late 1990's she performed numerous voice-overs for various television programs.

Sykes, Brenda (b. June 25, 1949, Shreveport, La.). Sykes made appearances on such television programs as *Room 222, The Streets of San Francisco*, and *Mayberry R.F.D.* A popular supporting actor of the 1970's, she played in such films as *The Liberation of L. B. Jones* (1970), *Black Gunn* (1972), and *Cleopatra Jones* (1973). She starred in such films as *Honky* (1971), *Mandingo* (1975) and *Drum* (1976).

Thigpen, Lynne (b. Joliet, Ill.). Thigpen landed her first major role in the stage version of *Godspell*, and also appeared in the 1973 film. She had roles in *Lean on Me* (1989) and *Tootsie* (1982), among other films. She appeared in several television series in the 1980's, and in the 1990's played a district attorney on *L.A. Law*, while also playing The Chief on the PBS children's show *Where in the World is Carmen Sandiego?* Thigpen also directed that geography quiz show. She appeared in several films during the 1990's: *Just Cause* (1995), *Random Hearts* (1999), and *The Insider* (1999).

Tyson, Cicely. *See main text entry.*

Uggams, Leslie (b. May 25, 1943, New York, N.Y.). Uggams first gained prominence in the early 1960's as one of the few African American performers on Mitch Miller's weekly variety television show, *Sing Along with Mitch*. Among her honors, Uggams won a 1968 Tony Award for her performance in the musical, *Hallelujah, Baby!*, and received an  Emmy nomination for her portrayal of Kizzy in the television miniseries *Roots* (1977). Uggams made sporadic appearances in television and films during the 1990's.

Washington, Fredi. *See main text entry.*

(continued)

Waters, Ethel. *See main text entry.*

Whitfield, Lynn (b. Baton Rouge, La.). Best known for her work in television, Whitfield won an Emmy Award for her portrayal of the title character in the HBO film *The Josephine Baker Story* (1991). She was also featured in such television films as *Johnnie Mae Gibson: FBI* (1986) and *The Women of Brewster Place* (1989), and in the series *Heartbeat* (1989), and *Equal Justice*, beginning in 1990. She has also appeared in *A Thin Line Between Love and Hate* (1996), *Eve's Bayou* (1997), and the television miniseries *The Wedding* (1998).

Williams, Vanessa. *See main text entry.*

Woodard, Alfre (b. Nov. 8, 1953, Tulsa, Okla.). Woodard has appeared in numerous films including *Remember My Name* (1978), *H.E.A.L.T.H.* (1979), *Cross Creek* (1983), *Crooklyn* (1994), *Down in the Delta* (1998), and *The Wishing Tree* (1999). She has also appeared in a number of television shows such as *Tucker's Witch* (1982-1983), *Hill Street Blues, Sara* (1985), *St. Elsewhere* (1985-1987), and *L.A. Law.*

ing, middle-class family and their quirky, adolescent neighbor, and NBC's *The Fresh Prince of Bel-Air* (1990-1996), which featured the cultural clash between a rich California family and their young relative (played by Will Smith) from the inner city in Philadelphia. In both these comedies, the stories revolved around typical family harmony issues and the challenges that came from balancing these issues amid the competing claims of sibling rivalry, marital spats, and romantic interests. Additionally, each program devoted some episodes to exploring issues related specifically to race. For example, both shows included episodes in which the teenage male characters confronted racism during encounters with law enforcement officers.

One family series that attempted to deal with racism on a fairly regular basis was the Fox television series *Roc* (1991-1994), in whi members of a blue-collar extended family consistently identified themselves as African American and openly disagreed about the "correct" perspective on a particular social issue while maintaining a comfortable level of family harmony. Many of the new situation comedies made a conscientious effort to include a variety of viewpoints, if only to set up a comedic punch line.

There were several comedies focusing on African American households that featured friends acting as surrogate families, often living under the same roof or in the same building. Among the most popular were ABC's *Hanging with Mr. Cooper* (1992-1996), which was dubbed a "crossover" comedy because of its popularity with both black and white audiences. The show featured three roommates who stuck by one another like family, and the male lead functioned as a big brother to his students and to neighborhood children. Two other notable comedies were aired on the Fox network: *Martin* (1992-1997), starring comedian Martin Lawrence as part of a couple sorting out the challenges of modern romance, and *Living Single* (1993-1998), featuring four single women depending on one another's support and candidness in coping with the demands of their careers, romances, and other personal issues. Criticism of programs such as *Martin* stemmed from the star's decision to create certain roles reminiscent of the caricatures of a previous era. In the case of *Living Single*, the program received initial criticism for the way in which its intelligent, career-oriented female characters focused much of their conversation on "men, men, men." The

(continued on page 2451)

Notable Male Television and Film Actors

Amos, John (b. Dec. 27, 1939, Newark, N.J.). Amos is well known for his Emmy-nominated role as the adult Kunta Kinte in the miniseries *Roots* (1977). He has many other television, stage, and film acting credits. Acting honors include a most outstanding performance nomination by the Los Angeles Drama Critics in 1971 for *Norman, Is That You?* and an IMAGE AWARD nomination in 1985 for best actor for *Split Second*. He also appeared in the hit film, *Boomerang* (1992). Amos continued his acting into the late 1990's with appearances in television movies and feature films.

Anderson, Eddie "Rochester." *See main text entry.*

Belafonte, Harry. *See main text entry.*

Blacque, Taurean. *See entry in Theater essay's stage actor table.*

Braugher, Andre (b. July 1, 1962, Chicago, Ill.). Braugher's film appearances include the feature film *Glory* (1989), the television film *Murder in Mississippi* (1990), and several Shakespearean productions: *Richard III, Measure for Measure,* and *Othello.* He is best known for his work on the television series *Homicide: Life on the Street* (1993). He left the series in 1998 and continued to appear in television and film roles.

Brooks, Avery (b. 1949, Evansville, Ind.). Brooks probably is best known as the gun-for-hire, Hawk, whom he played in two television series: *Spenser: For Hire* (1985-1988) and *A Man Called Hawk* (1989). He also appeared on the stage in *Spell 7* (1979), the opera *X: The Life and Times of Malcolm X* (1985), *Paul Robeson* (1988), and *Othello* (1991). Brooks was a regular in the television series *Star Trek: Deep Space Nine* (1993-1999).

Brown, Georg Stanford (b. June 24, 1943, Havana, Cuba): Stanford has many film, theater, and television appearances to his credit, including an Emmy-nominated role in the miniseries *Roots* (1977). He won a 1986 Emmy Award for directing an episode of the popular police show *Cagney and Lacey*.

Browne, Roscoe Lee (b. May 2, 1925, Woodbury, N.J.). Browne's stage work includes *Julius Caesar* (1957), *The Blacks* (1961), *The Dream on Monkey Mountain* (1971), and *Benito Cereno* (1974). He has appeared on film in *Black Like Me* (1964), *The Liberation of L. B. Jones* (1970), *The Cowboys* (1972), and *Legal Eagles* (1986). Television work includes *The Defenders* (1963), the miniseries *King* (1979), and *The Cosby Show* (1986). Throughout the 1990's Brown continued to appear in film and television roles.

Burton, LeVar (Le Vardis Robert Martyn, Jr.; b. Feb. 16, 1957, Landstuhl, West Germany). Burton gained fame by playing the young Kunta Kinte in the television miniseries *Roots* (1977) and in *Roots: The Gift* (1988). Throughout the late 1990's Burton portrayed the blind Lieutenant Geordi La Forge in television's *Star Trek: The Next Generation* and in feature films based on it.

Caesar, Adolph. *See entry in Theater essay's stage actor table.*

Cambridge, Godfrey (Feb. 26, 1933, New York, N.Y.—Nov. 29, 1976, Hollywood, Calif.). Cambridge gained fame in the 1960's as a stage actor, acerbic comedian, and screen star. He is known for his work in *Cotton Comes to Harlem* (1970) and its sequel, *Come Back, Charleston Blue* (1972). He also appeared in *Watermelon Man* (1970). Cambridge's career was cut short by his premature death from a heart attack.

AP/Wide World Photos

Casey, Bernie (b. June 8, 1939, Wyco, W.Va.). Casey starred in the 1977 film *Brothers* and has had featured roles in numerous films, such as *Guns of the Magnificent Seven* (1969), *Cleopatra Jones* (1973), *The Man Who Fell to Earth* (1976), *Bill and Ted's Excellent Adventure*

(continued)

(1989), *I'm Gonna Git You Sucka* (1988), and *The Glass Shield* (1994). He appeared in several television shows, including the miniseries *Roots: The Next Generations* (1979). Casey continued to appear in television and film roles in the late 1990's.

Chestnut, Morris (b. Jan. 1, 1969, Cerritos, Ca.). Chestnut has appeared in television movies and such feature films as *Boyz 'N the Hood* (1991), *The Inkwell* (1994), and *The Best Man* (1999).

Cosby, Bill. *See main text entry.*

Crosse, Rupert (1928, Nevis, British West Indies—Mar. 5, 1973, Nevis, British West Indies). Crosse starred in such films as *The Reivers* (1970), *Too Late Blues* (1961), *Shadows* (1961), and *Ride in the Whirlwind* (1965). He also appeared in numerous stage productions and on various television series.

Crothers, Scatman (Benjamin Sherman Crothers; May 23, 1910, Terre Haute, Ind.—Nov. 22, 1986, Los Angeles, Calif.). Best known for his role as Louie the garbage man on the popular television sitcom *Chico and the Man* from 1974 to 1978, Crothers also made memorable appearances in the films *One Flew over the Cuckoo's Nest* (1975), *The Shootist* (1976), *The Shining* (1980), and *Twilight Zone—The Movie* (1983). Crothers also had a part in the television miniseries *Roots* (1977).

AP/Wide World Photos

Davis, Clifton (b. Oct. 4, 1945, Chicago, Ill.). Davis began his acting career in a Broadway production of *Hello, Dolly!* in 1967. He appeared in numerous stage productions. Davis transferred his acting skills to the small screen with the series *That's My Mama* in the 1974-1975 television season and the series *Amen*, which debuted in 1986. Davis has also appeared in television movies, specials, and series, as well as films, such as *Any Given Sunday* (1999).

Davis, Ossie. *See main text entry.*

Davis, Sammy, Jr. *See main text entry.*

Diggs, Taye (Scott Diggs; b. 1972, Rochester, N.Y.). Diggs appeared in a soap opera before making the switch to the big screen. He has appeared in numerous films including *How Stella Got Her Groove Back* (1998), *The Wood* (1999) and *The Best Man* (1999).

Dixon, Ivan (b. Apr. 6, 1931, New York, N.Y.). Dixon has performed in numerous plays including *The Cave Dwellers* (1957) and *A Raisin in the Sun* (1959). His film appearances include *Porgy and Bess* (1959), *To Trap a Spy* (1966) and *Car Wash* (1976). He also appeared on the small screen in the television series *Hogan's Heroes* (1965-1970) and the teleplay *The Final War of Olly Winter* (1967). Beginning in the late 1960's, Dixon directed and worked on television programs through the 1980's.

Dorn, Michael (b. Lulling, Tex.). Following roles in nighttime television soap operas and the television series *CHiPs* (1980-1982), Dorn landed the role of Lieutenant Worf on *Star Trek: The Next Generation* in 1987. Worf's role as an alien raised by humans and the only Klingon officer in an interstellar federation dominated by humans, is laden with racial symbolism. Dorn also appeared in the film *Star Trek VI: The Undiscovered Country* (1991). He continued to make guest appearances on television shows throughout the 1990's.

Dutton, Charles S. *See entry in Theater essay's stage actor table.*

Epps, Omar (b. May 16, 1973, Brooklyn, N.Y.). Epps has appeared in a number of television programs. He has also starred in a number of films including *Juice* (1992), *Higher Learning* (1995), *Scream 2* (1997), *The Mod Squad* (1999), *The Wood* (1999), and *In Too Deep* (1999).

Esposito, Giancarlo (b. Apr. 26, 1958, Copenhagen, Denmark). Esposito began to appear in small roles on television shows such as *The Equalizer*, *Spenser: For Hire*, and *Miami Vice* during the 1980's and launched his film career with supporting roles in *Trading Places* (1983) and *The Cotton Club* (1984). He appeared in the films *School Daze* (1988), *Do the Right Thing* (1989), *Mo' Better Blues* (1990), *Malcolm X* (1992), *Fresh* (1994), and *Smoke* (1995). Through the late 1990's he had numerous film roles.

Evans, Michael Jonas (b. Nov. 3, 1949, Salisbury, N.C.). Best known for his role as Lionel Jefferson in the television series *All in the Family* from 1971 to 1975, he reprised that part in *The Jeffersons* in 1975 and again from 1979 to 1982. Evans also co-created the television series *Good Times* in 1974. He continued to appear in television roles through the mid-1990's.

Fetchit, Stepin. *See main text entry.*

Fishburne, Laurence, III. *See main text entry.*

Foxx, Redd. *See main text entry.*

Freeman, Albert Cornelius, Jr. *See entry in Theater essay's stage actor table.*

Freeman, Morgan. *See main text entry.*

Glover, Danny. *See main text entry.*

Gooding, Cuba, Jr. (b. Jan. 2, 1968, Bronx, N.Y.). Gooding has appeared in a number of films including *Boyz 'N the Hood* (1991), *A Few Good Men* (1992), *Outbreak* (1995), *Losing Isaiah* (1995), *Jerry Maguire* (1996), *As Good As It Gets* (1997), and *Instinct* (1999). He won a best supporting actor Academy Award for his role as a professional football player in *Jerry Maguire*.

Gossett, Lou, Jr. *See main text entry.*

Guillaume, Robert (b. Nov. 30, 1937, St. Louis, Mo.). Guillaume's theater credits include *Guys and Dolls* and *Purlie* (1970). He has also appeared in numerous television shows, and he is well known for his role as Benson, the butler of a governor, on *Soap* (1977-1981). He later starred in a spin-off series, *Benson* (1979-1986), in which Benson himself becomes lieutenant governor. For this role he received two Emmy Awards. Other series followed, including *The Robert Guillaume Show* (1989), *Pacific Station* (1991), and *Sports Night* (1998-   ). In addition, Guillaume has appeared in film and musical theater roles.

Hardison, Kadeem (b. c. 1966, Brooklyn, N.Y.). Hardison played the role of Dwayne Wayne on television's *A Different World* starting in 1987. He continued to appear in other roles after the series ended. He also appeared on *The Cosby Show* and in the films *School Daze* (1988) and *White Men Can't Jump* (1992), *Panther* (1995), and *The Sixth Man* (1997). He was part

of the ensemble cast of the short-lived series *Between Brothers* which debuted in 1997.

Harewood, Dorian (b. Aug. 6, 1950, Dayton, Ohio). Harewood first performed with the New York Shakespeare Festival in 1972 and appeared in various Broadway and Off-Broadway productions before touring in a production of *Jesus Christ Superstar*. Harewood landed television roles on *Roots: The Next Generations* (1979) and *Beulah Land* (1980) before appearing in the title role in the syndicated film *The Jesse Owens Story* (1984). His film credits include roles in *Against All Odds* (1984), *The Falcon and the Snowman* (1985), and *Full Metal Jacket* (1987). In 1989 he appeared in the Broadway production of *To Sir, with Love.* Harewood continued to appear in guest starring roles in various television series through the late 1990's.

Haynes, Lloyd (Oct. 19, 1935, South Bend, Ind.—Dec. 31, 1986, Coronado, Calif.). Haynes is best known for his portrayal of the benevolent high school history teacher, Pete Dixon, in the television series *Room 222* (1969-1974). His feature film credits include *Ice Station Zebra* (1968) and *The Greatest* (1977).

Hemsley, Sherman (b. Feb. 1, 1938, Philadelphia, Pa.). After playing several small parts, Hemsley landed the major role of Gitlow in the Broadway musical *Purlie* (1970). He is best known for his work on the television series *The Jeffersons* (1975-1985), one of the longest-running television shows with African Americans as central characters. Hemsley followed it with the successful series *Amen* (1986-1991). He continued to make television and film appearances during the 1990's.

Hernandez, Juano (1896, San Juan, Puerto Rico—July 17, 1970, San Juan, Puerto Rico). Hernandez's role as Lucas Beauchamp in *Intruder in the Dust* (1949) was the first definitive film portrayal of an African American who did not accommodate racial hatred and stood in defiance of it.

Hooks, Kevin (b. Sept. 19, 1958, Philadelphia, Pa.). The son of actor Robert Hooks, Kevin Hooks began his acting career with an appearance on his father's television series, *N.Y.P.D.* (1968). Subsequent roles include appearances in the teleplays *J.T.* (1970) and *Just an Old Sweet Song* (1976), the series *The White*

(continued)

Shadow (1978-1981), and the sitcom *He's the Mayor* (1986). Hooks appeared in the films *Sounder* (1972), *Aaron Loves Angela* (1975) and *A Hero Ain't Nothin' but a Sandwich* (1978). By the mid-1980's he turned from acting to directing. Between 1984 and 1987, he directed numerous television programs. In 1991 he directed his first feature film, *Strictly Business*. He continued to direct well into the 1990's with films such as *Passenger 57* (1992) and *Fled* (1996).

Hudson, Ernie (b. Dec. 17, 1945, Benton Harbor, Mich.). Hudson has portrayed a wide range of characters. His film roles include *Leadbelly* (1976), *Ghostbusters* (1984), *Weeds* (1986) *Ghostbusters II* (1989), *The Hand That Rocks the Cradle* (1992), *The Crow* (1994), *The Basketball Diaries* (1995), *Congo* (1995), and *The Substitute* (1996). Hudson continued to appear in television and feature films through the late 1990's.

Hyman, Earle. *See entry in Theater essay's stage actor table.*

Ice Cube. *See main text entry.*

Ingram, Rex (Oct. 20, 1895, Cairo, Ill.—Sept. 19, 1969, Los Angeles, Calif.). Ingram began his acting career as an African native in an early Tarzan film. After several bit parts, Ingram's breakthrough film role was "De Lawd" in *The Green Pastures* (1936). He also played the escaping slave Jim in *The Adventures of Huckleberry Finn* (1939). His best-known stage work was in *Cabin in the Sky* (1940).

Jackson, Samuel L. *See main text entry.*

Jacobs, Lawrence-Hilton (b. Sept. 4, 1953, New York, N.Y.). In addition to his role as wisecracking Freddie "Boom Boom" Washington in the television series *Welcome Back, Kotter* (1975-1979), Jacobs appeared in numerous films, including *Serpico* (1973), *Death Wish* (1974), *Cooley High* (1975), and *Youngblood* (1978). He continued to act into the late 1990's.

Jones, James Earl. *See main text entry.*

Kelly, Jim (b. May 5, 1946, Paris, Ky.). An international middleweight karate champion (1971), Kelly is best known for his roles in martial arts and action films of the 1970's, including *Enter the Dragon* (1973), *Black Belt Jones* (1974), and *Black Samurai* (1977). He continued to act in the 1990's.

Kennedy, Leon Isaac (b. 1949, Cleveland, Ohio). Kennedy is known for roles as an underdog boxer, particularly in the gritty films *Penitentiary* (1979), *Penitentiary II* (1982), and *Penitentiary III* (1987). Kennedy also starred in the 1981 remake film *Body and Soul*. Kennedy's other film appearances include *Hollywood Vice Squad* (1986), *Too Scared to Scream* (1982), and *Knights of the City* (1987).

Kirby, George (b. June 8, 1923, Chicago, Ill.). Kirby was featured on the short-lived weekly *ABC Comedy Hour* in 1972. He appeared in numerous episodes of such television series as *Gimme a Break; Murder, She Wrote; Fame; 227;* and *The Perry Como Show.* He also appeared in such films as *A Man Called Adam* (1966), *Trouble in Mind* (1985), and *Leonard Part 6* (1987). He is known for his more than one hundred impersonations.

Kotto, Yaphet. *See main text entry.*

LaSalle, Eriq (b. July 23, 1962, Hartford, Conn.). LaSalle has appeared in a number of films including *Coming to America* (1988). In 1994 LaSalle was cast in the television medical drama *ER*. LaSalle wrote, directed, and had a supporting role in the film *Psalms from the Underground* (1996).

Lee, Canada. *See main text entry.*

Lockhart, Calvin (b. Oct. 8, 1934, Nassau, Bahama Islands). In *Joanna* (1968), Lockhart introduced himself to film audiences as a sophisticated and confident character who falls in love with a white woman. He also appeared in *Cotton Comes to Harlem* (1970). He was relegated to supporting roles in *Uptown Saturday Night* (1974) and *Let's Do It Again* (1975). He continued to play relatively minor film and television parts and appeared as one of Diahann CARROLL's suitors on the television series *Dynasty* in the 1980's. He appeared in the films *Coming to America* (1988) and *Predator 2* (1990).

Lumbly, Carl (b. 1952?, Jamaica, West Indies). Best known for his role as detective Mark Petrie in the television series *Cagney and Lacey*, Lumbly also appeared in the series *Taxi*. His film credits include *Judgment in Berlin* (1988). In 1998 Lumbly appeared in the television mini series *The Wedding* and in the feature film *How Stella Got Her Groove Back*.

Marshall, William. *See entry in Theater essay's stage actor table.*

Mayo, Whitman (b. Nov. 15, 1930, New York, N.Y.). Mayo is best known for his role as Grady on the television series *Sanford and Son* (1973-1977) and the spin-off *Grady* (1975-1976). film credits include *The Main Event* (1979). He has appeared on stage in numerous plays, including *The Amen Corner* (1964), *Goin' to Buffalo* (1969), and *What If It Had Turned Up Heads* (1972). Mayo continued to appear in television and films during the 1990's. In 1991 he appeared in *Boyz 'N the Hood*.

AP/Wide World Photos

Morris, Garrett (b. Feb. 1, 1937, New Orleans, La.). Morris is best known as a member of the original ensemble cast of television's *Saturday Night Live* (1975-1980). He also appeared in numerous films and theater productions, including the films *Where's Poppa?* (1970), *Cooley High* (1975), and *Car Wash* (1976) and the plays *Ain't Supposed to Die a Natural Death* (1971) and *What the Wine Sellers Buy* (1973). In the 1990's Morris continued to make numerous television and film appearances. In 1996 he was cast in the television series *The Jamie Foxx Show*.

Morris, Greg (b. Sept. 27, 1934, Cleveland, Ohio-Aug. 28, 1996, Las Vegas, Nev.). Morris is best known as Barney Collier, the technical wizard of television's *Mission: Impossible* (1966-1973). He was one of the few black actors to appear as a dramatic series regular in the 1960's. His other television work includes episodes of *The Twilight Zone* (1963), *I Spy* (1966), *Sanford and Son* (1976), *Vega$* (1979-81), *The Jeffersons* (1983), and *The Jesse Owens Story* (1984). Among his film credits are *The New Interns* (1964) and *Sword of Ali Baba* (1965). He continued to appear in television and film roles until his death.

Morrison, Sunshine Sammy (b. Dec. 20, 1912, New Orleans, La.). When he was seven years old, E. Frederick Morrison became the first African American actor to sign with a Hollywood studio. His easy disposition and quick grasp of material endeared him to director Hal Roach, who dubbed him "Sunshine Sammy." Morrison earned 146 film credits in both silent and sound films. He was became noted as a dancer, comedian, and singer. He was inducted into the Black Filmmakers Hall of Fame in 1987.

Morton, Edna. A silent-film actor, Morton appeared in eight films from independent producers during the early 1920's. These included *The Burden of Race* (1921), *The Call of His People* (1922), *Easy Money* (1922), and *Wildfire* (1925).

Morton, Joe (b. Oct. 8, 1947, New York, N.Y.). Morton is perhaps best known for his leading role in the 1984 cult film *The Brother from Another Planet*. Morton has appeared in soap operas as well as other television series, and in a variety of other films. He was in *Tap* (1989), starring Gregory Hines, and was featured in *Between the Lines* (1977), *Crossroads* (1986), and *Trouble in Mind* (1986). He costarred in *Stranded* (1987). Morton has appeared on the television shows *Equal Justice*, and *Grady* (1975-1976), a spin-off from *Sanford and Son*. Some of his appearances in the 1990's include television's *Miss Evers' Boys* (1997) and the films *The Inkwell* (1994), *Speed 2: Cruise Control* (1997), and *Blues Brothers 2000* (1998).

Museum of Modern Art, Film Stills Archive

Mosley, Roger E. (b. Los Angeles, Calif.). Mosley appeared in such films as *Leadbelly* (1976), *Heart Condition* (1990), and *Unlawful Entry* (1992). From 1980 to 1988, he was featured on the television series *Magnum, P.I.* In the 1990's his television and film appearances included *A Thin Line Between Love and Hate* (1996).

Mr. T (Lawrence Tureaud or Tero; b. May 21, 1952, Chicago, Ill.). Before starring in the Sylvester Stallone film *Rocky III* (1982) as boxer Clubber Lang, Mr. T worked as a bodyguard for such celebrities as

(continued)

boxers Muhammad ALI and Leon Spinks and singer Donna SUMMER. He also played Sergeant Bosco "B. A." Baracus in the television series *The A-Team* (1983-1987). He changed his name officially in 1970. He continued to act in television and films during

Arkent Archive

the late 1990's, when he began experiencing serious health problems.

Murphy, Eddie. *See main text entry.*

Muse, Clarence (Oct. 7, 1889, Baltimore, Md.—Oct. 13, 1979, Perris, Calif.). As a film actor, Muse is best remembered for playing domestic roles in the 1930's with great dignity. In 1973 critics considered Muse's intelligent rendering of black characters worthy of his induction into the Black Filmmakers Hall of Fame. He appeared in such films as the all-black film *Hearts in Dixie*, *Huckleberry Finn* (1931), and the Civil War drama *So Red the Rose* (1935), as well as dozens of other films through the 1940's. In his later years, he appeared on screen only sporadically. His last three film appearances were in *Buck and the Preacher* (1972), *Car Wash* (1976), and *The Black Stallion* (1979).

O'Neal, Ron (b. Sept. 1, 1937, Utica, N.Y.). O'Neal is best known for his leading role as Priest in the film *Superfly* (1972). He re-created the character of Priest in *Superfly T.N.T.* (1973). He later acted in NEC productions including *Ceremonies in Dark Old Men* (1969) and *Dream on Monkey Mountain* (1971). His television appearances include recurring roles in *Bring 'Em Back Alive* (1982-1983) and *The Equalizer* (1986). In the late 1990's O'Neal continued to make appearances in films, such as *Original Gangstas* (1996).

Peters, Brock (Brock Fisher; b. July 2, 1927, New York, N.Y.). Peters's major stage credits include the touring productions of *The Great White Hope* (1969), *Lost in the Stars* (1972), and *Driving Miss Daisy* (1988). His film credits include *Carmen Jones* (1954), *Porgy and Bess* (1959), *To Kill a Mockingbird* (1962), *The Pawnbroker* (1965), *The Incident* (1967), the screen version of the musical *Lost in the Stars* (1974), and *Star*

Trek IV: The Voyage Home (1986). He has received numerous honors, including the L.A. Drama Critics Circle Award, three Image Awards, and lifetime achievement awards from the National Film Society and the Screen Actors Guild. Peters continued acting into

Museum of Modern Art, Film Stills Archive

the late 1990's with appearances in television movies and films such as *Ghosts of Mississippi* (1996).

Phifer, Mekhi (b. 1975, New York, N.Y.). Phifer has made guest appearances on the television shows *Homicide: Life on the Street* and *New York Undercover*. His film appearances include roles in the films *Clockers* (1995), *Soul Food* (1997), and *I Still Know What You Did Last Summer* (1998).

Poitier, Sidney. *See main text entry.*

Rasulala, Thalmus (Jack Crowder; Nov. 15, 1939, Miami, Fla.—Oct. 9, 1991, Albuquerque, N.M.). Rasulala's theater credits include *Fly Blackbird* (1962), *Hello, Dolly!* (1964-1969), and *One Is a Crowd* (1970). His film experience includes *Cool Breeze* (1972), *The Last Hard Men* (1976), *Above the Law* (1988), and *Life on the Edge* (1992). His television work include appearances in *T. J. Hooker*, *Cagney and Lacey*, *Simon and Simon*, *Duet*, and *Star Trek: The Next Generation*. He won a Theater World Award in 1968 for his work in *Hello, Dolly!*

Reid, Tim (b. Dec. 19, 1944, Norfolk, Va.). Reid is best known for his work on the hit television series *WKRP in Cincinnati* (1978-1982). He also appeared on the television series *Simon and Simon* (1983-1984). Reid hosted CBS's *Summer Playhouse* in 1987 and produced and acted in the critically acclaimed, but short-lived, television show *Frank's Place* (1987-1988). He also created, produced, and acted in *Snoops* (1988-1989). In the 1990's Reid was a star of the series *Sister, Sister* and also started to receive recognition as a director. Reid continued to act into the late 1990's.

Rhames, Ving (Irving Rhames; b. May 12, 1961, New York, N.Y.). Rhames has appeared in numerous film and television programs. His film credits and television guest appearances are extensive. His appearances include *Pulp Fiction* (1994), *Mission Impossible* (1996), *Rosewood* (1997), the cable movie *Don King: Only in America* (1997), *Out of Sight* (1998), and *Entrapment* (1999).

Robeson, Paul. *See main text entry.*

Rollins, Howard, Jr. (b. Oct. 17, 1951, Baltimore, Md.—Dec. 8, 1996, New York, N.Y.). Rollins's acting career began on the stage in 1967. The turning point in his television career came in 1978, with his work on the miniseries *King*. Among his other television credits are *Roots: The Next Generations* (1979), *A Member of the Wedding* (1982), *For Us, the Living* (1983), *The Wild Side* (1985), and *Johnnie Mae Gibson: FBI* (1986). His film work included roles in *Ragtime* (1981) and *A Soldier's Story* (1984). In 1988 he began his role on the successful television series *In the Heat of the Night*. He continued on the series until 1993.

Ross, Diana. *See main text entry.*

Roundtree, Richard (b. July 9, 1942, New Rochelle, N.Y.). Roundtree began his acting career in such NEC productions as *Mau Mau Room* (1968), *Kongi's Harvest* (1968), and *Man, Better Man* (1969). He is most recognized for his starring role in the film *Shaft* (1971). Roundtree starred in the film's two sequels, *Shaft's Big Score* (1972) and *Shaft in Africa* (1973). His other film appearances include roles in *Embassy* (1972), *Charley One-Eye* (1973), *Earthquake* (1974), *Diamonds* (1975), and *Man Friday* (1976). Roundtree delivered one of his strongest performances in the television miniseries *Roots* (1977). In the late 1980's and 1990's he was working primarily on television.

Shakur, Tupac. *See main text entry.*

Snipes, Wesley (b. 1962, Orlando, Fla.). In 1986 Snipes appeared in his first film role, as a high school football player in *Wildcats*. From 1986 to 1988, he performed in three theater productions in New York City: *Execution of Justice, Death and the King's Horseman,* and *The Boys of Winter*. His film work includes roles in *Mo' Better Blues* (1989) *New Jack City* (1991), *Jungle Fever* (1991), *White Men Can't Jump* (1992), *Passenger 57* (1992), *Demolition Man* (1993), *The Fan* (1996), *U.S. Marshals* (1998), and *Blade* (1998).

St. Jacques, Raymond (James Arthur Johnson; Mar. 1, 1930, Hartford, Conn.—Aug. 27, 1990, Los Angeles, Calif.). St. Jacques first gained prominence for his 1961 portrayal of the judge in the Broadway play, *The Blacks*. He later appeared in guest roles on numerous television series in the 1960's and 1970's. His film roles include appearances in *The Comedians* (1967) and *Cotton Comes to Harlem* (1970). He continued to act into the late 1980's.

Tate, Larenz (b. Sept. 8, 1975, Chicago, Ill.). Tate has appeared in several television programs such as *The Fresh Prince of Bel-Air* (1990) and *Family Matters* (1989). His film roles include appearances in *Menace II Society* (1993), *The Inkwell* (1994), *Dead Presidents* (1995), *love jones* (1997), and *Why Do Fools Fall In Love* (1998).

Taylor, Meshach (b. Apr. 11, c. 1947, Boston, Mass.). Taylor has had significant roles in two successful television shows, *Designing Women* and *Dave's World*. Taylor has appeared in numerous films including *Damien—Omen II* (1978), *The Howling* (1981), *One More Saturday Night* (1986), *House of Games* (1987), *Mannequin* (1987), *From the Hip* (1987), *Mannequin II* (1991), and *Class Act* (1992). In the late 1990's Taylor continued to appear in television roles.

AP/Wide World Photos

Thomas, Philip Michael (b. May 26, 1949, Los Angeles, Calif.). Thomas is best known for his role as a member of the multiracial ensemble cast of the hit television series *Miami Vice*, which began airing on NBC in 1984. After *Miami Vice* was canceled in 1989, Thomas starred in several made-for-television films, appeared in television infomercials, and was active behind the camera as a television director.

Turman, Glynn Russell (b. Jan. 31, 1947, New York, N.Y.). Turman has appeared in Broadway plays and
(continued)

films such as *The River Niger* (1975), *Cooley High* (1975), and *A Hero Ain't Nothin' but a Sandwich* (1977). In 1978 he received an Image Award for his achievements as an actor. In 1988 Turman returned to series television in *A Different World*. Through the late 1990's Turman continued to appear in television.

Underwood, Blair (b. 1964, Tacoma, Wash.). Underwood appeared in guest spots on *The Cosby Show*. In 1987 he began his stint on the hit series *L.A. Law*. Underwood also appeared in a cameo role on *A Different World* and has been featured in a series of NBC public service announcements about education. Throughout the 1990's he starred in various film and television roles. Underwood returned to television series acting with *City of Angels* (2000).

Warren, Michael (b. Mar. 5, 1946, South Bend, Ind.). After a successful basketball career at UCLA, Warren went into acting and had a regular role on the television series *Hill Street Blues* (1981-1987). He appeared in the films *Fast Break* (1979), *Norman, Is That You?* (1976), and *Drive He Said* (1970). He appeared in the television movies *The Child Saver* (1989) and *The Kid Who Loved Christmas* (1990). He produced and acted in the television pilot *Home Free* (1988). Warren's work on *Hill Street Blues* garnered him an Emmy nomination. During the 1990's Warren guested on various television programs. He appeared in the television drama *City of Angels* (2000).

Wayans, Keenen Ivory (b. June 8, 1958, New York, N.Y.). Wayans's acting career began with appearances in such television hits as *Benson*, *Cheers*, and *A Different World*. He collaborated with Robert Townsend on *Hollywood Shuffle* (1982), *Robert Townsend's Partners in Crime*, *Eddie Murphy Raw* (1987), and *The Five Heartbeats* (1991). He served as executive producer, writer, director, and star of *I'm Gonna Git You Sucka* (1989). He launched his own series *In Living Color* (1990-1992). In 1990 Wayans received the prestigious American Black Achievement Award for his contributions to dramatic arts. That same year, *In Living Color* won an Emmy Award

as the most outstanding variety, music, and comedy series and an Image Award as best variety show. Wayans directed, wrote, and starred in the film *A Low Down Dirty Shame* (1994). Wayans served as executive producer for the film *Don't Be a Menace in South Central While Drinking Your Juice in the Hood* (1996).

Weathers, Carl (b. Jan. 14, 1948, New Orleans, La.). Weathers is best known as boxer Apollo Creed in the first four films of the series that began with *Rocky* (1976). In 1986 he starred as the title character in the television series *Fortune Dane*. Into the late 1990's Weathers continued to act in series television and feature films.

Whitaker, Forest (b. July 15, 1961, Longview, Tex.). Whitaker has appeared in numerous films, including *Fast Times at Ridgemont High* (1982), *The Color of Money* (1986), *Platoon* (1986), *Good Morning, Vietnam* (1987), *Bird* (1988), *Johnny Handsome* (1990), *A Rage in Harlem* (1991), *The Crying Game* (1992), *Species* (1995), and *Light It Up* (1999). He has also received recognition as the director of several feature films.

Williams, Billy Dee (b. Apr. 6, 1937, New York, N.Y.). Williams made his professional stage debut at the age of seven in the musical *The Firebrand of Florence* (1945). He continued to star in such plays as *Slow Dance on the Killing* (1970), *I Have a Dream* (1976), and *Fences* (1988). He made appearances in the 1960's and 1970's on many television series. The turning point in his career came with his starring role as famed football player Gayle Sayers in the television movie *Brian's Song* (1970). Williams teamed with Diana Ross in *Lady Sings the Blues* (1972) and *Mahogany* (1975). He continued to appear in such films as *The Empire Strikes Back* (1980), *Return of the Jedi* (1983), and *Batman* (1989). He continued working steadily into the late 1990's.

Williams, Clarence, III (b. Aug. 21, 1939, New York, N.Y.). Best known for his role as Linc Hayes on the television series *The Mod Squad* (1968-1973). Williams has also appeared on the television shows *Daktari* (1967) and *Miami Vice* (1985), among others. His film credits include *Purple Rain* (1984) and *Deep Cover* (1992). Williams continued to act in films during the late 1990's. He appeared in *Hoodlum* (1997), *Life* (1999), and *The General's Daughter* (1999).

Williamson, Fred (b. Mar. 5, 1938, Gary, Ind.). A former professional football player, Williamson is best known for his starring roles as the hero of action films during the BLAXPLOITATION era of the 1970's. He appeared in such films as *Hammer* (1972), *The Legend of Nigger Charley* (1972), *Black Caesar* (1973), *Black Eye* (1974), *Three the Hard Way* (1974), and *Bucktown* (1975). Williamson appeared in guest spots on television throughout the 1970's and 1980's in such shows as *The Rookies* (1974), *Fantasy Island* (1980), *Lou Grant* (1981), and *The Equalizer* (1986). In the 1990's Williamson continued to appear in

AP/Wide World Photos

television and film roles, such as *Original Gangstas* (1996), and *Night Vision* (1998).

Wilson, Demond (b. Oct. 13, 1946, Valdosta, Ga.). Wilson's theater credits include his acting debut in *Green Pastures* in 1951 and *Five on the Black Hand Side* in 1970. However, he is easily best known for his role as Lamont on the television series *Sanford and Son* (1972-1977), in which he played Redd Foxx's son. He also co-starred in the short-lived *New Odd Couple* (1982-1983). He later became an evangelist in Southern California.

Winfield, Paul (b. May 22, 1940, Los Angeles, Calif.). Winfield has appeared in plays and television roles. His distinguished film career includes roles in *Sounder* (1972), *The Greatest* (1977), *A Hero Ain't Nothin' But a Sandwich* (1977), *Star Trek II: The Wrath of Khan* (1982), *The Serpent and the Rainbow* (1988), and *Presumed Innocent* (1990). His television credits include *The Sophisticated Gents*, *Backstairs at the Whitehouse*, *Roots: The Next Generations* and *Roots: The Gift*, and *The Women of Brewster Place*. Through the 1990's Winfield continued to appear in film and television roles such as *Mars Attacks!* (1996).

show's producers responded immediately with episodes that dealt with many issues affecting not only the women's lives but also the lives of their two male costars.

Other situation comedies of the 1990's included *Sister, Sister* (1994-   , with Tia and Tamera Mowry), *In the House* (1995-1998, with Debbie ALLEN and L.L. COOL J), *The Parent 'Hood* (1995-   , with Robert Townsend), *The Jamie Foxx Show* (1996-   ), *Malcolm and Eddie* (1996-   , with Malcolm-Jamal Warner and Eddie Griffin), *Moesha* (1996-   , with Brandy Norwood), *Sparks* (1996-   , with James Avery), and *The Steve Harvey Show* (1996-   ).

A number of television comedies that did not focus primarily on African American life displayed greater sensitivity in includingch black characters, weaving them in as interesting additions to the main casts. Criticism of comedy programs featuring African Ameri-

cans has been largely to raise questions about the continued presence of caricatures and stereotypes alongside the more realistic, complex characterizations, despite the fact that there have been exemplary comedic models that do not rely on caricature at all.

Drama Series

Since the 1965 premier of *I Spy*, African Americans have been featured as stars in television drama series. Drama series, outside of documentaries and features, have been the most receptive in including complex characterizations of African Americans. Nevertheless, drama series featuring all-black casts have been rare. Virtually all the dramatic portrayals of African Americans are to be found in drama series with primarily white, although integrated, casts. While this situation is likely to be simply a re-

(continued on page 2460)

Television Programs

Amen (NBC, 1986-1991). Pioneering situation comedy based on religion, starring Sherman Hemsley as a hot-headed Philadelphia church deacon and Clifton Davis as an eloquent minister romantically pursued by the deacon's daughter (Anna Maria Horsford).

Amos 'n' Andy. See main text entry

Arsenio Hall Show, The (1989-1994). Syndicated talk show. Hall emerged as a star and a staple of post-prime-time entertainment. He attracted personalities ranging from new faces to revered actors, entertainers, athletes, and other celebrities. However, Jay Leno's success at commandeering the retired Johnny Carson's *The Tonight Show* in 1992, coupled with the strong debut of *The David Letterman Show* shortly thereafter, sounded the death knell for Hall's show.

Baby, I'm Back (CBS, 1978). Situation comedy. Raymond Ellis (Demond Wilson) came home to Olivia (Denise Nicholas), the wife he had left seven years ago, only to find that she had just had him declared legally dead. Raymond spent the run of this series trying to reconcile with his wife, their two children (Kim Fields and Tony Holmes), and Olivia's mother, Luzelle (Helen Martin), as well as contending with Olivia's fiancé and attempting to have himself declared alive.

Barefoot in the Park (ABC, 1970-1971). Situation comedy. Neil Simon's story was a success first on Broadway and then as a 1967 film starring Robert Redford and Jane Fonda. It was then adapted for this short-lived, all-black television series. Scoey Mitchell and Tracey Reed played newlyweds Paul and Corie Bratter. Corie's mother, Mabel, was played by Thelma Carpenter, and Vito Scotti appeared as the eccentric building superintendent. Roles not included in Simon's original story were Paul's boss, Mr. Kendricks (Harry Holcombe), and Honey Robinson (Nipsey Russell).

Benson (ABC, 1979-1986). Situation comedy. The character of Benson DuBois (Robert Guillaume) originated as the calm, clear-thinking butler on the landmark series *Soap* (1977-1981). This spinoff portrayed Benson working for Governor James Gatling (James Noble) and living in the governor's mansion along with the governor's daughter, the housekeeper, and various staff members. Continually advising the somewhat befuddled governor in all aspects of life and work, Benson was eventually appointed state budget director, then elected lieutenant governor.

Beulah (ABC, 1950-1953). Situation comedy. *Beulah* originated as a spinoff from the popular RADIO comedy *Fibber McGee and Molly*. Working for the Hendersons—a stereotypical white middle-class family—maid Beulah constantly saved them from daily crises, calling "Somebody bawl fo' Beulah?" Ethel WATERS played the character until 1952, when she was replaced by Louise BEAVERS.

Bill Cosby Show, The (NBC, 1969-1971). Situation comedy. Comedian Cosby played high school physical education teacher and coach Chet Kincaid. Kincaid lived with his mother Rose, his brother Brian, and sister-in-law Verna. Set in a lower-middle-class Los Angeles neighborhood, this warm-hearted show focused on Chet's relationships with family, students and teachers, and friends.

Broadway Jamboree (NBC, 1948). Musical variety show. The first two broadcasts, titled *Broadway Minstrels*, were television's first programs to feature an entirely African American cast. The format then changed, with both black and white performers appearing on the third show.

Bustin' Loose (1987). Syndicated situation comedy. In this series based loosely on the 1981 motion picture of the same name, Jimmie Walker played Sonny Barnes, a con man sentenced to spend five years in community service, helping social worker Mimi Shaw (Vonetta McGee) raise four orphans. Sonny liked to boast of his relationships and adventures with celebrities, none of whom he actually knew.

Charlie and Co. (CBS, 1985-1986). Situation comedy. Flip WILSON and Gladys KNIGHT starred as Charlie and Diana Richmond, parents of three fast-talking, wise-cracking kids played by Fran Robinson, Kristoff St. John, and Jaleel White. The series had two false starts, in September, 1985, and again in January, 1986, then ran for three months that spring when Della Reese joined the cast as Diana's sarcastic Aunt Rachel.

Checking In (CBS, 1981). Situation comedy. *The Jeffersons'* wisecracking maid, Florence, checked into her own series for a short three-week stay. In this short-lived spin-off, Marla Gibbs's character became the executive housekeeper at a posh Manhattan hotel. Liz Torres played her efficient assistant, Elena, and Larry Linville portrayed her irritable and irritating boss, Lyle.

Cos (ABC, 1976). Comedy and variety show. Bill Cosby, known for his love of children, designed this hour-long, Sunday night series especially for two- to twelve-year-olds. Each show featured a monologue (which would be interrupted by one of the children), a "magic door" through which viewers could travel to various adventures, and guests that included sports and entertainment celebrities.

Cosby Mysteries, The (NBC, 1994). Detective drama. *The Cosby Mysteries* starred Bill Cosby as Guy Hanks, a criminologist and forensics expert who, despite winning the state lottery and taking early retirement, continued to work on difficult cases. The show was not renewed for a second season because of lower than expected ratings.

Cosby Show, The. See main text entry

Different World, A (NBC, 1987-1993). Situation comedy. In this spin-off series from the hugely popular *Cosby Show* (1984-1992), daughter Denise Huxtable (Lisa Bonet) attended the primarily African American Hillman College. Also included in the cast were Jasmine Guy (playing Whitley), Kadeem Hardison (Dwayne), Dawnn Lewis (Jaleesa), and Sinbad (Walter), all of whom later emerged as leads. (Bonet left after the first season.) With Debbie ALLEN serving as a producer and director, the cast portrayed the students and teachers, their families, and various other campus residents all struggling with the challenges of achieving goals in education, careers, and relationships.

Diff'rent Strokes (NBC, 1978-1985; ABC, 1985-1986). Situation comedy. When Philip Drummond's (Conrad Bain) housekeeper died, he took in her two orphaned sons to live with him and his daughter, Kimberly (Dana Plato). Willis (Todd Bridges) and Arnold (Gary Coleman) spent eight successful years as part of the Drummond household, which also included housekeeper Edna Garrett (Charlotte Rae,

who left in 1979 to star in the spinoff *Facts of Life*), Mr. Drummond's second wife, Maggie, and Maggie's son, Sam. Janet Jackson briefly played Willis's girlfriend, Charlene.

AP/Wide World Photos

Fame (NBC, 1982-1983; syndicated, 1983-1987). Drama. Based on the motion picture of the same name, this series was set in New York City's famous High School for the Performing Arts. The characters were students and teachers, all trying to "make it" in show business. Among the African American cast members were Debbie Allen, pictured; Erica Gimpel; Gene Anthony Ray; and Janet JACKSON.

Family Matters (ABC, 1989-1998). Situation comedy. Carl, played by Reginald Vel Johnson, headed the Winslow family. In addition to the usual challenges of maintaining a household, he had to deal with obnoxious neighbor Steve Urkel (Jaleel White). Kellie Shanygne Williams played his daughter, Laura Winslow, who endured Urkel's romantic attentions. The series finale ended on a high note as Urkel—now America's first student astronaut—returned from his perilous journey to the waiting arms of his now-fiancé, Laura.

Flip Wilson Show, The (NBC, 1970-1974). Comedy and variety show. In this enormous hit, which held the number-two spot in television ratings throughout its first two seasons, Wilson portrayed his numerous stock characters such as Geraldine Jones, the Reverend LeRoy of the Church of What's Happening Now, and Herbie the Good Time Ice Cream Man.

Frank's Place (CBS, 1987-1988). Situation comedy. Stuffy New England professor Frank Parrish (Tim Reid) inherited a small CREOLE restaurant in the heart of New Orleans. His staff of characters vacillated between resenting his presence and helping him adjust to his new life. His love interest, a mortician and embalmer named Hannah Griffin, was played by Reid's real-life wife, Daphne Maxwell-Reid.

(continued)

Fresh Prince of Bel-Air, The (NBC, 1990-1996). Situation comedy that won an NAACP IMAGE AWARD as best comedy series in 1992. Its main attraction was Grammy-winning rap artist Will SMITH. Smith played the visiting nephew of a wealthy African American lawyer and his family who lived in the wealthy Los Angeles neighborhood of Bel-Air. Although known as a mainstream, family-oriented show with humor that appeals to both black and white fans, the series was not afraid to tackle serious social issues affecting the African American community. Smith's decision to leave the show to pursue his film career led to its cancellation in 1996.

Get Christie Love! (ABC, 1974-1975). Police drama. Detective Christie Love, portrayed by African American actress Teresa Graves, played fast and loose with the rules of the job. Although a real female detective served as technical adviser, authenticity was sacrificed in order to show the female lead in the most flattering light.

Gimme a Break (NBC, 1981-1987). Situation comedy. Nell Harper (played by Nell Carter) was cook, housekeeper, and surrogate mother to the Kanisky family—a recently widowed police chief (Dolph Sweet) and his three daughters (Kari Michaelson, Lauri Hendler, and Lara Jill Miller). The series underwent several changes during its run: Jonathan Silverman joined as the middle daughter's husband, the Kaniskys adopted first a six-year-old orphan named Joey and later his little brother Matthew (Joey and Matthew Lawrence); the chief died; and Nell and her best friend, Addy (Telma Hopkins), moved to New York City, taking the Kanisky family with them.

Good Times (ABC, 1974-1979). Situation comedy. Producer Norman Lear's *All in the Family* was responsible for a number of hit spin-offs, including *Good Times*. In this series, Florida Evans (Esther Rolle), the former maid of Edith Bunker's cousin, Maude, and her husband, James (John Amos), lived with their three children (Jimmie Walker, pictured;

Bernadette Stanis; and Ralph Carter) in a Chicago ghetto. When Amos left the show in 1976, eldest son J. J. (Walker) turned to illegal means to support the family. Rolle, displeased with these story changes and their possible effect on impressionable viewers, left the show. She returned in the final season when promised that J. J.'s character would be portrayed as more respectable. During her absence, the part of Willona Woods (Ja'net DuBois), Florida's best friend, was expanded as she became surrogate mother to the Evans children and adoptive mother of an abused girl named Penny (Janet Jackson).

Hangin' with Mr. Cooper (ABC, 1992-1996). Situation comedy. Mark Curry starred as Mark Cooper, a high school coach/teacher, in a black 1990's version of the 1970's show *Three's Company*. He was single but living platonically with female roommates–until the series finale, which married him off to Vanessa, the roommate who was always looking for "Mr. Right."

Harris and Company (ABC, 1979). Family drama. Widowed father Mike Harris (Bernie Casey) tried to build a new life for himself and his children (David Hubbard, Renee Brown, Lia Jackson, Eddie Singleton, and Dain Turner), by moving from Detroit to Los Angeles and becoming a partner in a garage. Plots revolved around the problems encountered by a working single parent with a large family.

Hazel Scott (Dumont, 1950). Music show. This fifteen-minute program aired three nights a week during the summer of 1950. Singer and pianist Hazel SCOTT, a native of Trinidad and the wife of New York congressman Adam Clayton POWELL, Jr., performed songs for which she was known from her nightclub, radio, film, and Broadway work.

He's the Mayor (ABC, 1986). Situation comedy. When twenty-five-year-old Carl Burke (Kevin Hooks) found himself elected to the office of mayor, he organized his own personal "kitchen cabinet," consisting of his father (Al Fann), his best friend and chauffeur, Wardell (Wesley Thompson), and the janitor at City Hall.

Homefront (ABC, 1991-1993). Drama. *Homefront* was set in the small midwestern town of River Run, Ohio, circa 1945. Robert Davis (Sterling Macer, Jr.), who had been honored for his bravery overseas in WORLD WAR II, found himself less valued than white veterans when applying for work at the local factory. His parents, Abe and Gloria (Dick Anthony Williams and Hattie Winston), who did domestic work for the selfishly powerful owners of the factory, struggled to open a restaurant.

The Hughleys (ABC, 1998-   ). Situation comedy. In what has been called a 1990's version of *The Jeffersons*, a successful vending-machine magnate, Darryl Hughley (played by D. L. Hughley), moves his wife (Elise Neal) and two children into the white suburbs. Comedy ensues as Hughley struggles to hold onto his African American roots while living the elusive "American Dream." The show successfully deals with serious racial issues in a humorous manner.

I'll Fly Away (NBC, 1991-1993). Family drama. Set in the racially charged South of the late 1950's, the show focused on Lily (Regina Taylor), a black divorced mother who came to work for Forrest Bedford (Sam Waterston), a liberal prosecutor who needed help raising his three children after his wife was hospitalized for a nervous breakdown.

In Living Color (Fox, 1990-1994). Comedy and variety show. Keenen Ivory Wayans created, produced, wrote, and starred in this top-rated series, which attained popularity through its outrageous satires performed by an interracial cast. Controversial sketches provoked confrontations with television censors, and Wayans left the show as a result of a dispute with other producers and the Fox network over syndication rights. Controversy did not prevent the show from winning an Emmy Award, a People's Choice Award, and an NAACP Image Award. Wayans, his brother Damon, black comedian David Alan Grier, and white cast member Jim Carey all went on to success in films.

In the House (NBC, 1995-1998). Situation comedy. This lighthearted series with an all-African American cast featured Debbie Allen in the role of Jackie, a divorced mother of two who found herself suddenly single when her husband, undergoing a midlife crisis, left her for a younger woman. Rapper L.L. COOL J played Marion, her former football-player landlord.

I Spy (NBC, 1965-1968). Adventure series. Playing multilingual, highly educated undercover agent Alexander Scott, Bill Cosby became the first African American to star in an American dramatic series. His white partner, Kelly Robinson, was played by Robert Culp. Sometimes improvising dialogue, Cosby and Culp established a wisecracking, friendly rapport between their characters. Cosby won best-acting Emmy Awards three consecutive years while on the show.

It's Showtime at the Apollo (1987-   ). Syndicated musical variety show. Taped before a live audience at the famous APOLLO THEATER in Harlem, New York, this series featured guest hosts that included Bill Cosby, James BROWN, and Natalie Cole. A microcosm of the live Apollo experience, each program provided music, dance, and comedy performances, an "Amateur Night" segment, and tributes to Apollo legends such as Billie HOLIDAY, Sam COOKE, and Moms MABLEY.

Jacksons, The (CBS, 1976, 1977). Musical variety show. Michael, Jackie, Tito, and Marlon—four of the brothers in the original Jackson 5—along with their youngest brother, Randy, starred in this four-week summer program in 1976. Three of the Jackson sisters, Janet, LaToya, and Rebie (Maureen), joined them, as did a handful of supporting regulars and guest stars. The program appeared again in January through March of 1977.

Jamie Foxx Show, The (WB, 1996-   ). Situation comedy. Comedian Jamie Foxx starred as Jamie King, a Texan who moved to Hollywood in search of stardom. He spent his time working at Aunt Helen (Ellia English) and Uncle Junior's (Garrett Morris) King's Town Hotel and meddling in the lives of family and friends.

Jeffersons, The (CBS, 1975-1985). Situation comedy. A Norman Lear spin-off from *All in the Family*, *The Jeffersons* featured neighbors of the earlier show's Bunkers who moved from Queens to a Manhattan high-rise when their small dry-cleaning business expanded into a chain. The outrageously opinionated

(continued)

George (Sherman Hemsley, pictured) was kept in line by his wife, Louise (Isabel Sanford), and often by their maid, Florence Johnston (Marla Gibbs). Son Lionel (played by Mike Evans in 1975 and from 1979 to 1981 and by Damon Evans—no relation—from 1975 to 1978), dated, married, and eventually divorced Jenny Willis (Berlinda Tolbert), whose parents, Tom and Helen (Franklin Cover and Roxie Roker), were a racially mixed couple. *The Jeffersons* ranked among the top one hundred television series of the twentieth century in viewer ratings.

AP/Wide World Photos

Julia (NBC, 1968-1971). Situation comedy. This groundbreaking program successfully portrayed, for the first time, an African American female lead character. Singer and actress Diahann CARROLL played Julia Baker, a nurse who moved to Los Angeles after her husband was killed in Vietnam. She and her son, Corey (Marc Copage), lived in an integrated apartment building, and Julia worked at a prestigious medical office.

Living Single (Fox, 1993-1998). Situation comedy. This show featured four African American single women in their twenties who shared an apartment in New York City. Played by veteran performers Kim Coles, Kim Fields, Erika Alexander, and rap star QUEEN LATIFAH, the central characters were lifelong friends who relied on one another's candid commentary and support to cope with careers, love, and "sisterhood" in an urban setting.

Malcolm and Eddie (UPN, 1996-   ). Situation comedy. Malcolm McGee (Malcolm-Jamal Warner) and Eddie Sherman (Eddie Griffin) were longtime friends who shared everything, including girlfriends. Their antics often put their friendship to the test.

Martin (Fox, 1992-1997). Situation comedy. Comedian Martin Lawrence starred as the loud-mouthed, egocentric talk-show host Martin Payne. His wife, Gina, and a cast of friends had to constantly deal with his quick temper and its humorous consequences.

Melba (CBS, 1986). Situation comedy. Melba Moore played a divorced mother who worked at New York City's Manhattan Visitors' Center and lived with her nine-year-old daughter, Tracey (Jamilla Perry), and her mother, Rose (Barbara Meek). Gracie Harrison played Susan Slater, Melba's best friend and white "sister"—the two were reared together in the Slater house, where Mama Rose was once a housekeeper.

Mod Squad, The (ABC, 1968-1973). Police drama. This program featured three young adults who started out on the wrong side of the law but were recruited by Captain Adam Greer (Tige Andrews) for the police department's "youth squad." African American actor Clarence Williams III starred as Linc Hayes, a survivor of the 1960's Watts riots in Los Angeles. Hayes and his partners, Pete Cochran (Michael Cole) and Julie Barnes (Peggy Lipton), did not ignore, but rather analyzed, their differing cultural backgrounds. In 1979 the trio reappeared in the made-for-television movie *The Return of the Mod Squad*. In 1999 a theatrical film of the same title was released featuring a new set of young actors.

Moesha (UPN, 1996-   ). Situation comedy. Singing star Brandy Norwood plays the calm and collected Moesha Mitchell. The cast includes Moesha's father Frank (remarried after his wife's death), stepmother Dee, and brother Myles, all of whom seem to handle family life together with more ease than Moesha. Friends Niecy, Hakeem, Andell, and Kim are involved in her weekly predicaments as she tries to find her own place in the world.

The Montel Williams Show (Fox, 1991-   ). Talk-show host Montel Williams's empathetic and low-key approach encourages guests and audiences to seek rational explanations and positive solutions to problems.

AP/Wide World Photos

Nat "King" Cole Show, The (NBC, 1956-1957). Musical variety show. The first network series headlined by a major African American performer, it originally ran fifteen minutes, then was expanded to a half hour. Low ratings resulted in sponsor apathy. In an effort to keep it on the air, a host of entertainer friends of

Cole, both African American and Caucasian, appeared for minimal fees. These included Count BASIE, Mahalia JACKSON, Ella FITZGERALD, Sammy DAVIS, Jr., Peggy Lee, and Mel Torme. The show was nonetheless canceled in its fourteenth month.

New Bill Cosby Show, The (CBS, 1972-1973). Comedy and variety show. Each episode contained a monologue by Cosby, at least one musical number, and regular sketches including "The Wife of the Week" and "The Dude." It featured an impressive list of regulars and guest stars. Quincy Jones served as orchestra leader, and dancer Lola Falana was the announcer.

New Odd Couple, The (ABC, 1982-1983). Situation comedy. A reprise of the television show based on Neil Simon's Broadway play, the two wildly mismatched cohabitants in this African American version starred Ron Glass as the compulsively tidy Felix Unger, and Demond Wilson as Oscar Madison, his sloppy, poker-playing, sports-writer roommate.

One in a Million (ABC, 1980). Situation comedy. Shirley Hemphill's character from *What's Happening!!* was spun off into this series about a blue-collar working woman who inherited a multimillion-dollar, white-run conglomerate. The company's white executives had to

Capital Cities/ABC, Inc.

learn to contend with their new feisty and down-to-earth black boss.

Oprah Winfrey Show, The (1986-   ). Syndicated talk show. Consistently ranked as the number-one daytime talk show, this series was driven less by its topics than by its star—the producer and owner of the show as well as of the Harpo Entertainment Group. Oprah WINFREY repeatedly identified with her guests and audiences, revealing deeply personal aspects of her life and incorporating them into various segments. In the mid-1990's, she pointedly changed the show's direction away from the trashy, loud-mouthed format championed by her competitors. In 1996 she launched Oprah's Book Club, a national phenomenon that launched best-sellers and sold thousands of books.

Palmerstown, U.S.A. (CBS, 1980-1981). Drama. Nine-year-old Booker T. Freeman (Jermain Hodge Johnson) and his best friend, a white boy named David Hall (Brian Godfrey Wilson), grew up in the rural southern town of Palmerstown during the Depression. The boys united their families in friendship despite the overt racism of the time. Alex Haley, who coproduced the series with Norman Lear, described it as somewhat autobiographical.

Parent 'Hood, The (WB, 1995-   ). Situation comedy. Starring veteran actor and comedian Robert Townsend, this show featured a loving family of two professional parents and their four children, all of whom coped with the typical challenges of family life. An array of ever-present neighbors offered plentiful advice on parenting that heightened the chaos and comedy.

Paris (CBS, 1979-1980). Police drama. James Earl JONES portrayed Woody Paris, a highly principled police captain who also taught a university course in criminology. His understanding wife, Barbara, was played by Lee Chamberlain. Despite impressive reviews, the series lacked believability and failed to garner good ratings.

Pearl Bailey Show, The (CBS, 1971). Musical variety show. Bailey, famous for her work on the stage and for guest appearances on other television programs, starred in this short-lived series. Her husband, Louis Bellson, directed the orchestra, and guest stars included Bing Crosby, Louis ARMSTRONG, Andy Williams, Kate Smith, and B. B. KING.

Redd Foxx (ABC, 1977-1978). Comedy and variety show. Only after *Sanford and Son* proved successful was Foxx allowed to stage the type of show he had always wanted to do. Two regular segments were "Redd's Corner," in which he featured personal friends who might otherwise never have gotten a chance to perform on television, and "The History of the Black in America," in which his irreverent historical and political views were aired. Regulars included comedian Slappy White, singer Damita Jo, and Foxx's *Sanford and Son* costar LaWanda Page.

Redd Foxx Show, The (ABC, 1986). Situation comedy. Only the names and places were changed in this thinly disguised clone of *Sanford and Son*. Foxx again played a grumpy old codger who ran a small busi-

(continued)

ness in an inner-city neighborhood. The supporting characters, mostly neighborhood children, changed frequently during the series' half-season run.

Richard Pryor Show, The (NBC, 1977). Musical and variety show. Stand-up comedian and sometime talk-show host Richard PRYOR was already a success when he launched his first television series. A budding film career as well as network censorship problems meant that only five of the ten shows for which he was contracted were completed. Supporting regulars included fellow comics Robin Williams, Marsha Warfield, Tim Reid, and Sandra Bernhard.

Roc (Fox, 1991-1994). Situation comedy. The series featured Roc Emerson (Charles S. Dutton), a well-intentioned and hardworking trash collector, who, with his family and friends, struggled to make a decent living in Baltimore. The show had a realistic urban setting and tackled contemporary issues. Despite lobbying efforts by series cast members and even members of the CONGRESSIONAL BLACK CAUCUS, Fox network canceled the show because of unsatisfactory ratings.

Room 222 (ABC, 1969-1974). Drama. The title referred to the number of idealistic history teacher Pete Dixon's (Lloyd Haynes) homeroom at Walt Whitman High School. Denise Nicholas played Liz McIntyre, a school counselor and his girlfriend. The series was praised by educational and civil rights groups for its attention to problems such as prejudice and drug use.

Roots (ABC, 1977). Landmark dramatic miniseries. Alex HALEY spent twelve years writing *Roots: The Saga of an American Family* (1976), based on his own family tree, which he traced back to the mid-1700's in West Africa. Enormously controversial, the television adaptation of *Roots* drew praise as well as criticism from people of all colors for its fictionalized portrayal of the treatment of African American slaves by their owners and by their freed African American relatives. Eighty million viewers watched the show over its first seven nights—one hundred million viewed the finale. The star-filled cast included LeVar Burton, John Amos, Cicely TYSON, Maya ANGELOU, O. J. SIMPSON, Ren Woods, Louis GOSSETT, Jr., Madge Sinclair, Lawrence-Hilton Jacobs, Leslie Uggams, Olivia Cole, Scatman Crothers, and Ben Vereen.

Roots: The Next Generations (ABC, 1979). Drama miniseries. This sequel to the original *Roots* began in 1882 with the grandson of original main character, Kunta Kinte, and concluded with James Earl Jones playing the role of author Alex Haley. It depicted African Americans suffering at the hands of the KU KLUX KLAN; Haley's mother, Bertha, who was the first descendant of Kunta Kinte to enter college; and the author's interviews with important figures such as Malcolm X. The cast included Dorian Harewood, Ruby Dee, Rosey Grier, Paul Winfield, and Debbie Allen.

Royal Family, The (CBS, 1991-1992). Situation comedy. This series, featuring a much-anticipated return for Redd Foxx, was altered drastically by his sudden death one month after the show premiered. Six episodes already had been produced in which Foxx played newly retired Atlanta mailman Al Royal, who was looking forward to relaxing at home with his wife, Victoria (Della Reese). His solitude was interrupted, however, when the Royals' divorced daughter, Elizabeth (Mariann Aalda), moved in with her three children. After Foxx's death, Jackée (Harry) joined the cast.

Sammy and Company (1975-1977). Syndicated talk and variety show. In an attempt to bring Las Vegas to late-night television, entertainer Sammy Davis, Jr., hosted this ninety-minute program from various nightclub locales. Celebrity guests included Wayne Newton, Flip Wilson, Freddie Prinze, and Ray CHARLES.

Sanford and Son (NBC, 1972-1977). Situation comedy. Producer Norman Lear based this hit on a British television series entitled *Steptoe and Son*. The American version starred Redd Foxx as a crotchety and conniving old junk dealer and Demond Wilson as his ambitious but loving son. Slappy White, Hal Williams, Beah Richards, and LaWanda Page appeared in supporting roles.

AP/Wide World Photos

porting roles. Although rated in the top ten throughout its run, the series was canceled when Foxx left to work on a variety show.

Sanford Arms, The (NBC, 1977). Situation comedy spun off from the hit series *Sanford and Son*. Fred Sanford's chief antagonist, Aunt Esther Anderson (LaWanda Page), and other supporting players from that show enjoyed a brief reprise of their roles. New lead character Phil Wheeler (Theodore Wilson) starred as a widower with two children who purchased the Sanford home and businesses, including Aunt Esther's roominghouse. Without Redd Foxx and Demond Wilson, however, the series lasted less than a month.

Sinbad Show, The (Fox, 1994). Short-lived situation comedy. Comedian Sinbad starred as a video game designer struggling in the role of new father and foster parent to two lively kids. The show was intended to reflect Sinbad's personal interest in overcoming the misconception that black fathers run away from family responsibilities and fail to take care of their children. Targeted at family viewers, the show contained clean humor—in the tradition of comedian Bill Cosby—for mainstream appeal.

Sister, Sister (ABC, 1994-1995; WB, 1995-   ). Situation comedy. Starring real-life identical twins Tia and Tamera Mowry (as Tia Landry and Tamera Campbell), this series featured identical twins who were separated at birth and adopted by different families, then accidentally reunited as fourteen-year-olds. Tia had been reared in the projects by single mom Lisa (played by Jackée Harry), while Tamera had grown up in the suburbs with widower Ray (played by Tim Reid). The two families decided to share a house together as one uneasy extended family. When the series debuted on ABC, it was canceled because of low ratings. The producers, however, found a new home for it on the fledgling Warner Bros. (WB) television network.

Snoops (CBS, 1989). Detective drama. In this failed series, actor/producer Tim Reid and his wife, Daphne Maxwell-Reid, played a professor of criminology at Georgetown University and an assistant to the deputy chief of protocol at the State Department.

Sonny Spoon (NBC, 1988). Detective drama. Spoon, a private eye played by Mario Van Peebles, conducted his business from a public phone booth and employed friends and neighborhood residents as his informants. An expert at disguise, he sported several

personas in every episode, drawing from every race, age, and profession, and from both sexes.

Sparks (UPN, 1996-   ). James Avery (the father from *The Fresh Prince of Bel-Air*) played Alonzo, the father of two brothers, Maxey and Greg, who are law partners. They were also quarrelsome and polar opposites in personality. Sibling rivalry was the primary theme behind the show's humorous plots.

Star Trek: The Next Generation (1987-1994). Syndicated science fiction/adventure series. This popular sequel to the original *Star Trek*, set in the twenty-fourth century, featured a new starship *Enterprise* and an expanded multiethnic crew. African American actors portrayed three leading characters of different races—and from different planets. Human lieutenant Geordi La Forge (LeVar Burton) was a blind helmsman whose vision was enhanced by high-tech electronic glasses. Guinan (Whoopi GOLDBERG) was the alien proprietor of the ship's lounge as well as a close friend of the captain (Patrick Stewart). Lieutenant Worf (Michael Dorn), another alien, was the first Klingon ever to serve aboard a Federation starship; he eventually became its head of security. The popular spin-off series, *Star Trek: Deep Space Nine* (1992-1999), featured Avery Brooks as the African American Commander Benjamin Sisko. All these shows and the theatrical films that followed owed their multiracial heritage to Gene Roddenberry's original *Star Trek* (1966-1969), which featured black actress Nichelle Nichols as Lt. Uhura.

Steve Harvey Show, The (WB, 1996-   ). Steve Harvey portrayed a 1970's SOUL singer turned 1990's high-school music teacher. Accustomed to the luxuries of his former celebrity status, he struggled in adjusting to the demands of his new career and his troublesome but well-meaning students.

Sweet Justice (NBC, 1994-1995). Drama series. This widely acclaimed but short-lived series starred Cicely Tyson as Carrie Grace Battle, an African American defense attorney whose Louisiana law firm was known for taking on challenging, hopeless cases. She hired a white lawyer, Kate Delacroy (played by Melissa Gilbert), who had returned home to New Orleans after working in New York as a corporate attorney. Although much of the show revolved around the conflicts within the Delacroy family, the series was notable for Tyson's portrayal

(continued)

of an African American career woman from the South who had achieved success against overwhelming odds.

T. and T. (1987-1990). Syndicated detective drama. Actor Mr. T portrayed T. S. Turner, a detective and former boxer who worked for attorney Amanda Taler (Alex Amini). Although his character ostensibly preferred a suit and tie, Mr. T spent part of every episode pursuing criminals in studded leather gear.

Tenspeed and Brown Shoe (ABC, 1980). Detective drama. In this short-lived series, Broadway veteran Ben Vereen played E. L. Turner, better known as "Tenspeed," a con artist who chose to become a detective in order to meet his parole requirements. His white partner, Lionel Whitney, or "Brown Shoe" (Jeff Goldblum), was as naïve as Tenspeed was slick, and he depended on him to get through each case.

That's My Mama (ABC, 1974-1975). Situation comedy. When his father died, Clifton Curtis (Clifton Davis) inherited not only his father's Washington, D.C., barbershop but also his mother's meddlesome influence. "Mama" Eloise Curtis, portrayed by Theresa Merritt, continually pressured him to settle down and start a family.

227 (NBC, 1985-1990). Situation comedy. The show was named for the Washington, D.C., address where Mary Jenkins (Marla Gibbs) lived with her husband, Lester (Hal Williams), and their daughter, Brenda (Regina King). Among their neighbors were sexy Sandra Clark (Jackée), Mary's best friend and landlady, Rose Lee Holloway (Alaina Reed), and elderly and witty Pearl Shay (Helen Martin).

Under One Roof (CBS, 1995). Drama series. Developed by Thomas Carter, an award-winning black producer and director, this series was praised as the first to present a fully realized portrait of African American family life. Set in a middle-class Seattle neighborhood, it focused on typical family challenges, including child discipline, career changes, marital conflicts, and family discord. Ron Langston (played by Joe Morton) was a former Marine who moved his family in order to run his own hardware store. He and his wife, who returned to a career outside the home, dealt with rearing their two children.

Webster (ABC, 1983-1987). Situation comedy. As a result of his tiny size, twelve-year-old actor Emmanuel Lewis was able to portray the title character as a six-year-old. Webster was orphaned and taken in by his father's friend and colleague, George Papadapolis (Alex Karras), who knew almost as little about rearing a child as did his socialite wife, Katherine (Susan Clark). Webster brought out the best in them.

What's Happening!! (ABC, 1976-1979). Situation comedy. Raj (Ernest Thomas), Rerun (Freddie Berry), and Dwayne (Haywood Nelson) were friends who hung out at the local diner where Shirley (Shirley Hemphill) worked as a waitress. Raj's mother (Mabel King) was a loving but strict woman who often stopped fights between Raj and his little sister, Dee (Danielle Spencer). Six years after it was canceled by ABC, the series appeared in a new form in syndication as *What's Happening Now!!* (1985-1988). By this time Dee was in college, Dwayne and Rerun shared an apartment and struggled with careers, and Raj had become a writer, husband, and stepfather.

flection of American life, it also limits possibilities for examining cultural expressions that are unique to African American life but exist outside the topic range of common television fare.

Dramas featuring black cast members in the 1970's and 1980's included *Room 222* (1969-1974, with Lloyd Haynes and Denise Nicholas), *Paris* (1979-1980, with James Earl JONES), *Tenspeed and Brown Shoe* (1980, with Ben Vereen), *Palmerstown, U.S.A.* (1980-1981, with Jermain Hodge Johnson, Jonelle Allen, and Bill Duke), *Fame* (1982-1987, with Debbie Allen), *The A-Team* (1983-1987, with Mr. T), and *T. and T.* (1987-1990, with Mr. T).

In 1995 CBS launched the series *Under One Roof* in direct response to this challenge. Assembling a veteran cast of actors, headed by James Earl Jones, Joe Morton, and Vanessa Bell Calloway, under the supervision of Thomas Carter, an award-winning African American producer-director, the network developed the first series ever to present a fully developed portrait of an African American family. Critically acclaimed, the short-lived series featured a middle-class family consisting of an entrepreneur father, a working mother, two children, and a grandfather who lives with his other two children (one a foster child) in the same two-family home in suburban Washington State. Because of the various ages, experiences, and political beliefs of the characters, the series was able to explore not only a variety of situations that affect the typical middle-class household but also social issues such as single-parenting, health, and adult sibling rivalries. The series did not garner sufficient viewers to last beyond one season.

From 1991 to 1993, NBC aired the drama series *I'll Fly Away*. Although it focused on events from the late 1950's, the series was one of the few network dramas that attempted to examine black life alongside and intricately affected by a larger white society. It introduced a thoughtful, understated African American housekeeper (played by Regina Taylor) who kept a journal chronicling her experiences working in the household of a white district attorney (played by Sam Waterston) living in the South during a pivotal point in the Civil Rights movement. One of the program's strengths was its focus on African American family life, portraying the housekeeper as a loving mother, a devoted daughter, a supportive friend, and a sexual being—thus inverting the "mammy" stereotype.

Other popular dramas that have featured African Americans in modern (or futuristic) situations include the NBC hospital drama *ER* (1994-   ), the CBS community drama *Picket Fences* (1992-1996), and the syndicated science-fiction dramas *Star Trek: The Next Gen-*

eration (1987-1994) and *Star Trek: Deep Space Nine* (1992-1999). The most significant arena for overturning black stereotypes through complex characterizations on television has been the police drama. This phenomenon was evidenced by several popular series that aired during the 1990's: *In the Heat of the Night* (1988-1994), ABC's critically acclaimed *NYPD Blue* (1993-   ), and NBC's equally acclaimed *Law and Order* (1990-   ) and *Homicide: Life on the Street* (1992-1999). Each series featured African American men and women in prominent leading and supporting roles as police captains, lieutenants, commanders, detectives, judges, and lawyers. These characters were portrayed making crucial decisions and key discoveries—and often exercising final authority over white characters.

Some episodes also followed story lines in which race presented obstacles or challenges to decisions these characters have had to make professionally and personally. Virtually all these characters have been portrayed within the context of their personal and family lives.

Variety and Talk Shows

Variety shows, popular from the 1950's to the 1970's, offered another arena in which some black performers were able to showcase their talents. The trailblazing *Nat "King" Cole Show* (1956-1957) was the first entertainment program to be hosted by an African American. Later came *The Flip Wilson Show* (1970-1974), *The Pearl Bailey Show* (1971), *Cos* (1976, with Bill Cosby), *The Richard Pryor Show* (1977), *Redd Foxx* (1977-1978), and the syndicated program *It's Showtime at the Apollo* (1987-   ). A notable 1990's comedy and variety program featuring African American cast members was Fox's *In Living Color* (1990-1994), created by comedian Keenen Ivory Wayans and featuring many other members of his family, including brother Damon Wayans. *In Living Color* included comedic skits that explored race issues.

Cast of *In Living Color*, a Fox series that introduced several new African American performers to television. Top row, left to right: David Alan Grier, Kelly Coffield, Damon Wayans, and Keenen Ivory Wayans; bottom row: T'Keyah Crystal Keymah, Kim Wayans, Tommy Davidson, and Jim Carrey. *(AP/Wide World Photos)*

Cornelius Productions produced and syndicated the first *Soul Train Lady of Soul Awards* show in 1995 and the *Soul Train Twenty-fifth Anniversary Hall of Fame Special*, a retrospective.

Daytime Serials

Television programs airing during the daytime have also begun to feature more African American characters. Virtually every daytime soap opera airing in the 1990's featured an African American lead character. While often referred to as the "fluff" of television programming, daytime serials have courageously tackled many topical issues related to the African American community that have been circumvented or ignored by prime time series. For example, nearly every daytime soap that features African American characters explored the topics of racial bias, interracial romance and marriage, and biracial children. At the same time, these shows portrayed black characters who reflected popular urban styles, including dreadlocks, braids, hip-hop clothing, and other fashions.

Progress and Challenges

In the last decades of the twentieth century, television programming made significant strides in meeting the challenge of reforming its portrayals of African Americans. The comedies, dramas, and serials that are the most common offerings on commercial television successfully showcased black characters coping with the realities of American life in a formula that translated into advertising dollars.

In the 1990's, the presence of the cable BLACK ENTERTAINMENT TELEVISION (BET) and of networks such as Fox, the United Para-

Talk shows hosted by African Americans have included *Sammy and Company* (1975-1977, a talk and variety show hosted by Sammy Davis, Jr., and taped in Las Vegas), the phenomenally successful *Oprah Winfrey Show* (1986-   ), *The Arsenio Hall Show* (1989-1994), and *The Montel Williams Show* (1991-   ).

Another long-running program worthy of note hosted by an African American is Don Cornelius's syndicated music and dance program *Soul Train*. Cornelius created, produced, and hosted the show, featuring young adults who danced while records played and guest stars performed their hit songs. *Soul Train* began in 1970 as a local show in Chicago and later moved to Hollywood, California. Don

mount Network (UPN), and the Warner Bros. Network (WB), notable for ethnically diverse programming, indicated further changes in the industry. Children's programming, another highly competitive arena for networks and cable, seemed to have almost seamlessly developed a multiracial and multicultural look and content that reflected the changing demographics of the United States.

In the spring of 1999, however, the president of the NATIONAL ASSOCIATION FOR THE ADVANCEMENT OF COLORED PEOPLE (NAACP), Kweisi MFUME, took the four major broadcast networks (ABC, CBS, NBC, and Fox) to task for what he called a "virtual whitewash in programming" in that year's fall season. The lineup of twenty-six new shows did not feature any minority characters in leading roles, and there were very few in supporting roles. In his keynote address to the ninetieth annual meeting of the NAACP, Mfume outlined a wide range of protest measures that could be taken against the networks, including litigation and boycotts.

Network executives, stunned by the criticism, responded within hours with reassurances that they were concerned about and sensitive to the issue of ethnic diversity. Publicly, they acknowledged a need to do more minority casting. Privately, they scrambled to recast some of the new shows slated for the 1999 season. While the NAACP cautiously approved this step, Mfume also noted that television programming executives would face continuing scrutiny. The attack by the NAACP led some industry executives to argue that programming decisions simply boiled down to harsh economics rather than racism: There was not enough money in diversity to make it a priority. Nonetheless, network leaders had discussions with the NAACP in 1999, and in December the NAACP announced that it would not lead a boycott of the networks.

In another camp, some African American members of the entertainment community expressed concern that noble causes could actually hobble actors of color. Some activists, for example, insisted that nonwhites, and African Americans specifically, appear only in roles that portray positive images—a burden that white actors do not have to carry. As the controversy raged, the situation was summed up by Latino actor and activist Edward James Olmos: "No one will ever forget the television season of 1999."

—Monique S. Simón
—Updated by Cynthia Beres

See also: Comedy and humor; Comics, stand-up; Performing arts.

Suggested Readings:

Bogle, Donald. *Blacks in American Films and Television: An Illustrated Encyclopedia*. New York: Garland, 1988.

Brooks, Tim, and Earle Marsh. *The Complete Directory to Prime Time Network TV Shows: 1946-Present*. 4th ed. New York: Ballantine Books, 1988.

Dates, Jannette L., and William Barlow, eds. *Split Image: African Americans in the Mass Media*. 2d ed. Washington, D.C.: Howard University Press, 1993.

Fuller, Linda K. *The Cosby Show: Audiences, Impact, and Implications*. New York: Greenwood Press, 1992.

MacDonald, J. Fred. *One Nation Under Television*. New York: Pantheon Books, 1990.

McNeil, Alex. *Total Television: A Comprehensive Guide to Programming from 1948 to the Present*. 4th ed. New York: Penguin Books, 1996.

Torres, Sasha, ed. *Living Color: Race and Television in the United States*. Durham, N.C.: Duke University Press, 1998.

"TV's 'Moesha' Gives Positive View of Black Family Life." *Jet* (November 25, 1996): 56-59.

Woll, Allen L., and Randall M. Miller. *Ethnic and Racial Images in American Film and Television: Historical Essays and Bibliography*. New York: Garland, 1987.

Zook, Kristal B. *Color by Fox: The Fox Network and the Revolution in Black Television*. New York: Oxford University Press, 1999.

Temptations: Singing group of the 1960's and 1970's. Formed from members of several other groups, the Temptations formed in DETROIT, MICHIGAN, in 1961. By 1963 the group had signed with MOTOWN Records and taken the form that would produce most of its early hits: Paul Williams, Melvin Franklin, Otis Williams, Eddie Kendrick, and David Ruffin.

In 1964 the group scored its first hit, "The Way You Do the Things You Do," produced by Smokey ROBINSON, which went to number eleven on the charts. The following year, "My Girl" became the group's first number-one single. A series of other hits followed, with *Cloud Nine* (1968) winning a Grammy Award. In the early 1970's, both "Just My Imagination" (1971) and "Papa Was a Rollin' Stone" (1972) were number-one hits. By this time, the group had undergone major personnel changes, losing its two lead singers. Ruffin left the group in a dispute with Motown management in 1967 (being replaced by Dennis Edwards), and Kendrick left to pursue his own career in 1971. New members kept the group going into the 1980's and 1990's. In 1982 Ruffin and Kendrick rejoined the group for an album, *Reunion*, and a concert tour.

At their peak, the Temptations was among the most successful soul/rhythm-and-blues groups. Its mellow gospel background was nicely supplemented by Kendrick's falsetto and Ruffin's earthy baritone, giving the group considerable range. Most of the Temptations were former athletes, and the dance routines during live performances were among the most acrobatic in the business. Many considered the live shows to provide the best combination of music and visual entertainment of any soul group. In 1966 Norman Whitfield began producing the group's recordings and cultivated its versatility. In the later 1960's and 1970's, the group's style changed, with songs embodying greater use of brass in their instrumentation and subjects that were more topical. "Papa Was a Rollin' Stone" is considered by some critics to be one of rock music's most moving statements about the problems of inner-city families.

The Temptations in 1996: (left to right) Harry McGilberry, Ron Tyson, Theo Peoples, and Otis Williams. *(AP/Wide World Photos)*

Tennessee: The sixteenth state to join the union, Tennessee was one of the smallest slaveholding states before the CIVIL WAR. The last state to secede from the union, Tennessee was also the first to rejoin it following the war. In 1997, according to estimates of the CENSUS OF THE UNITED STATES, Tennessee's population was about 5.4 million, of whom about 884,000 were

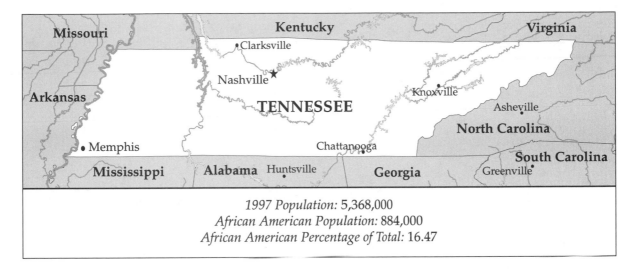

1997 Population: 5,368,000
African American Population: 884,000
African American Percentage of Total: 16.47

African Americans. Tennessee's African American community accounted for about 18 percent of the state's population, with more than 45 percent living in western Tennessee.

Settlers who entered eastern Tennessee from other Southern states in the late 1700's brought their slaves with them, and they continued to migrate to the fertile farmlands of West Tennessee, particularly the region around MEMPHIS, in the early 1800's. By 1860 African Americans accounted for roughly 25 percent of Tennessee's population and more than 45 percent of the population of Memphis.

The state's varied social, economic, and political climates led to conflicting events concerning its black citizens. In the nineteenth century Tennessee became both home to way stations on the UNDERGROUND RAILROAD, the route to freedom for runaway slaves, and the birthplace of the KU KLUX KLAN (in Pulaski). By the mid-1880's thirteen African Americans had won seats in Tennessee's General Assembly.

The early 1900's proved a time of increased racial turbulence in the state. In 1917 African Americans were plagued by a series of LYNCHINGS, riots, and other acts of white mob violence. The African American community reacted in various ways. Some people worked within the government to improve race relations. Others joined the GREAT MIGRATION northward, causing Tennessee's African American population to fall significantly.

A defining, and shocking, event for both Tennessee and the nation occurred when James Earl Ray assassinated Martin Luther KING, Jr., in Memphis following a 1968 speech in which King championed the cause of the city's striking sanitation workers. King's death led to a series of social and political changes in Tennessee. These changes came to fruition with the election of Representative Harold FORD of Memphis, who became Tennessee's first black representative to the U.S. Congress in 1974.

Tennessee houses the first museum dedicated to educating the public about the CIVIL RIGHTS movement. The National Civil Rights Museum is located in Memphis at the Lorraine Motel, where King was assassinated. Tennessee's history is filled with the achievements of African Americans who have distinguished themselves at all levels of society. These leaders include Robert Church, who became the South's first black millionaire in the late 1800's; Mary Church TERRELL, a feminist, a civil rights activist, and the first black woman to serve on the Washington, D.C., school board in 1895; and *Roots* (1976) author Alex HALEY, who encouraged African Americans to explore their family heritages with pride.

—*Kimberley H. Kidd*

Tennis: American tennis, like the society in which it is played, was segregated until after WORLD WAR II. African Americans competed under the auspices of the American Tennis Association, founded in 1916. Although an African American, Reginald Weir, played in the U.S. indoor tournament in 1948, blacks could not participate in major tournaments until the advent of Althea GIBSON. Because of her obvious abilities, the United States Lawn Tennis Association allowed her to enter the national tennis championships at Forest Hills, Long Island, in 1950.

Gibson became the first major black tennis star when she won the U.S. Open in 1957 and 1958. She won the Wimbledon doubles championship in 1956 and the women's singles crown at Wimbledon in 1957 and 1958. Frustrated at the lack of other opportunities for a black woman in amateur tennis, she turned professional in 1958.

A young Arthur Ashe gives a tennis demonstration to children in a Washington, D.C., park. *(National Archives)*

The greatest African American male player in the twentieth century was Arthur ASHE. Raised in Richmond, VIRGINIA, during the segregation era, Ashe competed as an amateur when he won the U.S. Open in 1968. Turning professional, he won the Australian Open in 1970 and, five years later, upset the heavily favored Jimmy Connors to win Wimbledon in 1975. He retired because of health problems in 1979. Always a commanding figure on and off the court, Ashe was one of the most popular and influential personalities in tennis. His death from ACQUIRED IMMUNODEFICIENCY SYNDROME (AIDS), which he had acquired from blood transfusions during a heart operation, saddened the tennis world.

In the post-Ashe era of the 1980's and 1990's, African American players such as MaliVai Washington and Byron Shelton among the men and Zina Garrison-Jackson and Lori McNeil among the women established creditable records. Washington and Garrison-Jackson each reached the finals of the Wimbledon championships.

The United States Lawn Tennis Association encouraged the development of black players in the United States. Obstacles remained, however. A lack of money for player development and the continuing presence of discrimination in tennis and country clubs contributed to limiting the number of talented African American players that emerged at the top ranks of the sport.

By the late 1990's, two new stars had burst upon the women's tennis scene. Sisters Venus and Serena Williams, coached by their father Richard Williams, brought impressive talent and engaging personalities to the women's tennis tour. The older of the two, Venus, first gained national attention with an impressive run to the women's singles final at the U.S. Open in 1997. She lost in

(continued on page 2468)

Notable Tennis Players

Allen-Selmore, Leslie (b. Mar. 12, 1957, Cleveland, Ohio). Winner of the Avon Championships of Detroit in 1981, Allen-Selmore was the first black woman since Althea GIBSON to win a singles title in a major tournament. In 1994-1995 she served as the tournament director for the U.S. Women's Hardcourt Championships, a U.S. Tennis Association event.

Ashe, Arthur Robert, Jr. *See main text entry.*

Garrison-Jackson, Zina (b. Nov. 16, 1963, Houston, Tex.). Winner of a bronze medal in singles and a gold medal in doubles with partner Pam Shriver in the 1988 Olympics. Garrison-Jackson won the U.S. Open and Wimbledon junior titles in 1981. By 1999 she had won seven U.S. Tennis Association junior titles—more than any other black player. In 1990 she was a singles runner-up at Wimbledon, becoming the first African American woman since Althea Gibson to reach a grand slam final.

Gibson, Althea. *See main text entry.*

Harmon, Rodney (b. Aug. 16, 1961, Richmond, Va.). In 1982, Harmon was a U.S. Open quarterfinalist, the first African American male to advance that far in the tournament since Arthur ASHE. He served as a U.S. Tennis Association coach from 1988-1995 and was a national coach from 1993 to 1995.

McNeil, Lori (b. Dec. 18, 1963, San Diego, Calif.). McNeil made history in 1986 when she and fellow African American Zina Garrison-Jackson made the finals of the Eckard Open in Tampa, Florida. McNeil prevailed, thereby placing two black women into the ranks of the world's top fifteen players. In 1994 she defeated top-ranked Steffi Graf in the first round of Wimbledon and reached the semifinals of a grand slam tournament for the second time in her career.

Rubin, Chandra (b. Feb. 18, 1976, Lafayette, La.). Rubin reached the 1996 Australian Open singles semifinals by defeating number-four-ranked Arantxa Sanchez Vicario in the longest women's match in the history of the tournament. In 1995 she was a French Open quarterfinalist.

Washington, MaliVai (b. June 20, 1969, Glen Cove, N.Y.). Washington's professional tennis career began in 1989 when he was named rookie of the year by *Tennis Magazine*. In 1993, he became the first African American man since Arthur Ashe named to the U.S. Davis Cup team; he was also on the team in 1996 and 1997. After defeating top-notch players in the early rounds of the competition, Washington was defeated in his first grand slam quarterfinal at the 1994 Australian Open. In 1996, Washington was defeated in the final round of Wimbledon by Richard Krajicek. In December, 1999, he announced his retirement from competition after failing to fully recover from knee surgeries.

AP/Wide World Photos

Washington, Ora (b. c. 1900, Philadelphia, Pa.). Washington's tennis career began in 1924. She remained undefeated until 1936, but her dream of playing the top-rated white tennis player of the day, Helen Wills Moody, was never realized because Moody refused her challenge. Washington also starred as a center on the *Philadelphia Tribune* women's basketball team for eighteen years and was a top scorer for the team.

Williams, Serena (b. Sept. 26, 1981, Saginaw, Mich.). The youngest of five sisters—including tennis star Venus Williams—Serena Williams was managed and coached by her father, Richard Williams. In 1998 she defeated five top-ten players more quickly than any player in the history of women's professional tennis. The 1998 Australian Open was her first grand slam singles event, at which she was defeated by Venus. In 1999 Williams won her first World Tennis Association title in the Open Gaz de France. She then lost to Venus in the Lipton Championships final, the first all-sister women's final in 115 years. In 1999 Williams became the first African American woman since Althea Gibson to win a Grand Slam title, at the U.S. Open.

Williams, Venus (b. June 17, 1980, Lynwood, Calif.). The older sister of Serena Williams, Venus began her formal tennis training with Rick Macci in Florida in 1990. She entered professional tennis at the age of

(continued)

fourteen. In 1997 she was the runner-up at the U.S. Open. She was the first African American woman since Althea Gibson to reach the U.S. championship and only the second woman ever to advance to the final in her U.S. Open debut. In 1999 she reached the quarterfinals of the Australian Open, thereby reaching at least the quarterfinal round in consecutive grand slam tournaments in eight career grand slam appearances. Williams and her sister, Serena, combined to win the 1999 U.S. Open doubles title. In July, 2000, Williams won the Wimbledon singles title and combined with Serena to win the women's doubles.

the finals to Martina Hingis but had established herself as a force on the tour. She continued to be so in 1998 and 1999. Venus and Serena each won several Grand Slam titles in mixed doubles in 1998, and in the early months of 1999 Serena won two tournaments in singles. Serena then won the women's singles title at the U.S. Open in 1999, the first African American woman since Althea Gibson to win a Grand Slam title. Together Venus and Serena won the 1999 U.S. Open doubles title.

Venus Williams in late 1994, shortly after she turned professional. *(AP/Wide World Photos)*

By the year 2000, the visible obstacles that black Americans had long faced in tennis were largely gone, but the sport had not yet captured the imagination of the majority of African Americans in the way that FOOTBALL and BASKETBALL had.

—*Lewis L. Gould*

Terrell, Mary Church (September 23, 1863, Memphis, Tennessee—July 24, 1954, Annapolis, Maryland): Civil and women's rights activist. Born into a wealthy family of former slaves, she was educated in Ohio. She graduated from OBERLIN COLLEGE in 1884 and completed an M.A. in 1888. She also studied languages in Europe; this background proved useful in her later political activities.

She taught at Wilberforce University and in Washington, D.C., schools before marrying school principal Robert Herbertson Terrell in 1891. The Harvard-educated Terrell was a lawyer and somewhat independent protégé of Booker T. WASHINGTON.

Terrell strengthened her public activities after her marriage, spurred on by the LYNCHING of her Memphis friend, Thomas Moss, in 1892. She gained appointment as one of the first black women on the District of Columbia school board (1895-1901 and 1906-1911), headed the prestigious Bethel Literary and Historical Society, and cofounded the Washington Colored Women's League. Later, Terrell worked with Margaret Murray Washington in national and international club movements. Terrell became the first president of the National Association of Colored

Mary Church Terrell, the founder of the National Association of Colored Women. *(Library of Congress)*

Women in 1896, retaining the office until 1901.

Terrell broke with Booker T. Washington over his acquiescence to Theodore Roosevelt's punishment of black soldiers after the BROWNSVILLE INCIDENT of 1906. She attended the founding conference of the NATIONAL ASSOCIATION FOR THE ADVANCEMENT OF COLORED PEOPLE, which both her husband and Washington avoided. She also participated in the woman's suffrage movement, entered into Republican Party politics, and attended international conferences on peace and women's rights.

Even into her eighties, Terrell maintained her life of protest against bigotry, waging a long, successful campaign to integrate the Washington Association of American University Women. She also chaired the Coordinating Committee for the Enforcement of the District of Columbia Anti-Discrimination Laws in 1949, seeking to revive antisegregation laws of the 1870's and picketing local establishments that discriminated against Af-

rican Americans. Terrell's autobiography, *A Colored Woman in a White World*, appeared in 1940. She wrote several other books about African American history.

Terry, Lucy (1730, West Africa—1821, Sunderland, Vermont): Poet. Terry was brought from Africa as a slave. She is considered to be the first African American poet, although Phillis WHEATLEY was apparently the first African American to have published poetry. She lived, sequentially, in the state of Rhode Island; Deerfield, Massachusetts; and Sunderland, Vermont. Only one of her poems, "Bars Flight," has survived. It was narrated by her to a second party in 1746 and published in 1893. It narrates an account of a settlement being attacked by Native Americans.

Texas: In the late 1990's, Texas was the second most populous state in the union, and African Americans composed a little over 12 percent of its population. In 1997 the CENSUS OF THE UNITED STATES estimated the total state population to be about 19.4 million and its African American population to be about 2.4 million. Through the years the state's geographic breadth, racial and economic diversity, and historical uniqueness have fostered a wide-ranging African American experience.

The exploration and occupation of the present southwestern United States in the sixteenth century brought the first African Americans to Texas. In 1528, Estaban, a slave, survived shipwreck on the eastern shore of Texas and explored the area with his master, Andres Dorontes, and Cabeza de Vaca. By the end of the eighteenth century, the Spanish had colonized Texas, and freed Africans and slaves were active in developing the area.

In the early nineteenth century, the conflict between Anglo dependence upon slaves to

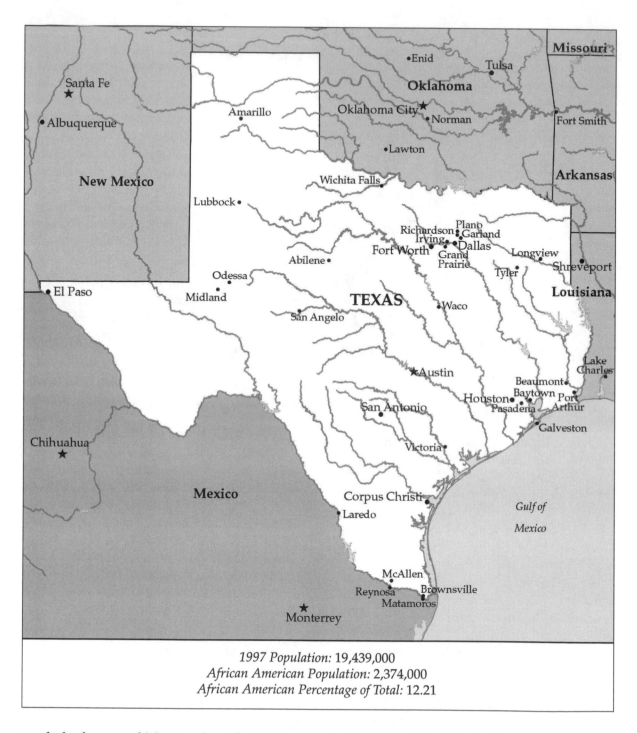

1997 Population: 19,439,000
African American Population: 2,374,000
African American Percentage of Total: 12.21

work the farms and Mexican laws forbidding slavery became one of the issues leading to the war for Texas independence from MEXICO. By the time Texas was annexed into the United States in 1845, the place of African Americans in Texas paralleled that of their counterparts in other southern states.

The black population grew to a quarter of a million during the CIVIL WAR. Little fighting took place in Texas, so many slave owners in more vulnerable Confederate states moved their slaves to Texas. When Union troops finally occupied Texas in June, 1865, the slaves were freed. Guaranteed CIVIL RIGHTS, however, were a long way off. The later nineteenth century and much of the twentieth century for African Americans in Texas mirrored, with few exceptions, the experiences of most blacks in the United States and especially those in southern states.

During RECONSTRUCTION, blacks achieved some political influence, mainly because of their support of and participation in the Republican Party, which at that time was the state's political power. Influential black leaders of the period included Norris Wright Cuney and George T. Ruby. Cuney held sev-

When the Dallas school system was desegregated in 1965, members of the American Nazi Party picketed the school district's administration building to express their objections. *(AP/Wide World Photos)*

eral elected and appointed political positions, most notably collector of customs for Galveston, the highest federal position in Texas at the time. Ruby was an elected representative to the state's 1869 constitutional convention and was later a member of the Texas Senate.

The nascent political influence of blacks had virtually collapsed by 1900 because of the rise in power of the DEMOCRATIC PARTY, the growth of white leadership among Republicans, and the passage of poll tax legislation in 1902. In addition, segregation, never absent, became the practice rather than the exception. Demographic change also occurred, as it did in many states for the same reasons. Industrialization and, especially in Texas, the burgeoning oil industry drew African Americans to the Gulf Coast cities.

The struggle to gain political and civil rights took place throughout the mid-twentieth century. While the violence that characterized the Civil Rights movement in southern states such as Alabama and Mississippi was less evident in Texas, the issues were the same. The ending of all-white primaries in 1944 and of the poll tax in 1965 initiated the return of black officeholders to local and state positions.

Texas has produced a large number of prominent African Americans. Heading the list in the political arena is U.S. congresswoman Barbara JORDAN. Musicians and actors include Jules Bledsoe, Zelma George, and RAGTIME composer Scott JOPLIN. Boxer Jack JOHNSON and baseball player Rube Foster, founder of the Negro National League, were prominent sports figures.

—Ann M. Thompson

Tharpe, Sister Rosetta (Rosetta Nubin; March 20, 1915, Cotton Plant, Arkansas—October 9, 1973, Philadelphia, Pennsylvania): Vocalist, guitarist, and pianist. Tharpe was the first African American GOSPEL MUSIC singer to extend her musical career beyond the confines of the black church community into the venues of nightclubs and lounges. Musically innovative, she popularized gospel by fusing it with jazz and blues rhythms. Classified as "pop gospel," her sound is credited with paving the way for the rhythm-and-blues era. She primarily sang gospel, but she successfully adapted her material to appeal to JAZZ, BLUES, and folk music audiences.

Tharpe was reared within a black Holiness church by her mother, Katie Bell Nubin, a traveling evangelist and a musician of considerable merit. Nurtured by an ecstatic religion that emphasized song and dance as a form of worship, Tharpe was, by the age of six, already a master of the guitar and the gospel repertoire. It was in this atmosphere of unbridled spiritual energy that Tharpe developed a unique style of showmanship that would provide the impetus for her lifelong career.

With the widespread acceptance in the 1930's of modern gospel, combined with the simultaneous rise of the recording industry and of radio, Tharpe's exuberant singing, enhanced by her blues-driven guitar accompaniment, was showcased on Decca records. Her first recording, "Rock Me/Lonesome Road," achieved pop status on Billboard's charts, instantly establishing her as a leading gospel singer. Astute in business, she capitalized on this success by touring with such jazz bands as Cab CALLOWAY's Cotton Club Revue, the Lucky Millinder Band, and Sammy Price's trio. She sang with a wide range of performers, from the DIXIE HUMMINGBIRDS and Madam Marie Knight to Benny Goodman, Muddy WATERS, and even country-and-western singer Red Foley. "Trouble in Mind," "Up Above My Head," and "God Don't Like It," among other recordings, earned her recognition as a jazz artist.

In the 1950's, Tharpe's bright career dimmed somewhat after she violated church ethics by singing the blues in nightclubs. Subsequently shunned by the black church community, she toured Europe for a year, where she sang her diverse repertoire to enthusiastic fans. Eventually, however, she returned to her church, though not with the same level of support as before. For the remainder of her career, she worked both by recording (one album earned her a Grammy nomination) and by touring, mostly in small rural churches in the South.

Theater: The first known appearance of an African American character in American theater was in 1769, when Lewis Hallam appeared in blackface in *The Padlock*. Other plays of the late eighteenth century featured a variety of African American characters. A play in 1798 called *The Triumph of Love* introduced a shuffling, cackling black servant, and an unfortunate stereotype was created.

The AFRICAN GROVE THEATER was formed in New York City in 1820 by James Hewlett and began performing Shakespearean dramas before mixed audiences in 1821. Hewlett was a fine tragic actor, but his company was forced to close because of attacks by white hooligans. With the destruction of that company and the departure of the great Ira ALDRIDGE for Europe came the end of an early opportunity to develop a significant African American theater.

The early nineteenth century also saw the beginning of the tradition of interspersing "black-dialect" songs into regular plays. By the 1820's, George Nichols had popularized "Zip Coon" and George Washington Dixon was impersonating African Americans in songs. In 1823 Edwin Forrest, a white actor, blackened his face in *The Tailor in Distress* and was praised as offering "the first realistic representation of the plantation Negro."

Minstrelsy

In 1828 Thomas "Daddy" Rice, a white performer, began to imitate the singing and shuf-

(continued on page 2476)

Notable Stage Actors

Aldridge, Ira Frederick. *See main text entry.*

Alice, Mary (Mary Alice Smith; b. Dec. 3, 1941, Indianola, Miss.). Alice has appeared in stage productions of such plays as *Julius Caesar, Nongogo, Fences* (1987), and *Having Our Say.* She appeared on the television series *A Different World* in 1987 and *I'll Fly Away.* Her

honors include Emmy, Obie and Tony Awards. She also appeared in the films *The Inkwell* (1994) and *Down in the Delta* (1998).

Avery, Margaret (b. 1940's, Okla.). Avery's first Hollywood appearances were in BLAXPLOITATION films and in television commercials. She also performed on stage in Los Angeles, Calif., where she formed the Zodiac Theater with her husband, Robert Gordon Hunt. Their production of the play *Does the Tiger Wear a Necktie?* won her the 1972 L.A. Drama Critics Circle Award for outstanding performance. Avery has also been in such films as *Cool Breeze* (1972), *Hell up in Harlem* (1973), *Which Way Is Up?* (1977), *The Fish That Saved Pittsburgh* (1979), *The Color Purple* (1985), *Blueberry Hill* (1988), and *Riverbend* (1989). Throughout the 1990's she appeared in numerous television shows and television movies

Blacque, Taurean (Herbert Middleton, Jr., b. May 10, 1946, Newark, N.J.). Best known for his performance as streetwise detective Neal Washington in television's *Hill Street Blues* from 1981 to 1987, Blacque also has numerous stage and television credits, including a role in the television serial *Generations.* He made his broadway debut in the Negro Ensemble Company production of *The River Niger.*

Anderson, Jim (b. 1929, Harlem, N.Y.). Born in HARLEM, Anderson was a Golden Gloves boxer and dockworker before becoming involved in the performing arts as an actor with the Living Theatre in New York. A staunch supporter of community self-help programs, he helped found the East Harlem Food Buying Federation to provide neighborhood food cooperatives with low-cost fresh produce and other groceries.

Bush, Anita (c. 1883, Washington, D.C.—Feb. 16, 1974, New York, N.Y.). A pioneer in the development of African American theater, Bush helped nurture black dramatic actors. As a member of the Williams and Walker VAUDEVILLE troupe from 1903 to 1909, she organized the Anita Bush Stock Company in 1915. A pioneer black dramatic group, it later became known as the Lafayette Players. Her acting credits include such Broadway musicals as *In Dahomey* (1902) and *Abyssinia* (1903), and such films as *The Crimson Skull* (1921) and *The Bull Doggers* (1922).

Caesar, Adolph (1934?, Harlem, N.Y.—Mar. 16, 1986, Los Angeles, Calif.). A longtime member of New York City's Negro Ensemble Company, Caesar won recognition in 1981 for his performance in *A Soldier's Play*, which earned him Obie and New York Drama Desk awards. He reprised his role of embittered Sergeant Vernon Walters in the 1984 film version, *A Soldier's Story*, and was nominated for an Oscar. He portrayed the old minister in the popular 1985 film *The Color Purple* and received a National Association for the Advancement of Colored People IMAGE AWARD in 1985.

Dee, Ruby (Ruby Ann Wallace; b. Oct. 27, 1923, Cleveland, Ohio). Dee's stage roles have included performances in *South Pacific* (1943), *Jeb* (1946), *Purlie Victorious* (1961), *A Raisin in the Sun* (1959), *Boesman and Lena* (1970), for which she won an Obie, and *Wedding Band* (1972). She also has the recognition of being the first African American woman to portray major roles with the American Shakespeare Festival—in *Taming of the Shrew* (1965) and *King Lear* (1965). In 1975 Dee was inducted into the Black Filmmakers Hall of Fame and in 1988 she was inducted into the Broadway Hall of Fame. She has appeared in numerous television shows and films. She has often worked with her husband, actor Ossie DAVIS, and performed on television and in films through the 1990's.

Dutton, Charles S. (b. Jan. 30, 1951, Baltimore, Md.). Convicted of killing a man in a brawl at age seventeen, Dutton spent eight years in and out of prison. While incarcerated, he grew interested in theater

(continued)

and worked in drama groups. In 1976 he entered the Yale School of Drama, where he trained under Lloyd RICHARDS, who later cast him in the 1986 Broadway production of *Ma Rainey's Black Bottom*. Dutton's performance earned him his first Tony nomination. Other theatrical successes included lead roles in *Joe Turner's Come and Gone* (1986) and *The Piano Lesson* (pr. 1987). His television credits include many guest appearances on series and made-for-television films. His film credits include *No Mercy* (1986), *An Unremarkable Life* (1989), *Q & A* (1990), *Mississippi Masala* (1992), *Alien 3* (1992) *The Distinguished Gentleman* (1992), *Rudy* (1993), and *Menace II Society* (1993). In 1991 he was cast in the lead role in the Fox situation comedy *Roc*, a realistic portrayal of a blue-collar African American family.

Foster, Gloria (b. Nov. 15, 1936, Chicago, Ill.). Foster has won such honors as the Obie Award, an AUDELCO Black Theater Award, and a place in the Black Filmmakers Hall of Fame. She is a graduate of Illinois State University, the Art Institute of Chicago, the University of Chicago Court Theater, and the University of Massachusetts at Amherst. She has made numerous film appearances and is acclaimed highly for her numerous Broadway and Off-Broadway performances in such plays as *The Cherry Orchard*, *A Midsummer Night's Dream*, *A Dream Play*, *The Trojan Women*, *Mother Courage and Her Children*, *Long Day's Journey into Night*, *Agamemnon*, and *Black Visions*.

Freeman, Albert Cornelius, Jr. (b. Mar. 21, 1934, San Antonio, Tex.). Freeman made his first appearance in 1954 at the Ebony Showcase Theater in Los Angeles, in the play *Detective Story*. Among his many roles are Richard Henry in *Blues for Mister Charlie* in 1964 and Paul Robeson in *Are You Now or Have You Ever Been* in 1972 at the Yale Repertory. He starred in the television series *Hot L Baltimore* in 1975 and appeared on THE COSBY SHOW in 1986.

Gilpin, Charles Sidney (Nov. 20, 1878, Richmond, Va.—May 6, 1930, Eldridge Park, N.J.). Gilpin won his greatest acclaim as the title character in Eugene O'Neill's *The Emperor Jones* (1920). He appeared with the Pekin Players in Chicago and the Lafayette Players in Harlem. He was cast as William Custis in Broadway's *Abraham Lincoln* (1919), notable since it was still atypical for African Americans to portray characters on the commercial stage.

Gunn, Moses (b. Oct. 2, 1929, St. Louis, Mo.). Gunn's stage credits include *The Blacks* (1961), *In White America* (1963), *Day of Absence* (1966), *Daddy Goodness* (1968), and *Sty of the Blind Pig* (1972). His honors include Obie Awards for his performances in *Titus Andronicus* (1967-1968) and *The First Breeze of Summer* (1975), and a Tony Award nomination for his role in *The Poison Tree* (1976). His greatest acclaim as a stage actor came with his portrayal of the title character in a production of *Othello* (1970). Gunn has also appeared on several television series and his film work includes *The Great White Hope* (1970), *Shaft* (1971), and *Ragtime* (1981). Gunn continued to act into the 1990's.

Harrison, Richard B. *See main text entry.*

Hooks, Robert (b. Apr. 18, 1937, Washington, D.C.). After appearing in several Off-Broadway plays, Hooks won a starring role in the drama *Dutchman* (1964). His other stage work includes roles in *Where's Daddy?* (1966) and *Hallelujah Baby!* (1967). He was instrumental in the 1967 founding of the Negro Ensemble Company, one of the most influential black companies in American theater. In addition to starring in the series *N.Y.P.D.* (1967-1969), Hooks has been a frequent guest star on a variety of television shows and has had featured roles in several made-for-television films. His screen credits include roles in *Trouble Man* (1972), *Aaron Loves Angela* (1975), and *Star Trek III: The Search for Spock* (1984). He continued to appear in guest starring roles on television and film. His film appearances include roles in *Posse* (1993) and *Fled* (1996).

Hyman, Earle (b. Oct. 11, 1926, Rocky Mount, N.C.). In 1965 Hyman received the Norwegian State Award for best actor as the title character in Eugene O'Neill's *The Emperor Jones*. He received an AUDELCO Pioneers Award in 1980 for his career-long contributions to African Americans in theater. Hyman is best known to television audiences as Russell Huxtable on *The Cosby Show* (1984-1992).

Jones, James Earl. *See main text entry.*

Little, Cleavon (June 1, 1939, Chickasha, Okla.— Oct. 22, 1992, Sherman Oaks, Calif.). Little's stage career began quickly when he appeared in *Jimmy Shine* (1968-1969), *Someone's Comin' Hungry* (1969), *Ofay*

Watcher (1969), *Dutchman*, and some half-dozen or more plays. In 1970, he won a Tony Award for best actor in a musical for his performance in *Purlie*. In 1985 he returned to Broadway in the hit play *I'm Not Rappaport* (1985) and he appeared in the one-man show *All God's Dangers* (1989). Little is perhaps most known, however, for his role as a black sheriff in Mel Brooks's farcical film *Blazing Saddles* (1974). He was also in more than fifteen other films.

Marshall, William (b. Aug. 19, 1924, Gary, Ind.). After being discharged from the Army because of a wound in 1943, Marshall joined the American Negro Theatre. In 1951 he played De Lawd in a Broadway revival of *The Green Pastures*. With his powerful, resonant voice and commanding physical presence, his performance caught film producer Darryl Zanuck's attention and led to film roles. In later years he played an African-prince-turned-vampire in *Blacula* (1972) and its sequel, *Scream, Blacula, Scream* (1973). Marshall was also the first African American actor to co-star in a dramatic television series, the locally produced New York show *Harlem Detectives* (1953-1954). He has also had frequent guest roles on many other series.

AP/Wide World Photos

McNeil, Claudia Mae (b. Aug. 13, 1917, Baltimore, Md.). At sixteen McNeil launched a singing career by appearing in a Greenwich Village nightclub. However, her career did not really develop until the early 1950's, when she joined Katherine DUNHAM's dance troupe as a dancer and featured singer. She made her first appearance on Broadway as a replacement in Arthur Miller's *The Crucible* in 1953. In 1959 she was cast as Lena, the family matriarch, in *A Raisin in the Sun*, a part for which she became well known. She reprised the part in 1975, and in 1981, she appeared again as Lena in the musical version, *Raisin*. Meanwhile, in 1962 she appeared on stage in *Tiger, Tiger Burning Bright*, for which she was nominated for a Tony award. In 1965, she appeared in James Baldwin's *The Amen Corner*. She also performed in such plays as *Winesburg, Ohio* (1958), *Something Different* (1968), *Her First Roman* (1968),

The Wrong Way Light Bulb (1969), and *Contributions* (1970). McNeil has also appeared in a variety of distinguished television dramas and won an Emmy for her performance in *The Nurses* in 1963.

Mills, Stephanie (b. Mar. 22, 1957, New York, N.Y.). Mills obtained her musical education at the Juilliard School of Music. Her first major success on Broadway came in her starring role in *The Wiz*. She has received seven Tony Awards for Broadway theater performance, recorded two gold albums, and won a 1980 Grammy.

Moore, Melba (b. Oct. 29, 1945, New York, N.Y.). In 1969 Moore was cast in a leading role in the rock musical *Hair* (1968), the first time that a female African American actor replaced a white actor on a Broadway stage. Her work in *Purlie* (1970) won for her a Tony Award for best supporting actress in a musical (1971). Moore also appeared in such screen musicals as *Lost in the Stars* (1974) and *Hair* (1980) and the television series *Melba*. She continued to act into the 1990's.

Richards, Beah (b. July 1, c. 1928, Vicksburg, Miss.). After an apprenticeship at San Diego's Globe Theater, Richards went to New York City. She made her professional stage debut in the Off-Broadway revival of *Take a Giant Step* (1954). While an understudy for the role of Lena Younger in *A Raisin in the Sun* (1959), she landed a role in the Broadway drama *The Miracle Worker* (1959). This was followed by another Broadway appearance in *Purlie Victorious* (1961). She received her greatest acclaim as Sister Margaret in James Baldwin's *The Amen Corner* (1965). That performance led to work in films, including *Hurry Sundown* (1967), *In the Heat of the Night* (1967), and *Guess Who's Coming to Dinner?* (1967), for which she received an Oscar nomination as best supporting actress. He other film credits include *Gone Are the Days* (1963), *Mahogany* (1975), and *Drugstore Cowboy* (1989). She has also been a frequent guest on television series. Her honors include the Theatre World Award for her work on *The Amen Corner* (1965), a 1986 IMAGE AWARD from the National Association for the Advancement of Colored People, and an Emmy Award (1988) for an appearance on *Frank's Place*.

Sands, Diana (Aug. 22, 1934, New York, N.Y.—Sept. 21, 1973, New York, N.Y.). A graduate of the New

(continued)

York High School of Performing Arts, Sands later studied with Lloyd Richards. She began her stage career in such Off-Broadway show as *An Evening with Will Shakespeare* (1953), *Major Barbara* (1954), and *The Egg and I* (1958), for which she won an Obie Award. Her performance as Beneatha Younger in *A Raisin in the Sun* in 1959) earned her an Outer Critics Circle Award. After re-creating the role in the film version, she returned to Broadway to perform in such shows as *Tiger, Tiger, Burning Bright* (1962), *Blues for Mister Charlie* (1964), *The Owl and the Pussycat* (1964), *Gingham Dog* (1969), and William Shakespeare's *Antony*

AP/Wide World Photos

and Cleopatra (1968), as Cleopatra. Her film career also continued into the early 1970's, until her untimely death at age thirty-nine. Two films in which she appeared, *Willie Dynamite* (1973), and *Honeybaby, Honeybaby* (1974), were released after her death. She also appeared in television series.

Simms, Hilda (Hilda Theresa Moses; b. Apr. 15, 1920, Minneapolis, Minn.). Simms's most memorable role was the title character in the AMERICAN NEGRO THEATRE production of *Anna Lucasta* (1944). She played the role in more than two thousand performances in New York, Chicago, and London. As Miss Ayres in television's *The Nurses* (1962-1965), Simms was one of the few African American women with a recurring role in a prime-time dramatic series before the 1970's.

Washington, Fredi. *See main text entry.*

fling of a black person and created a popular act called *Bone Squash*. He is credited with initiating the character of Jim Crow. Imitations of Rice followed. P. T. Barnum added Ethiopian "breakdowns" to his shows, and in 1843 Daniel Emmett brought his Virginia Minstrels to the New York stage. White men in its performances wore blackened faces and gala costumes, and they told jokes for white audiences. The era of minstrels was officially launched.

In minstrelsy, a large group of men sat or stood in a half circle, with a master of ceremonies in the middle acting as a straight man; on each side of him were the musicians. The language and music were parodies of the distinctive new styles that African Americans had developed in the nineteenth century.

African Americans as Theater Characters
African Americans also appeared as characters in the theater. In spite of the good intentions of the abolitionist play *Uncle Tom's Cabin*, it too helped to establish stereotypes, such as the mischievous Topsy and the all-forgiving

Uncle Tom. Another theatrical type was the "tragic mulatto," such as in Dion Boucicault's *The Octroon*. It further insulted blacks by establishing a "white" beauty standard. Other African American characters that appeared before and soon after the Civil War were mostly servants and minor personages.

By the 1880's and 1890's, a more balanced treatment slowly emerged, beginning with Steele Mackaye's play *A Fool's Errand* in 1881 and culminating with Edward Sheldon's *The Nigger* in 1910. Sheldon's was one of the few plays up to that time to appear on Broadway with a story line about an African American.

African American Actors
Theatrically, the most significant development following the Civil War was the appearance of African Americans as entertainers, at first in the minstrel tradition, where they were a caricature of a caricature, and later in their own unique form. In 1898 Bob Cole wrote, directed, and produced *A Trip to Coontown*, a musical with a plot that broke with the min-

(continued on page 2479)

Notable Musicals by and About African Americans

Ain't Misbehavin' (pr. 1978), Richard Maltby, Jr., book; Fats WALLER, music. The show is a tribute to Fats Waller and his musical style. It revived national interest in his music and led to the reissuing of many of his recordings. The Broadway version won three Tony Awards in 1978: for best musical; for best musical director (Richard Maltby, Jr.); and for best featured actress (Nell Carter).

Blackbirds of 1929 (pr. 1929), Lew Leslie, book; Eubie BLAKE, music; Andy Razaf, lyrics. Based on the book by Flournoy Miller and Al Richards, the work was one of Blake's numerous attempts to repeat the success of *Blackbirds of 1928*. The onset of the GREAT DEPRESSION meant failure at the box office, but the musical was praised by critics. Billed as "Glorifying the American Negro," the show starred Flournoy Miller and Ethel WATERS.

Bubbling Brown Sugar (pr. 1976), Loften MITCHELL, book. A young man, eager to leave HARLEM because he finds no history there and sees no future for himself, changes his mind after taking an imaginary tour of the city when it was prosperous. The show pays special attention to Harlem's all-black revues and features the music of Eubie Blake, Duke ELLINGTON, and Billie HOLIDAY.

Don't Bother Me, I Can't Cope (pr. 1970), Musical by Micki Grant. Using a wide variety of musical styles, including jazz, rock, blues, and gospel, the work depicts the difficulties that African Americans, and oppressed people everywhere, encounter as they deal with their realities and with the problems of life. It won the Outer Critics Circle Award, two Obie Awards, two Drama Desk Awards, and an IMAGE AWARD from the NATIONAL ASSOCIATION FOR THE ADVANCEMENT OF COLORED PEOPLE (NAACP).

Dreamgirls (pr. 1981), Tom Eyen, book and lyrics; Henry Krieger, music. Produced New York's Imperial Theatre, the musical depicts the story of a trio of talented black singers who become highly successful—much like the real-life SUPREMES.

Eubie! (pr. 1978), Julianne Boyd, book; Eubie Blake, music; Noble Sissle, Andy Razaf, Johnny Brandon, and F. E. Miller, lyrics. The work, which featured Gregory HINES and his brother Maurice Hines, is a tribute to Blake. It recounts his career from the 1919 to 1978.

Golden Boy (pr. 1964), William Gibson and Clifford Odets, book; Charles Strouse, music; Lee Adams, lyrics. Adapted from Odets's play of the same title, the musical brought Sammy DAVIS, Jr., back to the Broadway stage, tells the story of a talented young violinist who chooses to become a boxer. The was modified slightly to fit Davis's talents, and the setting was changed from an Italian one to an American one that reflects black boxing life.

In Dahomey (pr. 1902), Jesse A. Shipp, book; Will Marion Cook, music; Alex Rogers, lyrics. Although entitled *In Dahomey*, only part of the action of this work, the most successful of all the Bert WILLIAMS and George Walker shows, takes place in the West African republic (now Benin) of the title. Featuring a new RAGTIME musical style, the story recounts Williams and Walker's adventures searching for a silver box, then tells of their travels in Africa, where they remain.

Jelly's Last Jam (pr. 1991), George C. Wolfe, book. Based in part on the life and career of Jelly Roll MORTON, the work is set in 1941, the year Morton died. It recounts the ups and downs of his career and his attitude toward African Americans, to whom, as a CREOLE, he felt superior. The musical won three Tony Awards: Gregory Hines, best actor, musical; Tonya Pinkins, best featured actress; and Jules Fisher, best lighting designer.

Jesus Christ-Lawd Today (pr. 1971), Glenda Dickerson, book; Clyde Barrett, music. Produced by the Black American Theatre, the play was directed by Dickerson and choreographed by Debbie ALLEN. Set in an urban African American town, it depicts the story of Jesus Christ.

Mrs. Patterson (pr. 1954), Musical fantasy by Charles Sebree, with Greer Johnson. Adapted from Sebree's play *My Mother Came Crying Most Pitifully* (1949), the drama centers on a poverty-stricken black girl who fantasizes about being the wealthy white woman of the title, who is her mother's employer.

(continued)

Once on This Island (1990). Broadway show directed and choreographed by Braciela Daniele. Based on the 1985 novel *My Love, My Love, or the Peasant Girl* by Rosa Guy, it depicts a romance between a dark-skinned peasant girl, Ti Moune, and a light-skinned aristocratic mulatto, Daniel Beauxhomme. The destinies of the couple and their friends and neighbors are subject to the whims of the island's gods—a cheerful meddlesome bunch. This Caribbean fable unfolds with giddy simplicity, through song and dance, storytelling and mime, and vibrant calypso routines and ecstatic ritual dances. It is a fairy tale of life and death in which the lives of the characters become the stories they weave.

Porgy and Bess (pr. 1935), Dorothy and DuBose Heyward, book; George and Ira Gershwin, music and lyrics. The story is set in a tenement called Catfish Row and portrays Porgy (originally played by Todd DUNCAN), a black man with a physical disability, who seduces Bess and kills her former lover, Crown. The show also starred Abbie Mitchell and J. Rosamond Johnson. Although initially unpopular, the show developed into an outstanding success and, in many revivals, served as a vehicle for many African American singers and actors. A film adaptation produced in 1959 starred Sidney POITIER and Dorothy DANDRIDGE.

Prodigal Sister, The (pr. 1974), J. E. Franklin, book; Micki Grant, music; Franklin and Grant, lyrics. Based on Franklin's play *Prodigal Daughter* (1962), this modern version of the biblical story portrays a teenage girl who becomes pregnant and leaves her parents and hometown. She returns to her family's warmth and protection after enduring city life.

Show Boat (pr. 1927), Oscar Hammerstein II, book and lyrics; Jerome Kern, music. Originally staged in Florenz Ziegfeld's theater, the show was a great success. Its story is based on Edna Ferber's 1926 novel of the same title, which describes the era of floating theaters on major American rivers and their early attempts to introduce drama to settlers. The musical blended songs, dances, and jokes into the action. In 1927, the original production was significant for its sympathetic portrayal of southern blacks. The plot turns on the illegal marriage of the show boat's star, a MULATTO woman "passing" for white, to a white man. The first film version featured Paul ROBESON (1936) singing "Old Man River."

Shuffle Along (pr. 1921), Flournoy Miller and Aubrey Lyles, book; Eubie Blake, music; Noble Sissle, lyrics. Two friends, Sam and Steve, enter a mayoral race and promise each other that the winner will appoint the other as chief of police. Sam wins through questionable means, and a disagreement erupts between the two. A reform candidate who arrives on the scene for the next election vows to end corruption and wins, forcing Sam and Steve to leave town. The first black show written and produced by African Americans, *Shuffle Along* became an international success. It starred Josephine BAKER, Florence MILLS, and Caterina Jarboro.

Simply Heavenly (pr. 1957), Langston Hughes adapted this musical from his own play, *Simple Takes a Wife* (1955), which is based on the novel by the same title. Its story concerns Simple's efforts to save money to divorce his wife and marry his sweetheart. It was performed on Broadway at the Playhouse Theatre, and a British version played at London's Adelphi Theatre and toured the British provinces. In 1959, it was produced on American national television's *Play of the Week* series.

Sophisticated Ladies (pr. 1981), Donald McKayle, book; Duke Ellington, music. Performed in Broadway's Lunt-Fontanne Theater, the work, which was a hit, combines tap dancing with Ellington's mood music, ranging from the melodies of "Mood Indigo" and "Solitude" to the rhythms of "Cottontail." The show featured both black and white singers and dancers, including Gregory Hines and Judith Jamison.

Tap Dance Kid, The (pr. 1984), Musical by Charles Blackwell that addresses the frustrations and aspirations of a black middle-class family living in a Manhattan duplex and searching for upward mobility. A ten-year-old boy named Willie dreams of becoming a tap dancer when he grows up. His thirteen-year-old sister, Emma, wants to be a lawyer. Their father opposes Willie's ambitions because he believes that black people never got anywhere until they stopped dancing and started working.

Wiz, The (pr. 1975), William F. Brown, book; Charlie Smalls, music and lyrics. African American version of L. Frank Baum's children's story, *The Wonderful Wizard of Oz* (1900), about a girl from Kansas who is carried by a cyclone to the land of Oz, where she befriends strange characters. Producers used soft rock music and theater magic to replace film special effects, made famous in Metro-Golden-Mayer's 1939 *The Wizard of Oz*. *The Wiz* won six Tony Awards: best musical director (Geoffrey Holder); best musical composer and lyricist (Charlie Smalls); best musical production (Ken Harper); best choreography

AP/Wide World Photos

(George Faison); and performers Ted Rose and Dee Dee Bridgewater. A 1978 film version starred Diana Ross, Richard Pryor, Michael Jackson, Nipsey Russell, and Lena Horne.

Your Arms Too Short to Box with God (pr. 1976), Vinnette Carroll, book; Alex Bradford and Micki Grant, music and lyrics. The work, a black version of the Book of Matthew told in black idiom, was developed by Carroll and the Urban Arts Corps for presentation at the Festival of Two Worlds in Spoleto, Italy. Delores Hall won a Tony Award as best featured actress for her performance.

strel tradition by telling a story through music, song, and dance. Produced in New York City, it provided a model for others to follow.

After the beginning of the twentieth century, Bert Williams became one of the most popular black performers of all time, starring in such well-known shows as *Abyssinia* (1906), written by Jesse Shipp, *Bandana Land* (1908), *Mr. Lode of Kole* (1911), and various editions of the Ziegfeld Follies. The years 1909 to 1917 saw the rise of the Harlem theater movement, with shows by African American artists written for their own audiences at such theaters as the Crescent, the Lafayette, and the Lincoln.

With the production of Eugene O'Neill's *The Emperor Jones* in 1920, with Charles Gilpin cast as Brutus Jones, black characters played by black actors became accepted in the theater. Many other plays followed, including O'Neill's *All God's Chillun Got Wings* (1924), starring Paul Robeson, Paul Green's *In Abraham's Bosom* (1926), Dubose and Dorothy Heyward's *Porgy* (1927), and Lew Leslie's *Blackbirds of 1928*, which starred the great dancer Bill "Bojangles" Robinson and was followed by *Blackbirds of 1929* with Eubie Blake. Black theater flourished in the 1920's.

In 1930, although the Great Depression curtailed theatrical activity, some black plays were produced. One of the most successful was Marc Connelly's *The Green Pastures*. This was followed by worthy efforts such as Hall Johnson's *Run, Little Children* (1933), John Wexley's *They Shall Not Die* (1934), Langston Hughes's *Mulatto* (1935), and the musical *Porgy and Bess*.

The 1930's also saw a number of attempts to found a permanent African American theater. Such distinguished artists as Rose McClendon, Dick Campbell, Richard Huey, and Venezuela Jones contributed greatly to the effort. One of the most important organizations of the late 1930's was the Negro Unit of the Federal Theatre Project, which was an arm of the Works Progress Administration, President Franklin D. Roosevelt's program to put people back to work.

The numerous productions of the 1930's included such works as George McEntee's *The Case of Philip Lawrence*, J. Augustus Smith's *Turpentine*, Rudolph Fisher's *The Conjure Man Dies*, and William Dubois's *Haiti*. The most highly acclaimed production was the Orson Welles-John Houseman offering of *Macbeth*, setting Shakespeare's drama on a West Indian Island and featuring an all-black cast, among whom were Canada Lee, Jack Carter, and Edna Thomas. The Rose McClendon Players gave a noteworthy production of William

(continued on page 2484)

Notable Plays by and About African Americans

All God's Chillun Got Wings (pr. 1924). Eugene O'Neill, playwright. The work, first produced at the Provincetown Playhouse in New York City, portrays the tense marriage between a white woman and her black husband. It not only offers a commentary on American racism but presents a psychological study of its central characters.

Amen Corner, The (pr. 1954). James Baldwin, playwright. The work treats the collapse of the dichotomy between institutionalized religion, or "Temple," and moral integrity, or "Street," through the experiences of members of a Harlem church congregation.

Big White Fog (pr. 1938). Theodore Ward, playwright. Growing disillusioned with Marcus GARVEY's philosophy of black nationalism, Victor Mason embraces communism as a solution to his problems and the problems of all African Americans. Mason is later killed by the police when he resists eviction from his apartment. The play attempts to demonstrate that capitalism and Garvey's movement cannot rescue African Americans from their plight.

Black Girl, The (pr. 1971). J. E. Franklin, playwright. Set in a small TEXAS ghetto, this autobiographical play deals with an ambitious teenager who dreams of becoming a dancer. She struggles not only to achieve her goal but also to stay close to her family, especially her mother, who does not support her. Her two half-sisters do not have such high aspirations, and only her grandmother helps her fulfill her dream. The play won a Drama Desk Award.

Blues for Mister Charlie (pr. 1964). James Baldwin, playwright. Loosely based on a real murder that occurred in 1955, this protest drama concentrates on a young black man's white murderer and his acquittal, after which he confesses to the crime. It is an open condemnation of racial discrimination and racism in the criminal justice system.

Bronx Is Next, The (pr. 1970). Sonia Sanchez, playwright. The work criticizes poor housing and overcrowded ghettos in HARLEM and the Bronx. Black rebels vacate and burn down all underkept residences. One couple, a white man and a black woman, die in the fire. In the drama, Sanchez proposes that African Americans leave their disease-infested ghettos and start life anew in a land where they can live as human beings.

Brownsville Raid, The (pr. 1976). Charles Fuller, playwright. The work is a dramatization of an actual shooting incident that occurred in Brownsville, Tex., for which a black regiment was blamed. The play shows how interracial tension and hatred can lead to mass racial injustice.

Ceremonies in Dark Old Men (pr. 1965). Lonne Elder, playwright. The work explores the demoralizing effect of racism on a black family unable to advance in a white-dominated world. Humiliation and frustration lead its members to secure money through robbery and fraud.

Colored Museum, The (pr. 1986). George C. Wolfe, playwright. Hilarious work lampooning white Americans and African Americans alike. In a series of museum exhibits, it displays the stereotypical subjects of ridicule, including African wigs, EBONY magazine, and Josephine BAKER. It won the 1986 Dramatists Guild Award.

Day of Absence (pr. 1965). Douglas Turner Ward, playwright. Satirical drama exploring the turmoil in a southern town following the mysterious disappearance of its black population for one day. It ridicules white stereotypes of African Americans and demonstrates how dependent whites are on blacks. Ward received an Obie Award in 1966 for his performance in this play.

Divine Comedy (pr. 1938). Verse Owen Dodson, playwright. Drama revolving around the life and career of FATHER DIVINE (George Baker), the founder of the Peace Mission movement. The author of more than twenty plays, Dodson first presented this drama in two acts at the Yale University theater in New Haven.

Don't You Want to Be Free? (pr. 1937). Langston Hughes, playwright. Historical work with music recounting the history of African Americans: from slavery and emancipation through living within a white society. Combining Hughes's blues poems, JAZZ, and religious chants, the play was performed in 135 weekend shows over two years—a record run. The play was the first performance of Hughes's Harlem Suitcase Theater, which operated with unpaid actors.

Driving Miss Daisy (pr. 1987). Alfred Uhry, playwright. Dramatic work focusing on a southern Jewish woman and her black chauffeur. The woman wants to attend a banquet in honor of Martin Luther KING, Jr., but her son refuses to accompany her. She has a difficult time inviting her chauffeur to attend with her and is not able to do so until they arrive at the hotel where the banquet is being held. By then, however, his pride forces him to refuse the invitation. The play won the Pulitzer Prize in 1988 and two Obie Awards. A film version was released in 1989. Uhry won an Academy Award for his screenplay, Jessica Tandy won one as best actress, and Morgan Freeman received an Oscar nomination for reprising his stage role as the chauffeur.

Duplex, The (pr. 1970). Ed Bullins, playwright. Subtitled *A Black Love Fable in Four Movements*, this drama deals with the hopelessness of a young man's love for a woman married to a cruel man. When the young man attempts to rescue his loved one from her husband's brutality, he is beaten himself.

Dutchman (pr., pb. 1964). Amiri Baraka, playwright. The work focuses on the clash between a young black man traveling on a subway car and a white woman who sits next to him. The woman masquerades as a seductress, a psychologist, and a racist, then provokes the man into a rage and murders him. The play won an Obie Award in 1964 and the Off-Broadway Award for the best American play of 1963-1964.

Emperor Jones, The (pr. 1920). Eugene O'Neill, playwright. Drama dealing with the self-knowledge, fears, and final hours of an ex-convict who becomes emperor of an island in the WEST INDIES and exploits the superstitious islanders. In his attempt to flee the island after a revolt, he is haunted by the memory of his racial wrongdoings and is forced to relive the horrors of an auction block and a SLAVE SHIP.

Fences (pr. 1985). August Wilson, playwright. The work, set in the 1950's, centers on Troy Maxson, a black man scarred by racism. His explosive emotions and a struggle with his son lead to the family's collapse. The fences of the title symbolize the conflicts among family members and the psychological barriers that they erect to protect themselves and their differences. The play won the Pulitzer Prize in 1987, the New York Drama Critics Circle Award, and two Tony Awards.

for colored girls who have considered suicide/ when the rainbow is enuf (pr., pb. 1976). Ntozake Shange, playwright. Termed a "choreopoem" by Shange, this feminist work is a recital, with song and dance, of the lives of seven black women. The "colored girls" stereotype of the title and the poems of anguish and abuse that the women tell contrast with the colors of the rainbow with which they are dressed and that represent hope.

Funnyhouse of a Negro (pr. 1962). Adrienne Kennedy, playwright. Dream-like work exploring the double identity of a MULATTO woman whose internal conflict leads her to commit SUICIDE. It won an Obie Award in 1964.

Gold Through the Trees (pr. 1952). Dramatic revue by Alice Childress. The historical play, in eight scenes with music, examines the methods black people have used to fight oppression and discrimination. It traces their efforts beginning in Africa, proceeding to the United States, and ending in South Africa. It was produced by the Committee for the Negro in the Arts, at Club Baron, in Harlem.

Great White Hope, The (pr. 1967). Howard Sackler, playwright. Based on the career of Jack JOHNSON, the first black heavyweight BOXING champion, the play dramatizes the boxing world and tense race relations. The play won the Pulitzer Prize, a Tony Award, and the New York Drama Critics Circle Award for best play. James Earl Jones won Tony  and Drama Desk Awards for his performance as Johnson and he reprised the role in a film adaptation released in 1970.

(continued)

Harlem (pr. 1929). Wallace Thurman, playwright, with William Jordan Rapp. Opening at the APOLLO THEATER in New York City months before the great stock market crash, the melodrama was one of three plays by African American playwrights performed on Broadway during the 1920's. It offers a realistic description of black life in a railroad apartment in Harlem.

Home (pr. 1979). Samm-Art Williams, playwright. Set in the 1960's and 1970's, the play portrays the adventures of a black man who leaves his farm in Cross Roads, N.C., and travels to northern cities before returning to his hometown.

I'm Not Rappaport (pr. 1985). Herb Gardner, playwright. Two likable and eccentric octogenarians, one African American and the other white, sit on a park bench and exchange stories and one-liners. The former knows he might be forced to retire, so he avoids his employer. The white character is in love with confrontation politics but avoids his controlling daughter. The play was first produced at the Seattle Repertory Theater, then went Off-Broadway before being performed on Broadway. The play won three Tony Awards in 1986.

In Splendid Error (pr. 1954). William Blackwell Branch, playwright. Historical drama, first produced Off-Broadway at the Greenwich Mews Theatre. It explores the confrontation that between Frederick DOUGLASS and John BROWN over the best method to promote abolition and over the HARPERS FERRY raid by Brown, to which Douglass was opposed.

In the Wine Time (pr. 1968). Ed Bullins, playwright. First play in a projected series of twenty plays called the Twentieth-Century Cycle. Portrays black life in the northern ghettoes. It is also a criticism of black women who oppose black men's rejection of environmental and societal pressure.

Joe Turner's Come and Gone (pr. 1986). August Wilson, playwright. Set in a boardinghouse in 1911, this is the story of a black man who, having been freed after seven years of slavery, goes North with his daughter in search of his wife. The play depicts the transition of African Americans from slavery to freedom, their aimless wandering, and their search for solace.

Land Beyond the River, A (pr. 1957). Loften Mitchell, playwright. Set in Clarendon County, S.C., in 1949, the play dramatizes the true story of the Reverend Joseph A. DeLaine, who struggled to establish separate but equal school facilities and transportation for black children living in rural areas.

Ma Rainey's Black Bottom (pr. 1984). August Wilson, playwright. Produced on Broadway and set in 1927, this play treats the subservient position of BLUES singer Ma RAINEY and her musicians in the white-dominated entertainment world. They are subject to the whims of their exploitative and racist white managers, and they struggle financially and artistically. The play won the New York Drama Critics Circle Award.

Medal for Willie, A (pr. 1951). William Blackwell Branch, playwright. Set in a small southern town, the ironic play revolves around a memorial ceremony held in honor of a black American soldier killed in the KOREAN WAR while battling for freedom that he could not gain at home. His mother, sickened and insulted by the hypocrisy and bigotry of white people, refuses to accept the medal awarded to her son.

Moon on a Rainbow Shawl (pr. 1962). Errol John, playwright. Exploration of life in a Trinidadian family. It focuses on Charlie, the good-for-nothing husband; Sophia, the unyielding matriarch; and Esther, their daughter. James Earl Jones and Vinnette Carroll won Obie Awards for their performances in the play.

Mulatto (pr. 1935). Langston Hughes, playwright. The story of a young mulatto man who is the son of a wealthy plantation owner (Colonel Norwood) and his black mistress. After the young man returns from college in the North, he challenges his father and demands to be treated as a white son and to be a full heir to his father's estate. The father refuses and a fight ensues, resulting in Colonel Norwood's death and in the son shooting himself.

No Place to Be Somebody (pr. 1967). Charles Gordone, playwright. Subtitled *A Black-Black Comedy*, the play is set in Greenwich Village, New York, in an interracial bar, where racial tensions are running high. The bar's owner, Johnny Williams, who was once involved in fraudulent activities, is eagerly awaiting his friend's release from prison. The play reveals the frustrations inherent in black life and the violence that pervades the black community. The first play by an African American to win a Pulitzer Prize (1970), it also won the Drama Desk Award and an American Academy of Arts and Letters grant in 1971.

One Mo' Time (pr. 1979). Vernel Bagneris, playwright. Re-creation of a 1927 black VAUDEVILLE show in NEW ORLEANS, La., and presents a powerful depiction of life at the Theatre Owners Booking Association. The drama also examines the problems that often arose between white theater managers and black vaudeville troupers.

On Striver's Row (pr. 1939). Abram Hill, playwright. Set in Harlem's fashionable Striver's Row, the satiric comedy ridicules the snobbish conduct of the black bourgeoisie, always striving to move up the social ladder. The black family portrayed undergoes a crisis when the daughter, who is educated at Radcliffe, refuses to marry the "aristocratic" man who her mother thinks is best for her.

Photograph: Lovers in Motion, A (pr. 1977, as *A Photograph: A Still Life with Shadows; A Photograph: A Study*). Ntozake Shange, playwright. Set in San Francisco, Calif, explores a failed black photographer's sexual relationships with three artistic and professional women. He becomes a whole person after he learns to love himself and to be proud of his race.

Piano Lesson, The (pr. 1987). August Wilson, playwright. Set in 1936 in Pittsburgh, Pa., centers on a quarrel between two family members who cannot agree on what to do with the family's only notable heirloom, a bloodstained piano. The sister's desire to keep the piano represents her attachment to the past, while her brother's wish to sell the heirloom symbolizes his longing for a better future. The play received outstanding reviews and won the Pulitzer Prize.

Purlie Victorious (pr. 1961). Ossie Davis, playwright. Having failed to inherit five hundred dollars from a cousin to establish a church in a black community, Purlie, a black preacher, manages to pry the money from a white plantation owner who also is a staunch segregationist. The play, which opened in Broadway's Cort Theatre with Davis and his wife, Ruby Dee, in the leading roles, parodies black and white southern stereotypes. It was later filmed as *Gone Are the Days!* (1963) and was turned into the musical *Purlie* (1970).

Raisin in the Sun, A (pr. 1959). Lorraine Hansberry, playwright. Portrays a black family, with hopes for a better life, quarreling over life insurance money. The mother uses part of the money to buy a house in an all-white neighborhood, and her son spends the remainder on a business scheme, only to have one of his partners embezzle the money. The family reasserts its pride and unity after refusing to give in to segregation pressure. The New York Drama Critics Circle voted it best play of the year, and a musical adaptation in 1973, entitled *Raisin*, won a 1974 Tony Award as best musical of the year.

Rat's Mass, A (pr. 1966). Adrienne Kennedy, playwright. Surrealistic work portraying the difficulties of being black in a white world, the anguish caused by oppression and rejection, and the feelings of isolation and alienation experienced by African Americans. It is also a criticism of the apathy of organized religion.

Reckoning, The (pr. 1969). Douglas Turner Ward, playwright. Produced by the Negro Ensemble Company, the play centers on the dispute between the governor of a southern town and a black pimp. It won an Obie Award in 1970.

Rosalee Pritchett (pr. 1970). Carlton and Barbara Molette, playwrights. Set at an Atlanta bridge party in the midst of a race riot, the work is about an upperclass black woman who looks down upon black activists and who believes she is protected by her husband's professional influence. During the party, however, she is raped by a National Guard soldier.

Run, Little Chillun! (pr. 1933). Hall Johnson, playwright, with Lew Cooper. A pregnant black woman, attempting to force her lover, a pastor's son, to leave his wife and religion, is struck by lightning as she confronts him in a church. The religious folk drama centers on the conflict between the dual religious heritage in black culture, which includes African and Christian religious elements.

Seven Guitars (1995). Playwright August Wilson's sixth full-length play. Wilson once stated that he intended to write a play for every decade of the twentieth century, focusing in each on a critical aspect of the black experience in America. Typical of his dramaturgical approach, *Seven Guitars* uses music as a cultural metaphor. Set in Pittsburgh in 1948, the play portrays the final week in the life of guitar-

(continued)

playing scoundrel Floyd (Schoolboy) Barton as he is reunited with a group of fellow black musicians. Unlike Wilson's previous plays, *Seven Guitars* is a murder mystery. The play was nominated for the Pulitzer Prize in 1995.

Sign in Sidney Brustein's Window, The (pr. 1964). Lorraine Hansberry, playwright. Set in Greenwich Village, N.Y., the work is a study of a disillusioned intellectual and idealist who, having lost faith in his ability to create a better future, realizes that it takes commitment and responsible action to bring about constructive change. He upholds his integrity by confronting prejudice, immorality, and corruption in politics.

Slave, The (pr. 1964). Amiri Baraka, playwright. Revolutionary ritual drama set on a college campus during a black uprising, treating the issues of race, hatred, and anger. A black militant consumed by hatred and wanting to eliminate all that is white from his past, senselessly kills his white ex-wife's husband and lets her and his own children die in an explosion. The play won second prize for drama at the First World Festival of Dramatic Arts in Dakar, Senegal.

Soldier's Play, A (pr. 1981). Charles Fuller, playwright. Set during WORLD WAR II in Fort Neal, La., the play explores the murder in an all-black army company of a black noncommissioned officer by a black soldier, about the bigotry of the company's white commanding officer, and about the black military attorney investigating the crime. The play also examines the effect of hatred among African Americans themselves. It won the Pulitzer Prize in 1982.

Star of the Morning (pr. 1963). Loften Mitchell, playwright. Subtitled *Scenes in the Life of Bert Williams*, the historical play concerns the struggles and life experiences of entertainer and comedian Bert WILLIAMS, who starred in numerous black musicals with George WALKER.

Suicide, The (pr. 1967). Carol Freeman, playwright. This drama in one act is set in a ghetto apartment where a quiet vigil is being held to honor a death. A loud, disrespectful neighbor, however, refuses to turn down her radio, turning the wake into a noisy quarrel.

Taking of Miss Janie, The (pr. 1974). Ed Bullins, playwright. Set on a Southern California college campus, the drama centers on the rape of a California beach girl by her black friend. It won the New York Drama Critics Circle Award in 1975 as best American play of the year.

Tambourines to Glory (pr. 1963). Langston Hughes, playwright. A morality play set to GOSPEL MUSIC, the drama deals with the efforts of two women, Essie Belle Johnson and Laura Wright Reed, to establish a storefront church in Harlem. They are assisted in their efforts by a disguised devil.

Trouble in Mind (pr. 1955). Alice Childress, playwright. This drama of revolt portrays the emotions and epiphanies of a group of black actors who must play stereotypical black roles and demean themselves in order to please their white director. It won the Obie Award for the best original Off-Broadway play of the 1955-1956 season.

Two Trains Running (pr. 1990). August Wilson, playwright. Set in Pittsburgh, Pa., this comical drama takes place in a restaurant. The interaction of the black customers and employees reveals fragments of their lives that mirror the concerns of African Americans in society at large.

Wedding Band (pr. 1966). Alice Childress, playwright. Subtitled *A Love/Hate Story in Black and White*, the work portrays emotionally scarred characters who find themselves drawn into a dramatic interracial romance. It delicately examines their daily struggle and the effects their relationship has on them.

Ashley's *Booker T. Washington*, and *Mamba's Daughters* (1939) introduced the great Ethel WATERS.

In the 1940's, Richard WRIGHT's novel *Native Son* (1940) was adapted to the stage by Paul Green, with Orson Welles directing and Canada Lee playing the lead. Paul Robeson played the title role of *Othello* to great acclaim in 1943, Ethel Waters continued her career in

(continued on page 2486)

Notable Playwrights

Baraka, Amiri. *See main text entry.*

Bonner, Marita. *See main text entry.*

Bullins, Ed. *See main text entry.*

Davis, Ossie. *See main text entry.*

Dodson, Owen (Nov. 28, 1914, Brooklyn, N.Y.—June 21, 1983, New York, N.Y.). Educated at Bates College and Yale University, Dodson worked in many literary genres—opera, drama, short stories, verse plays, and novels. He taught drama at Spelman College and HOWARD UNIVERSITY. In 1949 he took the Howard Players on a successful European tour. Later he became head of the drama department at Howard. His works include *Boy at the Window* (1951), *The Confession Stone: Song Cycle* (1970), and *The Harlem Book of the Dead* (1978).

Elder, Lonne, III (Dec. 26, 1931, Americus, Ga.—June 11, 1996, Woodland Hills, Calif.). Elder's best-known play is *Ceremonies in Dark Old Men* (1965). His screenplays include *Sounder* (1972) and *Bustin' Loose* (1981). He wrote for the television series *N.Y.P.D.* (1967-1969) and *McCloud* (1970-1971) and worked on the made-for-television movies *A Woman Called Moses* (1978) and *Sounder, Part 2* (1976). His other plays include *Charades on East Fourth Street* (1967) and *Splendid Mummer* (1988).

Fuller, Charles (b. Mar. 5, 1939, Philadelphia, Pa.). Fuller is best known for *A Soldier's Play* (1981), which earned him the 1982 Pulitzer Prize for drama. He was the second African American to win this award. The film version of the play, *A Soldier's Story* (1984), received Academy Award nominations for best picture and best screenplay.

AP/Wide World Photos

Gordone, Charles (Oct. 12, 1925, Cleveland, Ohio–1995). A playwright, actor, director, and producer, Gordone is perhaps best known for his play *No Place to Be Somebody* (1969), which garnered the Drama Desk Award, the Drama Critics Circle Award, and most significantly, the 1970 Pulitzer Prize for drama, making him the first African American playwright to receive this prestigious award.

Hansberry, Lorraine. *See main text entry.*

Holland, Endesha Ida Mae. *See main text entry.*

Johnson, J. Rosamond. *See main text entry.*

Kennedy, Adrienne. *See main text entry.*

Mitchell, Loften. *See main text entry.*

Neal, Larry. *See main text entry.*

Richardson, Willis (Nov. 5, 1889, Wilmington, N.C.—Nov. 8, 1977, Washington, D.C.). In 1923 the premiere of Richardson's one-act play, *The Chip Woman's Fortune*, gave him the distinction of being the first African American playwright to have a serious nonmusical play produced on Broadway. With the exception of Randolph Edmonds, Richardson was the most published and produced African American dramatist before the 1960's.

Sanchez, Sonia. *See main text entry.*

Shange, Ntozake. *See main text entry.*

Ward, Theodore (Sept. 15, 1902, Thibodaux, La.—May 8, 1983, Chicago, Ill.). Ward was one of the earliest African Americans to have a play produced on Broadway, *Our Lan'* (1947). Ward's first acclaimed work, *Big White Fog* (pr. 1938), was produced by the Chicago unit of the Federal Theater Project. He received a Guggenheim Fellowship for creative writing (1947) and the AUDELCO Outstanding Pioneer Award for his contribution to the growth and development of black theater (1975).

Wilson, August. *See main text entry.*

Wolfe, George C. *See main text entry.*

Cabin in the Sky (1940), and *Carmen Jones* (1943) captivated New York audiences. Moreover, *Anna Lucasta* scored a big success on Broadway, *Deep Are the Roots* held a long run, and Robert Ardrey's *Jeb* received considerable attention. Experimentation took place Off-Broadway, giving a number of opportunities to black artists. The AMERICAN NEGRO THEATRE, founded in 1940, was part of this experimental movement.

Lorraine HANSBERRY's award-winning *A Raisin in the Sun* (1959), starring Sidney POITIER and directed by Lloyd Richards, brought black theater to international attention.

Black Theater Movements

In the 1960's, the African American theater movement arrived, accepting the integrity and dignity of the black experience and refusing to compromise with white sensibilities. In 1964 Amiri BARAKA and others founded the Black Arts Repertoire Theatre School (the BLACK ARTS THEATRE) in New York City and produced a number of black plays. Although it dissolved, it provided a model for black arts organizations across the country. In 1968 the Negro Ensemble Company was established, with Douglas Turner Ward as artistic director and thirteen permanent company members. It also instituted a training program for actors, directors, and playwrights. In 1967 the NEW LAFAYETTE THEATRE, headed by Robert Macbeth, was started in Harlem.

The 1960's and 1970's saw the advent of many new African American theater artists, including such writers and playwrights as James BALDWIN (*Blues for Mister Charlie*, 1964), Amiri Baraka (*The Toilet*, 1964; *Dutchman*, 1964), Lonne Elder III (*Ceremonies in Dark Old Men*, 1969), Charles Gordone (*No Place to Be Somebody*, 1969), and Ed BULLINS. Bullins won an Obie Award for *The Fabulous Miss Marie* and *In New England Winter*, produced together in 1971. In 1975 he won the New York Drama Critics Circle Award for best American play of the 1974-1975 season for *The Taking of Miss Janie*. Adrienne KENNEDY's *Funnyhouse of a Negro* (1964) won an Obie Award and a Stanley Drama Award. In 1967 her *The Lennon Play: In His Own Words* was produced; other plays include *A Rat's Mass* (1966) and *A Movie Star Has to Star in Black and White* (1976).

Ntozake SHANGE's 1976 poetic drama *for colored girls who have considered suicide/when the rainbow is enuf* was called a "choreopoem" by its author, and it interwove spoken words, dance, and music. Featuring seven female actors, the unique work won an Obie Award. Also in the 1970's Vinnette Carroll directed the Broadway hits *Don't Bother Me, I Can't Cope* (1972) and *Your Arms Too Short to Box with God* (1975), both written by Carroll. The plays were produced and performed by the URBAN ARTS CORPS, founded by Carroll in 1967.

Sidney Poitier (right) and Ruby Dee dance in the 1959 production of *A Raisin in the Sun*. (AP/Wide World Photos)

Playwright Adrienne Kennedy. *(Library of Congress)*

The 1980's saw the arrival of more African American theater talent. Charles Fuller's *A Soldier's Play* won the Pulitzer Prize for drama in 1982. One of the most important newcomers was August WILSON. His award-winning series of historical plays about African American life includes *Ma Rainey's Black Bottom* (1984), *Fences* (1985), *Joe Turner's Come and Gone* (1986), and *The Piano Lesson* (1987), each of which won the New York Drama Critics Circle Award for best play of the season in the year that it opened. *Fences* also won the Pulitzer Prize and four Tony Awards, including one for James Earl Jones, who played lead character Troy Maxson. (Jones had won his first Tony Award in 1969 for his portrayal of boxer Jack Jefferson in *The Great White Hope*.) Wilson's *Two Trains Running* (1991) and *Seven Guitars* (1996) continued the series. In the 1990's George C. Wolfe's *Spunk* and Richard Wesley's *The Talented Tenth* drew positive audience response.

—*Tony J. Stafford*

See also: Performing arts.

Suggested Readings:

Anadolu-Okur, Nilgun. *Contemporary African American Theater: Afrocentricity in the Works of Larry Neal, Amiri Baraka, and Charles Fuller.* New York: Garland, 1997.

Bean, Annemarie. *A Sourcebook on African-American Performance: Plays, People, Movements.* New York: Routledge, 1999.

Brown-Guillory, Elizabeth. *Their Place on the Stage: Black Women Playwrights in America.* New York: Greenwood Press, 1988.

Bloom, Harold, ed. *Black American Poets and Dramatists of the Harlem Renaissance.* New York: Chelsea House, 1995.

Bogumil, Mary L. *Understanding August Wilson.* Columbia: University of South Carolina Press, 1999.

Craig, E. Quita. *Black Drama of the Federal Theater Era: Beyond the Formal Horizons.* Amherst: University of Massachusetts Press, 1980.

Gavin, Christy. *African American Women Playwrights: A Research Guide.* New York: Garland, 1999.

Olaniyan, Tejumola. *Scars of Conquest/Masks of Resistance: The Invention of Cultural Identities in African, African-American, and Caribbean Drama.* New York: Oxford University Press, 1995.

Peterson, Bernard L. *The African American Theatre Directory, 1816-1960: A Comprehensive Guide to Early Black Theatre Organizations, Companies, Theatres, and Performing Groups.* Westport, Conn.: Greenwood Press, 1997.

Sanders, Leslie C. *The Development of Black Theatre in America: From Shadows to Selves.* Baton Rouge: Louisiana State University Press, 1988.

Thomas, Lundeana M. *Barbara Ann Teer and the National Black Theatre: Transformational Forces in Harlem.* New York: Garland, 1997.

Theatre Owners Booking Association: VAUDEVILLE circuit. The association was an

African American vaudeville circuit organized in Chattanooga, TENNESSEE, in 1920. The original theaters of the circuit were located primarily in the Midwest and South, in black sections of major cities. The circuit provided steady work for many famous entertainers, such as Pigmeat Markham, Ethel WATERS, and Bill "Bojangles" ROBINSON. Economic difficulties forced the circuit to disband during the GREAT DEPRESSION era.

Thirteenth Amendment: Constitutional amendment, ratified in 1865, that prohibited SLAVERY. It is one of the three Civil War Amendments, the others being the Fourteenth and Fifteenth Amendments.

During the CIVIL WAR (1861-1865), President Abraham Lincoln realized that the EMANCIPATION PROCLAMATION, which freed slaves in areas in rebellion against the Union, was regarded as a wartime measure that might be declared unconstitutional at the end of the war. (The proclamation had gone into effect on January 1, 1863.) Lincoln therefore sought passage of amendments to the U.S. Constitution that would limit or end slavery. He made proposals for such amendments even before the Emancipation Proclamation went into effect.

Congress did not act immediately on Lincoln's proposal, and it was not until 1864 that the U.S. Senate passed a proposed amendment that prohibited involuntary servitude except as punishment for crimes. In the House of Representatives, DEMOCRATIC PARTY members prevented passage of the amendment, which failed in June, 1864, by thirteen votes.

Collage celebrating emancipation drawn by noted *Harper's Weekly* cartoonist Thomas Nast. *(Associated Publishers, Inc.)*

During the 1864 elections, REPUBLICAN PARTY members adopted a platform that called for passage of an amendment banning slavery. Republican victories in the elections ensured that they had the votes to pass it after newly elected members of Congress took their seats in March, 1865.

Lincoln, however, wanted the amendment to pass with bipartisan support, and he urged the House to reconsider it. Using political pressure and promises of government offices to the lame-duck Democrats who would soon be leaving Congress, the Lincoln administration secured the votes necessary to pass the amendment in January, 1865. People cheered, cannons were fired, and the House adjourned for the day to mark the event. Some members of the AMERICAN ANTI-SLAVERY SOCIETY favored disbanding the organization, arguing that the amendment's passage meant that their work was done.

The Constitution requires that three-quarters of the states ratify a proposed amendment for it to go into effect. All the Union states except for New Jersey, Kentucky, and Delaware quickly ratified the proposed amendment. The southern states of Louisiana, Arkansas, and Tennessee, which were largely under Union control, also ratified the amendment. It still required the approval of three more states. After the Civil War had come to an end and Lincoln was assassinated in April, 1865, Lincoln's successor in the White House, Andrew Johnson, let it be known that he considered ratification of the Thirteenth Amendment a condition for recognizing the new southern state governments and readmitting them to the union. As a result, most southern states ratified the amendment, which became law in December, 1865. Despite considerable pressure from Johnson, Mississippi refused to ratify the amendment, an ominous sign for the future of race relations in that state.

The Thirteenth Amendment constituted a victory for African Americans because it en-sured that they could not be returned to bondage. However, in the years that followed its ratification, white southerners found ways to evade the spirit of the amendment. Many used threats, violence, and indebtedness to force African Americans to work the land for low or nonexistent wages. The amendment did not play a significant role in the CIVIL RIGHTS struggles that ensued in the years after the Civil War ended. A century later, however, in 1968, the U.S. SUPREME COURT cited the Thirteenth Amendment in its ruling on the case of JONES V. ALFRED H. MAYER CO. The Court maintained that the amendment gave Congress the authority to legislate against private RACIAL DISCRIMINATION, in this particular case relating to the sale of a house.

—*Thomas Clarkin*

See also: Fifteenth Amendment; Fourteenth Amendment.

Suggested Readings:

Maltz, Earl M. *Civil Rights, the Constitution, and Congress, 1863-1869.* Lawrence: University of Kansas, 1990.

Mayer, Harold Melvin. *A More Perfect Union: The Impact of the Civil War and Reconstruction on the Constitution.* Boston: Houghton Mifflin, 1973.

Thomas, Bettye Collier (b. 1943, Macon, Georgia): Historian, museum director, and educator. Thomas is best known for her scholarly endeavors in African American women's history. From 1977 to 1989, she developed and administered the Bethune Museum and its archives in Washington, D.C. In 1979 she coordinated the first national scholarly research conference on black women's history, held at the museum and funded by the National Endowment for the Humanities. In 1989 she became the first director of the Center for African American History and Culture at Temple University in Philadelphia. Her book *Freedom and*

Community: Nineteenth Century Black Pennsyl-vania was published in 1992.

Thomas, Clarence (b. June 23, 1948, Pin Point, Georgia): U.S. SUPREME COURT justice. Clarence Thomas's father abandoned his family when Thomas was two years old, and Thomas was sent to be reared by his maternal grandparents at the age of seven. Thomas was educated at an all-black Catholic grade school and later at a boarding-school seminary. He attended college at Immaculate Conception Abbey for one year before transferring to Holy Cross College. Thomas graduated with honors from Holy Cross and received his B.A. degree in 1971. He was admitted to Yale Law School and received his J.D. degree in 1974. Upon graduation, Thomas moved to MISSOURI, where he was admitted to the state bar. He served as assistant attorney general for Missouri under Attorney General John C. Danforth from 1974 to 1977. In 1977 he became an attorney for the Monsanto Company, serving until 1979.

Thomas's career in WASHINGTON, D.C., began when Danforth, who had since been elected as a senator from Missouri, selected him to serve as his legislative assistant from 1979 to 1981. Upon Danforth's recommendation, President Ronald Reagan appointed Thomas to serve as assistant secretary for civil rights in the U.S. Department of Education. In 1982 Thomas was appointed chairman of the U.S. EQUAL EMPLOYMENT OPPORTUNITY COMMISSION (EEOC). He served in this post until 1990. President George Bush appointed Thomas to the federal bench on March 6, 1990. Thomas became U.S. circuit judge for the District of Columbia Circuit of the U.S. Court of Appeals.

Thomas's next judicial appointment came in July of 1991, when President Bush announced that he had selected Thomas to replace retiring justice Thurgood MARSHALL on the U.S. Supreme Court. Senate Judiciary Committee hearings on Thomas's appointment began shortly thereafter, and Thomas's judicial record and positions on such issues as affirmative action, school prayer, and abortion were scrutinized.

The confirmation hearings became the focus of national attention when a FEDERAL BUREAU OF INVESTIGATION report was leaked to the press. The report contained allegations of sexual misconduct and harassment by Thomas, made by Anita Hill, an African American professor of law at the University of Oklahoma who had been an assistant to Thomas when he was the head of the EEOC. As a result of the ensuing controversy, the committee reconvened the hearings to investigate Hill's charges. The Senate panel was unable to determine Thomas's guilt or innocence and voted by a narrow margin to recommend to the full Senate confirmation of Thomas's nomination. Thomas was confirmed by a vote of 52 to 48 in the full Senate on October 15, 1991. The Thomas confirmation hearings provoked strong partisan responses from many quarters, and a number of book-length works in the early 1990's assessed the hearings.

Following his tumultuous and highly publicized confirmation hearings, observers described Thomas's personal life as intensely private. Public appearances were rare, even by the traditional low-profile standards of Supreme Court justices. During Supreme Court sessions he was quiet, seldom speaking or asking questions.

Despite his difficulties during his confirmation hearings, Thomas asserted himself judicially during his first term (1991-1992) on the Court, writing nine opinions for the majority, four concurring opinions, and eight dissents, seen as relatively numerous for a newcomer on the court. He voted with the majority or plurality 75 percent of the time. He quickly emerged as a strongly conservative justice who wrote forceful and outspoken opinions.

By the close of the 1994-1995 term, observers described Thomas's judicial record as consistently conservative and characterized him as a rule-oriented judge who believed that courts should not attempt to solve social problems that should, he believed, be handled by the legislative or executive branches. He was seen as a believer in a color-blind society and in literal interpretations of the Constitution, refraining from reading into it any protections or rights not specifically stated. For example, he dissented in the

Justice Clarence Thomas signing autographs after speaking at a meeting of the National Bar Association in July, 1998. *(AP/Wide World Photos)*

court's 5-4 decision (*U.S. Term Limits Inc. v. Thornton*, 1995) overturning the attempt by states to establish congressional term limits, arguing that the Constitution was silent on this question so there was nothing to deprive states of the power to establish eligibility requirements.

Regarding brutal prison conditions and prisoners' rights, Thomas argued in a dissent that the Eighth Amendment's prohibition of "cruel and unusual punishment" applied to sentencing, not to conditions in a prison. In a 1995 case (*Miller v. Johnson*) concerning racial districting for U.S. congressional districts in the state of GEORGIA, Thomas joined the court's five-member majority in stating that the use of race as a predominant factor in creating electoral districts was a misinterpretation of the Voting Rights Act of 1965.

Some observers of the Court long viewed Thomas as being somewhat in the shadow of Justice Antonin Scalia, the Court's other staunch conservative. In 1999, however, Thomas, more than before, began to elaborate on his own views and to vote differently from Scalia. Both remained strongly conservative

but sometimes expressed different rationales for their votes. In the 1999 case *Saenz v. Roe*, the Court held that states could not provide lesser welfare benefits for new residents in the state than for established residents. Thomas dissented, writing that the Court's majority opinion "raises the specter that the Privileges or Immunities Clause will become yet another convenient tool for inventing new rights."

In another 1999 case, *Cedar Rapids Community School District v. Garret F.*, he voted against requiring public schools to provide a wide range of medical care to students with disabilities; he wrote that the Court must "interpret Spending Clause legislation narrowly, in order to avoid saddling the states with obligations that they did not anticipate."

As the second black justice on the Supreme Court, replacing the liberal Thurgood Marshall, Thomas dismayed many African Americans and civil rights groups with positions and opinions that appeared to threaten civil rights gains. However, at the same time that critics accused him of forgetting his roots, supporters challenged this intolerance of Thomas's nonconformity, saying that he was consistent in applying his judicial philosophy that judges should not broaden the terms of the Constitution.

Thomas was invited to deliver a speech at the convention of the NATIONAL BAR ASSOCIATION, an association of mostly liberal African American attorneys, in 1998. Receiving both boos and applause, he spoke forcefully about his right to vote as his own belief and conscience dictated, saying "I reserve the right not to have my views assigned to me." About his continuing opposition to affirmative action programs, he said that any policy that accepts the idea "that blacks are inferior is a nonstarter with me."

—*Updated by Forest L. Grieves*

Suggested Readings:

Danforth, John C. *Resurrection: The Confirmation of Clarence Thomas.* New York: Viking Press, 1994.

Flax, Jane. *The American Dream in Black and White: The Clarence Thomas Hearings.* Ithaca, N.Y.: Cornell University Press, 1998.

Gerber, Scott D. *First Principles: The Jurisprudence of Clarence Thomas.* New York: New York University Press, 1999.

Hill, Anita, and Emma C. Jordan, eds. *Race, Gender, and Power in America: The Legacy of the Hill-Thomas Hearing.* New York: Oxford University Press, 1995.

Mayer, Jane, and Jill Abramson. *Strange Justice: The Selling of Clarence Thomas.* Boston: Houghton Mifflin, 1994.

Phelps, Timothy M., and Helen Winternitz. *Capitol Games: Clarence Thomas, Anita Hill, and the Story of a Supreme Court Nomination.* New York: Hyperion, 1992.

Ragan, Sandra L. *The Lynching of Language: Gender, Politics, and Power in the Hill-Thomas Hearings.* Urbana: University of Illinois Press, 1996.

Smith, Christopher E. *Critical Judicial Nominations and Political Change: The Impact of Clarence Thomas.* Westport, Conn.: Praeger, 1993.

Smitherman-Donaldson, Geneva, ed. *African American Women Speak Out on Anita Hill-Clarence Thomas.* Detroit: Wayne State University Press, 1995.

Thomas, Debi (b. March 25, 1967, Poughkeepsie, New York): Figure skater. Approximately sixty million American television viewers watched "The Battle of the Carmens" in the 1988 Winter Olympics in Calgary, Alberta, Canada. The combatants were Thomas and 1984 Olympic champion Katarina Witt of East Germany. Each skated to music from Georges Bizet's *Carmen*. At the end of the competition, Witt took the gold medal and Thomas finished behind Canada's Elizabeth Manley to earn a bronze.

Thomas's career prior to the 1988 Olympics was one of great achievement. That she was

Debi Thomas performing in the short program during the 1988 Winter Olympics in Calgary. *(AP/Wide World Photos)*

the first African American—in fact, the first person of African ancestry—to achieve such a level of success in figure skating is only part of her significance. She was one of the most accomplished figure skaters of her generation, something borne out by her many championships. Thomas won the U.S. national championships in 1986. That same year, she went on to win the gold medal at the World Championships, defeating Witt. The following year, plagued by problems with her Achilles tendons, Thomas won the silver medal at both the U.S. and World championships. In 1988 Thomas became the first dethroned national champion in fifty-four years to reclaim her title at the U.S. championships.

After her retirement from amateur competition in 1988, Thomas returned to Stanford University to complete her studies; she also made professional figure skating appearances. In 1992, after winning several professional championships, she announced that she planned to retire from skating and to realize her other ambition, going to medical school. In 1997 she graduated from Northwestern University's medical school.

Thomas, Franklin A. (b. May 27, 1934, Brooklyn, New York): Corporate executive and attorney. The youngest of six children born to parents who came from the WEST INDIES, Thomas grew up in the Bedford-Stuyvesant neighborhood of Brooklyn. An outstanding high school basketball player who was offered several sport scholarships, Thomas accepted an academic scholarship to attend Columbia University. He participated in the school's ROTC program and completed his bachelor's degree in 1956. Thomas went on to serve in the U.S. Air Force as a navigator with the Strategic Air Command, reaching the rank of captain before being discharged in 1960. He went on to earn his LL.B. from Columbia Law School in 1963.

After passing the bar examination, Thomas served as assistant U.S. attorney for the Southern District of New York from 1964 to 1965. Next, he worked for the NEW YORK CITY police department, serving as deputy police commissioner in charge of legal matters from 1965 until 1967. That year, Senator Robert F. Kennedy appointed Thomas to serve as president and chief executive officer of the Bedford-Stuyvesant Restoration Corporation, a newly created community development organization. The organization's work served as a model for other community redevelopment projects. After heading up the corporation's projects for ten years, Thomas returned to the private practice law in 1977. In 1979 he accepted a post as head of the prestigious Ford Foundation.

In his new position, Thomas used the foundation's assets to help needy communities, finance cultural institutions, and support education and civil rights endeavors. As president, Thomas slimmed down the foundation's staff from nearly 450 to 324, freeing up resources to be used to support charitable efforts. While serving as head of the Ford Foundation, Thomas was invited to serve as a trustee and director on the boards of several major American corporations, including AT&T. From 1985 to 1987, he served as a member of the Secretary of State's Advisory Commission on South Africa. Using foundation assets said to stand at $5.8 billion in the early 1990's, Thomas continued to support worthy causes and founded the Local Initiative Support Corporation within the foundation to support neighborhood revitalization efforts.

Thompson, Era Bell (August 10, 1906, Des Moines, Iowa—December 30, 1986, Chicago, Illinois): Journalist. Thompson is best known as editor of *Negro Digest* and Ebony magazines. She grew up in Iowa and in an ethnically diverse farming community in North Dakota. At

North Dakota State University, she wrote for the college paper and served as correspondent to the Chicago Defender, writing features on social issues as well as a lighthearted column under a cowboy pseudonym. After graduating from Iowa's Morningside College in 1933, she moved to Chicago to work and study journalism at Northwestern University.

Between 1933 and 1945, Thompson worked for the Works Progress Administration, the Chicago Relief Administration, and many other public organizations. To combat discontent at work, Thompson utilized her tongue-in-cheek humor to write the *Giggle Sheet*, a one-page newspaper that poked fun at fellow employees.

In 1945 Thompson received the Newbery Fellowship to write her autobiography. Published a year later, *American Daughter* is an optimistic story of growing up that has been recognized for its warmhearted treatment of family relationships and rural life, as well as for its racial tolerance. The book earned Thompson the Patron Saints Award from the Society of Midland Authors in 1968. Thompson explored her African heritage in a second book, *Africa: Land of My Fathers* (1954), and coedited *White on Black: The Views of Twenty-two White Americans on the Negro* (1963) with Herbert Nipson.

In 1947 Thompson joined the JOHNSON PUBLISHING COMPANY as an associate editor of *Negro Digest* (later called *Black World*); in 1951, she was named comanaging editor of *Ebony*. She served in that position until 1964, when she became international editor for *Ebony*, specializing in on-the-spot coverage of foreign places and personalities. She traveled extensively, interviewing leaders in thatched huts and palaces and examining racial relations worldwide. Until her retirement in the 1980's, Thompson wrote features on such topics as Ugandan martyrs, Indian gurus, and problems facing the children of black soldiers in Asia. Thompson's honors include a Bread Loaf Writer's Fellowship in 1949 and a National Press Club citation in 1961. Her portrait was hung in the North Dakota Hall of Fame in 1977.

Thornton, Big Mama (December 11, 1926, Montgomery, Alabama—July 25, 1984, Los Angeles, California): Singer. After winning an amateur talent contest at age fourteen, Willie Mae "Big Mama" Thornton traveled to ATLANTA, GEORGIA, where she worked as a dancer and comedienne in a number of VAUDEVILLE shows. After successful stints with various show bands, she left for HOUSTON, TEXAS, where she recorded for various labels and eventually began a long tenure with the Johnny Otis R&B Caravan shows. Her big break came when she met songwriters Mike Leiber and Jerry Stoller, who provided her with "Hound Dog," which she recorded in 1953 with the Johnny Otis Band as backup.

Three-strikes laws: State and federal legislation mandating life sentences for three-time convicted offenders. These so-called three-strikes laws fall into the broader category of mandatory sentencing laws.

In response to a perceived fear of crime on the part of the public, and following several high-profile incidents, such as the kidnapping and 1993 murder of twelve-year-old Polly Klaas in Northern CALIFORNIA, politicians rushed to offer a variety of "get tough" proposals intended to provide solutions to the crime problem. Given the fact that the U.S. prison population is disproportionately made up of African American men, many of whom have multiple convictions, the passage of these three-strikes laws inevitably created situations that penalize African American and other minority offenders and affect their families and communities more severely than other groups within American society.

Background

Crime became a national political issue at least as early as the 1964 presidential election, when REPUBLICAN PARTY presidential candidate Barry Goldwater challenged President Lyndon Johnson for being "soft on crime." Goldwater, like other conservative politicians, were seen as encouraging the tendency to identify racial protest movements with crime and using the phrase "law and order" as a code for maintaining the status quo. Since the mid-1960's, candidates for public office have typically turned away from addressing the causes of crime or social injustice and tried to outdo their opponents by offering to support punitive measures, such as mandatory sentences and the abolition of parole.

Mandatory sentences appealed to a variety of critics of the criminal justice system. Some complained that judicial discretion (allowing judges to set the amount of jail or prison time a convicted criminal must serve) resulted in "coddling criminals." Others found that sentencing disparities revealed racial bias. Mandatory penalties, especially for drug-related offenses, became part of federal crime legislation in 1984 and 1986, and the states followed suit. It was soon found that some mandatory sentence provisions, rather than erasing racial bias, served to institutionalize it. For example, the mandatory federal penalty for selling 5 grams of crack cocaine is the same as for selling one hundred times as much powdered cocaine. In drug cases involving crack, as opposed to powdered cocaine, more than 80 percent of defendants are black.

During the 1988 presidential campaign, Republican candidate George Bush ran a television advertisement that used the case of African American convict Willie Horton to condemn his Democratic opponent Michael Dukakis for supporting the MASSACHUSETTS policy that allowed convicted felons to participate in a furlough program. While on leave from prison, Horton had raped a white woman. For many, the case seemed a symbol of the misguided leniency of the criminal justice system.

The 1993 murder of Polly Klaas provided the impetus for California to pass a "three strikes and you're out" law in March, 1994. The previous November, the state of WASHINGTON had passed a law providing life imprisonment without parole for "persistent offenders" convicted of a third "serious felony." By mid-1995, a total of fourteen states and the federal government had three-strikes laws on the books. By 1997 twenty-four states had enacted some form of mandatory sentencing law.

Legislation

The federal three-strikes provision was part of the Violent Crime Control and Law Enforcement Act signed by President Bill Clinton in September, 1994. It required life imprisonment for a person convicted on two previous occasions of two serious violent felonies or one serious violent felony and a serious drug offense. The definition of "serious violent felony" was broad enough that it could include such crimes as burglary and prostitution. Convictions that occurred before the law went into effect on January 1, 1995, were included in the "strikes."

The Washington law defined persons as "persistent offenders" if they were convicted of three crimes within the "most serious felony" category. The category includes crimes that range from promoting prostitution to second-degree manslaughter to murder.

California required a mandatory life sentence for a third felony, with a minimum of twenty-five years or triple the normal sentence to be served. (For the second felony, the prison sentence was doubled.) According to the California law, serious felonies include offenses from burglary to murder, a felony using a firearm, and giving or selling drugs to a minor.

Compared with the federal, Washington, and California statutes, GEORGIA legislation

Nation of Islam minister Tony Muhammad (left) listens as private investigator Jan B. Tucker (center) denounces California's three-strikes law at a September, 1999, news conference. *(AP/Wide World Photos)*

seemed to go even further, allowing only two strikes and providing for life imprisonment after the second "serious violent felony." Unlike the others, however, the Georgia law included a shorter list of eligible crimes, all of them clearly violent, such as murder, armed robbery, kidnapping, and rape, or utterly reprehensible, such as child molestation.

The vagueness of mandatory sentencing statutes' definitions of serious crimes is illustrated in the California "pizza thief" case, in which Jerry Williams, a twenty-seven-year-old black man, was convicted of stealing a slice of pizza, normally a misdemeanor. Williams was charged with a felony for the theft, however, and because he had two prior felony convictions, the three-strikes provision went into effect. As a result, Williams automatically received a sentence of twenty-five years to life for the crime. The tendency to mandate punishments out of proportion to the crime is one serious potential result of three-strikes laws.

Consequences

Both scholars and criminal justice professionals expected that the three-strikes laws would have unintended—but not entirely unforeseen—effects on the criminal justice system. Prosecutors predicted that, given the extremely serious consequences of a third conviction, accused offenders would be much more likely to refuse a plea bargain and to insist on a trial. Jurisdictions would face both the high cost of more criminal trials and, because these cases must take precedence in the courts, the likelihood that nonfelony cases would become even more backlogged in the system.

The 1990's prison population in the United States stood at roughly 1.3 million, and that population was disproportionately made up of African American men. The incarceration rate of whites was 306 per 100,000, while for blacks the rate was 1,947 per 100,000—more than six times as high. Many observers predicted that under the three-strikes laws, the prison population could more than double within ten years and that the racial imbalance would persist.

Some critics assert that three-strikes laws have inherent, if perhaps unintentional, racial biases. One example relates to the harsh sentencing that accompanied the nation's zero-tolerance approach to drug trafficking. A large proportion of African Americans who have been convicted of felonies in federal courts have been charged as dealers or accomplices in the drug trade. Because cases against these small-time operators are easier to prosecute than cases against wealthier high-level traffickers (many of whom are white), more cases involving black defendants are prosecuted under the jurisdiction of federal mandatory sentencing laws that require five- and ten-year minimum sentences even for first offenders.

Evidence regarding whether increasingly severe penalties during the 1980's and 1990's had a significant impact on the crime rate is ambiguous and inconclusive. The cost of building and maintaining prisons, however, increased dramatically. At the federal level, spending for prisons was seven times as high in the mid-1990's as it had been in 1980; in California the increase was 373 percent. One consequence of the growth in corrections spending is the reduction in resources available for other public services, ranging from housing to education to drug prevention programs.

Debate

Like other mandatory sentencing plans, the three-strikes laws promise a simple solution to the complex problems of violent crime and the national prevalence of drug abuse. Critics argue that in doing so they shift attention and resources from the causes and conditions that foster violent behavior, as well as from other important components of the criminal justice system such as juvenile justice, diversion, or early intervention programs.

By the late 1990's, although hardly any politicians were willing to speak publicly against mandatory sentencing laws, debate was growing behind the scenes as to their effectiveness and their tendency to promote sentences out of proportion to the crime. A few states began to scale back mandatory sentencing, and many judges and crime experts were expressing their opposition to the laws. In 1978 Michigan had instituted a law nicknamed the "650 lifer law" that required a life-without-parole sentence for possession of 650 grams or more of heroin or cocaine with intent to distribute the drug. In 1998 the state's Republican governor signed a law allowing people sentenced under this law to be eligible for parole after fifteen years. Utah (in 1995) and Georgia (in 1996) also voted for changes to their mandatory sentencing laws.

—*Mary Welek Atwell*

See also: Crime and the criminal justice system.

Suggested Readings:

Benekos, Peter J., and Alida V. Merlo. "Three Strikes and You're Out: The Political Sentencing Game." *Federal Probation* 59 (March, 1995): 3.

Edwards, Margaret. "The Issues: Mandatory Sentencing." *The CQ Researcher* 5 (May 26, 1995): 467.

Griset, Pamala. *Determinate Sentencing: The Promise and the Reality of Retributive Justice.* Albany: State University of New York Press, 1991.

Mann, Coramae R. *Unequal Justice: A Question of Color.* Bloomington: Indiana University Press, 1993.

Shichhor, David, and Dake K. Sechrest, eds. *Three Strikes and You're Out: Vengeance as Public Policy.* Thousand Oaks, Calif.: Sage Publications, 1996.

Thurman, Howard (November 18, 1900, Daytona Beach, Florida—April 10, 1981, San Francisco, California): Theologian and educator. Thurman received his B.A. degree from Morehouse College and the M.Div. degree from Colgate Rochester Divinity School. As a Kent Fellow at Haverford College, he studied under mystic scholar Rufus Jones. He began his career as a pastor in Oberlin, Ohio, in 1925. From 1929 to 1932, he was director of religious life and professor of religion at Morehouse and SPELMAN colleges in ATLANTA, GEORGIA. He was dean of Rankin Chapel and professor of theology at HOWARD UNIVERSITY from 1932 to 1944. In 1944 he cofounded the Church for the Fellowship of All Peoples in San Francisco. He served as pastor until 1953. From 1953 to 1964, Thurman was a professor in the school of religion and dean of Marsh Chapel at Boston University. He was that university's first full-time black professor. He established the Howard Thurman Educational Trust in San Francisco following his retirement.

Throughout his career, Thurman devoted

Howard Thurman in 1952. *(AP/Wide World Photos)*

and one hundred outside North America. Among his numerous awards are membership in Phi Beta Kappa and fourteen honorary doctorates from Ivy League colleges and universities.

Thurman, Wallace Henry (August 16, 1902, Salt Lake City, Utah—December 22, 1934, New York, New York): Novelist, editor, and screenwriter. Thurman was a controversial figure associated with the HARLEM RENAISSANCE. He first gained attention with his literary quarterly *Fire!!* It showcased younger black writers but gained little support from more-established African Americans. His novel *The Blacker the Berry* (1929) concerns the psychologically distorting effects of colorism and race-consciousness. *Infants of the Spring* (1932), one of his more controversial works, satirizes several writers of the Harlem Renaissance as "infants" who produced little of value. It was republished in the Northeastern Library of Black Literature in 1992.

himself intensely to meditation, study, reflection, and experience of the religious life and to sharing his findings with others for enhancement of their religious experiences. His lifelong quest was for an inclusive community and "common ground" among people. He sought to fulfill this dream through pastoring, teaching, writing, lecturing, and other ventures. He attracted tremendous followings of students, professionals, and religious, social, and political leaders throughout the United States and in other parts of the world. Many graduate students, both black and white, in ethics, sociology, psychology, philosophy, theology, and literature have written dissertations and published books and articles on his life and teachings.

Thurman published more than twenty books and hundreds of journal articles. He held numerous guest and visiting lectureships at prestigious institutions, both in the United States and abroad. He addressed audiences at four hundred institutions in the United States

Till, Emmett (July 25, 1941, Chicago, Illinois—August 28, 1955, Tallahatchie, Mississippi). LYNCHING victim. Emmett Till's tragic fate had a direct impact on the development of antilynching legislation and federal involvement in CIVIL RIGHTS.

In August of 1955, fourteen-year-old Emmett "Bobo" Till traveled by train from CHICAGO to visit with his cousins in LeFlore County, MISSISSIPPI. On the evening of August 24, Till went with a group of teenagers to the small town of Money. On a dare, this self-confident adolescent from the North—an outsider unfamiliar with the mores of the JIM CROW South—entered the general store to buy bubble gum and to ask the twenty-one-year-old white storekeeper, Carolyn Bryant, for a date. (Bryant's husband, Roy, was away on business.) Rebuffed and leaving the store, Till was said to have "wolf-whistled" at her. Even as a minor, Till had transgressed a southern code of behavior that forbade any association between black men and white women.

His sense of honor violated, Roy Bryant and his half-brother, J. W. Milam, abducted Till from his great-uncle's home. Taken aback by the youth's behavior and shocked to discover that he carried a photograph of a white girl in his wallet, the men pistol-whipped him, shot him in the head, and dumped his body in the Tallahatchie River. Three days later, Till's badly beaten, decomposing corpse was pulled from the river with a cotton gin fan tied by barbed wire to the victim's neck. During the

Emmett Till. *(Library of Congress)*

subsequent trial, an all-white male jury acquitted Bryant and Milam of murder charges.

Receiving substantial national and international publicity, the Till lynching and the men's acquittals became significant issues in the CIVIL RIGHTS MOVEMENT of the 1960's.

—Kevin Eyster

See also: Dyer antilynching bill.

Tindley, Charles Albert (July 7, 1856, Berlin, Maryland—July 26, 1933, Philadelphia, Pennsylvania): Minister and GOSPEL MUSIC composer. Tindley was born to slave parents and taught himself to read and write. In 1873 he met and married Daisy Henry. Together they moved to PHILADELPHIA, where Tindley worked as a hod carrier at Bainbridge Street Methodist Episcopal Church to support himself while in school. He studied at the Brandywine Institute in preparation to enter the Methodist ministry and took correspondence courses with Boston Theological Seminary. Tindley became a sexton of the Bainbridge Street Church and passed his ministerial examinations in 1885.

After he was ordained a minister, Tindley spent seventeen years as an itinerant preacher, appointed to pastorates in NEW JERSEY, MARYLAND, and DELAWARE. In 1902 he returned to Philadelphia as the pastor of the Bainbridge Street Church. His popularity as a preacher helped increase the church's membership to more than ten thousand, and he made preaching tours throughout the United States. After his death, the Bainbridge Street congregation renamed the church Tindley Temple in his honor.

Tindley was well versed in the chorus and refrain tradition of black spirituals, and he began to compose gospel music songs based on this tradition as early as 1901. He wrote more than fifty compositions, including "I'll Overcome Someday" (1901), "We'll Understand It Better By and By" (1905), "Stand By Me"

(1905), and "Let Jesus Fix It for You" (1923). His songs were published in *Soul Echoes* (1905) and *Gospel Pearls* (1921), two compilations of gospel hymns that included Tindley's compositions along with older hymns and spirituals popular in both white and black churches. His own collection of gospel music was published in Philadelphia under the title *New Songs of Paradise* in 1916. In addition to being popular with black Methodist and Baptist congregations, Tindley's gospel hymns were adopted enthusiastically by fundamentalist black Pentecostal congregations of the early 1900's, which also were drawn to the songs' messages of comfort to the poor and oppressed who suffered hardships on earth but looked forward to the joys of the afterlife.

Tokenism: As applied to equal opportunity and desegregation efforts, tokenism refers to efforts to show accommodation to a demand or principle without actually accommodating. The term also implies compliance with programs or requests in a visible but shallow manner. The term first surfaced in the early and mid-1960's, when school desegregation was being implemented. "Token" numbers of African American students were enrolled in predominantly white schools that wished to be perceived as implementing integration without actually doing so. The few African American students enrolled were tokens, or symbols, of integration efforts.

Tokenism is a result, in part, of the language used in defining equal opportunity and antidiscrimination programs. For example, the language used in legislating certain practices or kinds of conduct is frequently open to interpretation. "Representation" is one ambiguous term that is used commonly. When a community has a specific ethnic makeup, each ethnic group is supposed to be represented adequately in areas such as law enforcement agencies and public-sector employment, as well as in the political arena. It is not clear what form representation must take. Employment representation, for example, can be achieved by hiring members of targeted ethnic groups only at the lowest employment grades or categories. They are thus left unrepresented at higher levels. Tokenism might take place at those higher levels. An agency or firm may employ a member of a targeted ethnic group in a highly visible, but actually unimportant, capacity with the intention of conveying an impression that it employs many minority-group members at high levels. A 1960's term for an African American in such a position was "token Negro."

Political representation may take the form of single minority-group members in various political groups, as token members, or may take the form of officeholding by ethnic-group members who do not in fact hold the opinions of the majority of the group whom they supposedly represent. On the surface, however, minority groups are represented, because their members hold office.

Tokenism also can be found in the history of school integration in the United States, especially in the Deep South. Under court orders to desegregate, southern school districts often employed their own strategies of token desegregation. They spread the process of desegregation over many years or administered tests of dubious value as a means of denying or limiting admission. In ways such as these, districts made token efforts to desegregate but in fact had little intention of doing so.

Tolliver, Melba (b. 1939, Rome, Georgia): Television broadcaster. Before moving to an NBC affiliate as a newscaster in 1977, Tolliver worked at an ABC affiliate from 1968 to 1976 as a reporter for *Eyewitness News*, anchor and associate producer for *Sunday Hours News*, cohost for the show *Like It Is*, and host of her own show, *Melba Tolliver's New York*. She won

Melba Tolliver in 1973. *(AP/Wide World Photos)*

the Outstanding Woman in Media award in 1975 and a National Endowment for the Humanities Fellowship in 1976.

Tolson, M. B. (February 6, 1898, Moberly, Missouri—August 29, 1966, Guthrie, Oklahoma): Poet. Known as a modernist, Melvin Beaunorus Tolson published *Rendezvous with America* in 1944. He was named poet laureate of LIBERIA in 1947 and was commissioned to write a poem for Liberia's centennial; he wrote *Libretto for the Republic of Liberia* (1953). In *Harlem Gallery: Book I, The Curator* (1965), Tolson explores the relationship of the artist with his community. In 1966 Tolson won the Arts and Letters Award in literature from the American Academy and Institute of Arts and Letters.

Toomer, Jean (December 26, 1894, Washington, D.C.—March 30, 1967, Doylestown, Pennsylvania): Writer. Nathan Eugene "Jean"

Toomer earned his reputation as one of the major artists of the HARLEM RENAISSANCE with his book *Cane* (1923), a remarkable collection of short stories, poems, sketches, and drama that captured the poetic spirit of African Americans.

He was the son of Nathan Toomer, a GEORGIA planter, and Nina Pinchback. Shortly after Toomer's birth, his father deserted the family, and Toomer was raised in the household of his maternal grandparents. His grandfather was the mulatto RECONSTRUCTION politician P. B. S. PINCHBACK, who had served as acting governor of Louisiana and was twice elected to, but denied a seat in, the U.S. Senate.

In WASHINGTON, D.C., Jean lived in both white and black neighborhoods, and he came to consider himself neither white nor black, but rather as American. In a letter to *The Liberator* magazine, he wrote, "I am naturally and inevitably an American. I have strived for a spiritual fusion analogous to the fact of racial

Jean Toomer. *(Beinecke Rare Book and Manuscript Library, Yale University)*

intermingling. Without denying a single element in me, with no desire to subdue one to the other, I have sought to let them function as complements." Resentful of his grandfather for allegedly driving his father away, Toomer turned to his uncle Bismarck for intellectual stimulation. His uncle encouraged his interest in science and in literature. Toomer enrolled in a variety of universities in several different majors, never staying long enough to earn a degree.

In 1921, as acting principal of an industrial and agricultural school in Sparta, Georgia, Toomer at least temporarily found the harmony he sought. In the rural South, he learned to love the land, to admire the farmworkers' dignity in the face of oppression, and to value the songs they sang. His emotional response to the experience was *Cane*. In it, Toomer experimented with language and revealed his dissatisfaction with post-WORLD WAR I society, typical attributes of American writing of the 1920's. In 1924 he became attracted to the philosophy of George Ivanovitch Gurdjieff, who sought to cure the division between body, mind, and soul that tormented modern man. Toomer's most famous work after *Cane*, the poem entitled "Blue Meridian" (1936), combines Gurdjieff's utopianism with Toomer's own long-standing conception of America as a new culture in which racial boundaries would be dissolved into a new spiritual synthesis.

In 1932 Toomer married Margery Latimer, a white member of a Gurdjieff group he had organized in Wisconsin. She died less than a year later, giving birth to their daughter. In 1934 he married Marjorie Content, another white woman, and moved to Doylestown, Pennsylvania. He was never again to achieve the literary success of *Cane*, despite attempts to have other works published. His prose and poetry were collected and edited by Darwin T. Turner as *The Wayward and the Seeking* (1980).

Toote, Gloria E. A. (b. November 8, 1931, New York, New York): Businesswoman and political appointee. Toote received her J.D. degree from HOWARD UNIVERSITY School of Law in 1954 and earned her LL.M. degree from Columbia University Graduate School of Law in 1956. She was an attorney in private practice in Englewood, NEW JERSEY, from 1954 to 1971. In 1965 she helped open the Town Sound Recording Studios in Englewood with the aid of a Small Business Administration loan. Toote became president of Toote Town Publications, Inc., and was a member of the editorial staff of the national affairs section for *Time* magazine. In 1973 she was appointed assistant secretary of the Department of HOUSING AND URBAN DEVELOPMENT (HUD), serving until 1975. After leaving HUD, she returned to private law practice and became an author and public lecturer.

Toussaint-L'Ouverture (François Dominique Toussaint; c. 1743, Breda, Saint-Domingue, now Haiti—April 7, 1803, Fort-de-Joux, France): Leader, patriot, and martyr of HAITI's independence movement. Toussaint-L'Ouverture fought for the abolition of SLAVERY in the European colonies of the Caribbean.

Toussaint-L'Ouverture was born a slave on the French-ruled part of the island of San Domingo in the Caribbean. His father, the son of a West African chieftain, had been captured during a tribal war and sold to European slave traders. Encouraged by his godfather, a freedman who had converted to Catholicism, Toussaint-L'Ouverture learned the French language. He also converted to the Catholic faith.

During his teenage years, Toussaint-L'Ouverture became a favorite of Bayou de Libertas, the PLANTATION manager. Libertas spared the young man the cruelty of field labor, assigning him less strenuous positions such as livestock handler, coachman, and eventually steward of all the livestock. Legally freed in 1777, paid a salary, and given a plot of

Contemporary engraving of Toussaint-L'Ouverture. *(Library of Congress)*

land, Toussaint-L'Ouverture soon gained the respect of both slaves and plantation owners. At age forty, he married a widow who bore him two sons.

When a slave revolt erupted on the island in 1791, Toussaint-L'Ouverture was initially reluctant to join the rebellion, choosing instead to assist whites and MULATTOES in their escape. He did, however, join the rebel leaders some weeks later. Then, frustrated with the inaction of the insurgents, Toussaint-L'Ouverture began organizing his own army and training it in the tactics of guerrilla warfare. France and Spain went to war in 1793, and Toussaint-L'Ouverture and his army joined with Spain, occupier of the eastern two-thirds of the island. The union was brief, however, as Toussaint-L'Ouverture soon opted to join with the French, whose revolutionary government had abolished slavery.

Then, in an unprecedented act of goodwill, Toussaint-L'Ouverture allowed many planters to return to the western side of the island, using military discipline to force the former slaves to work on the plantations. Part of his strategy was based on his belief that if a black republic in the Americas was to succeed economically, the people had to learn from the island's successful white and mulatto businessmen. A portion of plantation profits was distributed to the former slaves who worked the plantations.

After controlling all of the western side of the island by 1801, Toussaint-L'Ouverture liberated blacks in the island's Spanish-held territory. Napoleon Bonaparte, who by then controlled France, was outraged by his actions. Toussaint-L'Ouverture, as ruler of the entire island, declared a constitution that established him as a virtual dictator for life with near absolute power. Catholicism was declared the state religion. VOODOO was outlawed, and anyone caught practicing it was severely punished.

Bonaparte, despite acts of goodwill on the part of Toussaint-L'Ouverture, saw him as an obstacle to the restoration of French San Domingo as a profitable French colony. In January of 1802, a large French military force landed on the island and successfully occupied strategic coastal towns. Facing defeat, Toussaint-L'Ouverture and his followers agreed to surrender in exchange for promises that slavery would not be restored. Toussaint-L'Ouverture retired to his plantation at Ennery for a brief period before he was accused of plotting an uprising and imprisoned. He was later sent to Fort-de-Joux in the French Alps, where he died in prison. In death, Toussaint-L'Ouverture became a martyr in the ongoing struggle for the independence of Haiti.

—*Donald C. Simmons, Jr.*

Suggested Readings:

Griffiths, Ann. *Black Patriot and Martyr: Toussaint of Haiti.* New York: Julian Messner, 1970.

James, C. L. R. *The Black Jacobins: Toussaint L'Overture and the San Domingo Revolution.* New York: Vintage Books, 1963.

Korngold, Ralph. *Citizen Toussaint.* Reprint. New York: Hill and Wang, 1979.

Towns, Ed (b. July 21, 1934, Chadbourn, North Carolina): New York politician. Edolphus "Ed" Towns graduated from North Carolina Agricultural and Technical University in 1956, then spent two years in the Army. He later settled in NEW YORK CITY. He earned a master's degree in social work from Adelphi University in 1973. He subsequently worked as a teacher, a hospital administrator, and a professor at Medgar Evers College in Brooklyn.

Towns's political career grew out of his involvement in DEMOCRATIC PARTY politics in Brooklyn. In 1976 he was named deputy borough president of Brooklyn. In 1982 he won his party's nomination for Congress on his first attempt and then was elected to represent New York's Eleventh District, a multicultural district in which African Americans and Hispanics were the two largest groups. Subsequently, he was reelected by large margins.

In Congress, Towns developed a low-key but effective style marked by strong ties to the Democratic leadership. His voting record was characterized by liberal positions, party loyalty, and opposition to the Ronald Reagan and George Bush administrations, including a vote against the use of force against Iraq in 1991. Service on the House Energy and Commerce and Governmental Operations Committees as well as on the Select Committee on Narcotics Abuse and Control gave Towns the opportunity to deal with issues of vital importance to his urban constituents. Another issue on which Towns played a major role was his cosponsorship of legislation under which colleges were required to make available the graduation rates of scholarship athletes. He was also prominent on legislation that involved inner-city health care, having played a key role in keeping open federally funded community and migrant health centers.

In 1991 his quiet effectiveness was recognized by his election as chairman of the CONGRESSIONAL BLACK CAUCUS. In 1992, however, his congressional record was sullied by the House check-bouncing scandal. Towns, it was revealed, had written 408 checks on insufficient funds, and he was named by the House Ethics Committee as one of the abusers of the chamber's banking privileges. Towns continued to serve in Congress through the 1990's and was a member of the Commerce Committee and the Government Reform and Oversight Committee.

Congressman Ed Towns (right) with Vice President Al Gore at a meeting on urban revitalization in Brooklyn in June, 1996. *(AP/ Wide World Photos)*

Townsend, Willard Saxby (December 4, 1895, Cincinnati, Ohio—February 3, 1957, Chicago, Illinois): Labor union official. Townsend served as president of the United Transport Service Employees of America (UTSEA) from 1940 to 1957. Along with A. Philip RANDOLPH, he was elected a vice president of the American Federation of Labor-Congress of Industrial Organizations on December 5, 1955.

After graduation from Walnut Hills High School in OHIO in 1912, Townsend took a railroad job as a "red cap." He served in the military during WORLD WAR I, then returned to the railroads as a dining car waiter, based in CHICAGO. He wanted to escape the railroads' employment system, which closed the better jobs to black workers, so he entered the University of Toronto's premed course. After two years, he transferred to the Royal Academy of Science in Toronto, where he earned a degree in chemistry.

Townsend taught high school in TEXAS briefly but was unable to find work as a chemist. He reentered the railroad industry in 1932. Townsend was determined that black railroad workers, many of whom had college educations, would get the opportunities they deserved. In 1936 Townsend was elected vice president of an American Federation of Labor (ALF) red cap local union. He had organized red cap workers at five Chicago train stations, in opposition to AFL practices of barring blacks from unions or attempting to remove them from the railroad industry. In 1937 he was elected president of the International Brotherhood of Red Caps.

After the Fair Labor Standards Act of 1937 was passed, white workers sought to have the red caps declared as independent contractors, and thus as ineligible for union organization, because they worked mainly for tips. The red caps won status as employees under the railway labor act by appealing to the Interstate Commerce Commission. Railroad managements fought against granting bargaining rights, but Townsend's union continued to expand, bringing in train porters and Pullman laundry workers. The union was renamed the UTSEA in 1940, with Townsend still its president.

In 1942 Townsend led his union out of the AFL and into the CIO (Congress of Industrial Organizations). He joined the CIO executive board as its first black member. He was the only black leader of a national union that had white members. By 1944 his union's membership had reached about fifteen thousand. The union was successful in getting railroads to pay red caps a salary. Managements tried to count tips against salaries, finally settling on accepting a small "service charge" from each red cap for each bag handled.

Townsend continued to believe in the value of education. He earned an LL.B. and a J.D. through correspondence and night courses at the Blackstone College of Law in Chicago. He lectured on human and industrial relations at the Seabury Western Theological Seminary in Evanston, Illinois, and in 1942 he won the Race Relation Leadership Award from the Arthur Schomburg Collection of the New York Public Library. He was part of numerous labor conferences and was commissioned by the U.S. State Department as a labor adviser to the international labor office conference held in Mexico City, Mexico, in 1946.

The UTSEA declined after World War II as economic and technological changes affected the railroad industry and as other modes of transportation competed. When the AFL merged with the CIO in 1955, Townsend was elected as a vice president of the new organization. By 1972 the UTSEA had a membership of less than two thousand. It then merged with a railway clerks union.

Track and field: Contests in running, jumping, and throwing have a long and distinguished history. For centuries, these skills were part of a young African boy's passage into manhood, and slaves in early America engaged in physical contests during their brief recreational periods. In 1864 the first international competition in the one-mile run was held, and in the years following the Civil War, track and field events began to be staged on college campuses across the United States. The commencement of the modern Olympic Games in 1896 in Athens, Greece, propelled the sport to prominence.

Early Black Olympians

The first African American to win an Olympic medal was George Poage, a hurdler and quarter-miler who had established a college record at the University of Wisconsin in the 440-yard dash and low hurdles. Poage won the bronze medal in the 400-meter hurdles and came in fourth in the 400-meter run at the 1904 Olympics in St. Louis.

On the national scene, African American athletes began to dominate in certain track and field events. In 1912 Howard P. Drew won national titles in the 100-yard dash and the 220-yard dash. Sol Butler won the Amateur Athletic Union title in the broad jump in 1920, beginning the domination of African American men in the event.

Eddie Tolan won gold medals in the 1932 Olympics in the 100-meter dash and the 200-meter dash. Tolan went on to compete in more than three hundred meets, losing just seven times. One of Tolan's teammates on the 1932 American Olympic team was Ralph Metcalfe. Metcalfe finished second to Tolan in the 100-meter race and third in the 200 meters. Four years later, Metcalfe placed second in the 100 meters again, this time to the legendary Jesse Owens.

Jesse Owens

At the 1936 Olympics, Germany, under the leadership of Adolf Hitler, hoped to demonstrate the superiority of its people. The "Black

The first African American to win the decathlon in the Olympics, in 1960, Rafer Johnson was given the honor of lighting the Olympic torch at the 1984 Summer Games in Los Angeles. *(AP/Wide World Photos)*

Auxiliaries"—as the African American members of the U.S. Olympic team were called—performed with excellence, however, thus challenging Hitler's "master race" concept. Jesse Owens became the first athlete in modern Olympic history to win four gold medals at a single Olympics, setting three records and tying a fourth. Moreover, John Woodruff disproved the myth that African American runners could compete only in the sprints by winning the gold medal in the 800-meter run.

While the Olympics were interrupted by World War II, African American athletes con-

(continued on page 2510)

Notable Track and Field Athletes

Ashford, Evelyn (b. Apr. 15, 1957, Shreveport, La.). A member of five U.S. Olympic teams (1976-1992), Ashford dominated the women's 60-yard, 100-meter, and 200-meter dashes in the late 1970's, but the U.S. boycott kept her from competing in the 1980 Olympics. In 1984 she won Olympic gold medals in the 4×100-meter relay and the 100-meter run. She won a silver medal in the 1988 Olympics in the 100-meter run, and

AP/Wide World Photos

gold medals in the 4×100 relay in 1988 and 1992. In 1998 she was inducted into the Track and Field and Woman's Sports halls of fame.

Bailey, Donovan (b. Dec. 16, 1967, Jamaica). Like Ben JOHNSON, a Jamaican-born Canadian sprinter, Bailey set a world record (9.84) in the 100 meter dash in the 1996 Olympics and was a member of Canada's gold medal-winning 4×100 relay team. The following year he defeated Olympic 200-meter champion Michael JOHNSON in a special "world's fastest man" challenge race set at 150 meters.

Beamon, Bob (b. Aug. 29, 1946, New York, N.Y.). Beamon won the 1968 Olympic gold medal in the long jump, setting a world record of 29 feet 2½ inches, nearly 2 feet farther than the previous world record. His incredible record stood until 1991, when Mike Powell jumped 29 feet 4½ inches.

Boston, Ralph (b. May 9, 1939, Laurel, Miss.). Trained at Tennessee State College by coach Ed Temple, Boston won a gold medal at the 1960 Olympic Games with a jump of 26 feet 7¾ inches. He won the silver medal in the long jump in the 1964 Olympics and a bronze medal in 1968. Through the course of his career, Boston set seven world long jump records.

Brown, Earlene (b. 1934 or 1935). Shot put and discus thrower. The 250-pound Brown struggled against crippling poverty to compete with the world's best athletes. She was the first American woman to exceed 50 feet in the shot put and the first athlete to reach the finals in the shot put in three consecutive Olympics (1956, 1960, and 1964). In the 1960 Olympics she won the bronze medal in the shot put with a throw of 53 feet 10¼ inches.

Burrell, Leroy (b. Feb. 21, 1967, Philadelphia, Pa.). Often compared to his friend and fellow Santa Monica Track Club sprinter Carl Lewis, Burrell lowered the world record for the 100-meter dash to 9.90 seconds in 1990. After a disappointing individual performance in the 1992 Olympics, he helped the U.S. 4×100-meter relay team to a gold medal and world record time of 37.4 seconds. In a 1991 meet, he lowered the 100-meter record to 9.85 seconds.

Carlos, John (b. June 5, 1945, New York, N.Y.). Carlos's finest sprint performance was at the 1968 final Olympic trials, where he ran the 200 meters in 19.7 seconds. However, this mark was never ratified because he wore illegal spikes. When he won a bronze medal in the 200-meter dash in the 1968 Olympics finals, he and gold medalist Tommie Smith protested the treatment of African Americans on the victory stand by refusing to acknowledge the American flag and raising black-gloved fists in a black power salute. Their gesture led to their immediate expulsion from the Olympics. Carlos later competed in the professional International Track Association from 1973 to 1975.

Coachman, Alice. *See main text entry.*

Davenport, Willie D. (b. June 8, 1943, Troy, Ala.). Considered the world's premier high hurdler throughout the late 1960's, Davenport set an Olympic record of 13.3 seconds for the 110-meter hurdles on his way to a gold medal in the 1968 Olympics. He was also a pusher for the U.S. four-man bobsled team during the 1980 Winter Olympics, making him one of the few athletes to compete in both summer and winter Olympic Games. He was elected to the National Track and Field Hall of Fame in 1982 and the Olympic Hall of Fame in 1991.

Devers, Gail (b. Nov. 19, 1966, Seattle, Wash.). After battling Graves' disease, Devers reemerged on the track scene in 1991. That year, she broke the American record in the 100-meter hurdles, with a time of

(continued)

AP/Wide World Photos

12.48 seconds. She won gold medals in the 100-meter dash in both the 1992 and 1996 Olympics, and was the 1993 world champion in that event. At the 1999 World Championships she won the 100-meter hurdles title in 12.37 seconds, establishing a new American record.

Gourdin, Edward Orval (Aug. 10, 1897, Jacksonville, Fla.—July 21, 1966, Quincy, Mass.). The first man in history to jump more than 25 feet in a college international meet, Gourdin set a world record in the event at the Harvard/Yale vs. Oxford/Cambridge meet in 1921 with a jump of 25 feet 3 inches. He won a silver medal in the 1924 Olympics with a jump of 23 feet 10¼ inches. Gourdin later became a U.S. district attorney and a Massachusetts supreme court justice.

Greene, Maurice (b. July 23, 1974, Kansas City, Kans.). Greene started racing at the age of eight and broke Leroy Burrell's world record in the 100-meter dash in 1999 with a time of 9.79 seconds. He also won gold medals in the 100- and 200-meter races at the 1999 World Championships in Seville, Spain.

Griffith-Joyner, Florence. *See main text entry.*

Hayes, Bob (b. Dec. 20, 1942, Jacksonville, Fla.). Known as "the world's fastest human," Hayes was an Olympic sprinter and later a receiver for the Dallas Cowboys football team. He set world records for the 100-yard and 60-yard dashes. In the 1964 Olympics, he won gold medals in the 100-meter dash and the 400-meter relay race. During his professional football career (1965-1974), he led the National Football League in average yards per catch in 1965 and 1971.

Hubbard, William DeHart (Nov. 25, 1903, Cincinnati, Ohio—June 23, 1976, Cleveland, Ohio). The holder of national and collegiate titles in the long jump and triple jump while competing for the University of Michigan, Hubbard became the first African American in Olympic history to win a gold medal in an individual event, with a jump of 24 feet 5 inches at the 1924 Games in Paris. In 1925 he set a world record of 25 feet 10¼ inches. The following year he tied the world record in the 100-yard dash with a time of 9.6 seconds.

Jackson, Nell (July 1, 1929, Athens, Ga.—Apr. 1, 1988, Vestal, N.Y.). A member of the 1948 U.S. Olympic team, Jackson later went to the 1951 Pan-American Games, and won a silver medal in the 200-meter run and a gold medal in the 400-meter relay. In 1956 she became the first black female head coach of the U.S. women's Olympic track and field team. She went on to coach the 1969 and 1972 women's track and field teams. She was inducted into the Black Athletes Hall of Fame in 1977 and the National Track and Field Hall of Fame in 1989.

Johnson, Ben *See main text entry.*

Johnson, Michael. *See main text entry.*

Johnson, Rafer (b. Aug. 18, 1935, Hillsboro, Tex.). After winning 13 varsity letters in four different sports in high school, Johnson focused on track and field when he entered the University of California at Los Angeles, As a nineteen-year-old freshman, he won the decathlon in the 1955 Pan-American Games. He broke the world record in the event later in the year and won a silver medal in it at the 1956 Olympics in Melbourne, Australia, despite a serious stomach injury, which forced him to withdraw from the regular long jump competition. After dominating the decathlon over the next four years, Johnson won a gold medal in the event at the 1960 Olympics in Rome, with an Olympic record of 8,392 points. In the opening ceremonies of the 1984 Olympics in Los Angeles, Johnson had the honor of lighting the Olympic torch.

Jones, Marion (b. Oct. 12, 1975, Belize). The premier female American track and field competitor of the late 1990's, Jones was also a basketball star at the University of North Carolina. She won the 100-meter dash in the 1997 and 1999 World Championships and was named woman athlete of the year by *Track & Field News* in 1997 and 1998.

AP/Wide World Photos

Joyner-Kersee, Jackie. *See main text entry.*

Lewis, Carl (b. July 1, 1961, Birmingham, Ala.). A sprinter and long jumper, Lewis had a career of exceptional achievement and length that netted him an unparalleled eight World Championships and nine Olympic gold medals. In the 1984 Olympics, he matched Jesse OWENS's 1936 achievement by winning gold medals in the long jump, 100- and 200-meter dashes, and 400-meter relay, while setting Olympic records in the last two events. In 1988 he won gold medals in the 100 meters and long jump and a silver medal in the 200 meters; his 100-meter time was an Olympic record. Gold medals in the long jump at the 1992 and 1996 Olympics made him the first person to win that event four times. Although a world record in the long jump eluded him, he had more jumps of 28 feet or more than any athlete in history. He eventually exceeded Bob Beamon's long-standing record of 29 feet 2½ inches, but only after Michael Powell had raised the record to 29 feet 4½ inches.

Metcalfe, Ralph (May 30, 1910, Atlanta, Ga.—Oct. 10, 1978, Chicago, Ill.). During the 1930's Metcalfe broke or equaled every men's sprint record between 40 and 220 yards. In 1949 he was named athletic commissioner of Illinois. Metcalfe was seated on the Chicago City Council from 1954 to 1970, then was elected as representative of the Illinois First Democratic District.

Mims, Madeline Manning (b. 1948, Cleveland, Ohio). The first American woman to win the 800-meter running event in the Olympics, Mims won her gold medal in 1968 in an Olympic record time of 2:00.9. At the 1972 Olympics she won a silver medal in the 4×400-meter relay. She held the American record for 800 meters (1:57.9) from 1976 to 1983. She was named to the All-Time, All-Star Indoor Track and Field Team in 1983 and is a member of the U.S. Track and Field Hall of Fame, the National Track and Field Hall of Fame, and the Olympics Track and Field Hall of Fame.

Moses, Edwin (b. Aug. 31, 1955, Dayton, Ohio). Generally considered the best 400-meter hurdler in history, Moses set numerous records in the event. In 1983 he received the Sullivan Award as outstanding amateur athlete in the United States. He won gold medals in the 1976 and 1984 Olympics and won the

bronze medal in the 1988 Games. From 1977 to 1987, he was undefeated in 122 consecutive races.

O'Brien, Dan (b. July 18, 1966). The premier decathlon athlete in the world during the 1990's, O'Brien won the event at the world championship meets in 1991, 1993, and 1995. In 1992 he missed qualifying for the U.S. Olympic team when he failed to clear a height in the pole vault after waiting for the bar to rise above 17 feet before he made his first try. Nevertheless, he set a world record in the event later the same year and won the Olympic decathlon in 1996.

Owens, Jesse. *See main text entry.*

Powell, Michael (b. Nov. 10, 1963, Philadelphia, Pa.). At the 1991 World Championships, Powell set one of the most remarkable records in the history of sports by long jumping 29 feet 4½ inches to beat a world record Bob Beamon had set when Powell was less than four years old. At the 1992 Summer Olympics in Spain, he finished second to Carl Lewis. Undaunted, he went on to win twenty-three consecutive meets through August of 1993 and dominated the long jump in international competition leading up to the 1996 Olympics—at which Lewis again won the long jump.

Rudolph, Wilma. *See main text entry.*

Smith, Tommie C. *See main text entry.*

Stoakes, Louise (b. Malden, Mass.). Stoakes was the first African American woman to make a U.S. Olympic team but was never was allowed to compete. After qualifying for the 1932 Olympic 400-meter relay team, she and Tyde Pickett were replaced by two white runners whom they had beaten in time trials. U.S. coaches replaced Stoakes with a white athlete again for the 1936 Olympics.

Torrence, Gwendolyn L. (b. June 12, 1965, Atlanta, Ga.). At the 1988 Olympics, Torrence finished fifth in the 100-meter finals and sixth in the 200-meter event. At the 1992 summer Olympic Games in Barcelona, she won three medals, including a gold in the 200-meter dash, which she ran in 21.81 seconds. She earned a gold medal as a member of the women's 4×100-meter relay team and a silver medal on the 4×400-meter teams. At the 1996 Olympic Games, she
(continued)

won the bronze medal in the 100-meter dash and a gold as anchor of the 4×100 relay team.

Tyus, Wyomia (b. Aug. 29, 1945, Griffin, Ga.). Tyus was the first athlete—male or female—in Olympic history to win the same sprint event twice. At the 1964 Olympics she took the gold in the 100 meters in a world record time of 11.49 seconds; she also won a silver medal for the 4×100-meter relay. At the 1968 Olympics she won gold medals in the

AP/Wide World Photos

100 meters, again with a world-record time (11.08) and the 4×100-meter relay, which the team also won in world-record time (42.88). Tyus was inducted into the Women's Sports Hall of Fame in 1981 and the U.S. Olympic Hall of Fame in 1985.

White, Willye B. (b. Jan. 1, 1939, Money, Mich.). The winner of a silver medal at the 1956 Olympics in the long jump, White became the first female track and field athlete to represent the United States in five Olympics, from 1956 to 1972. A member of the Black Sports Hall of Fame and of the President's Commission on Olympic Sports, White was awarded the Pierre de Coubertin International Fair Play Trophy in 1965, the first individual to receive the award.

tinued to excel at domestic track meets. The Penn and Drake Relays, along with the Millrose Games, gave them the opportunities to display their talents. John Borican twice beat the legendary Glenn Cunningham in the

1,000-yard run, and Frank Dixon won the Millrose Mile.

The Olympic Games following World War II saw African American men begin to dominate in the dashes, short runs, hurdles, and long

One of the most stirring moments in the 1960 Olympics in Rome was Wilma Rudolph's victory in the 200-meter dash, which made her the first American woman to win both sprints in one Olympiad. *(AP/Wide World Photos)*

jump and as members of the 400- and 1,600-meter relay teams. In 1936 Tidye Ann Pickett, a hurdler, became the first African American woman to compete in the Olympics; Alice Coachman, however, was first to win a medal, a gold in the high jump in the 1948 games. African American athletes won seventeen of the thirty-nine gold, silver, and bronze medals amassed by the U.S. team in the 1956 Summer Games.

For decades, African American colleges and universities had produced a number of exceptional track and field athletes. Ed Temple, track coach at Tennessee State College, helped to develop the talents of a number of young men and women, including long jumper Ralph Boston, who won a gold medal at the 1960 Olympics and a silver medal at the 1964 games. A short time later, Boston set a world record with a jump of 27 feet 4¾ inches. Two other Temple protégés were Wilma RUDOLPH and Wyomia Tyus. In the 1960 games, Rudolph became the first American woman to win three gold medals in a single Olympics, winning in the 100- and 200-meter dashes and as the anchor of the 400-meter relay team.

The 1968 Olympics

The 1968 Olympics were held in Mexico City, and African Americans saw an opportunity to dramatize the Civil Rights movement on the international stage. A group was formed called the Olympic Committee for Human Rights that included such CIVIL RIGHTS leaders as Martin Luther KING, Jr., Louis Lomax, and Floyd McKISSICK, the director of the CONGRESS OF RACIAL EQUALITY (CORE). The committee's demands included calls for the removal of Avery Brundage—who was alleged to be antiblack and anti-Semitic—from the International Olympic Committee, for the banning of all-white teams from South Africa and Rhodesia from athletic competitions in the United States and the Olympics, for there to be

black U.S. Olympic coaches and black members on the U.S. Olympic Committee, and for desegregation of the New York Athletic Club.

The demands were not met that year, but a threatened boycott of the games by African American athletes never materialized. The 1968 Olympics were a great triumph for African American athletes, both for the number of medals they won and for the records they set.

Two African American sprinters, Tommie Smith and John Carlos, made certain that no one watching the games would forget the struggle for racial equality and justice. After being presented with their medals—the gold and the bronze in the 200-meter dash—the two men raised their black-gloved fists in a Black Power salute as "The Star-Spangled Banner" was played. The two were immediately banned from the Olympic Village and ordered out of Mexico; most of the other African American athletes protested the exclusion of Smith and Carlos by wearing black-colored clothing either while competing in their respective events or when receiving their medals.

In the 1970's, African American athletes continued to dominate the shorter races—including the hurdles—and the long jump. They emerged as contenders in the decathlon and began to win in the triple jump. Black men from the Caribbean island nations and from Africa had also established themselves as premier runners, with the latter excelling at the long distances, including the marathon.

Boycotts of the 1980's

The Olympics are the ultimate goal of most track and field athletes, but in 1980, international politics short-circuited the aspirations of athletes from the United States. Led by the United States, sixty-two countries boycotted the Moscow Games to protest the Soviet Union's invasion of Afghanistan.

Four years later, American athletes were able to compete in the Olympics in Los An-

(continued on page 2514)

Track and Field World Records Established by African Americans

Note: Asterisk indicates that world record was set in the Olympics

Women's 100 Meters

1960	Wilma Rudolph	11.3 seconds*
1961	Wilma Rudolph	11.2 seconds
1964	Wyomia Tyus	11.2 seconds*
1965	Wyomia Tyus	11.1 seconds
1967	Barbara Ferrell	11.1 seconds
1968	Wyomia Tyus	11.08 seconds*
1983	Evelyn Ashford	10.79 seconds
1984	Evelyn Ashford	10.76 seconds
1988	Florence Griffith-Joyner	10.49 seconds*

Women's 200 Meters

1960	Wilma Rudolph	22.9 seconds
1988	Florence Griffith-Joyner	21.34 seconds*

Women's 4 × 100 Meter Relay

1952	Mae Faggs	45.9 seconds*
	Barbara Jones	
	Catherine Hardy	
1960	Martha Hudson	44.4 seconds*
	Lucinda Williams	
	Barbara Jones	
	Wilma Rudolph	
1961	Willye White	44.3 seconds
	Wilma Rudolph	
	Ernestine Pollard	
	Vivian Brown	
1964	Willye White	43.9 seconds
	Wyomia Tyus	
	Marilyn White	
	Edith McGuire	
1968	Wyomia Tyus	42.88 seconds*
	Barbara Ferrell	
	Margaret Bailes	
	Mildrette Netter	
1968	Barbara Ferrell	43.4 seconds
	Mildrette Netter	
	Wyomia Tyus	
	Margaret Bailes	

Women's Heptathlon

1986	Jackie Joyner-Kersee	7,148 points
1986	Jackie Joyner-Kersee	7,161 points
1988	Jackie Joyner-Kersee	7,291 points*

Women's High Jump

1956	Mildred McDaniel	5 feet, 9¼ inches*

Women's Long Jump

1984	Jackie Joyner-Kersee	24 feet, 3½ inches*

Men's 100 Meters

1912	Howard Porter Drew	10.4 seconds
1929	Eddie Tolan	10.4 seconds
1932	Eddie Tolan	10.3 seconds*
1933	Ralph Metcalfe	10.3 seconds
1934	Eulace Peacock	10.2 seconds
1936	Jesse Owens	10.2 seconds
1948	Barney Ewell	10.2 seconds
1956	Ira Murchison	10.2 seconds
	Willie Williams	10.1 seconds
	Ira Murchison	10.1 seconds*
	Leamon King	10.1 seconds
1959	Ray Norton	10.1 seconds
1964	Bob Hayes	10.06 seconds*
1968	Jim Hines	9.95 seconds*
	Charles Greene	10.0 seconds
	Ronnie Ray Smith	9.9 seconds
	Charles Greene	9.9 seconds
	Oliver Ford	10.0 seconds
1972	Eddie Hart	9.9 seconds
	Rey Robinson	9.9 seconds
1974	Steve Williams	9.9 seconds
1976	Harvey Glance	9.9 seconds
1983	Calvin Smith	9.93 seconds
1991	Carl Lewis	9.86 seconds
1994	Leroy Burrell	9.85 seconds
1999	Maurice Greene	9.79 seconds

Men's 110 Meter High Hurdles

1948	Harrison Dillard	13.6 seconds
1960	Lee Calhoun	13.2 seconds
1967	Earl McCulloch	13.2 seconds
1969	Willie Davenport	13.2 seconds
1972	Rodney Milburn	13.24 seconds*
1979	Renaldo Nehemiah	13.16 seconds
	Renaldo Nehemiah	13.00 seconds
1981	Renaldo Nehemiah	12.93 seconds

Men's 200 Meters

1929	Eddie Tolan	21.1 seconds
1933	Ralph Metcalfe	21.1 seconds
1936	Jesse Owens	21.1 seconds
	Jesse Owens	20.7 seconds

1951	Andrew Stanfield	20.6 seconds		Charles Greene	
1960	Ray Norton	20.6 seconds		Melvin Pender	
	Stone Johnson	20.5 seconds		Ronnie Ray Smith	
	Ray Norton	20.5 seconds	1972	Eddie Hart	38.19 seconds*
1962	Paul Drayton	20.5 seconds		Gerald Tinker	
1963	Henry Carr	20.3 seconds		Robert Taylor	
1964	Henry Carr	20.2 seconds		Larry Black	
1966	Tommie Smith	20.0 seconds	1977	Steve Riddick	38.03 seconds
1968	Tommie Smith	19.83 seconds*		Steve Williams	
1979	James Mallard	19.8 seconds		Bill Collins	
1980	James Sanford	19.7 seconds		Cliff Wiley	
1996	Michael Johnson	19.32 seconds*	1977	Emmitt King	37.86 seconds
				Willie Gault	

Men's 400 Meters

1916	Ted Meredith	47.4 seconds		Calvin Smith	
1916	Binga Dismond	47.4 seconds		Carl Lewis	
1936	Archie Williams	46.1 seconds	1984	Sam Graddy	37.83 seconds*
1955	Lou Jones	45.4 seconds		Calvin Smith	
1956	Lou Jones	45.2 seconds		Ron Brown	
1960	Otis Davis	44.9 seconds*		Carl Lewis	
1967	Tommie Smith	44.5 seconds	1992	Mike Marsh	37.40 seconds*
1968	Lee Evans	43.86 seconds*		Leroy Burrell	
	Lawrence James	44.1 seconds		Dennis Mitchell	
	Lee Evans	43.86 seconds*		Carl Lewis	
1988	Butch Reynolds	43.29 seconds	1993	Jon Drummond	37.40 seconds
1999	Michael Johnson	43.18 seconds		Andre Cason	
				Dennis Mitchell	
				Leroy Burrell	

Men's 1500 Meters

1985	Sydney Maree	3:29.77

Men's 4 × 200 Meter Relay

1994	Mike Marsh	1:18.68 minutes
	Leroy Burrell	
	Floyd Heard	
	Carl Lewis	

Men's 400 Meter Hurdles

1976	Edwin Moses	47.64 seconds*
1977	Edwin Moses	47.45 seconds
1980	Edwin Moses	47.13 seconds
1983	Edwin Moses	47.02 seconds
1992	Kevin Young	46.78 seconds*

Men's 4 × 400 Meter Relay

1960	Otis Davis	3:02.2 minutes*
1964	Ulis Williams	3:00.7 minutes*
	Henry Carr	

Men's 4 × 100 Meter Relay

1936	Jesse Owens	39.8 seconds*	1966	Lee Evans	2:59.6 minutes
	Ralph Metcalfe			Tommie Smith	
1956	Ira Murchison	39.60 seconds*		Therin Lewis	
	Leamon King		1968	Lee Evans	2:56.16 minutes*
1961	Hayes Jones	39.1 seconds		Vincent Matthews	
	Paul Drayton			Ronald Freeman	
	Charles Frazier			Lawrence James	
1964	Bob Hayes	39.06 seconds*	1993	Andrew Valmon	2:54.29 minutes
	Paul Drayton			Quincy Watts	
	Richard Stebbins			Butch Reynolds	
1967	Earl McCulloch	38.6 seconds		Michael Johnson	
	O. J. Simpson		1998	J. Young	2:54.20
1968	Jim Hines	38.24 seconds*		A. Pettigrew	

(continued)

			Men's Long Jump		
	T. Washington		1921	Edward Gourdin	25 feet, 3 inches
	Michael Johnson		1925	William DeHart	
				Hubbard	25 feet, 10¾ inches
Men's Decathlon			1935	Jesse Owens	26 feet, 8½ inches
1955	Rafer Johnson	7,758 points	1960	Ralph Boston	26 feet, 11¼ inches
1958	Rafer Johnson	7,896 points	1961	Ralph Boston	27 feet, ½ inch
1960	Rafer Johnson	8,063 points		Ralph Boston	27 feet, 2 inches
1992	Dan O'Brien	8,891 points	1964	Ralph Boston	27 feet, 3¼ inches
				Ralph Boston	27 feet, 4¼ inches
Men's High Jump			1965	Ralph Boston	27 feet, 5 inches
1936	Cornelius Johnson	6 feet, 9¾ inches	1968	Bob Beamon	29 feet, 2½ inches*
	Dave Albritton	6 feet, 9¾ inches	1991	Mike Powell	29 feet, 4½ inches
1937	Melvin Walker	6 feet, 10¼ inches			
1953	Walter Davis	6 feet, 11½ inches	*Men's Triple Jump*		
1956	Charles Dumas	7 feet, ½ inch	1985	Willie Banks	58 feet, 11½ inches
1960	John Thomas	7 feet, 1½ inches			
	John Thomas	7 feet, 1¾ inches			
1964	John Thomas	7 feet, 1¾ inches*			

geles, but the Soviet Union and its allies pulled out of the competition in response to the 1980 boycott. Although African American athletes performed with distinction in the 1984 games, it was not until 1988 that America's premier athletes were again able to compete in the Olympics against athletes from the Eastern Bloc countries.

Leroy Burrell (left) lunges at the finish line to beat Carl Lewis in the 100-meter race at the 1990 Goodwill Games. *(AP/Wide World Photos)*

Memorable Feats

As in other sports, whenever African American men and women were able to participate in track and field events, they aimed at excellence. Their individual feats are legendary: Jesse Owens's four gold medals in the 1936 Olympics, Carl Lewis's matching four golds in the 1984 games, and Wilma Rudolph's three gold medals in the 1960 games are among the most memorable achievements in track and field history. Many other black athletes have set track and field records as well. Edwin Moses dominated the 400-meter hurdles for more than a decade and set the world record at 47.02 seconds. Florence GRIFFITH-JOYNER set world records in both the 100- and 200-meter dashes. Bob Beamon leaped two feet beyond the world long jump record in the 1968 Olympics, setting a new record of 29 feet 2½ inches, which was not surpassed until 1991, when Mike Powell jumped 29 feet 4½ inches. Willie Banks set the record in the triple jump at 58 feet 11½ inches, and Rafer Johnson's record of 8,392 points amassed in the decathlon at the 1960 Olympics stood for twenty-four years.

African American athletes who have been inducted into the National Track and Field Hall of Fame include Dave Albritton, Bob Beamon, Ralph Boston, Lee Calhoun, Milt Campbell, Alice Coachman (Davis), Willie Davenport, Harrison Dillard, Charles Dumas, Lee Evans, Barney Ewell, Mae Faggs (Starr), Bob Hayes, Jim Hines, DeHart Hubbard, Edward Hurt, Nell C. Jackson, Rafer Johnson, Hayes Jones, Ralph Metcalfe, Madeline Manning-Mims, Jesse Owens, Wilma Rudolph, Mel Sheppard, Tommie Smith, Andy Stanfield, John Thomas, Eddie Tolan, Wyomia Tyus, LeRoy Walker, Willye White, Mal Whitfield, and John Woodruff.

—*Philip G. Smith*

See also: Olympic gold medal winners.

Suggested Readings:
Archdeacon, H. C., and Kenneth G. Ellsworth, eds. *Track Cyclopedia*. 10th ed. Omaha, Neb.: Simmons-Boardman Books, 1985.
Ashe, Arthur. *A Hard Road to Glory: A History of the African American Athlete*. 3 vols. New York: Warner Books, 1988.
Henderson, Edwin B. *The Negro in Sports*. Washington, D.C.: Associated Press, 1939.
Johnson, Rafer, and Philip Goldberg. *The Best That I Can Be: An Autobiography*. New York: Doubleday, 1998.
Lewis, Carl, and Jeffrey Marx. *Inside Track: My Professional Life in Amateur Track and Field*. New York: Simon & Schuster, 1990.
Matthews, Peter. *Track and Field Athletes: The Records*. Enfield, England: Guinness Superlative, 1985.
Rust, Art, Jr., and Edna Rust. *Art Rust's Illustrated History of the Black Athlete*. Garden City, N.Y.: Doubleday, 1985.

TransAfrica: Pan-Africanist lobbying organization. In 1977 Randall ROBINSON, a Harvard Law School graduate and an assistant to Michigan congressman Charles DIGGS, founded TransAfrica, an organization devoted to securing human and civil rights for black people worldwide. TransAfrica was particularly successful in orchestrating American opposition to the apartheid regime of South Africa. By the 1990's the group claimed about eighteen thousand members.

Objectives and Functions

From its inception, TransAfrica had a simple but profound mandate: to advocate and pursue activities designed to influence U.S. policies toward the continent of AFRICA and the WEST INDIES. TransAfrica thus epitomizes the efforts to strengthen the ties that bind African Americans to blacks around the globe.

TransAfrica is headquartered in Washington, D.C. It is headed by an executive director who conducts the daily business of the organization and is assisted by a legislative director and several legislative assistants; the executive director reports to a board of directors elected by the general membership. While much of its work is done in Washington, TransAfrica has chapters across the United States that work in conjunction with the national office.

Disseminating Information

Perhaps the most important function of TransAfrica has been advising the U.S. government on matters and issues affecting Africa and the West Indies. The information generated by TransAfrica on those reigons has become relied on in Washington and beyond. The organization established a newsletter,

TransAfrica News. The newsletter and Trans-Africa's news releases were intended to provide information for the general public and official Washington on political, social, and economic conditions of the African world. The organization is able to obtain timely information on such matters in large part because of the strong and cordial ties that TransAfrica has fostered with the peoples and leaders of Africa and the Caribbean.

TransAfrica's reputation as a source of accurate, reliable information has done much to improve ways in which Africa has been portrayed. In 1981 TransAfrica created Trans-Africa Forum, its educational and research-oriented arm. The forum, with its own board of directors, sponsors symposia on topics pertaining to Africa and the Caribbean and publishes *TransAfrica Forum: A Quarterly Journal of Opinion on Africa and the Caribbean.*

TransAfrica also incorporates a letter-writing system in its lobbying. The system allows TransAfrica to trigger a letter-writing campaign to produce quick mass mailings in selected congressional districts. Such shows of strength can be crucial when specific members of Congress are targeted on a particular issue or legislation.

TransAfrica is funded from sources that include membership dues; contributions from corporations, foundations, and individuals; and subscriptions to the journal. The organization sponsors a yearly dinner at which the Nelson Mandela Courage Award is bestowed.

Success and Challenges

As the premier African American lobbying group for Africa and the Caribbean, Trans-Africa has has a number of successes. It has continually lobbied for increases in U.S. assistance to the African world, and it was instrumental in getting Congress to pass the Clark Amendment, which barred the Central Intelligence Agency (CIA) from assisting any insurgency movement in Angola during that country's struggle for independence. TransAfrica was also active in prodding the U.S. government to work for black liberation in Zimbabwe. TransAfrica has played a middleman role in many instances when leaders from Africa and the Caribbean have needed to be introduced to the American public.

Role in Abolishing Apartheid

One of TransAfrica's biggest successes was the role it played in the transition to a post-apartheid South Africa. TransAfrica succeeded in mobilizing grassroots American anti-apartheid efforts. In 1984, with the help of other anti-apartheid groups, TransAfrica established and coordinated the activities of the Free South Africa Movement (FSAM). The work of the FSAM eventually led to congressional action in 1986 that placed U.S. economic sanctions on South Africa. The legislation, passed over the veto of President Ronald Reagan, played a major role in pushing the South African government into undertaking such far-reaching measures as releasing Nelson Mandela and other anti-apartheid leaders from jail, repealing bans on major anti-apartheid organizations, repealing the legal pillars of apartheid, and ultimately creating a new, democratic South Africa with a new constitution.

Randall Robinson remained director of TransAfrica through the 1980's and 1990's. In 1993 the group moved into a new Washington headquarters, and by the mid-1990's it had an annual budget of over $1 million. In the mid-1990's, TransAfrica lobbied the government to change its policies toward the government of Nigeria; it also urged the U.S. government to assist in returning Jean-Bertrand Aristide to power in HAITI and to grant refugee status to fleeing Haitians.

Funding in the 1990's came partly from large corporations such as Reebok, Coca-Cola, and Philip Morris, and the involvement of celebrities such as Danny GLOVER and Harry BELAFONTE helped raised public awareness of the group's concerns. In 1999 TransAfrica Forum began a capital-raising campaign to which Glover contributed $1 million and author Walter MOSLEY contributed $100,000.

—*Akwasi Osei*

See also: Africa and African American activism; Diaspora, African; South African boycott.

Suggested Readings:

Chapelle, Tony. "Randall Robinson and TransAfrica: Standing on the Frontline." *The Black Collegian* (September/October, 1990): 96-98.

Hadjor, Kofi B. *Africa in an Era of Crisis*. Trenton, N.J.: Africa World Press, 1990.

Robinson, Randall. "TransAfrica Explores New Challenges." Interview with Frank McCoy. *Black Enterprise* (August, 1992): 52-58.

Miller, Jake C. *The Black Presence in American Foreign Affairs*. Washington, D.C.: University Press of America, 1979.

Robinson, Randall. *Defending the Spirit: A Black Life in America*. New York: E. P. Dutton, 1998.

Shepherd, George W., Jr., ed. *Racial Influences on American Foreign Policy*. New York: Basic Books, 1971.

Transracial adoption: With growing numbers of children needing homes in which to live, and adoption being considered more socially acceptable, many childless couples and professional people who want to start families, with or without partners, are choosing to adopt. In some cases, families that have previously chosen to adopt children are choosing to adopt again.

In 1994 there were 500,000 children in the foster care system. Of this number, roughly 100,000 children were eligible for adoption nationwide. Within this adoptable population, 40 percent were African American children. At the same time, the majority of couples waiting to adopt a child were white. Without a great surplus of African American homes for these children to go to, many of these children remained in the foster care system. In California, African American children in the foster care system were only one-third as likely to be adopted as white children.

While the median length of waiting time for a child to be adopted was two years and eight months, in 1994, the waiting time for an African American child was often twice as long. Those who are not adopted are lucky to find a good placement early in their foster care lives. For some, this at least provides some stability. Those who are not so lucky often circulate through the system, living in several different homes or facilities throughout their early years of life. Rather than subject a child to the instability of continuous moving, some foster care and adoption professionals would prefer to arrange transracial adoptions. Some modern taboos concerning "race-mixing" have kept thousands of African American children out of caring homes. There are a variety of arguments in favor of and against transracial adoptions.

Opponents of Transracial Adoptions

In 1972 the National Association of Black Social Workers (NABSW) took a public stance against transracial adoptions. They went so far as to call it "cultural genocide." According to the NABSW, transracial adoptions have several detrimental affects on African American children. First, they argued that transracial adoptions prevented African American children from developing positive black identities. They concluded that African American children reared in white homes suffered identity confusion and might wish they were white. An example given to illustrate this point was a 1947 study conducted by Kenneth and Mamie Clark which indicated that African American children who were given black and white dolls chose white dolls when asked which doll was nice; they also chose the white doll when asked which doll they most resembled. Presumably, a child's early exposure to cultural differences may have some confusing effect.

Second, it was stated that white parents could not provide African American children with survival techniques to cope with racial inequities unless they are specifically trained to do so. Since many adoption agencies do not offer special training classes in racial sensitivity, many transracial adoption parents learned through trial and error. In the eyes of the NABSW, this is detrimental to the child.

Third, the NABSW said that African American children that grew up in white homes grew up unable to relate to other African Americans and must deal with the pain of not being fully accepted by the white community. According to the NABSW this places many transracial adoptees in a position to be rejected by both sides. Finally, the NABSW argued that the African American community needed its own children to build a strong nation. Transracial adoptions were said to weaken African American family structures and communities.

In 1983 the NABSW presented information to Congress to gain support for the federal prohibition of all black-white adoptions. Instead of transracial adoptions, they supported the preservation of existing African American homes and reunifying broken homes. They believe that families that were broken could be given the resources and skills to come back together. In addition, more recruitment should be directed toward African American families.

Proponents of Transracial Adoptions
Persons who support transracial adoptions say that the goal of adoption agencies should be to place children in loving, supportive homes as quickly as possible, regardless of race. Senator Howard Metzenbaum of Ohio initiated a bill in 1993 called the Multiethnic Placement Act. This bill was designed to deny federal financing to any agency that used race as the only factor in adoptive placements. Under the bill's provisions, a white family could not be denied access to the adoption of an African American child based on racial differences alone. Senator Metzenbaum especially opposed the removal of an African American foster child from a white home when the agency became aware of the white family's desire to adopt. While not opposed to same-race adoptions, Senator Metzenbaum made it clear that transracial adoptions should not be totally denied. Unfortunately, the bill, which initially took a strong stance against delaying the adoption process because of race, was later changed to race not causing "undue delay." In addition, the clause about transracial adoption being preferred to foster care was changed to "may be a preferable alternative."

Other arguments in favor of transracial adoptions are basically rebuttals to the NABSW rationale as to why transracial adoptions should not exist. First, several studies have indicated that transracial adoptees became emotionally stable and well-adjusted adults who were comfortable with their racial identity. Although in some cases there were tendencies to deemphasize one's racial identity, most transracial adoptees were secure with their racial identity. Second, when it came to preparing African American children to cope with racial hostility or inequalities, parenting skills became more of an issue than race. An adoptive parent's willingness to confront a child's frustrations and hurt feelings, without ignoring such realities, was the most important factor.

Critics say there is no guarantee that parents of the same race would even address racially sensitive issues. Some same-race parents may be so inured to racial injustices that they ignore their child's negative racial experiences altogether. Third, when it came to African American children being able to relate to their own race, those white families that exposed their adoptive children to racially diverse schools and neighborhoods fared well.

In the 1995 film *Losing Isaiah* Halle Berry (left) played a young black woman struggling to regain custody of her son (Marc John Jeffries), whom she had given up to a white couple. *(Museum of Modern Art, Film Stills Archive)*

In addition to being reared in racially diverse settings, regular family interactions with members of all races helped the adopted child relate better to all races, not just his or her own. Finally, proponents of transracial adoption stated that love and a secure home were more important than the politics of skin color. Most supporters of transracial adoptions agreed that same-race adoptions would be preferred next to family reunification, but when that was not an option, transracial homes were seen as better than no home at all. Supporters of transracial adoption say innocent children should not have to pay for adult intolerance regarding race.

Laws Regarding Transracial Adoption

In 1968 transracial adoptions became legally sanctioned, during the peak of the Civil Rights movement. Although there were no federal records kept of either transracial or same-race adoptions after 1975, varied reports conveyed that transracial adoptions were at an all-time high during the early 1970's but declined significantly thereafter.

A 1995 film entitled *Losing Isaiah* addressed the legal side of transracial adoptions. The film's plot centered on what was in the best interest of an African American child when it came to living with a biological parent who could not properly care for the child or living with a white parent who was emotionally and financially able to care for the child. In the film, the courts ruled in favor of the biological mother, even though the child had obviously bonded with the white mother who had adopted him. The issue that determined the final verdict was the belief that the child, Isaiah, needed to be around people of his same racial background in order to gain a healthy racial identity and learn of his ethnic heritage. The white adoptive mother was viewed as being unable to provide this for Isaiah. After being placed into the custody of his biological mother, Isaiah had adjustment problems that reaffirmed his need for love and care without regard for race. This argument of what is in the best interest of the child is being acted out every day through court decisions.

Since 1991, states such as California, Arizona, and Minnesota passed laws in preference of same-race adoptions. In CALIFORNIA, for example, social workers are required to seek out adoptive parents of the same race, before allowing prospective parents of a different race to adopt the child. In a 1984 court case in Florida, known as *Palmore v. Sidoti*, a state court judge awarded custody of a white child to her white father, after the child's mother married an African American man. The U.S. SUPREME COURT later reversed this decision. From these legal battles it is apparent that socially sanctioned segregation remains in place when it comes to who should care for whose children.

There are several legal hurdles one must consider when adopting across racial lines. First, race plays a part in the overall consideration of what is in the best interest of the child's welfare. Although one might think the court systems are color blind, white parents, no matter how loving, may be denied adoption if a judge thinks it is to the child's advantage to remain in a same-race household. A second issue is that a local authority policy, such as a same-race policy, is not the final word of the law. Local authority policies are lawful only if they do not override other equally important factors, such as religion or cultural background. Another important factor is that the biological parents are entitled to be informed about their child until the adoption process is completed. Once the child is adopted, the biological parents may still be able to have a contact order made in their favor. This may even be the case when it is obvious that the child's best interest is served with the adoptive parents. Finally, foster parents who have reared a child for three or five years may apply for adoption without the consent of the local authority or biological parent. In any case, the welfare of the child is the most important factor in deciding where the child will live.

Adoption Options

When children are removed from their biological families, and there is no hope of reunifying these children with their parents, a decision must be made as to what is the next "least detrimental" option. Some would argue that foster care appointments involving members of the same race would be the next best option; others favor transracial adoption, if a same-race adoption was not first available; still others would say that race should not be an issue. When looking at the adoption option interracially, there are several steps agencies can take to encourage a more natural transracial transition for both the child and the adoptive parents. These steps include providing literature on racial awareness, providing training sessions on how to deal with racial and cultural differences, providing support systems and networks for white parents rearing African American children, and encouraging white parents to live in racially integrated communities as well as regularly engaging in activities with diverse racial groups. In addition to these practices, an agency might require white parents to go through an evaluation interview session with an African American counselor, to help determine the potential parents' sensitivity toward racial concerns. Some of these practices have been put into effect at various agencies, but many people believe that these practices should become the rule rather than the exception.

Organizations such as the Institute for Black Parenting, based in Los Angeles, and Harambee: Service to Black Children, located in Cleveland, promote black adoptions within

African American communities. Other organizations, such as One Church, One Child, encourage African American churches to adopt African American children. Some adoption agencies targeting African American families have even eased their eligibility criteria to make it easier for more African American children to be adopted. Such things as lower income requirements and fewer restrictions for single people to adopt have made it easier for African American families to adopt children of their own race.

Transracial Outlook

In determining the future of transracial adoptions, the value of love and a commitment to caring will have to be weighed along with racial differences and cultural preferences. In deciding whether an African American child who grows up listening to rap music is any better or worse off than one who does not, the community will limit the possibilities and outcomes of what each individual takes from a situation or experience. While one adopted African American child who grows up in the inner city with African American parents may blame his or her failures on the lack of opportunities that were presented to him or her, another African American child growing up with white adoptive parents in a racially mixed neighborhood may view his or her success as being directly linked to the opportunities that were provided through the adoptive parents. Each child is different, and each case must be considered on an individual basis.

—*Kimberly Battle-Walters*
See also: Biracial and mixed-raced children.

Suggested Readings:

"All in the Family: Remove the Barriers to Transracial Adoption." *The New Republic* (January 24, 1994): 6-7.

Courtney, Mark E. "The Politics and Realities of Transracial Adoption." *Child Welfare* 76 (November/December, 1997): 749-779.

Craven-Griffiths, Jennifer. "The Law and Transracial Families." In *In the Best Interests of the Child: Culture, Identity and Transracial Adoption*, edited by Ivor Gaber and Jane Aldridge. London: Free Association Books, 1994.

Davis, Molly. "Transracial Adoption." *The Crisis* (November/December, 1992): 20-21.

Kaeser, Gigi, and Peggy Gillespie. *Of Many Colors: Portraits of Multiracial Families*. Amherst: University of Massachusetts Press, 1997.

Kallgren, Carl A., and Pamela J. Caudill. "Current Transracial Adoption Practices: Racial Dissonance or Racial Awareness?" *Psychological Reports* 72 (1993): 551-558.

Kennedy, Randall. "Orphans of Separatism: The Politics of Transracial Adoption." *Current* (October, 1994): 8-13.

Simon, Rita J., Howard Altstein, and Marygold Melli. *The Case for Transracial Adoption*. Washington, D.C.: American University Press, 1994.

Solnit, Albert, Barbara Nordhaus, and Ruth Lord. *When Home Is No Haven: Child Placement Issues*. New Haven, Conn.: Yale University Press, 1992.

Tizard, Barbara, and Ann Phoenix. "Black Identity and Transracial Adoption." In *In the Best Interests of the Child: Culture, Identity and Transracial Adoption*, edited by Ivor Gaber and Jane Aldridge. London: Free Association Books, 1994.

Travis, Dempsey Jerome (b. February 25, 1920, Chicago, Illinois): Business executive. Travis owned numerous companies involved in the real estate, securities, and mortgage industries. As a piano player, he led his own orchestra at the age of fifteen, and he joined the musicians union at the age of sixteen. He graduated from Chicago's Du Sable High School in 1939 and entered the U.S. Army, learning business skills while managing Post Exchanges. After his discharge, he tried to gain admission to Roosevelt University, but he failed the entrance examination. He realized how deficient his high school education had been, even though his grades were high. Travis attempted to get his high school music combo back together, but its members had scattered and the dime-a-dance establishments where he had played had gone out of style.

Travis decided to pursue his education, taking classes in accounting and social science at night at Englewood High School while working for the Veterans Administration. His efforts earned him admission to Wilson Junior College, where he earned an A.A. degree in 1948. He earned his B.A. from Roosevelt University in 1949 and a certificate from the Northwestern University School of Mortgage Banking in 1969. He enrolled in the Kent College of Law but dropped out when he realized

Dempsey Travis.

that African Americans were limited almost entirely to practicing criminal law.

Travis formed the Sivart ("Travis" spelled backward) Mortgage Company in 1945. At one time, it was the largest mortgage company owned by an African American, and in 1961, it was the first such company to be approved by the Federal Housing Administration and the Veterans Administration. This approval opened a large range of lending opportunities.

Travis founded the Travis Realty Company in 1949, even though he was struggling and had difficulty raising the $50 for a broker's license. He did not buy property for himself until he had been in the business for seven years. Although he advocated borrowing to buy property, paying off part of the mortgage, then using the property as collateral for more loans, he did not follow his own advice, preferring to pay substantial parts of the purchase price of his own properties in cash.

Travis founded the United Mortgage Bankers of America (UMBA) in 1960 and served as its president. The association of black mortgage bankers unfortunately brought in clients who were the least likely to qualify for loans and the worst prospects to repay them. Travis lost money on residential mortgages made through the group and sold the residential portfolio of Sivart Mortgage Company in 1974 at a loss. The UMBA already had dissolved. Travis remained interested in the problems of black property owners. He had testified in 1969 to the Senate Antitrust and Monopoly Subcommittee that insurance companies used the threat of race riots as an excuse to deny coverage at standard rates to automobile and property owners in ghetto areas. He began serving on the advisory committee of the Federal National Mortgage Association in 1971 and was a director of the National Housing Conference, Inc.

Travis, who had to take remedial reading as a condition of college enrollment, became a published author. He wrote books about black jazz, housing in Chicago, Chicago history, and former Chicago mayor Harold WASHINGTON, among other topics. He won the Society of Midland Authors Award in 1982 and was the group's president from 1988 to 1990.

Trinidad and Tobago: Independent island nation. Trinidad and Tobago are together the southernmost islands of the WEST INDIES. Trinidad lies 7 miles east of Venezuela, separated from the mainland by the Gulf of Paria. Tobago is 19 miles northeast of Trinidad. Both islands are mountainous. In 1991 Trinidad had a population of 1,245,000, of which approximately 40 percent was black, 40 percent Indian from India, 15 percent mixed, 1 percent white, and 1 percent Chinese. The population of Tobago, almost 50,000, was predominantly black.

Christopher Columbus discovered Trinidad on his third voyage in 1598, but few Spanish people settled there. In 1784 Spain permitted colonization from the French West Indies. The French brought black slaves and began sugar PLANTATIONS. The number of black slaves increased from about two hundred to more than ten thousand between 1783 and 1797.

Trinidad was ceded to Great Britain in the 1802 Treaty of Amien. Five years later, Britain abolished the slave trade, increasing the labor shortage that already existed on the island. The problem worsened in 1834 when Britain granted emancipation. Blacks left the sugar estates to live in towns or on their own small holdings in the interior.

In 1845 indentured laborers from India were imported to supply labor on the sugar estates. Between 1845 and 1917, when the program was ended, almost 144,000 Indians were brought to Trinidad. The island was divided by race and religion: There were English Protestants and French ROMAN CATHOLICS, Hindu and Muslim Indians, middle-class blacks and black laborers, and people of color and whites. In Tobago sugar became less profitable beginning around 1820. Blacks left the plantations. They moved onto unoccupied lands and produced cocoa, coconuts, coffee, and food products. The economy was barely above self-sufficiency.

Britain united Trinidad and Tobago into a single colony in two stages in 1889 and 1898. Tobago became a ward or county of Trinidad. Britain gradually granted self-government and adult suffrage to its colony between 1924 and 1950. The Great Depression, combined with slow progress in achieving self-government, caused riots in 1937, and political parties based on race and religion emerged. The People's National Movement (PNM), organized by Eric WILLIAMS, an Oxford-educated black, was the party of middle-class blacks and emphasized economic development. Williams led Trinidad and Tobago to independence in 1962 and continued in power until his death in 1981.

In the twentieth century, oil production changed both the economy and the residential patterns of Trinidad. Blacks became concentrated in the oil fields of the south and in towns. Indians worked on the sugar estates or on their own small holdings. The oil profits of the 1970's enabled the government to buy a major portion of the economy, and by the end of the 1970's the government employed two-thirds of the workers.

Economic diversification and improvements in education, housing, and social services have generally been successful, especially in the cities and the regions near the oil fields. With the decline in oil prices in the 1980's Trinidad and Tobago experienced economic problems and dissatisfaction. The divisions in society still prevented unified action by labor.

Tobago was never satisfied with its union with Trinidad and has demanded concessions. Greater autonomy, but not independence, was granted in the 1990's.

—*Robert D. Talbott*

Suggested Readings:

Brereton, Bridget. *A History of Modern Trinidad 1783-1962*. Port of Spain, Trinidad: Heinemann, 1981.

Rogozinski, Jan. *A Brief History of the Caribbean from the Arawak and Carib to the Present*. New York: Meridian, 1992.

Trotter, William Monroe (April 7, 1872, Boston, Massachusetts—April 7, 1934, Boston, Massachusetts): CIVIL RIGHTS activist. Trotter was one of the most outspoken critics of racial discrimination in the United States. He founded the militant newspaper the *Boston Guardian* in 1901 as his primary vehicle for advancing his views on the lack of socioeconomic and political rights for African Americans. He had little tolerance for groups and individuals he considered to be too moderate or accommodating to white society.

Trotter was one of the organizers of the NIAGARA MOVEMENT (1905), the forerunner of the NATIONAL ASSOCIATION FOR THE ADVANCEMENT OF COLORED PEOPLE (NAACP). Many of the Niagara movement proposals, such as equal educational and political rights for African Americans, were adopted at the founding of the NAACP. Trotter, however, refused to join the NAACP because he considered it to be moderate and incapable of advancing the real best interests of African Americans. He and his newspaper had always been critical of the accommodationist policies of NAACP organizer Booker T. Washington. This dissatisfaction led Trotter to found the National Equal Rights League, which adopted positions closer to his own beliefs than those adopted by the NAACP, under Moorfield Storey and W. E. B. DU BOIS.

After the conclusion of WORLD WAR I, world leaders gathered in 1919 for the Paris Conference, at which they were to draft proposals designed to prevent further conflicts. Trotter took this opportunity to try to convince the conference to pass a law outlawing racial discrimination. The U.S. State Department denied him a passport, but he got to Paris by taking a job as a cook on a ship. Representing his National Equal Rights League, he supported an unsuccessful Japanese petition to include a prohibition against discrimination in the covenant of the League of Nations.

Trotter influenced the Civil Rights movement of the 1950's and 1960's by his legacy of strategies, such as demonstrating against racist entertainment and getting arrested, to draw public attention to his cause. He urged nonviolent protest but was passionate in his beliefs. President Woodrow Wilson once dismissed him from a conference for use of insulting language. Trotter had shaken his finger at the president to emphasize a point.

Truman administration: More than any twentieth century president before him, Harry S Truman was determined to address the problems of RACIAL DISCRIMINATION in the United States. After assuming office following the death of Franklin D. Roosevelt in April, 1945, he believed that the time had come for the chief executive to speak out on CIVIL RIGHTS.

Truman appointed a Civil Rights Commission in 1946, composed of a group of distinguished black and white Americans, to study civil rights in America. Their report, entitled *To Secure These Rights*, revealed that the country still had serious racial problems and called for federal programs to help eliminate discrimination and segregation.

On June 29, 1947, Truman delivered an address to the NATIONAL ASSOCIATION FOR THE ADVANCEMENT OF COLORED PEOPLE (NAACP) from the steps of the Lincoln Memorial. It was one of the strongest presidential statements on civil rights delivered up to that time. He called for a guarantee of full civil rights and freedom for all Americans, state and federal action against LYNCHINGS and poll taxes, and an end to inequality in education and employment. On February 2, 1948, the president prepared and submitted to Congress the most ambitious civil rights program ever proposed by an American president. Along with the recommendations outlined in his NAACP speech, he asked for the establishment of a federal Fair Employment Practices Commission, an end to JIM CROW LAWS in interstate transportation, and the protection of the right to vote.

President Truman meeting with members of the 1948 U.S. Olympic team, including high jump champion Alice Coachman (second from right). *(AP/Wide World Photos)*

The Civil Rights Commission's recommendations became part of the 1948 DEMOCRATIC PARTY presidential platform. Many observers thought that Truman's strong commitment to civil rights would be political suicide, but he was determined to do more than simply lend moral support for equality. In another bold move, Truman, against the advice of his military advisers, signed EXECUTIVE ORDER 9981 on July 26, 1948, ordering the integration of the U.S. armed forces. That same day he issued a second executive order guaranteeing fair employment in the federal civil service. He told Congress that

> the principles on which our government is based require a policy of fair employment through the federal establishment without discrimination because of race, color, religion, or national origin.

Truman's actions on behalf of civil rights created an uproar in the South. When the 1948 Democratic presidential nominating convention adopted a strong civil rights plank, the southern delegates walked out. Southern conservatives founded the States' Rights, or "Dixiecrat," Party and nominated segregationist Strom Thurmond of South Carolina for president. In spite of the party split over the issue of civil rights, Truman remained firm, and he went on to win the nomination and the presidential election in 1948.

In 1952, as his term in the White House was coming to an end, Truman said in a commencement speech at Howard University that there should be a civil rights program backed by "the full force and power of the federal government" to end discrimination in the United States. He declared that the more the nation put into practice its stated belief in equality, "the stronger, more vigorous, and happier" it would become.

—*Raymond Frey*

See also: Dixiecrats; Roosevelt administration, Franklin D.

Suggested Readings:

McCullogh, David. *Truman.* Simon and Shuster, 1992.

Miller, Merle. *Plain Speaking: An Oral Autobiography of Harry S. Truman.* Greenwich House, 1985.

Truth, Sojourner (Isabella Van Wagener; c. 1797, Ulster County, New York—November 26, 1883, Battle Creek, Michigan): Evangelist and ABOLITIONIST MOVEMENT leader. Born a slave in rural NEW YORK STATE, Sojourner Truth emancipated herself in 1826, walking away from the farm of her master, John Dumont, early one morning. After a stay of some years in NEW YORK CITY as a freed woman, in June, 1843, she left New York, carrying a pillowcase stuffed with personal items and a basket of provisions, to begin her mission—preaching and lecturing on the promise of humanity.

Before leaving New York City, a place she described as the "second Sodom," Isabella stopped at the residence of a former employer to inform her that her name was now "Sojourner." She further reported that "the Spirit" had called her to the service of humanity. Later, she accounted for the name "Truth" by explaining that, during her travels, she would be declaring the truth to the people. The predominant image of Truth as recorded by her contemporaries is that of a deeply spiritual woman with great oratorical ability and immense energy for affecting change.

Her mission lasted for more than twenty-five years and included missionary efforts and calls for abolition, women's rights, temperance, CIVIL RIGHTS, and the welfare of freed people. Among other activities, the former slave traveled thousands of miles, lectured and preached in many states, addressed Congress, visited President Abraham Lincoln, and stood fast in the face of mobs of bigots. Illiterate and poor, Truth succeeded in her endeavors at various reforms where many had failed.

(She often stated that she had never determined to do anything and failed.) Her memory is celebrated by African American groups, women's groups, and others because her life is a testament to the boundless energy of the human spirit.

Early Life

The actual date of Truth's birth is unknown, but she was born to James Baumfree and Elizabeth, also affectionately known as "Mau-Mau Bett," who were both slaves of one Colonel Hardenbergh of Ulster County, New York. Elizabeth was the third wife of James Baumfree and was believed to have borne some ten or twelve children, most of whom were sold before Truth was old enough to retain any memory of them; Truth was the next to youngest child. Truth's recollections of her childhood, as dictated to various biographers, began at about age five. At that time, she lived with her father, her mother, and the family's youngest child in a cellar beneath the hotel and home of then-master Charles Hardenbergh, along with other slaves. The conditions of the cellar encouraged rheumatism, fever sores, and palsy, among other afflictions that would aggravate Truth throughout her later life.

Her family reportedly spoke only a form of Dutch, the language of the Hardenbergh family. In some accounts, Truth's parents and Truth herself were captured in Africa. Other accounts suggest that Truth's mother's parents came from the Guinea Coast and that her paternal grandmother was a Mohawk Indian. Yet another account of Truth's life identifies her father as hailing from Africa, having received passage from the Gold Coast via an African trader.

Truth's religious awareness began with ideas related by her mother, Mau-Mau Bett. In the evening, after the completion of work on the estate, Truth's mother provided instruc-

A woman with great oratorical ability, Sojourner Truth had immense energy for effecting change. *(Associated Publishers, Inc.)*

tion in an open-air worship service. At such times, Truth learned something of the nature of God as Creator, transcendent, and immanent—ideas of traditional African origin. While both parents might have been instructed in some of the tenets of a Western religion, it is doubtful that theirs was a full-blown theological knowledge of any Western religion. Hence, whatever the truth of the origin of her parentage, her family retained traditional African beliefs that were communicated to Truth in her early life.

As human chattel, Truth passed from the hands of Colonel Hardenbergh to his son Charles, to John Neely, to Martin Scriver, to John Dumont. During her sojourn with Neely, an Englishman who did not understand her Dutch language, she was beaten severely. At the time, she began her petitions to God (as instructed by her mother) in earnest. With her next master, her biographers report, she all but abandoned the religious life in favor of the libertine, secular life led by Martin Scriver, a fisherman and tavern keeper. In 1810, at the age of thirteen, she was sold to John Dumont for the sum of seventy pounds.

Marriage and Emancipation

During her service to Dumont, Truth married a man named Thomas with whom she seems to have had five children. Their youngest child, Peter, is frequently mentioned in accounts of Truth because his illegal sale out of the state of New York gave occasion to the expression of Truth's demonstration of the power she appropriated as hers through her belief in God. Truth remained with Dumont until she was emancipated in 1827. She acquired the name Van Wagener from a Quaker who bought her services from Dumont in response to Dumont's threat to have Truth returned to him by force.

Thomas, much older than Truth, remained enslaved until freed in 1828. In poor health and advanced in age, he lived only a few years after his emancipation, leaving Truth with two children for whom to provide (the others had been sold away earlier). Truth was in her early thirties when she took the youngest child, Peter, with her to New York City, leaving the eldest child, Diana, in Ulster County.

Religious Instruction

Before her sojourn in New York City, Truth had contact with the QUAKERS, who aided her endeavors to become reunited with her son Peter. With the Quakers, she was exposed to two of the sect's fundamental doctrines: the notion of an "inner light" (each individual was said to possess a spark of divinity) and the principle of mutual aid.

In New York City, she was witness to the METHODIST moral reform movement within the city and aided women in their missionary efforts. Yet she insisted that she could develop no affinity for their prayer meetings, which she viewed as boisterous and exhausting.

Her experiences with various sects continued when in 1832 she met Robert Matthews (later Matthias), whom she mistook for Jesus Christ. Truth fell victim to Matthews's delusion and subsequently contributed her earnings to his cause. Matthias declared that the spirit of God dwelt in him and preached the idea that the spirits of the former saints would enter the bodies of the present generation. Matthias's philosophies presumably proved attractive to Truth, insomuch as animism appeared to be an essential part of the traditional belief system embraced by her mother. After a scandal following the death of a former employer and benefactor of Matthias, and after Matthias's exoneration of the charge of murder and subsequent removal to the far West, Truth's liaison with Matthias ended.

Shortly thereafter, Truth felt her call to leave the city. On June 1, 1843, armed with an understanding of the principles of several sects and religions, Truth ordained herself as preacher—believing she needed no other authority—and left on her mission.

Her Legacy

Described by her contemporaries as in possession of "personal presence," "magnetism," and "magical influence," Truth is the prototype of the strong African American woman endowed with spiritual command. Hers was a strong belief in the power of God as being accessible to the individual. Anecdotes of her life experiences abound. She was able to reason to a group of anxious men at a women's rights convention that if the first woman God ever made was strong enough to turn the world upside down, then surely the group gathered was more than strong enough to turn it right side up. After Frederick DOUGLASS expressed his lack of hope in justice from whites, suggesting bloodshed as a means to freedom,

Truth queried, "Frederick, is God dead?" Perhaps she is best remembered for her famous "Ain't I a Woman?" oration delivered at the Akron women's rights convention of 1851.

Charitable Work

In addition to the fame Truth garnered from her moving orations at antislavery and women's rights meetings, and in addition to the stirring sermons Truth delivered at camp meetings and churches, she also provided humanitarian aid to those in need, including efforts to provide shelter, food, and clothing to runaway slaves. With the commencement of the CIVIL WAR in 1861, Truth raised money to buy gifts for soldiers and frequented their camps. After the Civil War, she campaigned on behalf of education and improved conditions for the freed people.

Fanciful depiction of Sojourner Truth's meeting with President Abraham Lincoln. *(Library of Congress)*

Advanced age and poor health eventually forced her to retire to a Battle Creek, Michigan, sanatorium, but by then, Truth had made a great impact on nineteenth-century America. In a society that enslaved her and denied her humanity, Truth was able to forge a formidable identity owing to the supreme spirituality that empowered her missions. She died at about age 86.

—*Adele S. Newson*

See also: Tubman, Harriet.

Suggested Readings:

Braxton, Joanne M. *Black Women Writing Autobiography*. Philadelphia: Temple University Press, 1989.

Fitch, Suzanne P., and Roseann M. Mandziuk. *Sojourner Truth as Orator: Wit, Story, and Song*. Westport, Conn.: Greenwood Press, 1997.

Mabee, Carleton, and Susan M. Newhouse. *Sojourner Truth: Slave, Prophet, Legend*. New York: New York University Press, 1993.

McKissack, Pat, and Frederick McKissack. *Sojourner Truth: Ain't I a Woman?* New York: Scholastic, 1992.

Ortiz, Victoria. *Sojourner Truth, a Self-Made Woman*. Philadelphia: J. B. Lippincott, 1974.

Painter, Nell I. *Sojourner Truth: A Life, a Symbol*. New York: W. W. Norton, 1996.

Pauli, Hertha E. *Her Name Was Sojourner Truth*. New York: Appleton-Century-Crofts, 1962.

Stetson, Erlene, and Linda David. *Glorying in Tribulation: The Lifework of Sojourner Truth*. East Lansing: Michigan State University, 1993.

Tuberculosis: Disease caused by the mycobacterium tuberculosis, or tubercle bacillus. The disease, which usually attacks the lungs, spreads on airborne droplets

Homeless men gather around a steam vent seeking relief from near-freezing weather in Washington, D.C., in 1994. The unhealthful conditions associated with homelessness make the homeless especially susceptible to tuberculosis and other diseases. *(AP/Wide World Photos)*

and usually enters the body through the air passages. Anyone sharing a poorly ventilated space with a victim can contract the disease. Once North America's leading cause of death, the disease affected a disproportionately large number of African Americans, whose impoverished living conditions and inadequate health care made them its most likely targets.

From the post-CIVIL WAR era through the early decades of the twentieth century, public health officials, physicians, and black leaders cited pulmonary tuberculosis as the major threat to black health. Reports of health boards from urban centers repeatedly attributed high rates of morbidity and mortality among blacks to the ravages of tuberculosis. Moreover, sanitarians and reformers attending race conferences held at ATLANTA UNIVERSITY, HAMPTON INSTITUTE, and TUSKEGEE INSTITUTE at the beginning of the twentieth century agreed that black mortality from tuberculosis posed a major threat to the well-being of African Americans. Many of these reformers believed that the excessive morbidity and mortality resulting from tuberculosis could be prevented.

Accordingly, during the early twentieth century, African Americans began a battle against tuberculosis. From 1907 to 1909, antituberculosis leagues were formed by black medical societies in Louisiana, Alabama, Virginia, and the District of Columbia. At its organizational meeting in 1908, the National Association of Colored Graduate Nurses discussed both the high incidence of black tuberculosis mortality and methods to control the disease. In addition, in 1910, the NATIONAL MEDICAL ASSOCIATION (composed primarily of blacks) appointed a special commission on tuberculosis which would attempt to educate African Americans about the disease. In 1915 Booker T. WASHINGTON of Tuskegee Institute initiated Negro National Health Week, focusing attention on tuberculosis and other health problems in the black community.

By the 1960's, tuberculosis was all but forgotten, as powerful drug therapy used during the 1950's had subdued it. The ACQUIRED IMMUNODEFICIENCY SYNDROME (AIDS) epidemic beginning in the 1980's and the increasing number of homeless people caused a resurgence of the disease. AIDS victims, a disproportionate number of whom are African Americans, are also the most likely victims of tuberculosis. Homelessness is also disproportionately prevalent in the black community. The unsanitary conditions associated with homelessness put the homeless at special risk of contracting tuberculosis.

Tubman, Harriet (Araminta Ross; c. 1820, Bucktown, Dorchester County, Maryland—March 10, 1913, Auburn, New York): Abolitionist movement leader. Dubbed the greatest conductor of the Underground Railroad by abolitionists and sympathizers, "Moses" by the fugitive slaves she led to freedom, and "General Tubman" by abolitionist John Brown, Tubman made a great impact on nineteenth-century American life. Among other activities, the illiterate runaway slave made nineteen trips to the South, where she liberated more than three hundred people from slavery, including all but one member of her own family. During the Civil War, Tubman also served in the Union army, without remuneration, as a spy, scout, and nurse. After the war, she established a hospital for old and disabled freed people.

Like Sojourner Truth, Tubman forged an invincible persona with the aid of a belief that hers was an intimate and immediate relationship with God. The predominant image of Tubman as recorded by her contemporaries is that of a physically powerful woman, entirely African in features, possessing an abundance of spirituality. Sarah Bradford, Tubman's first biographer, described her as possessing "the strange familiarity of communion with God." She was given to premonitions (she called them "intimations"), which she believed warned her of impending dangers in her work as conductor of the Underground Railroad and as Union spy. Reasoning early in her life that she (as well as all people of African descent) had the right to liberty or death, she then proceeded to live her life of activism accordingly. At one point, slaveholders offered a reward of forty thousand dollars for her capture, dead or alive.

Early Life
Tubman's parents, Benjamin Ross and Harriet Green, were said to have been full-blooded Africans. Tubman's Maryland master named her Araminta, but Tubman later took her mother's first name. In addition to Tubman, her mother bore some ten other children. Beginning at age six, Tubman was subjected to a series of temporary masters, because her owner frequently hired her out to local planters and families. She was first taken away to learn the trade of weaving, and while in her early teens, she was hired out as a field hand. Tubman developed amazing strength and fortitude as she learned the tasks of the field hand. Additionally, her father taught her the medicinal value of roots derived from his understanding of his African past. Both apprenticeships would later serve her well in her endeavors to lead fugitive slaves to freedom.

During Tubman's adolescence, an overseer struck her head with a two-pound weight; the effect of the blow was to plague Tubman for

In June, 1999, this statue of Harriet Tubman leading slaves to freedom was unveiled in Boston's South End neighborhood. *(AP/Wide World Photos)*

the rest of her life. She suffered from occasional lethargy and stupors. Once, she was made to work in the home of a woman who used her as a maid by day and a child's nurse by night, affording Tubman virtually no hours of rest. Her mistress often beat her savagely, and the discipline thus learned and hardship thus endured prepared Tubman for a life of activism that would involve enforced wakefulness and endurance. Eventually, Tubman was returned to her master battered and ill.

In 1844 she married John Tubman, but the couple had no children. By 1849 her young master died; aware of an impending sale, she then resolved, at the age of twenty-nine, to escape, and she convinced her two remaining brothers on the plantation to accompany her. After a while, the two brothers found the way north too foreign and fraught with dangers to continue. They abandoned the journey and returned to the plantation. With the North Star as her guide and with the good fortune of finding sympathetic blacks and whites alike, she continued alone.

The Underground Railroad

Tubman reached PHILADELPHIA, where she worked for two years to save enough money to return to the South to liberate her family. Between 1850 and 1860, she made about twenty trips to the South and liberated some three hundred people, among the last of whom were her elderly parents. Because of the infirmity owing to their age, Tubman reasoned that they were in no immediate danger of being sold. Also, the journey with her parents proved most perilous, because they had to be transported much of the way by wagon. Tubman's efforts established her as the most able of those who led fugitive slaves to freedom via the Underground Railroad, a network of way stations that helped slaves to escape from the South to the free states.

Tubman effected escapes by traveling at night, hiding by day, drugging babies with opium to quiet their cries, and carrying a revolver for recalcitrant sojourners. In 1851, two years after her escape, Tubman returned for her husband, but she discovered that he had remarried and preferred to remain with his new wife. She then gathered a group of fugitives in the area and led them to Philadelphia. With the 1850 passage of the FUGITIVE SLAVE LAW, Tubman began to lead fugitive slaves to Canada. By 1852 famous abolitionists such as Thomas Garrett knew of Tubman; they often donated great sums of money to her cause. John Brown met with Tubman on many occasions, consulting and sharing with her, among other things, his plans for his attack on HARPERS FERRY, West Virginia.

The late 1850's marked the beginning of Tubman's lecturing activity. Beginning with an appearance at an antislavery meeting in BOSTON, Tubman traveled the nation calling for the abolition of slavery and for women's rights.

The Civil War

During the early years of the Civil War, the governor of Massachusetts sent for Tubman to engage her services as a spy, scout, and nurse for the Union army. At the time, Tubman lived on an Auburn, New York, farm with her parents. Leaving her parents and farm to the care of neighbors and friends, she went to war. Her labors included leading armies through swamps, gaining the confidence of recently liberated slaves (who often feared northern whites more than they feared their former owners), nursing soldiers, using the knowledge of roots and herbs acquired from her father, and passing through enemy lines as a spy. After the war, she returned to Auburn, where she found her farm being sold to satisfy delinquent mortgage payments.

Declining Years

By the war's end, Tubman was some forty-five years old and penniless. She also continued to

During her last years, Harriet Tubman converted her own house into a home for the aged and used her meager government pension money to support her work. *(Library of Congress)*

suffer from the wound inflicted to her head during her youth. In 1867 Sarah Bradford wrote Tubman's biography, the proceeds from which Tubman used to aid aged freed slaves. Her first husband had died shortly after the war; in 1869 she married Nelson Davis, a war veteran.

Tubman continued to lobby for the establishment of a home for the indigent aged blacks of Auburn. During the years that funds were insufficient for such a project, she converted her own home into a shelter for the aged. In 1897, more than thirty years after the end of the Civil War and after decades of asking the federal government, Tubman was awarded a pension of twenty dollars a month. Much of her pension she used to help shelter and care for the aged. The people of Auburn, moved by her selflessness, eventually rallied to her aid and established the Harriet Tubman Home for Aged and Indigent Negroes in 1908. After her death in 1913, Auburn erected a monument in her honor as a testament to her indomitable will.

Biographies and Writings About Tubman
During her long life, Tubman was well known to many famous personages, including statesmen, abolitionists, and literary figures. Records of her activities are found in the memoirs and writings of many famous people of the nineteenth century—William H. Seward, Gerrit Smith, Frederick Douglass, Elizabeth Stanton, Susan B. Anthony, and others. The first edition of Sarah Bradford's biography of Tubman appeared in 1869, and an expanded edition appeared in 1886; both were privately printed by Bradford, who donated the book's proceeds to Tubman.

—*Adele S. Newson*

Suggested Readings:

Conrad, Earl. *Harriet Tubman: Negro Soldier and Abolitionist*. New York: International Publishers, 1942.

Heidish, Marcy. *A Woman Called Moses: A Novel Based on the Life of Harriet Tubman*. Boston: Houghton Mifflin, 1976.

Loewenberg, Bert J., and Ruth Bogin. *Black Women in Nineteenth-Century American Life*. University Park: Pennsylvania State University Press, 1976.

Schroeder, Alan. *Minty: A Story of Young Harriet Tubman*. New York: Dial Books for Young Readers, 1996.

Scruggs, O. M. "The Meaning of Harriet Tubman." In *Remember the Ladies*, edited by Carol V. R. George. Syracuse, N.Y.: Syracuse University Press, 1975.

Woodward, Helen B. "Aren't I a Woman?: Sojourner Truth and Harriet Tubman." In *The Bold Women*. Freeport, N.Y.: Books for Libraries Press, 1953.

Tucker, C. DeLores (b. October 4, 1927, Philadelphia, Pennsylvania): PENNSYLVANIA politician. Cynthia DeLores Nottage Tucker served as vice chairperson of the Pennsylvania state DEMOCRATIC PARTY and served on the executive committee of the Democratic National Committee. She was a member of the National Women's Political Caucus and a member of the Pennsylvania Commission on Women. Tucker was also the first African American woman to hold the office of secretary of state for Pennsylvania, serving from 1971 to 1977. During her term of office, Tucker was secretary of the National Association of Secretaries of State.

As a result of her achievements, Tucker was named by EBONY magazine to its list of the one hundred most influential black Americans in 1973, 1974, and 1975. She served as president of the Federation of Democratic Women in 1977 and as chair of the Democratic National Committee Black Caucus in 1984.

Tucker was drafted as one of fourteen candidates to run for lieutenant governor of Pennsylvania in 1987—the first African American candidate ever selected—but she lost the primary election. In 1989 she became national vice president of the board of trustees of the NATIONAL ASSOCIATION FOR THE ADVANCEMENT OF COLORED PEOPLE (NAACP) and was named vice president of the *Philadelphia Tribune.*

As the chair of the National Political Congress of Black Women, in the 1900's Tucker launched a crusade against gangsta RAP music's encouragement of violence, misogyny, and licentious disrespect in young people. Her efforts brought her in contact with William J. Bennett, a conservative Republican politician who was secretary of education in the REAGAN ADMINISTRATION and drug czar with the BUSH ADMINISTRATION. Their unlikely partnership persuaded many leading record labels, including Time Warner entertainment, to reconsider their marketing and endorsement of gangsta rap artists and albums. Time Warner, in fact, severed its business relationship with Interscope, a label with prominent gangsta rap artists.

Pennsylvania politician C. DeLores Tucker. (© Roy Lewis Archives)

Tucker made enemies in the music business and even reported receiving death threats. Gangsta rapper Tupac SHAKUR released an album, *All Eyez on Me* (1996), containing vulgar lyrics about her. In 1997 she sued Interscope, its subsidiary Death Row, and the estate of Tupac Shakur for defamation of character and damages. "It is the gangstas in the suites, not those in the streets, that I am after," she said. Nonetheless, she dropped the charges against all except Shakur's estate in 1998, and the case was dismissed in 1999.

—*Updated by Dorothy C. Salem*

Tucker, Lem (May 26, 1938, Saginaw, Michigan—March 2, 1991, Washington, D.C.): Broadcaster. A broadcaster for decades, Lemual "Lem" Tucker culminated his career as medical and science correspondent for *CBS Evening News with Dan Rather* from 1984 until his retirement in 1988. During his last years at CBS news, he garnered two Emmy Awards, for his reporting on black families in the 1981-1982 season and for coverage of the Iceland summit meeting in the 1986-1987 season. He also won an Emmy for a series on hunger in America for the 1968-1969 season.

Walter Tucker III confronts the news media after his conviction on extortion and tax evasion charges in November, 1995. *(AP/Wide World Photos)*

Tucker, Walter, III (b. May 28, 1957, Los Angeles, California): CALIFORNIA politician. Tucker was reared in Compton, California. He graduated as valedictorian of Compton Senior High School in 1974, attended Princeton University, and earned a B.A. with honors in political science from the University of Southern California in 1978. Tucker went on to earn his law degree at Georgetown University in Washington, D.C., in 1981. He worked for a law firm in Washington, then returned to California. Tucker passed the California bar exam and served as deputy district attorney for Los Angeles County from 1984 to 1986. He opened a law practice in 1986, specializing in criminal law.

Tucker was active in politics from an early age. Beginning in 1969, he worked on his father's campaigns for the school board and city council. He coordinated his father's last two campaigns for the mayoralty of Compton. Tucker had worked for the Los Angeles County district attorney's office, and at one time he pleaded no contest to misdemeanor charges connected to altering official documents.

Tucker's father died on October 1, 1990, while serving his third term as mayor of Compton. Tucker won the special election to succeed his father on April 16, 1991, and became Compton's youngest mayor. He immediately began campaigns to benefit to city's youth, improve police services and community involvement, and foster intracommunity cooperation. He organized the First Annual Unity Festival and Summit Conference in Compton. An ordained Christian minister, Tucker also taught Sunday school at his church, the Bread of Life Christian Center.

Tucker's star rose higher when he was elected to the U.S. Congress in 1992. In 1994, however, he was indicted on charges of accepting bribes while he was mayor of Compton. He was convicted of extortion and bribery in late 1995 and resigned from Congress.

See also: Congress members; Electoral politics; Mayors; Politics and government.

Reconstruction-era politician Benjamin S. Turner. *(Associated Publishers, Inc.)*

Turner, Benjamin S. (March 17, 1825, near Weldon, North Carolina—March 21, 1894, Selma, Alabama): RECONSTRUCTION-era politician. Born into slavery, Turner was among the first African Americans to serve in Congress. During the RECONSTRUCTION era he was a representative from ALABAMA in the 1871-1873 term. He was one of five African Americans to serve in Congress during that session. Following his defeat for the successive term, he retired from politics. Before becoming a congressman, he had served as a tax collector, a councilman in Selma, and an independent businessman.

Turner, Darwin T. (May 7, 1931, Cincinnati, Ohio—1991, Iowa City, Iowa): Educator. Darwin Theodore Troy Turner had a distinguished career as a university teacher, literary critic, anthologist, and pioneer of the study of African American history and culture within higher education. He began his academic career precociously, earning a B.A. in English from the University of Cincinnati in 1947 and an M.A. in 1949. From 1949 to 1951, he taught at Clark College in ATLANTA, GEORGIA, as an assistant professor of English. His Ph.D. in English and American drama was from the University of Chicago (1956).

His academic path involved several moves. He taught at Morgan State College in BALTIMORE, MARYLAND, from 1952 to 1957, then was chair of the English department at Florida A&M State University from 1957 to 1959. From 1959 to 1970, he was first chair of English then dean of the graduate school at North Carolina A&T University of Greensboro. His last positions were at the University of Iowa, where he was professor of English, chair of African American studies (1972-1991), and Iowa Foundation Distinguished Professor (1981).

Turner served on an array of national education committees, including those of the Modern Language Association, the National Committee of Teachers of English, the Rockefeller Committee on the Humanities, and Phi Beta Kappa. He built a deserved reputation as a kindly, committed educator and director of African American literary and cultural research. His own scholarly work equally made its mark.

Perhaps his best-acclaimed volume is *In a Minor Chord: Three Afro-American Writers and Their Search for Identity* (1971), a lucid critique of Jean TOOMER, Countée CULLEN, and Zora Neale HURSTON. The Hurston chapters caused some controversy. For example, Turner described Hurston as superficial and shallow in her artistic and social judgments. Other representative publications include Turner's journal essays (he also served as a contributing editor to the *College Language Association Journal*), his own poetry in *Katharsis* (1964), the three-volume collection *Black American Literature: Essays, Poetry, Fiction, Drama* (1970), *Black*

Drama in America: An Anthology (1971), and his edited works *The Wayward and the Seeking: A Collection of Writings by Jean Toomer* (1980) and *The Art of Slave Narrative: Original Essays in Criticism and Theory* (1982, with John Sekora).

Turner, Henry McNeal (February 1, 1834, Abbeville, South Carolina—May 8, 1915, Windsor, Ontario, Canada): Religious leader and activist. Henry McNeal Turner's cry in response to the 1884 DEMOCRATIC PARTY's presidential victory was, "A man who loves a country that hates him is a human dog and not a man." In this speech, which ended with his famous slogan "Respect Black," Turner summarized the central tenets of his writings, works, and beliefs: that African Americans should act and think proudly for themselves and, if thwarted, should resist and protest or should find freedom in Africa.

In a long life, Turner served as a preacher, organizer, and bishop for the AFRICAN METHODIST EPISCOPAL CHURCH (AME), as a GEORGIA legislator, as a political critic, and as an active proponent of the AMERICAN COLONIZATION SOCIETY and its interests in LIBERIA. Above all, he was a crusader urging blacks to fight for their rights against the increasing inroads of JIM CROW legislation and racism at the beginning of the twentieth century. While Booker T. WASHINGTON proposed harmonious cooperation between the races and W. E. B. DU BOIS argued the intellectual case for African American equality, Turner used a biblical vision and rhetorical eloquence to appeal to a more popular audience.

Youth and Religious Training
Henry Turner was born to free parents in slave SOUTH CAROLINA, a society then in the process of constraining black opportunities in the wake of the Denmark VESEY and Nat TURNER uprisings. Despite the restrictions imposed on black EDUCATION, Henry Turner learned reading, writing, and basic arithmetic in his adolescence while working at a variety of trades before pursuing his education while employed by a medical college in Baltimore. According to his first biographer, Mongo Ponton, Turner also believed himself descended from African royalty through his mother, Sarah Greer Turner, a belief that may have influenced his continuing interest in African colonization and study.

Turner joined the Methodist Episcopal Church, South, in 1851 and was licensed to preach in 1853. He relinquished his membership in this white-dominated denomination in the late 1850's after a dramatic meeting in NEW ORLEANS with Dr. Willis B. Revels of the African Methodist Episcopal Church; the African church's black autonomy appealed more to Turner's temperament. Despite difficulties caused by his educational background, he was admitted to work in Baltimore with the support of Bishop Daniel A. PAYNE. Shortly thereafter, in 1862, Turner and his wife, Elizabeth Ann Peacher, moved to a church in WASHINGTON, D.C., where Turner's sermons and political views gained him more public attention.

Civil War and Political Work
In 1863 Abraham Lincoln commissioned Turner as chaplain of the First Regiment, U.S. Colored Troops, making Turner the first black U.S. Army chaplain. In 1865 he became a regular chaplain. He was also assigned to duty with the Georgia Freedmen's Bureau. In Georgia, he served the church by building AME churches and organizations; he claimed to have received more than fourteen thousand members into the church. Turner also spent five years in stormy political activities in the Georgia legislature and federal Republican patronage posts. His legislative career, for example, became embattled through white Georgians' 1868 rejection of black legislators and refusal to ratify the FIFTEENTH AMENDMENT. Turner also resigned federal posts in

Macon and Savannah, Georgia, after intense harassment. His speech arguing for political franchise, "On the Eligibility of Colored Members to Seats in the Georgia Legislature," circulated as a pamphlet, as did many of his later political and social arguments.

Church Publications and College Presidency
When not yet forty, Turner retired from politics to a pastorate in Savannah, and thereafter his political and critical base became the AME Church. He became a bishop (1880-1892), general manager of the AME Book Concern, and a regular contributor to *The Christian Recorder.* He also served for twelve years as president of Morris Brown University. Turner proved active as a publicist and author for the church and as founder and editor of publications such as *The Southern Recorder* (1886-1888), *The Voice of Missions* (1893-1900), and *The Voice of the People*

During his long and varied career, Henry McNeal Turner became the first African American chaplain in the U.S. Army. *(Associated Publishers, Inc.)*

ple (1901-1907). Among his books were *The Negro in All Ages* (1873), *The Genius and Theory of Methodist Polity: Or, the Machinery of Methodism* (1885), *African Letters* (1893), and *Turner's Catechism* (c. 1917, also translated into French).

From the AME pulpit, Turner continued to criticize the political compromises that reconstituted segregation and black oppression in the South in the second half of the nineteenth century. He claimed in *The Christian Recorder*, for example, that the U.S. SUPREME COURT's 1883 reversal of the Civil Rights Act of 1875 "absolves the negro's allegiance to the general government" (November 8, 1883) and attacked black leaders who adopted accommodationist positions. He also criticized the Republican Party's growing abandonment of black suffrage and civil rights.

Emigrationist Work
As early as the mid-1870's, Turner showed sympathy to supporters of the COLONIZATION MOVEMENT who saw the future of American blacks in a return to Africa. He argued in 1876 that

> there is no instance mentioned in history where an enslaved people of an alien race rose to respectability upon the same territory of their enslavement and in the presence of their enslavers, without losing their identity or individuality by amalgamation. Can any result be hoped for the negro in the United States? I think not.

Turner himself first visited Sierra Leone and Liberia in 1891, returning to Africa in 1893, 1895, and 1898. In the last trip, as senior bishop of the AME Church, he arranged affiliation for emergent black congregations in South Africa. His letters and editorials praised the opportunities of Liberia, although his critics noted that he himself never moved there. His vision was made clear in an 1880 letter to his son, John P. Turner, to whom he wrote:

If you want your name woven into song and history when you are dead, become an African explorer, geologist, mineralogist or something that will enlighten the world upon her resources, and make you her benefactor.

Colonization, however, faced many practical problems and never proved a mass success.

As Turner's seniority and international fame grew, he received honorary doctorates from the University of Pennsylvania (1872), Wilberforce University (1873), and the College of Liberia (1894). A family man as well, he remarried twice in the 1890's and again before his death. His commentary on American life and politics grew ever more acid. In reference to the 1896 presidential election, for example, he wrote in *The Voice of the Missions*, "Vote any way in your power to overthrow, destroy, ruin, blot out, divide, crush, dissolve, wreck, consume, demolish, disorganize, suppress, subvert, smash, shipwreck, crumble, nullify, upset, uproot, expunge, and fragmentize this nation until it learns to deal justly with the black man." Turner opposed black participation in the Spanish-American War for the same reason. Moreover, in 1898, to the consternation of the white press, he declaimed that "God is a Negro."

Later Life
As the twentieth century began, Turner maintained his office and residence in ATLANTA, GEORGIA. His career, however, was tempered by health problems. He was accorded recognition for his service by the AME Church in 1905. Still, in his final decade, he was quoted in the *Atlanta Constitution* of February 16, 1906, as saying, "Without multiplying words, I wish to say that hell is an improvement upon the United States where the Negro is concerned."

After Turner's death in Canada, his body was brought back in state to Big Bethel Church in Atlanta for burial. More than fifteen thousand people attended the ceremony. Booker T. Washington died in the same year.

Turner's influence persisted in a variety of black movements, including the AME Church. His Christian radicalism was influential on Marcus GARVEY and Garvey's UNIVERSAL NEGRO IMPROVEMENT ASSOCIATION as well as on others who demanded a radical reassessment of black opportunities in the United States. Although Turner's colonization projects failed, the congregations and spirit of the African Methodist Episcopal Church that he spread along the Atlantic coast also became a bulwark for later nationalist identity. Thus Gayraud Wilmore, a prominent historian of African American religion and politics, considers Turner to have been the American black of his era of most lasting impact on the future of Africa, even beyond his rich legacy of actions and words in the United States.

—*Gary W. McDonogh*

Suggested Readings:

Angell, Stephen W. *Bishop Henry McNeal Turner and African-American Religion in the South*. Knoxville: University of Tennessee Press, 1992.

Coulter, E. Merton. "Henry M. Turner: Georgia Negro Preacher-Politician During the Reconstruction Era." *Georgia Historical Quarterly* 48 (December, 1964): 371-410.

Perdue, Frank. *The Negro in Savannah, 1865-1900*. New York: Exposition Press, 1973.

Redkey, Edwin S. *Black Exodus: Black Nationalist and Back-to-Africa Movements, 1890-1910*. New Haven, Conn.: Yale University Press, 1969.

_____, ed. *Respect Black: The Writings and Speeches of Henry McNeal Turner*. New York: Arno, 1971.

Wilmore, Gayraud S. *Black Religion and Black Radicalism: An Interpretation of the Religious History of African Americans*. 3d ed. Maryknoll, N.Y.: Orbis Books, 1998.

Turner, James Milton (May 16, 1840, St. Louis County, Missouri—November 1, 1915, Ardmore, Oklahoma): Educator and government official. Turner was born a slave in MISSOURI. He and his mother were purchased from slavery by his father, John Turner, when he was four years old. Turner was largely self-educated but learned to read at a secret slave children's school conducted by nuns at the St. Louis Catholic Cathedral. In his early teen years, he attended a day school in Brooklyn, Illinois, and at age fourteen he studied at the preparatory school at OBERLIN COLLEGE.

During the CIVIL WAR Turner served as valet to a Northern officer. He was wounded in the hip during the Battle of Shiloh, causing a limp that he retained for the rest of his life. After the war, Turner became active in public life, promoting the cause of EDUCATION for African Americans. In 1866 the Kansas City school board appointed him to teach in Missouri's first tax-supported school for black students. He helped to solicit money from black soldiers in the South for a new school. These funds, along with those collected by black infantry units, were the basis for Jefferson City's Lincoln Institute, which since 1921 has been known as LINCOLN UNIVERSITY. Turner joined Lincoln's board of trustees in 1868.

In view of the contributions of black soldiers, Turner in 1870 urged the Missouri state legislature to appropriate funds for schools based on the number of students enrolled, without regard to color. He was appointed as assistant state superintendent of schools, responsible for establishing free public schools for black students.

Turner emerged as Missouri's leading radical politician during the RECONSTRUCTION era, largely as a result of his tours on behalf of Lincoln Institute and the Equal Rights League. He helped obtain the support of black voters for the election of Ulysses S. Grant to the U.S. presidency. Grant rewarded Turner by naming him as minister resident and consul-general at Monrovia, LIBERIA, on March 1, 1871. This appointment made Turner the first black U.S. DIPLOMAT accredited to an African country. James W. Mason had been named as minister in March, 1870, but never traveled to his post.

Turner spent seven years in Liberia. Numerous tribal uprisings and changes in government there led him to oppose colonization by black people from the United States. He also thought that the equatorial climate of the country was unsuitable. He returned to the United States, and during the "Great Exodus" movement of 1879 he established a refuge depot in St. Louis for African Americans on their way to Kansas. As president of the Freedmen's Oklahoma Association of St. Louis, he circulated information about the free land that was available to homesteaders. During the 1880's, Turner worked as an attorney on behalf of black members of various Native American nations. Those members often were denied their share of money granted to the nations by the U.S. government in compensation for land taken from the nations.

Turner, Nat (October 2, 1800, Southampton County, Virginia—November 11, 1831, Jerusalem, Virginia): Slave revolt leader. In 1831, Nat Turner led a major slave revolt in Southampton County, VIRGINIA, variously known as "Nat's Fray," the "Southampton Insurrection," and the "First War" (the CIVIL WAR being regarded as the second war). Turner planned the insurrection, which involved between sixty and eighty slaves and free blacks and in which between fifty-five and sixty-five whites were killed. Turner's revolt was important because it disproved the myth of the happy slave, showed that slaves were willing to die for freedom, and demonstrated that slaves were capable of organizing a movement themselves. It inspired many African Americans who would later strive for freedom and justice.

Early Influences

Turner spent his entire life in Southampton County. The county is in the tidewater area of southeastern Virginia, near the NORTH CAROLINA border. The county seat was the town of Jerusalem (later Courtland). The region underwent an economic depression in the 1820's; there was widespread white apprehension concerning possible slave revolts, as whites were outnumbered by blacks, and as the well-publicized abortive slave insurrection of GABRIEL Prosser had occurred near Richmond in 1800.

Turner was born October 2, 1800, to a slave called Nancy, who had been kidnapped from Africa in 1793 and purchased by Benjamin Turner. There is a legend that Nancy tried to kill Nat just after his birth to prevent him from being subjected to a life of slavery. Turner's father's name is unknown, but he was the son of another Turner farm slave and ran away when Nat was eight or nine.

During his boyhood, Nat Turner learned to read and write, an unusual accomplishment for a slave child. He also learned about Christianity. He came to associate religion with freedom and to feel fervently about both. Turner had religious visions throughout his life. Once he reported hearing a voice tell him to seek the "Kingdom of Heaven," a phrase he interpreted to mean an end to servitude. He believed that it was his destiny to lead his fellow slaves to freedom.

Upon Benjamin Turner's death, Nat Turner was inherited by Benjamin's son, Samuel Turner. Samuel Turner hired a harsh overseer, and Nat Turner ran away. A month later, Nat returned and gave himself up. He reported having had a vision in which "the Spirit" chided him for being selfish. This may have caused him to see his destiny as the pursuit of freedom for his people, not merely himself.

In 1821 Nat Turner married a slave named Cherry. They had two sons and one daughter, but the family was split up as a result of the death of Samuel Turner in 1822. Nat was sold to Thomas Moore, whereas Cherry and the children were sold to Giles Reese, a neighbor of Moore.

Nat the Prophet

Between 1825 and 1830, Turner became a popular preacher in a circuit of African American churches. His sermons were impassioned and poetic. He vividly described visions of conflict and liberation and said that the judgment day was at hand. His followers came to believe that he was a prophet. During these years, he formulated a secret plan for insurrection.

In 1828 Thomas Moore died, and Turner was inherited by Moore's nine-year-old-son, Putnam Moore. Thomas Moore's widow, Sally Moore, married a carriage maker named Joseph Travis, who moved to the farm and supervised Nat and sixteen other slaves.

Plans for Revolt

Turner's travels as a preacher allowed him to learn things necessary to prepare an insurrection. He found out which slaves to trust and the location of roads and hiding places. He assembled a close group of followers, but he did not tell them his plans for rebellion until 1828, when he experienced a vision. A spirit told him he was soon to fight against "the serpent." His close followers included four other slaves and two free blacks.

Another sign came to Turner in February of 1831; he interpreted an eclipse of the sun as meaning that it was time to prepare his revolt. He assigned tasks to the members of his inner circle, who recruited followers, arranged for horses and mules, and prepared weapons. Turner chose July 4, 1831, for the revolt. When he became ill, though, the insurrection was postponed. Another vision came to him on August 13, 1831, when he saw a dark spot moving on the sun and told his followers that blacks would pass over the earth just as the spot had passed across the sun. The insurrection was then set to begin in the early morning of August 22, 1831. All whites, regardless of age or sex, were to be killed. As the rebels traveled from farm to farm, slaves would be recruited and weapons confiscated.

Insurrection

The revolt began with an attack on the Travis household by Turner and his close followers. Nat Turner drew the first blood, attacking Joseph Travis. Soon all the family were slain. Until the revolt was overcome by white resistance forty hours later, Turner directed his followers' actions. He reminded them to view themselves as soldiers rather than as outlaws and to keep liberation in mind.

Contemporary depiction of Nat Turner's capture by Benjamin Phipps. *(Library of Congress)*

The rebels used the cover of night to make surprise attacks on several farms. Whites were killed, and guns, horses, mules, and food were taken. There was no torture or rape. The rebels spared the home of Giles Reese, where Turner's wife and children were slaves, as well as the farm of a boyhood friend of Turner's. Also spared was a poor white family that did not own slaves.

When one member of the slave army urged the group to turn back because of the superior force of the whites, Turner pointed out that they could expect ruthless treatment if they gave up. He argued that death was acceptable because they had tasted freedom. Turner's view prevailed, and the group moved on. By noon, there were about sixty in the slave army, many mounted. Turner's goal was to take the town of Jerusalem, as it held a large store of ammunition.

Word of the revolt had spread throughout the area by mid-morning. Whites rushed to town for protection, and armed resistance was mobilized. The rebels and white militia clashed at the Battle of Parker's Field. After attack and counterattack, Turner led a retreat into a cover of woods. He rallied a force of twenty, which tried unsuccessfully to cross a bridge into Jerusalem from the south. Turner's force camped that night near a large plantation from which he hoped to recruit more slaves. At dawn, there was an ambush in which many of his men were wounded. The weakened slave army moved to another farm, where the militia waited. Only Turner and four others escaped, and soon only Turner was at large. All the coconspirators either died in the battles with militia or went to trial. Between fifteen and twenty men and a small number of women were hanged, and other Turner followers were sold to plantations in the Deep South or the Caribbean. There was a massive effort to find the missing leader, including the offer of a five-hundred-dollar reward.

Capture

After two months in hiding, Turner was captured and taken to the authorities by a poor white, Benjamin Phipps. Under heavy guard to prevent a LYNCHING, Turner was questioned by two judges in Jerusalem. He answered them calmly and frankly and did not repent; he said that he had done as God had commanded. He expressed no remorse over the killing of women and children, saying he thought such terror was necessary to win freedom from slavery. While in jail awaiting trial, he gave a statement to Thomas Gray, which Gray later published.

The trial began November 5, 1831. Turner's lawyer, William Parker, entered a not-guilty plea, but Turner did not deny the deeds with which he was charged. His statement to Gray was read. Turner acknowledged the statement and said he had nothing to say beyond it. Turner was found guilty and sentenced to hang on November 11, 1831. The hanging was a public spectacle; many in the crowd expected a show of cowardice, but Turner was calm.

Aftermath

There were more than one hundred lynchings of blacks in the area prompted by white anxiety and a desire for revenge. Thus, at least twice as many blacks as whites died as a result of the rebellion. Repressive laws were passed intended to suppress further rebellion, including rules against selling liquor to slaves and against allowing slaves to possess arms. Slaves, on the other hand, became still more restless and more determined to end their servitude.

—*Nancy Conn Terjesen*

Suggested Readings:

Aptheker, Herbert. *Nat Turner's Slave Rebellion.* New York: Grove Press, 1966.

Baker, James T. *Nat Turner: Cry Freedom in America.* Fort Worth: Harcourt Brace, 1998.

Davis, Mary K. *Nat Turner Before the Bar of Judgment: Fictional Treatments of the Southampton Slave Insurrection.* Baton Rouge: Louisiana State University Press, 1999.

Foner, Eric, ed. *Nat Turner.* Englewood Cliffs, N.J.: Prentice-Hall, 1971.

Lindsay, Jack. *Turner.* Chicago: Academy Chicago Publishers, 1981.

Oates, Stephen B. *The Fires of Jubilee: Nat Turner's Fierce Rebellion.* New York: Harper & Row, 1975.

Stone, Albert E. *The Return of Nat Turner: History, Literature, and Cultural Politics in Sixties America.* Athens: University of Georgia Press, 1992.

Tragle, Henry. *The Southampton Slave Revolt of 1831.* Amherst, Mass.: 1971.

Turner, Thomas Wyatt (April 16, 1877, Hughesville, Maryland—April 21, 1978, Washington, D.C.): Scientist and religious activist. Turner had a distinguished career as a biologist and dean of HOWARD UNIVERSITY (1914-1920) and HAMPTON INSTITUTE (1924-1945). Primarily, however, Turner was the leading opponent of racism in the ROMAN CATHOLIC Church. In 1924 he founded the Federation of Colored Catholics. He bitterly fought its absorption in 1935 into the Catholic Interracial Council, which he regarded as white-dominated and passive. Turner remained a militant yet loyal Catholic. He was also a charter member of the NATIONAL ASSOCIATION FOR THE ADVANCEMENT OF COLORED PEOPLE.

Turner, Tina (Anna Mae Bullock; b. November 26, 1939, Brownsville, Tennessee): Rock and SOUL MUSIC singer. Turner was born in Brownsville, TENNESSEE's Haywood Memorial Hospital, at which African American patients were treated in the basement. Shortly after her birth, she was sent back to Nut Bush, Tennessee, where the Bullock family lived. She was the second child of Floyd Richard Bullock, who worked as a manager for a cotton plantation and served as a deacon of the

Woodlawn Baptist Church, and Zelma Bullock. Her older sister, Alline, was nearly three years old at the time of Turner's birth. The Bullocks were divorced when Turner was eleven years old. After the divorce, the two girls moved in with their grandmother.

Turner began singing and dancing when she was a schoolgirl. In class talent shows, she would excel at singing ballads and operatic numbers. Normally a shy child, she found singing to be a wonderful outlet. In the church choir, she got a chance to sing gospel hymns, but it was the blues songs that she belted out at picnics that she really loved. After her grandmother died in the mid-1950's, Turner and her sister moved to St. Louis, MISSOURI, to live with their mother. In St. Louis, they frequented nightclubs where rhythm and blues

Tina Turner performs at a song contest in San Remo, Italy, in February, 2000. *(AP/Wide World Photos)*

was played. It was at one of these nightclubs in 1956 that Turner met guitarist Ike Turner and his band, the Kings of Rhythm. It took almost a year of her pestering before Ike gave her a chance to sing. He was so impressed by her voice that he allowed her to sing with the band on occasional engagements. When she did join the band, she used the name "Little Ann."

In 1962 the couple married. Shortly thereafter, Ike convinced Anna to change her name to Tina. Turner eventually got her chance to sing lead at a recording session when the scheduled vocalist failed to show up. The single that was recorded, "A Fool for Love," became a hit, selling 800,000 copies. Ike decided to transform their band into the Ike and Tina Turner Revue, with Tina becoming the lead singer and the focal point of the group. Under Ike's supervision, the Revue blended gospel, rock, blues, and even country music into a powerful mix. During the 1960's, the Ike and Tina Turner Revue had a number of hits, including "It's Gonna Work Out Fine," "River Deep, Mountain High," and "Proud Mary." Tina Turner was an electrifying performer and in 1973 wrote the hit song "Nut Bush City Limits." Ike and Tina separated in 1976 and were divorced in 1978. Tina Turner related in her 1986 autobiography, *I, Tina*, that Ike was an abusive husband.

After a number of years of floundering, Turner, with the help of such friends as the Rolling Stones and Rod Stewart, began to rebuild her singing career in the early 1980's. In 1984 she released the album *Private Dancer*, which became a huge success. The album included the hit songs "Better Be Good to Me" and "What's Love Got to Do with It." Turner won a number of Grammy Awards for *Private Dancer*. She also attempted to build an acting career, appearing in the Who's rock opera film *Tommy* (1975) and in *Mad Max Beyond Thunderdome* (1985).

Released in 1986, Turner's second solo album, *Break Every Rule*, went platinum. She followed it with a concert tour album, *Tina Live in Europe* (1988), and other successful albums. Her best-selling autobiography was adapted to a successful film, *What's Love Got to Do with It* in 1993. Three years later her album *Wildest Dreams* launched her on a worldwide tour. Meanwhile, she was inducted into the Rock and Roll Hall of Fame in 1991.

Tuskegee Airmen: African Americans trained at Tuskegee Institute during WORLD WAR II to become pilots in the U.S. Air Force. In early 1941, responding to pressure from African American organizations, the U.S. Army established a special unit at Tuskegee, ALABAMA, to train African American pilots. Despite the racism that hampered their training, the Tuskegee Airmen became distinguished pilots during World War II.

As members of the 332d Fighter Group and as graduates of the segregated pilot training program at Tuskegee, Alabama, the Tuskegee Airmen accomplished unmatched aerial feats in World War II. Two of their records were still standing in the 1990's: First, during more than two hundred missions as heavy bomber escorts, they never lost an escorted bomber to enemy fighters; second, in a unique instance of aerial gunnery, they managed to sink a German navy destroyer with aircraft gunfire. After World War II, a select group of black fighter pilots from the 332d took first place in the first National Gunnery Meet in Las Vegas, Nevada.

Fifty years after the unit's daring work, the accomplishments of the Tuskegee Airmen have received wider public attention. As part of its commemoration of the fiftieth anniversary of the end of World War II, the Department of Defense sponsored the dedication of a Tuskegee Airmen World War II Living Memorial at Arlington National Cemetery. In addition, a made-for-television film entitled *Tuskegee Airmen* was aired on the Home Box

Cadets in the first group of airmen to train at Tuskegee line up for review in early 1942. *(AP/Wide World Photos)*

Office cable channel in 1995. The film's cast included Laurence Fishburne, Malcolm-Jamal Warner, Courtney Vance, Allen Payne, and Cuba Gooding, Jr. Based on a script written by Trey Ellis, along with Ron Hutchinson and Paris H. Qualles, the film accurately depicts the many accomplishments of the "Fighting" Ninety-ninth Pursuit Squadron of the 332d Fighter Group. Producer Robert W. Williams, a veteran of the 332d Fighter Group, worked with director Robert Markowitz to create a powerful history that premiered at the Tuskegee Airmen National Convention held in Atlanta, Georgia, in August of 1995, and later was viewed at the White House.

Museums nationwide are also featuring the Tuskegee Airmen in their aviation, World War II, and African American history activities. For example, the Smithsonian Institution's "The Dream to Fly Collection" and the Chicago Oral History Project include repositories of oral history gathered from Tuskegee Airmen. In turn, the National Museum of the Tuskegee Airmen (located in Detroit, Michigan), the Wright Patterson Air Force Base Museum (located in Ohio), the Cantigny Museum (located in Chicago, Illinois), the U.S. Air Force Academy, and other institutions have created prominent displays dedicated to the Tuskegee Airmen. As part of their own efforts to educate the public about their role in the war effort, the Tuskegee Airmen themselves have taken their story directly out to schools, churches, and community centers through their speakers bureau and national and international press coverage.

To keep the dream of flight alive among American youth, the Tuskegee Airmen also provide academic scholarships and support flying programs. For example, the Chicago chapter has sponsored monthly airplane rides for up to one hundred junior high school boys and girls. The Detroit chapter sponsors extensive flight programs that include ground

Pilots of the Fifteenth U.S. Army Air Force being briefed before a mission over Italy in September, 1944. *(National Archives)*

Future general Benjamin O. Davis, Jr., climbs into a training plane in January, 1942. *(National Archives)*

school training and twelve hours of flying. In other school-related activities, local chapters have also provided long-term mentor and academic programs. Moreover, the organization National Tuskegee Airmen, Inc., provides $1,500 scholarships to thirty-six students every year. The national and local chapter scholarships are open to high school seniors and are primarily based on financial need and grades.

—*Yolandea M. Wood*

Suggested Readings:

Dryden, Charles W. *A-Train: Memoirs of a Tuskegee Airman*. Tuscaloosa: University of Alabama Press, 1997.

Francis, Charles E. *The Tuskegee Airmen: The Men Who Changed a Nation*. Boston: Branden, 1988.

McGee Smith, Charlene E., and Adolph Caso. *Tuskegee Airman: The Biography of Charles E. McGee, Air Force Fighter Combat Record Holder*. Boston, Branden, 1999.

Osur, Alan M. *Blacks in the Army Air Forces During World War II: The Problem of Race Relations*. Washington, D.C.: Office of Air Force History, 1977.

Rose, Robert A. *Lonely Eagles: The Story of America's Black Air Force in World War II*. Los Angeles: Tuskegee Airmen, Los Angeles Chapter, 1980.

Scott, Lawrence P., and William M. Womack. *Double V: The Civil Rights Struggle of the Tuskegee Airmen*. East Lansing: Michigan State University Press, 1994.

Tuskegee experiments: Medical experiments conducted on African American men by the federal government between 1932 and 1972. In 1932 the U.S. Public Health Service (PHS) began a study of the effects of untreated syphilis on human beings. The study was performed in the area around Tuskegee, Alabama. African American men in advanced stages of syphilis infection were promised free medical attention, hot meals, and burial insurance in exchange for their participation in the study. An uninfected control group, again composed of African American men, was created for comparison purposes. All told, some six hundred black men, almost all of them poor and uneducated, took part in the study.

Because the experiment was designed to increase understanding of the effects of syphilis, the participants were not treated for their illness. In its final stages, syphilis can cause paralysis and mental derangement, and it leads to death. PHS officials later claimed that the participants were told that they had syphilis, but this assertion was contradicted by reports from both doctors and patients. In any case, the subjects of the experiment were denied medical care appropriate for their condition.

Stories concerning the Tuskegee experiment appeared in medical journals on occasion, but the study did not become public knowledge until a reporter published a story about it in 1972. In response to the ensuing furor, some PHS officials defended the study.

President Bill Clinton (right) and Vice President Al Gore assist Herman Shaw at a 1997 news conference, during which Clinton apologized to Shaw and other men whose syphilis had been left untreated by government doctors participating in the Tuskegee experiments. *(AP/Wide World Photos)*

They maintained that the medical treatments for syphilis available in 1932 would have done little to help men infected with the disease. They also claimed that providing the subjects with penicillin, which became the standard treatment for syphilis during the 1940's, might have harmed them because they had suffered from the disease for so long.

These defenses did not impress critics, who argued that the Tuskegee experiment violated medical ethics and evidenced racism on the part of government officials. Some compared the study to the gruesome medical experiments that were conducted in Nazi Germany. The claim that the study's originators withheld medical care during the 1930's because available treatments were not effective (or, in some cases, were dangerous) did not explain why only poor African Americans were in-cluded in the study. The refusal to offer the men penicillin was found to have no medical basis. In an effort to remedy the damage that the revelation of study had caused, the U.S. government guaranteed complete health care for the surviving members of the study. However, it did not offer any compensation, so study participants responded with a class action lawsuit. The government settled out of court, offering cash payments to the survivors and to the heirs of participants who had died.

The Tuskegee experiment did not contribute to the medical understanding of syphilis, and it provided no information regarding treatment or possible cures. The only positive effect of the study was the revision of federal guidelines for medical studies involving human beings. Within the African American community, the study increased suspicions and anger concerning the racism prevalent in American society and among government officials.

—*Thomas Clarkin*

Suggested Readings:

Jones, James H. *Bad Blood: The Tuskegee Syphilis Experiment*. Rev. ed. New York: Free Press, 1993.

Tuskegee Institute (Tuskegee, Alabama): School established in 1881 by Booker T. WASH-INGTON. Now a professional and technical university, the institute evolved from a modest beginning as an industrial school with thirty students in one shanty room. The campus encompasses five thousand acres. About three thousand students attended in 1992, and more than fifty-seven thousand had graduated from the institute since its inception. The school's history is significant to the understanding of the American dual system of education.

After the CIVIL WAR, the battle for control over the education of African Americans continued. In the 1880's, industrial philanthropists who realized the importance of shaping postsecondary training for African Americans expanded programs of industrial education. These curricula did not meet the educational aspirations of African Americans; black schools, however, could not afford to ignore the availability of philanthropic funds. This new focus represented a pragmatic move rather than a commitment to the social and educational philosophy of industrial training.

Industrial education was the core agenda at Tuskegee in its early years, consisting of masonry, carpentry, printing, skilled trades, domestic arts for women, and character development. Botanist George Washington CARVER joined the faculty in 1896 and stayed for forty-seven years, until his death. Christian dogma, moral sense, dignity of labor, self-reliance, thrift, and industry were among the middle-class values that Booker T. Washington tried to instill, hoping to achieve racial equality for his people. His accommodationist views explain why whites made him the spokesperson for African Americans and why his adversaries adamantly opposed him. W. E. B. DU BOIS, his toughest critic, believed that "education makes men, not workers"; through a liberal arts curriculum, schools should articulate the sources of oppression, identify the aspirations and struggles of African Americans, and lead toward greater freedom and justice.

Tuskegee Institute was seen as a model by

Booker T. Washington, the founder of Tuskegee Institute. *(Arkent Archive)*

Uniformed Tuskegee students in 1906. *(Library of Congress)*

first saw service in the Spanish-American War at Daiquiri, near Guantánamo Bay, in Cuba. On July 1, 1888, a battalion of the infantry attacked the El Caney garrison and won the position. *See also:* Military.

Twenty-fourth Infantry: Black U.S. Army unit in service during the Indian wars, the SPANISH-AMERICAN WAR, WORLD WAR I, and WORLD WAR II. The unit spent more than a month in combat in CUBA in 1888 before being ordered back to Siboney. Yellow fever had broken out there, and members of the Twenty-fourth Infantry responded to a call for volunteers to nurse the sick and dying and to bury the dead. More than 60 of the approximately 450 men volunteered. The regiment also helped capture the New Georgia Islands from Japan in May, 1942, and won one of the first victories in the KOREAN WAR. The unit was deactivated on October 1, 1951. It was the last all-black unit in the U.S. Army and had been one of the first four such units created.
See also: Military.

white southerners and philanthropic northerners. From RECONSTRUCTION to the GREAT DEPRESSION era, HIGHER EDUCATION for African Americans took the form of training for industrial jobs rather than for changing social conditions. Two years of contention and unrest led to changes in the model in 1929. Students proclaimed that their "Du Bois ambition" could not be mixed with a "Washington education," and their demand for standard institutions of higher learning soon materialized.

The main emphasis at Tuskegee became science and technology. The school offered students a choice of forty-five undergraduate degrees in 1992, along with twenty-five master's degrees and a doctorate in veterinary medicine. Students could also gain experience and financial assistance by working in industry through a program of cooperative education. *See also:* Hampton Institute; Historically black colleges.

Twenty-fifth Infantry: Black U.S. Army unit in service during the Indian wars, the SPANISH-AMERICAN WAR, and WORLD WAR I. The unit

2 Live Crew: RAP group. The group's lead rapper, Luther Campbell, grew up as the youngest of four brothers in Liberty City, a ghetto neighborhood in Miami, FLORIDA. Campbell's father worked as a custodian, and his mother helped to support the family by working as a hairdresser. Campbell began his music career during his teens as a street deejay, using the name "Luke Skyywalker." He graduated from Miami Beach High School in 1978 and played football as a linebacker on the school's team.

Campbell became involved as a rap promoter for shows at Miami area schools, parks, and recreational facilities that featured popular groups such as RUN-D.M.C. and the Fat Boys. He started on the local rap circuit as the frontman for the group Ghetto Style DJs and made his own solo recordings as a rapper before joining a Southern California crew called the 2 Live Crew in 1985. 2 Live Crew was one of the first to popularize the Miami rap sound. The group became known for its hard-core lyrics, often containing sexually explicit language and misogynistic themes. Its first hit, "Throw the D." (1986), was recorded on Campbell's own record label, called Skyywalker Records, and sold approximately 250,000 copies. *2 Live Is What We Are* (1986) and *Move Somethin'* (1987) sold almost one million copies each.

2 Live Crew's precedent-setting album *As Nasty as They Wanna Be* (1989) sold nearly two million copies and was the first record declared legally obscene in an American court of law. Although some listeners accused the group of promoting serious hard-core pornography, most critics noted that 2 Live Crew's live performances—while crude and risqué—had the atmosphere of a raunchy stag party. As a result of the album's notoriety, *Star Wars* filmmaker George Lucas filed a $300 million lawsuit to prevent Campbell from using the name "Luke Skyywalker" as his record label. Campbell changed the label's name to Luke Records and was able to settle the Lucas lawsuit out of court with a settlement of $300,000. The obscenity ruling against *As Nasty as They Wanna Be* was overturned by a federal appeals court in Florida in 1992.

The title single from the group's 1990 album, *Banned in the USA*, addressed the issue of the court battles. Bruce Springsteen gave his written consent for the group to use the melody from his hit song "Born in the USA." In an effort to protect musical artists from what it viewed as creeping censorship, Atlantic records agreed to release the group's single and negotiated a partnership deal to distribute new recordings by artists on Campbell's Luke Records label. Campbell had stated his concerns that his company had been singled out unfairly because of its independent status and reiterated his claim that he had always labeled the group's albums as containing explicit lyrics in accordance with guidelines proposed by parents' groups. By mid-1990 Campbell's corporation had grossed more than $17 million in record sales alone. 2 Live Crew's 1991 album, *Sports Weekend: As Nasty as They Wanna Be II*, was released with a warning label stating "Parental Advisory—Explicit Lyrics." The group also recorded the song "In the Dust" for the sound track of the film *New Jack City* (1991).

Tyner, McCoy (b. December 11, 1938, Philadelphia, Pennsylvania): Pianist. Alfred McCoy Tyner began studying music at an early age, starting his formal studies at the age of thirteen and then moving on to take theory

McCoy Tyner in 1977. *(AP/Wide World Photos)*

Tyson, Cicely

lessons at the Granoff School of Music. Among his early influences was the work of Richie and Bud Powell, Art TATUM, and Thelonius MONK. Tyner joined the Benny Golson-Art Farmer Jazztet in 1959, then went on to play with John COLTRANE's quartet from 1960 to 1965.

In addition to his work with Coltrane and others, Tyner made a series of recordings under his own name for the Blue Note and Impulse labels, including *Inception* (1962) and *The Real McCoy* (1967). After a brief lull in the later 1960's, his career surged when he began to record for Milestone in 1972. He released *Sahara* in 1972, *Supertrio* in 1977, and *Four Times Four* in 1980. He toured and recorded with the Milestone Jazzstars in 1978, and in the mid-1980's, he led a quintet including Gary Bartz and John Blake. A volume of his transcriptions, *Inception to Now*, was published in 1983.

Tyson, Cicely (b. December 19, 1939, New York, New York): Stage, television, and FILM actor. Tyson earned acclaim for her work in theater, film, and television. She grew up in the Upper East Side of Manhattan, the youngest of three children of a couple from Nevis, one of the Leeward Islands in the WEST INDIES. The impoverished family found various means to support itself. Cicely's father, William, worked as a carpenter and painter and, at times, sold fruit from a pushcart. Her mother, Theodosia, worked as a domestic. At age nine, Tyson also helped to support the family by selling shopping bags on the streets.

When Tyson was eleven, her parents divorced, and her mother retained custody of the children. A fundamentalist religious woman, her mother forbade Tyson to date before the age of seventeen and prohibited her from attending films or the theater. Tyson spent most of her spare time at church, where she enjoyed the religious and social life of the congregation.

Upon graduating from Manhattan's Charles Evans Hughes High School, she obtained a secretarial position with the Red Cross but soon grew tired of the monotony of her work. One day she decided, "I know God did not put me on the face of this earth to bang on a typewriter for the rest of my life." Shortly afterward, she began working as a model, appearing in such magazines as *Vogue* and *Harper's Bazaar*. Her interest in acting was encouraged by the producers of an independent film, "The Spectrum." The film was never completed, but Tyson decided she would seek training for her newfound career.

Career Beginnings
Tyson studied briefly at New York University and with director Lloyd Richards. Director Vinnette Carroll cast her in her first starring role as Barbara Allen in a 1957 production of *Dark of the Moon*. After winning the position of understudy for Eartha KITT in a 1959 production of *Jolly's Progress* and performing in a variety showcase on Broadway called *Talent '59*, she undertook roles in several television shows, including productions of *Between Yesterday and Today* in 1959 and *Brown Girl, Brownstones* in 1960. Her first film role was little more than a bit part in *Odds Against Tomorrow* (1959).

After a minor role in a 1960 production of *The Cool World*, Tyson played a prostitute, Virtue, in Jean Genet's controversial 1961 play *The Blacks*. The drama proved to be the biggest break of her career, as she was cast with such actors as James Earl JONES, Roscoe Lee Browne, and Godfrey CAMBRIDGE. Catching the notice of critics, she won the Vernon Rice Award for outstanding achievement in Off-Broadway theater. A year later, she won the award again for her portrayal of another prostitute, Mavis, in the 1962 production of Errol John's *Moon on a Rainbow Shawl*.

Impressed with her performance in *The Blacks*, actor and director George C. Scott encouraged her casting in a role as his secretary on the critically acclaimed but short-lived television series *East Side/West Side*. Tyson became the first black actor with a continuing role in a dramatic TELEVISION SERIES.

Throughout the 1960's, Tyson continued to hone her craft in such plays as *Tiger, Tiger Burning Bright* (1962), *Trumpets of the Lord* (1963), and *To Be Young, Gifted, and Black* (1969). She was one of the few black actors to work regularly on television, with guest appearances on such shows as *Slattery's People*, *I Spy*, *Medical Center*, and *The Courtship of Eddie's Father*. She won critical acclaim for her film roles in *A Man Called Adam* (1966), *The Comedians* (1967), and *The Heart Is a Lonely Hunter* (1968).

Breakthrough Roles

Tyson had to wait for four years after the release of *The Heart Is a Lonely Hunter* before she found a film role that she felt was not demean-

ing to black women. She found that role in the character of Rebecca Morgan in the 1972 film *Sounder*. The film centers on a black Louisiana sharecropping family (Sounder is their dog's name) and their struggle to survive and maintain their integrity amid the economic and racial hardships of the Depression. The film endeared itself to audiences. Black audiences were particularly impressed, because they rarely saw themselves depicted in close and nurturing relationships. Portraying the family's parents, Tyson and costar Paul Winfield received widespread praise, and both received Academy Award nominations. Tyson won best actor awards from the Atlanta Film Festival and the National Society of Film Critics.

In 1974 Tyson's success in *Sounder* was followed by a challenging television role. In *The Autobiography of Miss Jane Pittman*, Tyson portrayed a black woman from the age of nineteen

Cicely Tyson's performance in *Sounder* (1972) earned her numerous honors, including an Academy Award nomination. *(Museum of Modern Art, Film Stills Archive)*

Cicely Tyson in 1973. *(AP/Wide World Photos)*

to her 110th birthday. Through the life history of the woman, the film dramatized the social and political changes experienced by African Americans from the Civil War to the 1960's Civil Rights movement. Both the teleplay and Tyson's performance won the Critics Consensus Award for exceptional contributions to television. Her work also won Tyson an Emmy Award as best leading actor in a television special.

Other Roles

After her role as Jane Pittman, Tyson often appeared in theater, television, and film in works of uneven quality. Her performances in the drama *The Corn Is Green* (1983) and the films *The River Niger* (1976) and *Bustin' Loose* (1981) were overshadowed by criticism of the overall quality of the works. Television productions provided her most noteworthy roles, showcasing her ability to portray strong, dignified women. She played Coretta Scott KING in

King (1977) and Kunta Kinte's mother in the miniseries of Alex HALEY's *Roots* (1977). She won an Emmy nomination for her work on *Roots*. Tyson portrayed Harriet TUBMAN in *A Woman Called Moses* (1978) and Marva COLLINS in *The Marva Collins Story* (1981); she was also part of the female ensemble cast of *The Women of Brewster Place* (1989).

Tyson found few film scripts worthy of her attention until she was cast in *Fried Green Tomatoes* (1991). In 1994 Tyson won another Emmy Award, this time for her lead role as a savvy New Orleans defense attorney and civil rights defender in the NBC television series *Sweet Justice*.

In the late 1990's Tyson remained active in film (*Hoodlum*, 1997) and television (*Bridge of Time*, 1997; *Ms. Scrooge*, 1997; *Always Outnumbered*, 1998).

Personal Life and Awards

Tyson and jazz trumpeter Miles DAVIS were married in 1981 at the home of Bill COSBY. Former U.N. ambassador and Atlanta mayor Andrew YOUNG married the couple, and Cosby served as best man. Tyson was later divorced from Davis, who died in 1991.

In addition to acting, Tyson was one of the founders and board members of the DANCE THEATER OF HARLEM; she served on the board of governors of Urban Gateways, an arts program for children; and as a trustee for the American Film Institute and Human Family Institute. For her accomplishments as an actor and humanitarian, Tyson received National Association for the Advancement of Colored People (NAACP) IMAGE AWARDS in 1970, 1982, and 1986; honorary degrees from Atlanta, Loyola, and Lincoln Universities; and the Wonder Woman Foundation's Roosevelt Women of Courage Award (1983). In 1977 she was inducted into the Black Filmmakers Hall of Fame.

—*Addell Austin Anderson*
—*Updated by Dorothy C. Salem*

Suggested Readings:

Bogle, Donald. *Brown Sugar: Eighty Years of America's Black Female Superstars*. New York: Harmony Books, 1980.

Davis, Marianna W., ed. *Contributions of Black Women to America, Volume I: The Arts, Media, Business, Law, Sports*. Columbia, S.C.: Kendey Press, 1982.

Ebert, Alan. "Inside Cicely." *Essence* (February, 1973): 40-41.

Robinson, Alice M., Vera Mowry Roberts, and Milly S. Barranger, eds. *Notable Women in the American Theatre*. New York: Greenwood Press, 1989.

Robinson, Louie. "Cicely Tyson, a Very Unlikely Movie Star." *Ebony* (May, 1974): 33-36.

Tyson, Cicely. "Talking with . . . Cicely Tyson." Interview with Natasha Stoynoff. *People* (November 9, 1998): 31.

Tyson, Mike (b. June 30, 1966, Brooklyn, New York): Boxer. Michael Gerard "Mike" Tyson, the youngest of three children in a single-parent family, grew up in the impoverished Brownsville section of Brooklyn. After winding up in a reform school as a teenager, Tyson learned BOXING skills and attracted the attention of the famous trainer Gus D'Amato. D'Amato became Tyson's legal guardian and worked closely with the young fighter to refine his talents.

In 1981 and 1982, Tyson won Junior Olympiad championships, and in 1983 and 1984 he was a U.S. Junior Champion. Also in 1984, Tyson won the National Golden Gloves heavyweight championship, but he lost a spot on the 1984 U.S. Olympic Team when he was defeated by Henry Tillman at the Olympic trials. (Tyson would later defeat Tillman as a professional.)

Heavyweight Championship and Prison
In early 1985, Tyson turned professional and rapidly earned the attention of the boxing world. A stocky five-foot, eleven-inch fighter with explosive punching power, he won twenty-three of his first twenty-five professional fights by knockout. In November, 1986, Tyson knocked out Trevor Berbick to win the World Boxing Council (WBC) heavyweight title. At twenty years of age, he was the youngest heavyweight champion in history. In 1987 he unified the heavyweight title by defeating the champions of the World Boxing Association (WBA) and the International Boxing Federation (IBF).

A series of widely publicized personal troubles, including an acrimonious divorce from actor Robin Givens, did not seem to affect Tyson's performance in the ring, where he continued to awe fans and intimidate opponents with his ferocity and power. In February,

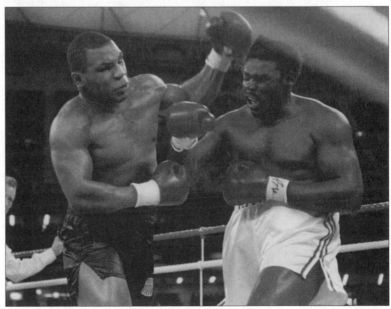

In March, 1988, Mike Tyson (left) knocked out challenger Tony Tubbs in the second round of a title defense in Tokyo. *(AP/Wide World Photos)*

Tyson leaving the Indiana courthouse where he was arraigned on criminal rape charges in September, 1991. *(AP/Wide World Photos)*

Tyson's status as a convicted rapist created controversy soon after his release. Tyson fans in New York's HARLEM district planned a parade honoring the boxer and thanking him for donating one million dollars to local charities. Angered that Tyson was to be celebrated as a hero, protesters organized a candlelight vigil against violence the night before the parade. Tyson refused an invitation to attend the event. The conflict caused parade supporters to cancel the event and merely offer a "salute" to Tyson instead.

1990, however, Tyson was knocked out by James "Buster" Douglas, who was so lightly regarded that most oddsmakers refused to accept bets on the fight. Then, while waiting for a match with Evander Holyfield, who took the title from Douglas in October, 1990, Tyson was indicted by an Indiana grand jury on charges that he had raped a beauty-contest competitor. He was convicted of rape and other charges on February 10, 1992, and sentenced to several twenty-year prison terms.

Tyson served four years in an Indiana penitentiary. Although he continued to claim that he was innocent of the rape charge, he acknowledged that he had put himself in an awkward position that left him open to such an accusation. While in prison, Tyson continued his physical training and read extensively, developing an interest in black history. He had been baptized by the Reverend Jesse JACKSON into the BAPTIST faith in 1988, but he turned to ISLAM during his incarceration. After his release in March of 1995, he went directly to a mosque to offer prayers to Allah.

Return to Boxing

Although Tyson was eager to return to boxing, commentators questioned his ability to compete professionally, pointing to his 1990 loss to Douglas as evidence that he had been in decline before entering prison. They also questioned Tyson's business relationship with Don King, a controversial boxing promoter accused by many of cheating Tyson out of millions of dollars. King remained Tyson's exclusive promoter despite these accusations.

Tyson declared his intention to regain the undisputed heavyweight championship, which meant that he had to defeat several boxers who held titles from various boxing associations. Tyson fought Peter McNeeley in a nontitle bout in August of 1995. He knocked McNeeley down twice before McNeeley's manager entered the ring to stop the fight. Lasting only eighty-nine seconds, the match angered fans, who argued that either the fight was fixed or King was scheduling Tyson against easy opponents in order to make money. Tyson reportedly earned $25 million for the McNeeley bout.

In his next nontitle bout, Tyson fought James "Buster" Mathis, Jr. Mathis lasted three rounds, far longer than most sportscasters had predicted. Tyson's victory over Mathis convinced many that "Iron Mike" still retained the ability and desire to consolidate the various titles and regain his position as the best heavyweight boxer in the world. In his first title bout since his release from prison, Tyson defeated British boxer Frank Bruno on March 16, 1996, and regained the World Boxing Council (WBC) heavyweight title.

In June, 1997, however, Tyson shocked the boxing world during his title bout with Evander Holyfield: He bit off a part of Holyfield's ear. Tyson was fined almost $3 million, and his boxing license was revoked (he would be eligible to reapply for his license in a year). In 1998 Tyson sued promoter King, alleging that King had cheated him out of millions of dollars; later that year his license to box was reinstated. In February, 1999, Tyson defeated Francois Botha in Las Vegas. Two weeks later he was sentenced to jail for assaulting two motorists after a traffic accident. He was released in June, 1999. In October of that year Tyson fought Orlin Norris in Las Vegas; the fight was halted after Tyson threw an illegal punch at his opponent after the bell had rung to end the first round. Unable to obtain a license to fight in the United States, Tyson fought next in Great Britain in early 2000.

—*Updated by Thomas Clarkin*

Suggested Readings:

Berger, Phil. *Blood Season: Mike Tyson and the World of Boxing*. 2d ed. New York: Four Walls Eight Windows, 1996.

Gutteridge, Reg. *Mike Tyson: The Release of Power*. Toronto: Warwick, 1996.

Hoffer, Richard. *A Savage Business: The Comeback and Comedown of Mike Tyson*. New York: Simon and Schuster, 1998.

U

Ujamaa: Term taken from the Swahili language. It refers to familyhood, communal life, or communal development and is often associated with the African concept of socialism. Ujamaa is also the fourth day of the week-long KWANZAA holiday. It commemorates the goals of cooperative economics and of building and maintaining business enterprises to be profited from collectively.

Uncle Tom's Cabin (1852): Novel by Harriet Beecher Stowe (1811-1896). *Uncle Tom's Cabin: Or, Life Among the Lowly* reflects New Englander Stowe's strong antislavery sentiments. The book was based on her observations of the lives of slaves during a trip she made to the South. It was also based in her deep-seated belief that, as a Christian, it was her calling to expose the evils of SLAVERY in her writing.

The novel centers on a noble African American slave, Tom, who is a devout Christian. Tom is owned by the Shelby family, which has to sell him because of financial problems. Tom then spends two happy years in the household with a young girl named Eva and her father. After both Eva and her father die, Tom is sold by Eva's mother at auction to a cruel planter, Simon Legree. When Tom refuses to reveal the hiding place of two female slaves, he is beaten to death. Shortly before he dies, the son of his original owner arrives, hoping to buy Tom

Illustration from the first edition of *Uncle Tom's Cabin*, depicting Little Eva reading to Uncle Tom from the Bible. *(Library of Congress)*

back so he can free him. After Tom dies, the young man returns to Kentucky and frees all his family's slaves.

Because it is a southerner who sees the light and frees his slaves and it is a former northerner, Legree, who personifies the evils of slave ownership, many contemporary readers regarded Stowe's book as a balanced treatment of its subject matter. Initially serialized in a magazine in 1851-1852, *Uncle's Tom Cabin*, was an immediate success, and it was a runaway bestseller in book form throughout the 1850's.

Uncle Tom's Cabin was one of the most influential works in the United States in the mid-nineteenth century, and it helped stir abolitionist fervor in the North. After the CIVIL WAR ended in 1865, President Abraham Lincoln is supposed to have met with Stowe and told her that she had written a book that "started a big war." The novel has been one of the most frequently translated and republished works in American literature.

The novel has been criticized for presenting a false picture of how African American slaves felt about slavery. Many twentieth century African American writers and scholars, including Richard WRIGHT and James BALDWIN, wrote essays challenging the authenticity of the book's portrayal of the African American experience. Nonetheless, Stowe did the best she could to depict for her readership the devastating effects of slavery on slave families, the brutality of slavery, and the lengths to which slaves would go to escape. Because of Uncle Tom's willingness to acquiesce to his masters, the term "Uncle Tom" has come to refer to a black person who, in order to please white society, turns away from African American culture.

—*Qun Wang*

Underground Railroad: Vast informal network of paths through southern fields and woods, fords across rivers, and safe houses where slave runaways could hide while fleeing to free territories in the north. The Underground Railroad helped thousands of southern slaves escape to freedom. It had many "conductors" or agents—men and women, blacks and whites—who aided and hid runaways along their routes. Some of these conductors became so famous that their names are still known; many others worked in anonymity.

The railroad north became a network of "stations" located about a day's journey apart. Conductors told runaways how to reach the next station; sometimes they personally escorted the escapees. As the Underground Railroad grew, so did the "grapevine telegraph": Word was passed from station to station to prepare transportation and safe hiding places for new fugitives. From 1820 to 1860, an average of perhaps twenty-five hundred—possibly more—slaves reached freedom every year via the Underground Railroad.

The Runaways

Of all the heroes involved in the railroad, the bravest were the runaways themselves. William Still, an underground agent in PHILADELPHIA, wrote that

> guided by the north star alone . . . penniless, braving the perils of land and sea, eluding the keen scent of the blood-hound as well as the more dangerous pursuit of the savage slavehunter . . . [surviving] indescribable suffering from hunger and other privations, the fugitives made their way to freedom.

Most slaves walked their way to freedom, but a few concocted ingenious escapes. Henry "Box" Brown, for example, had been a model slave in Richmond, VIRGINIA, but he grew resentful as his life slipped away in servitude. Then, disaster struck: His wife and children were sold to a new owner in NORTH CAROLINA. Crushed, he decided to run away. He turned to a white Virginian, Samuel A. Smith, who was a conductor of the Underground

Railroad. They found a box big enough to hold a man. Brown got in; Smith handed him a few biscuits and a water bag before nailing down the box lid. Smith then shipped Brown to the Philadelphia Vigilance Committee, an abolitionist group. The runaway eventually arrived safely, even though he had traveled upside down for part of his trip.

Men under thirty years of age were most likely to run away, although young women often joined them. Usually slaves escaped alone or in small groups. Slaves were most likely to run during the warm months of late spring, summer, and early fall. The desire for freedom was so strong that not only field hands but also relatively well-treated domestics and artisans left. As the Underground Railroad became more fully developed from the 1840's onward, entire families, including children, ran together.

Once slaves were on the run, they would typically seek slaves along their route who seemed trustworthy and who would supply the runaways with food and with geographical information. Some white groups were also likely to aid escapees. In southern TEXAS, antislavery Germans of the hill country frequently helped runaways get to the Rio Grande, where Mexicans helped them cross to freedom. In the upper South, some QUAKERS became conductors for the Underground Railroad. Disguised as peddlers or census takers, abolitionists frequently roamed the South, trying to make contacts with potential runaways.

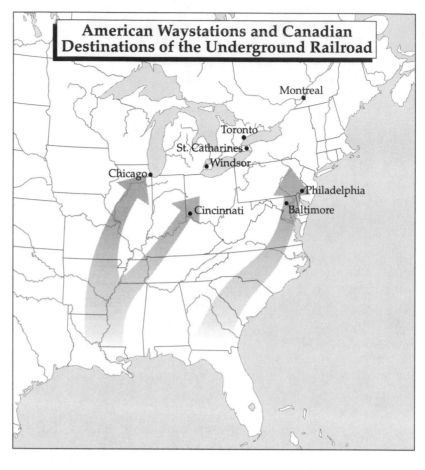

American Waystations and Canadian Destinations of the Underground Railroad

Development of the Underground Railroad
As early as the mid-1780's, George Washington wrote that Quakers had organized the Abolition Society of Pennsylvania and that its members harbored runaways. The society's membership included such non-Quakers as Thomas Paine, Benjamin Franklin, and the Marquis de Lafayette, all heroes of the AMERICAN REVOLUTION.

Although records are sparse regarding the early work of the Underground Railroad, it is known that by 1787 Isaac T. Hopper, while still a teenager, had settled in Philadelphia, where he began a systematic, well-organized program to free slaves. Soon he was contacting abolitionist leaders in other Pennsylvania towns. He also included many New Jersey villages within his range. Hopper's work led to the liberation of hundreds of slaves even before the beginning of the nineteenth century and well before the emergence of militant abolitionism in the 1820's.

A particularly dramatic event occurred in 1804. General Thomas Boude, a veteran of the Revolution, bought a slave named Stephen Smith. Boude took Smith to Columbia, Pennsylvania, the general's home, and freed him. Soon Smith's mother arrived at the Boude home; she had escaped from slavery in order to find her son. A few weeks later, the owner of Smith's mother came to Columbia and demanded that Boude return her. Boude refused the woman's demand, and the entire town resolved to support the general and to champion the cause of all fugitives who came their way.

Slowly, the network grew, and by 1815, conductors could be found as far west as OHIO. By 1831 all the northern states adjacent to the slave South had flourishing stations, conductors, and means for fast travel—farm wagons, some especially built with closed compartments, covered wagons, and closed carriages. Passage of the FUGITIVE SLAVE LAW of 1850, which officially recognized the right of southern slaveowners to retrieve runaways from the North, made freedom in the North more precarious. As a result, after 1850 Canada became the major destination of fugitives on the Underground Railroad.

Destinations

There were several Underground Railroad routes. Slaves in western LOUISIANA, Texas, and western slave territories usually headed south for MEXICO. Those from eastern Louisiana, Mississippi, Alabama, and Tennessee usually moved westward until they came to the Mississippi River. They then followed it to the Ohio River and crossed into freedom in one of the states in the Old Northwest Territories land; some continued on to Canada from there. KENTUCKY slaves also headed for the Old Northwest and Canada. From GEORGIA and FLORIDA, runaways most often headed for the Florida Keys, where they hoped that they could find a ship captain to sail them to freedom. From the Carolinas northward to the MASON-DIXON LINE, escapees traveled straight north, hoping to reach Pennsylvania, New Jersey, the New England states, and Canada.

The Conductors

Many former slaves who escaped became Underground Railroad conductors because they sought freedom for their family and friends. A former slave known to history only as Ben, for example, escaped from Kentucky by crossing

Virginia house near Manassas used on the Underground Railroad. *(Library of Congress)*

the Ohio River and hiding in Ohio. Subsequently, he made several trips back to Kentucky in the 1830's to rescue others, but he was finally caught and reenslaved. Many free African Americans also hated the institution of slavery so much that they helped slaves escape.

The most famous conductor of the Underground Railroad was Harriet Tubman. Born a slave on MARYLAND's Eastern Shore in 1821, she was severely abused by her owner. Once he almost killed her. In 1849, at the age of twenty-eight, she decided to run away. She traveled by night and hid in caves and graveyards by day; she walked upstream in creeks and rivers to escape dog packs. She ultimately reached Philadelphia and freedom. Because she missed the friends and family that she had left behind, she became a conductor. Between 1849 and 1861, she made nineteen trips back to the South and liberated more than three hundred slaves. Becoming a legendary figure, and finally having a forty-thousand-dollar reward on her head, Tubman took pride that she never lost a single "passenger."

Although many conductors were black, others were white. A white conductor named Calvin Fairbanks operated in Kentucky, where he assisted slaves trying to get to the Northwest. There they could be placed in the hands of Levi Coffin, a Quaker who became known as the "president" of the Underground Railroad. Beginning in 1844, Fairbanks sent several slaves to Coffin, but Kentucky authorities caught Fairbanks in 1845 and sentenced him to fifteen years' imprisonment. He received a pardon in 1849 on condition that he leave Kentucky. He ignored the warning and continued to work in the state, "liberating," as he said, "slaves from hell." Arrested again in 1852, Fairbanks again faced a fifteen-year sentence—this time at hard labor. Not released until 1864, Fairbanks spent more than fifteen years of his life in prison as a consequence of his zeal.

Native Americans and Europeans also served as conductors. Ottawa chief Kinjeino in western Ohio was among the earliest Indian friends of slave runaways. Seminoles in Florida harbored runaways, intermarried with them, and accepted them into their tribes. Portuguese and other European fishermen sometimes allowed slaves living on the Atlantic Coast to come aboard ship and then took them to freedom.

At its peak in the 1850's, the Underground Railroad had at least thirty-two hundred active conductors (and probably thousands more whose names and personal histories have been lost). Indirectly, conductors did more than free thousands of slaves each year; they also kept the issue of slavery in the national focus, always condemning the institution as an abomination.

—*James Smallwood*
See also: Fishermen and whalers.

Suggested Readings:
Bial, Raymond. *The Underground Railroad.* Boston: Houghton Mifflin, 1999.
Blockson, Charles L. *Hippocrene Guide to the Underground Railroad.* New York: Hippocrene Books, 1994.
Breyfogle, William A. *Make Free: The Story of the Underground Railroad.* Philadelphia: J. B. Lippincott, 1958.
Buckmaster, Henrietta. *Let My People Go: The Story of the Underground Railroad and the Growth of the Abolition Movement.* New York: Harper & Brothers, 1941.
Gorrell, Gena K. *North Star to Freedom: The Story of the Underground Railroad.* Toronto: Stoddart, 1996.
Harding, Vincent. *There Is a River: The Black Struggle for Freedom in America.* New York: Vintage Books, 1983.
Runyon, Randolph, and William A. Davis. *Delia Webster and the Underground Railroad.* Lexington: University Press of Kentucky, 1996.

Scherman, Tony. "Uncovering the Underground Railroad." *American Legacy: Celebrating African-American History & Culture* 5 (Summer, 1999): 22-28.

Still, William. *The Underground Rail Road: A Record of Facts, Authentic Narratives, Letters, &c, Narrating the Hardships, Hair-breadth Escapes and Death Struggles of the Slaves in Their Efforts for Freedom.* Philadelphia: Porter & Coates, 1872.

Tobin, Jacqueline, and Raymond G. Dobard. *Hidden in Plain View: The Secret Story of Quilts and the Underground Railroad.* New York: Doubleday, 1999.

Undocumented workers: The nature of U.S. immigration laws and the composition of the nation's undocumented immigrants changed radically after 1965. That year, changes were made to U.S. immigration policies, many of which had been in place since before WORLD WAR I. As a result, the United States maintained a relatively open immigration policy in the 1980's and early 1990's. A large number of people of African descent, primarily from the Caribbean (the WEST INDIES) and South America, entered the country both legally and illegally during these decades.

The CENSUS OF THE UNITED STATES estimated the undocumented immigrant population in 1980 at two million. During the 1980 census, the U.S. government estimated that about 55 to 65 percent of undocumented workers were from MEXICO. The census also indicated a growing representation of immigrants from the WEST INDIES (including blacks from CUBA and HAITI), CENTRAL AMERICA and South America (including blacks from Guatemala, Belize, Honduras, Costa Rica, Panama, and Brazil), and, to a lesser extent, AFRICA.

The federal government's estimation of undocumented immigrants was believed by many to be inaccurate. It is difficult to assess the nature and magnitude of undocumented immigration because there are different kinds of undocumented immigrants and workers.

In the census, the government basically distinguished two groups of undocumented immigrants. The first group represented persons who entered the United States without any legal documentation. The second group consisted of persons who entered the United States but remained beyond the authorized time limit accorded them by the Immigration and Naturalization Service (INS). The majority of black undocumented immigrants fell under the second category. The federal government further divided the second group into subgroups. The first subgroup was referred to as "sojourners": undocumented immigrants who intended to return to their countries of origin at a later time. Black undocumented immigrants have usually intended to return to their countries of origin. Nevertheless, a small group of undocumented black immigrants were referred to as "settlers"— undocumented immigrants intending to reside in the United States permanently.

Problems Faced by Undocumented Workers

The African American community provided a safe environment for these immigrants. Although there were notable cultural differences, racial similarities provided a sense of brotherhood and unity. The undocumented black workers who migrated to the United States tended to settle in primarily African American cities because of an inherent commonality—a commonality established by color. The undocumented black worker accepted the reality that, in the United States, society passes judgment on an individual because of his or her color. Undocumented black workers found solidarity of some sort in African American communities because color made them look like American-born citizens of African descent.

A large majority of black undocumented workers is from the English-speaking world of the Caribbean. In the 1990's, however, the number of French-speaking black Haitian immigrants increased, primarily in large FLOR-IDA cities. During the 1990's, in large metropolitan areas such as NEW YORK CITY and Miami, the number of undocumented immigrants was equal to or sometimes greater than the legal immigrant population.

The undocumented black workers within the African American community faced a strenuous process of being incorporated into American life. In most cases, they entered a society far more prosperous than the ones they left. As a result, they were able to find employment possibilities, although the jobs were usually menial. These workers suffered tremendous social, political, and economic indignities while they sojourned in the United States as part of a minority within a minority. These inequalities and indignities were further compounded by the precarious legal position occupied by undocumented black workers. Without citizen status, these black workers had no clearly defined legal and political rights.

Lack of Political Voice
The hardships endured by undocumented workers are invariably justified in some quarters because these individuals had broken federal immigration laws when they entered the United States illegally. Such arguments generally hold that, because of this violation, undocumented immigrants waived all rights normally given to persons in the United States. As a result of renewed anti-immigrant feeling that flared up during the 1990's, more Americans expressed the opinion that the U.S. government should not extend protection to any individual who entered and remained in the United States illegally. The irony is that discrimination on the basis of one's legal status is against the law. The discrimination against the black undocumented immigrants can be described as a triple burden combining race, class, and citizenship discrimination.

By living in and around the African American community, black undocumented workers joined the ranks of America's most consistently oppressed minority group. Undocumented black workers suffered further indignities because their status precluded them from participating in the political process. As a group, undocumented black workers can be aptly described as an invisible minority group. In essence, by choosing to exist as a shadow underclass to avoid deportation, undocumented black immigrants collectively became the most powerless of any group in the United States.

The political plight of undocumented workers is partly the result of their lack of an official status. This lack of an official status came about because the undocumented worker represents the least attractive constituent for politicians. Although undocumented immigrants developed social networks, they still could not participate in American politics. Politicians are less inclined to work diligently for any group that is politically disfranchised by the laws of the United States. Although the number of undocumented workers has grown, there is little need for politicians to court this group, since undocumented workers are never considered potential voters. Organizations created by undocumented workers were effective in absorbing the trauma of cultural adaptation in America, but the fact that these organizations were formed by noncitizens limited their political effectiveness.

Undocumented immigrants do have some specific rights accorded to them in the American legal process. The life and status of undocumented immigrants can be equated to the conditions under which blacks lived in the antebellum South. Noncitizens have always enjoyed certain political rights under American law. While illegal aliens are unable to vote, this group at least has been able to rally others in the political process and to persuade them to seek their interest. Unable to protect their political interests directly, undocumented immigrants have had limited success in seeking redress through indirect political participation.

Political invisibility has limited the opportunities of undocumented immigrants for political acceptance in the United States. The fear of deportation reduces the opportunity of undocumented immigrants to capitalize on their rights as stated in the U.S. CONSTITUTION and in federal and state laws. In reality, most federal and state laws agree that undocumented immigrants are entitled to many statutory rights unrelated to their violation of American immigration laws. Nevertheless, members of this silent minority group have lived in the background of the American political process and have accepted exploitation because of their vulnerable status.

—*Abdul Karim Bangura*
See also: Census of the United States; Immigration and ethnic origins of African Americans.

Suggested Readings:
Barbour, William, ed. *Illegal Immigration.* San Diego: Greenhaven Press, 1994.

Davis, Darien J. *The African Dimensions in Latin American Culture.* Wilmington, Del.: Scholarly Resources, 1992.

Jones, Maldwyn A. *American Immigration.* Chicago: University of Chicago Press, 1992.

O'Neill, Teresa, ed. *Immigration: Opposing Viewpoints.* San Diego: Greenhaven Press, 1992.

Portes, Alejandro, and Ruben G. Rumbaut. *Immigrant America: A Portrait.* Berkeley: University of California Press, 1990.

Union American Methodist Episcopal Church: Church with early nineteenth-century roots. In 1805 Peter Spencer, William Anderson, and forty other black members of the Asbury Methodist Church in Wilmington, DELAWARE, left that church after being denied full participation in church rites. The group established itself as the Ezion Methodist Episcopal Church and held services under the direct supervision of the Asbury Church. When a white elder was appointed to preach in the Ezion Church in 1812, Spencer, Anderson, and others left Ezion in protest and constructed another church building which was dedicated in 1813. They severed all ties with the AFRICAN METHODIST EPISCOPAL CHURCH in PHILADELPHIA and established the Union Church of African Members.

After 1816 thirty congregations of the Union Church split, eventually incorporating as the African Union American Methodist Episcopal Church in the United States and Elsewhere. The church is Methodist in doctrine and Episcopal in governance, and it has a strong tradition of lay participation. The church also has a long-standing position in favor of licensing women to preach.

United American Free Will Baptist Denomination: Denomination that traces its origins to a general conference of Free Will Baptists organized in 1827. In one of its first sessions, the general conference of Free Will Baptists decided to ordain African Americans to the ministry. The church also adopted a strong antislavery posture that attracted a number of African Americans to the organization in the nineteenth century. In 1901 African American members split from the Free Will Baptists and established their own denomination.

United Golfers' Association: Sports group founded in the 1920's. GOLF was long a rigidly segregated sport, and the United Golfers' Association was created to organize tournaments for African American golfers and to promote African Americans' right to play golf.

United Holy Church of America: Pentecostal group founded in 1886 in Method, North Carolina, by Issac Cheshier. Most notable among early church organizers were the Reverend C. C. Craig and Mrs. E. E. Craig. The church was first known as the Holy Church of North Carolina, then as the Holy Church of North Carolina and Virginia. In 1916 the name of the church officially was changed to United Holy Church of America, Inc. Major rites include baptism, foot washing, communion, and divine healing. The church has a number of congregations in countries other than the United States.

United Negro College Fund: Organization founded to provide financial support to historically black colleges and universities. Begun in the 1940's, the United Negro College Fund was the brainchild of Tuskegee Institute president Frederick D. Patterson. Like other heads of historically black colleges, Patterson understood the peculiar problems affecting these institutions, particularly fiscal problems. Located throughout the South, these schools educated the overwhelming majority of African American college students before the Civil Rights movement of the 1960's and 1970's opened the doors of other schools. They relied upon limited state funds and contributions from alumni and philanthropists. During the Great Depression of the 1930's and its aftermath, these sources became inadequate as donors reduced their contributions.

Determined to maintain the Tuskegee Institute and other schools as centers for educating African American youth, Patterson devised a scheme that he introduced in his weekly column in the Pittsburgh Courier, a high-circulation black newspaper. He suggested that funds for black state and private colleges might be solicited from all segments of the population. He reasoned that everyone stood

William H. Gray III, president of the United Negro College Fund, discussing education at a ceremony hosted by Microsoft chairman Bill Gates, at which Gates announced the creation of the Gates Millennium Scholarship Fund in September, 1999. *(AP/Wide World Photos)*

to gain if more African Americans received college degrees. Moreover, he was impressed with the American National Red Cross and the National Foundation for Infantile Paralysis, both of which raised funds through mass appeals.

Patterson persuaded the majority of black college heads of the soundness of his plan. To raise money for operating costs, he used the John Price Jones consulting firm of New York City, which assisted him in securing $100,000. Half of that sum was provided by the Rosenwald Fund and the General Education Board, both of which had funded several black education projects. The United Negro College Fund held its opening fund-raiser at the Waldorf Astoria hotel. John D. Rockefeller, Jr.'s generous endorsement started the organization on a sound footing.

The fund selected New York City as the site of its headquarters. In 1944 William J. Trent, a Livingstone College alumnus and holder of an M.B.A. from the Wharton School at the University of Pennsylvania, became the first executive director. Patterson agreed to serve as the first president of the fund even though he was still president of Tuskegee. During its first year, the fund raised $760,000 of its one-million-dollar goal. By 1950 the fund had launched its first capital campaign, with a goal of $25 million. The first $5 million was given by the Rockefeller family.

Although significant numbers of African Americans were attending white colleges by the late 1970's, the United Negro College Fund continued to support black colleges and still relied on funding from all segments of the population. One of its most successful fundraisers has been a series of telethons. The fund became even more successful in providing financial resources to about three dozen historically black institutions, mostly in the South. These institutions were then better able to provide financial aid to deserving students. In 1973 Christopher EDLEY was named the fund's president and chief executive officer. The same year, the UNCF launched its national advertising slogan, "A Mind Is a Terrible Thing to Waste." The UNCF ran a number of award-winning television spots revolving around the slogan.

Edley retired in 1990, but not before obtaining a major grant for the UNCF from philanthropist Walter H. Annenberg. William H. GRAY III assumed the presidency of the fund in 1991. In 1998 the UNCF received the largest single gift in its history, a $42 million grant from the Lilly Endowment. The UNCF stated that the grant would help finance building and renovation projects as well as add to the funding available for scholarships and faculty positions.

United Steelworkers of America v. Weber: AF-FIRMATIVE ACTION case decided by the U.S. SUPREME COURT in 1979. This case was heard by the Supreme Court along with the case *Kaiser Aluminum and Chemical Corporation v. Weber,* and the decision is sometimes referred to by that name.

Brian Weber, a white worker, challenged a voluntary affirmative action plan created by the United Steelworkers of America (USWA) union and the Kaiser Corporation. A quota of 50 percent of new skilled craft trainees were to be African American until the percentage of African Americans in Kaiser's Louisiana plant equaled the percentage of blacks in the local labor force.

Lower federal courts ruled that this affirmative action plan violated Title VII of the Civil Rights Act's prohibition making it unlawful to discriminate because of race against persons such as Weber in job training programs.

The U.S. Supreme Court reversed the lower court decisions and ruled that Congress did not intend to prohibit all voluntary race-conscious affirmative action plans designed to eliminate patterns of racial segregation in the workplace.

—*Steve J. Mazurana*

Universal Negro Improvement Association: Organization founded by Marcus Garvey. One of the most important figures in African American history, Garvey founded the Universal Negro Improvement Association (UNIA) in 1917 in New York City. A Jamaican immigrant, he intended the UNIA to be the vehicle for realizing his dream of a self-sufficient, powerful African American community that would liberate Africans worldwide. With that in mind, the UNIA raised funds to establish small businesses in Harlem and elsewhere, started a newspaper, the Negro World, and built a huge assembly hall for its meetings and rallies. The

While the head of the Universal Negro Improvement Association during its glory years, Marcus Garvey styled himself the "provisional president of Africa" and dressed accordingly in annual UNIA parades. *(AP/Wide World Photos)*

among millions of African Americans in the early 1920's.

The UNIA's reach exceeded its grasp. It was unable to gain a foothold on the African continent as a consequence of the hostility of the European powers that still controlled much of Africa and the suspiciousness of the weak government of LIBERIA. The UNIA was also the target of surveillance and harassment by law-enforcement agencies.

The UNIA and Garvey eventually fell victim to the failure of their major project, the Black Star Line. Its bankruptcy led to Garvey's prosecution on mail-fraud charges. With its leader convicted and sentenced to federal prison, the UNIA began to die. Its members were able to obtain a commutation of Garvey's sentence, but he was deported to Jamaica. With its charismatic leader gone, the UNIA faded into insignificance in the United States. Garvey was unable to continue the organization in Jamaica and died penniless in London in 1940. The UNIA lived on into the 1990's, but only as a shadow of its early glory.

UNIA also established the Black Cross Nurses, the African Orthodox Church, and the Black Star Line steamship line.

At the UNIA's height in the early 1920's, Garvey claimed it had more than a million members. However, the organization's actual membership—as W. E. B. DU BOIS estimated in an article in THE CRISIS—was probably more on the order of 20,000. Nevertheless, the UNIA commanded an enormous amount of support from African American communities at large and was a major social, political, and economic force. The UNIA's message of race pride, love of Africa, and economic and political self-sufficiency struck a responsive chord

Upward Bound program: Program established in 1964 to provide various forms of assistance to low-income high-school students so that they are able to attend college. A program of the U.S. Department of Education, Upward Bound emphasizes peer counseling and hands-on acquaintance with a college and its faculty and students. Students are selected from urban schools, usually from the inner city, or from rural areas, often very remote, and are then given weekly counseling and tutoring by student advisers at their intended colleges. They also participate in workshops and skill-development programs and are given assistance in career planning and counseling. These weekly sessions are conducted throughout the academic year.

For those students who have demonstrated a commitment to the program, the college becomes the site of residence for approximately six weeks during the summer. Students live on campus, usually in the dormitories, and attend classes for which they receive high school credit. Classes typically include writing, math, science, and preparation for the Scholastic Aptitude Test, as well as various electives. Sports and games play a large part in the program, as do field trips and explorations of the immediate and close environments of the campus.

The success of the Upward Bound program can be measured perhaps by its endurance. Originating in 1964 from the Economic Opportunity Act that was part of President Lyndon B. Johnson's Great Society, as Johnson's programs sometimes were called by those working to establish reform, it remained in the 1990's a popular and respected program. Because the groups of students at each campus tend to be small, usually less than one hundred, and because each campus program is autonomous, bureaucratic problems are avoided. The program is untainted by grandiose promises and unrealistic goals. Few can dispute the wisdom and integrity of a program that furnishes promising young people with a prospect of a future uncontaminated by poverty and that allows a glimpse of a life not ordinarily visualized in the inner city or within rural zones of poverty.

Urban Arts Corps: NEW YORK theater company. The company's objective is to develop the professional skills of minority writers, performers, and composers. Founded in 1967 by Vinnette Carroll, the organization used a workshop format to create plays, using source material from folktales, the Bible, and Western classic and modern literature. The company is best known for its productions of Carroll's plays *Don't Bother Me, I Can't Cope* (1972) and *Your Arms Too Short to Box with God* (1975).

Urban Bush Women: NEW YORK-based dance theater company established in 1984 by Jawole Willa Jo Zollar. The company performs "stage collages" using dance, narrative and imagistic texts, live music, and a cappella singing. Critics and audiences interpret the company's works variously, seeing them as spiritual, political, avant-garde, feminist, or as a fusion of modern and traditional African dance.

Urbanization: In 1900 approximately 90 percent of the African Americans in the United States lived in the South. By 1990 about 50 percent of African Americans were living in the northern, north central, or western states of the United States. The term most often used to describe this exodus from the southern states is the GREAT MIGRATION. One of the most profound demographic changes in American society during the twentieth century, it took place initially during and after WORLD WAR I. It continued, however, especially after WORLD WAR II. In both eras of relocation, the major impetus was economic: Southern blacks looked particularly to the northeastern and north central states for economic relief from POVERTY and unemployment.

A major characteristic of this great migration of southern blacks was a shift from rural to urban living. The eras of northern migration around the times of the world wars were the times when African Americans began to live in cities in large numbers. By the end of the twentieth century, African Americans had become one of the most urbanized ethnic communities in the United States.

Black Americans had traditionally lived in rural areas or in small towns; this contrasted with the American experience of many of the immigrant groups who were to become their urban neighbors. Irish, Puerto Rican, and European Jewish immigrants, for example, did not have the long-term American rural or small-town experience that African Americans had as their primary living contexts. The established rural traditions and styles of life of African Americans were challenged as they moved from South to North and from rural to urban life.

Backgrounds of the New Black Urbanites
African Americans from the rural South were offered economic opportunities by northern-based factories that produced goods for both world wars. Industrial production had to be expanded for the United States to fight these wars successfully, and the increased demand for factory workers was accompanied by a decrease of the cheap labor that had traditionally immigrated from the southern and eastern portions of Europe. Initially, around 1910, this decrease was the result of European hostilities that made immigration of the European poor very difficult. During the 1920's, the decrease was largely the result of legislation that restricted immigration from the poorest European countries. In response to this labor shortage, northern industries found a large human resource in the poorly paid African Americans who were living and working in southern rural areas.

The socioeconomic backgrounds of the new urbanites from the South have been debated by scholars. Certainly, southern rural economies offered few opportunities to their black populations. Many were confined to tenancy status on agricultural lands owned by whites; their surplus production was profit for the farm owners. Others lived in small towns and were hired primarily as unskilled laborers. African American women were largely limited to domestic service in nonblack homes.

The exceptions largely consisted of clergy and teachers, a relatively small group unrepresentative of the majority of southern African Americans. They had been able to attain middle-class status in the South largely because they were less dependent on white employers. The rural ministers were the corporate heads of their own congregations, which whites did not join. Many teachers taught in rural schools that were wholly black attended and did not have white supervision or financial support. Nonetheless, the characteristics of rural African Americans migrating north were largely those of displaced farmers; they had been sharecroppers with limited formal education and virtually no knowledge of urban living.

Social Effects
The northern communities that began to receive the migrants quickly developed negative perceptions of them, stereotypical perceptions that were perpetuated by whites and by some northern blacks as well. Many northern-born African Americans resented the arrival of the southern blacks. They sometimes claimed, along with their white counterparts, that the migration was responsible for a wide range of social difficulties in northern cities, including higher rates of crime, delinquency, ALCOHOLISM, and venereal disease. Considered most threatening was the idea that the southern rural blacks in northern cities were responsible for a disintegration of the family.

Early black sociologists such as E. Franklin Frazier, and later white scholars such as Daniel Patrick Moynihan, saw urbanization as a major cause of a deterioration of the black family. They argued that the adjustment to urban life was overwhelming for southern rural blacks and that the result was the disorganization of black families. Suggested particular difficulties include the newness of anonymity, personal isolation, limited primary affiliations, and problems in establishing the appropriate social bonding to support family security.

Later sociologists, black sociologists in particular, have challenged this characterization. Among them is Andrew BILLINGSLY, in *Black Families in White America* (1968). According to his research, the multitude of social problems experienced by blacks upon urbanization did not lead to disorganization of the family. The problems resulted instead in the development of, or strengthening of, modes of adaption to the new lifestyle. These scholars contend that urbanization has not been as damaging as previously interpreted but may actually have helped in maintaining certain family characteristics. Such characteristics include relatively well-organized roles, such as gender roles, and the continuation of the African American extended family model. In this model, relatives and other providers and care givers beyond the nuclear family are included as "family" for the welfare of all members.

Discrimination

Most analysts of black urbanization agree that African American immigrants from rural areas faced an overwhelming obstacle that most immigrants (from Europe, especially) did not encounter: the bias of the white communities to which they migrated against them because of their color. Color alone often meant that migrating African Americans were in a disadvantaged position in relation to obtaining jobs. Moreover, since a majority of the new black urbanites had previously been farmers and untrained laborers, they did not have skills that could conceivably have helped them overcome job discrimination. Unemployment and underemployment led to personal despair and ultimately to new adaptation processes, some of them illegal. New roles for the urban black man led to a kind of personal capitalism that for some involved pimping (maintaining a group of prostitutes) and for others meant participation in gambling and illegal alcohol and drug trafficking.

The concentration of urbanized African Americans in so-called GHETTOS remained high in American cities throughout the latter twentieth century. In 1990 the CENSUS OF THE UNITED STATES described ghettos as areas with a poverty rate of at least 20 percent. African Americans living in cities throughout the nation were more highly concentrated in such areas than either whites or persons of Hispanic origin. Over 50 percent of all blacks who lived in central city areas at that time lived in designated poverty areas, even if many individual black families in those areas were not determined to be at socioeconomic levels considered impoverished.

Central city areas often are at great distances from developing industries, which have largely relocated to suburbs. Mass transit is often inadequate to transport workers from the central city to outlying areas. Therefore, a kind of hypersegregation usually is characteristic of ghettos, and the families who reside in these areas are often limited to consumer status rather than production functions that would provide alternatives to them.

Migration, Urbanization, and Political Power

Migration and urbanization, although most dramatic from south to north, also occurred from south to west and from the rural South to southern cities. Western and midwestern cities such as Los Angeles and San Francisco, California, as well as Denver, Colorado, and Kansas City, Missouri, all became receiving cities of black migrants from the South during the twentieth century. At the same time, rural African Americans were migrating to southern cities. Their proportions of those cities' populations rose significantly, especially in urban areas such as Charlotte, North Carolina; Birmingham, Alabama; Jackson, Mississippi; Memphis, Tennessee; Jacksonville, Florida; and Savannah and Atlanta, Georgia.

The black populations of West Coast cities have never been proportionately as high as those of major southern metropolitan areas, where they were frequently between 40 and 50 percent. However, the African American political impact was shown in the elections of black governmental officials in these regions during the last quarter of the twentieth century. Most major American cities have had African American MAYORS; among these cities are New York, WASHINGTON, D.C., Cleveland, CHICAGO, DETROIT, Charlotte, ATLANTA, BIRMINGHAM, and NEW ORLEANS. A number of western cities, including Los Angeles and San Francisco, have also elected African American mayors. Urbanization therefore can be said to have resulted in organized community strength, as shown in the progress blacks have made in the political arena in urban communities.

Affluence

Black urbanites have not always remained in central cities, nor have they always experienced high poverty levels. While black affluence grew during the last part of the twentieth century, African American migration from central cities to nearby urban or suburban areas also increased. In the book *Black Corona* (1998), Steven Gregory describes the growth of a black neighborhood in the Queens section of New York City. Corona is atypical in that its growth as a black neighborhood began early, shortly after World War I. Queens was developing rapidly at the time.

Blacks began to move to Corona from Harlem or predominantly black areas of the Bronx; many were professionals, but others were personal service workers or semiskilled laborers. Initially they lived in racially mixed blocks with first- and second-generation Italian and German immigrants. Corona represented the chance to leave the congestion and problems of central New York City but also the chance for home ownership and the possibil-ity of upward social mobility. By the 1950's, black Corona had grown to be a thriving working-class and middle-class community of about nine thousand. It was surrounded by predominantly white residential areas. The Corona experience would be replicated in many other American metropolitan areas in the last half of the twentieth century.

Urban Opportunity

The many problems of major American cities have been analyzed and detailed thoroughly not only by scholars but also by the media. The social and economic drawbacks of urban life, including poverty, crime, and drug use, are widely known.

Nevertheless, the magazine *Black Enterprise* claimed in August, 1995, that the larger metropolitan areas of the United States were the most advantageous places for African Americans to live. It based this statement largely on the median income of black families, the larger percentages of blacks employed in metropolitan regions, and the power of African American political organizations to effect changes.

Black Enterprise had stated in May, 1987, that the best places for African Americans (based on the above criteria), were Atlanta, Chicago, and Los Angeles. Significantly, none of these cities is northeastern. In 1995 this business and entrepreneurial-oriented magazine named five metropolitan areas that it considered best urban living areas based on median family income. Ranked in preferred order, they were Washington, D.C.; NEWARK, NEW JERSEY; LOS ANGELES, CALIFORNIA; BALTIMORE, MARYLAND; and Atlanta, Georgia. The *Black Enterprise* analysis stated not only that urban life was more advantageous than rural life but also that life in a very large city was more advantageous than smaller city life for African Americans.

—*William Osborne*

See also: Moynihan Report; Suburbanization.

Suggested Readings:

Betten, Neil, and Raymond Mohl, eds. *Urban America in Historical Perspective*. New York: Weybright and Talley, 1970.

Billingsley, Andrew. *Black Families in White America*. Englewood Cliffs, N.J.: Prentice-Hall, 1968.

Connolly, Harold. *A Ghetto Grows in Brooklyn*. New York: New York University, 1977.

Fainstein, Susan. *The City Builders*. Cambridge, Mass.: Blackwell, 1994.

Gregory, Steven. *Black Corona: Race and the Politics of Place in an Urban Community*. Princeton, N.J.: Princeton University Press, 1998.

Katznelson, Ira. *City Trenches: Urban Politics and the Patterning of Class in the United States*. New York: Pantheon, 1981.

Kelly, Robin D. G. *Race Rebels: Culture, Politics, and the Black Working Class*. New York: Free Press, 1994.

King, Mel. *Chain of Change: Struggles for Black Community Development*. Boston: South End, 1981.

Massey, Douglas, and Nancy Denton. *American Apartheid: Segregation and the Making of the Underclass*. Cambridge: Harvard University Press, 1993.

Ward, David. *Poverty, Ethnicity, and the American City, 1940-1925*. Boston: Cambridge University Press, 1989.

Usry, James L. (b. February 2, 1922, Macon, Georgia): NEW JERSEY politician. Usry earned his B.A. degree in 1946 from Lincoln University in Pennsylvania. He attended graduate school at Glassboro State University in New Jersey. After earning his master's degree, he did further studies at Temple University in Philadelphia.

A VIETNAM WAR veteran, Usry was also a professional athlete who competed with the New York Rens and the HARLEM GLOBETROTTERS. After his basketball career, Usry became active in politics and education in Atlantic City, New Jersey. His career in education included positions as teacher, principal, and assistant superintendent of schools. He also joined the Board of Education. He was elected MAYOR of Atlantic City, serving from 1984 until 1990. He served as a member of university boards and as an active member of political and educational organizations. His awards for public and professional service include the Omega Psi Phi man of the year (1986) and the Bob Douglas Hall of Fame (1984).

Utah: Although African Americans have never composed more than 1 percent of Utah's population, the policies of the state's predominant CHURCH OF JESUS CHRIST OF LATTER-DAY SAINTS (Mormons) regarding African Americans have sometimes focused national attention on Utah. In 1997 the CENSUS OF THE UNITED STATES estimated the state's population to be a bit under 2.1 million and its African American population to be about 18,000.

Three African American slaves were with the first Mormons who entered the Salt Lake Valley in 1847, and members of the Church of Jesus Christ of Latter-day Saints continued to bring slaves into the territory. A law officially authorizing SLAVERY was passed in 1852. Freed African American Mormons also came in the nineteenth century. Other blacks came to work on the railroad, in mines, and for the military. In 1886 the NINTH CAVALRY established a fort to settle disputes between settlers and Ute Indians. The black TWENTY-FOURTH INFANTRY came to Fort Douglas near Salt Lake City in 1896.

A chapter of the NATIONAL ASSOCIATION FOR THE ADVANCEMENT OF COLORED PEOPLE (NAACP) was established in 1919 and revived during WORLD WAR II. Utah's African Americans had limited access to housing and entertainment until the U.S. Congress passed CIVIL RIGHTS legislation during the 1960's and the state legislature adopted similar measures.

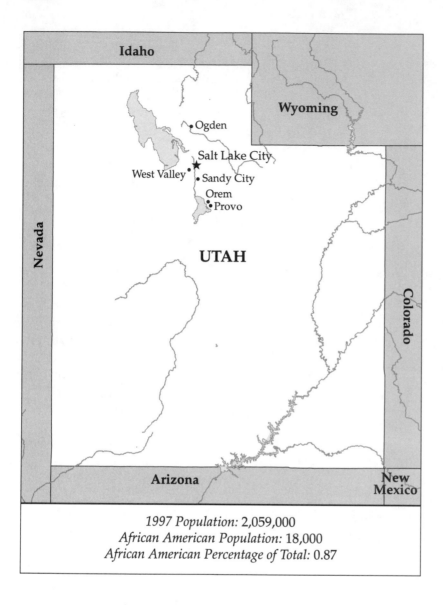

1997 Population: 2,059,000
African American Population: 18,000
African American Percentage of Total: 0.87

Attitudes toward blacks gradually improved in the 1960's and 1970's. In 1978 the Mormon Church announced that blacks could be ordained into the lay priesthood. Martin Luther KING, Jr.'s birthday (Human Rights Day) became a state holiday in 1986.

African American athletes at the state universities and on its professional basketball team, the Jazz, have received press attention. Reverend Francis Davis of the Calvary Baptist church, state senator Terry Williams, Judge Tyrone Medley, and University of Utah professor Ronald Coleman have played important roles in the state.

—*Jessie Embry*

V

Van Der Zee, James (June 29, 1886, Lenox, Massachusetts—May 15, 1983, Washington, D.C.): Photographer. James Augustus Van Der Zee is best known for his sensitive photographic portraits of both the celebrities and the common people who enjoyed the heyday of HARLEM during its renaissance of the 1920's.

Van Der Zee taught himself the art of photography. He worked as a busboy, waiter, and musician. He married Kate Brown in 1906, and they were divorced in 1914. Van Der Zee became a darkroom assistant for Gertz Department Store in NEWARK, NEW JERSEY, in 1915. In 1923 he remarried. He operated his own studio, Guarantee Photos (later GGG Photo Studio), in Harlem from 1916 to 1968. Often sought after to photograph weddings, funer-

James Van Der Zee during the early 1980's, when he came out of retirement to photograph figures such as Muhammad Ali. *(AP/Wide World Photos)*

als, and other auspicious occasions, Van Der Zee was the official photographer for Marcus GARVEY's UNIVERSAL NEGRO IMPROVEMENT ASSOCIATION. He became well known outside Harlem after his work was featured in the 1967 Metropolitan Museum of Art exhibition *Harlem on My Mind: Cultural Capital of Black America, 1900-1968.*

Van Der Zee's photographs are marked by warmth, grace, and dignity that reflect his sensitivity to his subjects. A man of Harlem himself, he found through his camera's lens the energy and pride of the black community in that city. His portraits are usually posed and capture the deeper, psychological character of his subjects, sometimes with the aid of his skillful air brush and double-printing techniques.

Among his many professional awards are the American Society of Magazine Photographers Award (1969), Life Fellowship at the Metropolitan Museum of Art (1970), the Pierre Toussaint Award for outstanding service to humanity (1978), the International Black Photographers Award (1979), and the Living Legacy Award (1979), presented by President Jimmy Carter. He received honorary doctorates from Seton Hall University in 1976 and from Haverford College (Pennsylvania) in 1980.

In 1983 Van Der Zee died while visiting Washington, D.C., to receive an honorary doctorate from HOWARD UNIVERSITY. The product of his long career as a professional photographer is a visual record of Harlem's most creatively energetic and prosperous era.

Van Peebles, Melvin (b. August 21, 1932, Chicago, Illinois): FILM DIRECTOR, producer,

Melvin Van Peebles in 1998. *(AP/Wide World Photos)*

writer, actor, and composer. Van Peebles is credited with being one of the first African Americans to make Hollywood aware of the dollar potential and appeal that black films and filmmakers could have for a large African American audience. After graduating from Ohio Wesleyan University, Van Peebles spent time as a navigator in the U.S. Air Force. In 1959, while living in Hollywood, CALIFORNIA, Van Peebles, frustrated because he could not break into the film business, decided to move his family to Holland, where he studied at the University of Amsterdam and acted with the Dutch National Theatre.

He then moved to France but found that breaking into filmmaking in France was no easier than in America. Van Peebles decided that the only way to get into filmmaking was to become a writer. With that determination, he wrote five novels. He used a screenplay adapted from his novel *Story of a Three Day Pass* as a vehicle to take the French Film Center's examination for directors, required for entry into the French directors' union.

Shot on a budget of $200,000, *Story of a Three Day Pass* debuted at the San Francisco In-

ternational Film Festival in 1967. The film's success prompted critics and the press to call Van Peebles, inaccurately, America's first black film director. Van Peebles capitalized on this attention by directing 1970's *Watermelon Man* for Columbia Pictures.

In 1971, with no studio backing and a modest budget of $500,000, Van Peebles made the celebrated *Sweet Sweetback's Baadasssss Song*, a radical, political, sexually graphic, and violent picture. Van Peebles found it impossible to get publicity through the channels of the film industry, which had given the film an X rating. Van Peebles decided to market the film directly to the black public himself. He used the communication systems within the black community and word of mouth.

Sweet Sweetback's Baadasssss Song opened in sixty New York theaters and in one hundred fifty other film houses around the country. The extraordinary success of the film caught the interest of the press, and Van Peebles took advantage of the opportunity. He dressed in street styles and used street language to recount his problems as a black man trying to break into the film business and the obstacles he faced getting this particular picture made. The media loved this new black militant, and Hollywood realized that there was an audience of African Americans who would pay to see themselves on screen.

After the success of his film and his rise to fame, Van Peebles put together two Broadway plays, *Ain't Supposed to Die a Natural Death* in 1971 and *Don't Play Us Cheap* in 1972. He made an unsuccessful film version of his 1972 play. In 1976 he surfaced in television as the writer of *Just an Old Sweet Song*, a mild family drama which was very different from his early works. In 1981 he wrote another television drama, *Sophisticated Gents*, which addressed the concerns of blacks trying to achieve in white society.

In the 1980's Van Peebles became an options trader in the stock market, and he wrote two books about his approach to, and successes in, the options market. In 1993 he appeared in the film *Posse*, a Western directed by his son, Mario Van Peebles.

Vasquez v. Hillery: U.S. SUPREME COURT discrimination case on JURY SELECTION decided in 1986. In 1962 a Superior Court trial jury in Kings County, California (in the San Joaquin Valley), convicted Booker T. Hillery of first-degree murder in the stabbing of a fifteen-year-old girl.

Hillery, a black man, had moved before trial to quash his indictment on grounds that blacks were systematically excluded from the grand jury that indicted him; for twenty-three years he continued his challenge. State courts sustained Hillery's indictment and conviction, although they noted that no black had ever served on the grand jury in Kings County.

A final federal writ of habeas corpus brought Hillery's case, on appeal of prison warden Daniel Vasquez, to the U.S. Supreme Court, which (6-3) reversed Hillery's conviction. Justice Thurgood MARSHALL's opinion for the Court held that systematic exclusion of blacks from the grand jury that indicted an accused tainted the prosecution beyond a condition simply purged by conviction at trial. The ruling extended the ban against RACIAL DISCRIMINATION on juries begun with STRAUDER v. WEST VIRGINIA (1880) as an element of equal protection under the FOURTEENTH AMENDMENT.

—*Thomas J. Davis*

Vaudeville: Theatrical entertainment form that proliferated between 1905 and 1925; the first American popular entertainment to cross racial and class boundaries. Vaudeville emerged in the last quarter of the nineteenth century, a hybrid of performance styles ranging from music halls and burlesque to circus acts and minstrel shows. A vaudeville show was a variety show composed of numerous individual acts (a typical bill consisted of nine acts, but the number was variable). Vaudeville was the predominant form of popular entertainment in America through the mid-1920's, when it was eclipsed by the growing popularity of motion pictures and radio.

The rise of vaudeville was a direct outgrowth of the increasing diversity of American life; not only were many of vaudeville's most popular acts (such as juggling and slap-

Vaudevillian Bert Williams in a publicity still for the *Ziegfeld Follies of 1910. (Library of Congress)*

stick comedy) able to transcend a language barrier, but also the content of the acts themselves served as lessons in socialization. Through the use of comedy, music, and theatrical presentations, vaudeville shows addressed concerns about ethnicity, gender roles, social problems, and other issues.

Vaudeville was controlled by theatrical chains, which operated the shows and owned the chains of theaters across the country in which the vaudeville shows played. There were numerous major chains and several smaller ones as well. The THEATER OWNERS BOOKING ASSOCIATION (TOBA) was white-owned but employed only black entertainers and played to primarily black audiences. Its theater chain, known as the TOBA circuit, extended through the South but also included houses in such cities as CHICAGO, BALTIMORE, and WASHINGTON, D.C. At its peak, the TOBA circuit encompassed more than forty theaters, including the famous APOLLO THEATER in New York's HARLEM. While the TOBA circuit enjoyed popular success, the performers themselves were subject to the racial injustices of the times. They had to pay their own travel expenses, stay in segregated accommodations, and abide by curfews.

Many of the musical and dance styles of vaudeville, and much of its humor and narrative, was appropriated from traditional African American entertainment forms. Much of the material in the vaudevilles, both white and black, relied on racial stereotypes and the use of blackface makeup. Many black vaudeville performers assumed control of the stereotypes through inversion: the CAKEWALK, a dance style created by blacks but popularized by whites, mocked white dancing, while RAGTIME was an antidote to traditional European music.

The performance styles of black vaudeville stars, including Bill (Bojangles) ROBINSON and Bert WILLIAMS, set a standard for black entertainers in the post-vaudeville era and influenced popular white performers such as Al Jolson and Eddie Cantor. Vaudeville paved the way for many popular black performers to enter the mainstream of American entertainment, performing and innovating on Broadway, in films, and in the music industry, in the years following the GREAT DEPRESSION.

—*Christine J. Catanzarite*
See also: Comedy and humor; Minstrels; Theater.

Suggested Readings:

Lhamon, W. T., Jr. *Raising Cain: Blackface Performance from Jim Crow to Hip Hop.* Cambridge, Mass.: Harvard University Press, 1998.

Lott, Eric. *Love and Theft: Blackface Minstrelry and the American Working Class.* New York: Oxford University Press, 1993.

Slide, Anthony. *The Encyclopedia of Vaudeville.* Westport, Conn.: Greenwood, 1994.

Vaughan, Sarah (March 27, 1924, Newark, New Jersey—April 3, 1990, Los Angeles, California): JAZZ singer. Vaughan received her first musical training as a choir member of Mount Zion Baptist Church, where, at the age of twelve, she became an organist. In 1942 she won an amateur contest at HARLEM's famed APOLLO THEATER. This led to an engagement with Earl Hines's big band as a pianist and singer. This affiliation led to her association with singer and bandleader Billy ECKSTINE, whose orchestra she joined. She first recorded with the orchestra in 1944.

Vaughan's associations with instrumentalists were not limited to big bands and orchestras. She frequently sang with bebop musicians of the era. Her recording of "Lover Man" established her as a jazz singer of the highest order. She recorded with Dizzy GILLESPIE and with John Kirby in the 1940's. Most of her subsequent work was as a soloist, performing and touring with small groups. She became known as a singer who used her voice as an-

Sarah Vaughan in 1952. *(AP/Wide World Photos)*

other instrument, not simply as a vehicle for words or sentiments. Her contralto voice, with its extraordinary range and timbre, seemed receptive to every kind of musical statement. She could, and did, record popular, more commercial tunes. She also performed and recorded jazz with such important musicians as trumpeter Clifford Brown and saxophonist Cannonball ADDERLEY. She recorded numerous songs by Duke Ellington and by George Gershwin. She won a 1982 Grammy Award for best female jazz vocal performance for her album *Gershwin Live!*

Vaughan's tours were always marked by enthusiastic audiences, with crowds cheering her splendid style and a musicianship that brought to each work a dynamic unsurpassed by other performers. Usually accompanied by a trio of piano, double bass, and drums, she unfolded to both new and experienced audiences the wonders of her versatility. Occasionally, she would perform with a symphony orchestra or a big band, but her preference seemed to reside in small combos, in which each musician is allowed the freest sort of range of expression.

Vermont: Although Vermont is the second largest of the six New England states in area, it is one of the nation's smallest states in population. In 1997 it had approximately 589,000 residents, according to the CENSUS OF THE UNITED STATES. Only about 0.5 percent of those residents, or 3,000 people, were African Americans. Sixty-eight percent of the population lived in rural areas, the highest percentage of any state. Vermont's capital city is Montpelier; its largest city, with approximately forty thousand residents, is Burlington.

Vermont is bordered on the north by the Canadian province of Quebec, and many of its settlers were French Canadians. Settlers also came northward from the southern New England states and New York. In 1777 Vermont became the first state to abolish SLAVERY. In the 1840's, Vermont, along with Massachusetts, passed a personal liberty law forbidding state officials from imprisoning fugitive slaves or assisting in their capture. Also in the early nineteenth century, Vermont was one of only eight states (of thirty-eight) that did not have a law prohibiting racial intermarriage. In 1861 Vermont was the first state to volunteer troops to participate in the CIVIL WAR. Vermont sent 33,288 troops to fight; included among them were 120 black men.

Burlington is the home of the University of Vermont. It was there, in 1877, that George Washington Henderson became the first African American elected to Phi Beta Kappa. Henderson continued to excel, and he gradu-

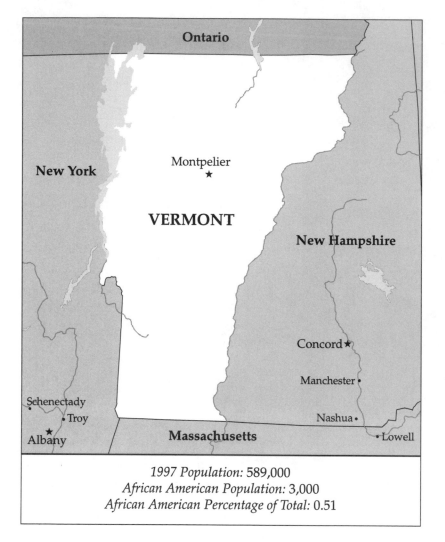

New York

Ontario

Montpelier
★

VERMONT

New Hampshire

Concord ★

Manchester •

Nashua •

Schenectady •
Troy •
★
Albany

Massachusetts

• Lowell

1997 Population: 589,000
African American Population: 3,000
African American Percentage of Total: 0.51

lion in American history. Local officials, uncovering and suppressing the conspiracy at the last moment, were deeply shaken by it and soon implemented policies that strengthened their commitment to preserve slavery.

Biographical Background
Denmark Vesey was born about 1767, either in Africa or on the Caribbean island of St. Thomas. By 1781 he lived on St. Thomas, where he was purchased by a Bermuda slave trader named Joseph Vesey, who was impressed with his appearance and intelligence. Transported immediately to the booming French sugar colony of St. Domingue (later HAITI) and sold to a planter, Denmark Vesey faced a short life of relentless labor in the cane fields and refineries. Denmark, though, was soon found unfit to labor because he showed signs of epilepsy, and Captain Vesey was required by law to buy him back a year later.

Denmark then became a hand on Vesey's ship and began a long relationship with the slavetrader. He worked alongside sailors of various nationalities and visited numerous ports in the WEST INDIES, experiences that doubtless contributed to his facility with English, French, Dutch, and Spanish. During this period, he also probably accompanied the captain to the west coast of Africa to buy Africans and became familiar with all aspects of the infamous Atlantic slave trade. By 1783, when Captain Vesey decided to settle in

ated at the top of his class from the university. He went on to Yale Divinity School, graduated, and became a minister and a professor. Henderson had been born a slave, and he was brought north by an alumnus of the University of Vermont.

—Betsy L. Nichols

Vesey, Denmark (c. 1767—July 2, 1822, Charleston, South Carolina): SLAVE RESISTANCE leader in SOUTH CAROLINA. In 1822 Denmark Vesey, a free black carpenter, plotted a slave revolt in Charleston, South Carolina, that would have led to the largest such rebel-

Charleston, South Carolina, as a slave merchant, there was little about the brutal slave world of the Caribbean to which the mobile Denmark had not been exposed.

Opportunities for slave merchandising, however, were not then good in South Carolina, as commerce slowed after the AMERICAN REVOLUTION and the state restricted trade in slaves. Captain Vesey soon shifted to the ship supply business, in which he appears to have remained for the balance of the century. Throughout this time, Denmark continued with him as his slave.

After a slave revolt exploded in St. Domingue in 1793 and led to the creation in 1804 of independent Haiti, many French colonials and their slaves fled the tumult and sought asylum at ports in the Caribbean and the southern United States. In Charleston, Joseph Vesey helped form a society to assist the beleaguered emigrants, giving Denmark many opportunities to talk with slaves who had witnessed or been directly involved in the uprising. The vision of slaves rising successfully against their overlords was vividly impressed upon him, and he would repeatedly use the example of Haiti to rally his recruits in 1822.

In 1800 Denmark's long servitude came to a startling end: He won fifteen hundred dollars in a local lottery, bought his freedom, and opened a carpenter's shop with the balance. He then became one of the hundreds of free blacks in Charleston, and in the following years, his industriousness allowed him to become a homeowner, gain financial security, marry several times, and have numerous children.

Denmark Vesey's Conspiracy

Vesey's hatred of slavery and of the sway whites held over the lives of blacks appears only to have grown after his MANUMISSION. In 1817 Morris Brown and other black associates formed a Charleston branch of the AFRICAN METHODIST EPISCOPAL CHURCH after having become angered over local white METHODISTS' mounting efforts to curtail the black congregants' liberty to supervise their religious affairs. By late 1817, more than four thousand blacks had left the white churches and joined Brown's. Local authorities, threatened by this symbol of black autonomy, regularly harassed the church and intended to close it, but by early 1822 had still not succeeded.

First thoughts of revolt began with the bitter resentment this harassment engendered. Of the seventy-one individuals involved in the plot for whom trial transcripts remain, thirty-six were members of what was called the African Church. Among the inner circle of conspirators, most members, including Vesey, had been class leaders in the church. The right to independence in churches and in biblical interpretations was critical to the members, and their church soon became a focal point of the conspiracy. In the latter stages of organizing, religious classes were used to disseminate information and biblical doctrines favorable to revolt. Vesey used his fervent faith in Christianity and its democratic tenets, such as the essential equality of all before God, to excoriate the slavery that prevented blacks from exercising freedom and dignity and to defend a revolt against such a devilish institution.

The most active phase of organizing for the rebellion began in late December, 1821, and continued through June, 1822. Fearing spies and traitors, Vesey gathered around him a small core of conspirators in whom he had complete trust: Peter Poyas; "Gullah" Jack Pritchard; Ned, Rolla, and Batteau Bennett; Mingo Harth; and Monday Gell. All were skilled slaves who were trusted by their owners and allowed to hire out their own time: As long as they regularly paid a large portion of their wages to their owners, they were at liberty to rent their own quarters and come and go as they chose. Vesey deliberately chose them because they had the mobility to recruit blacks throughout Charleston and the surrounding countryside without arousing the suspicions of their trusting masters. Some blacks whom Vesey believed could become zealous rebels at first feared joining the conspiracy, but he inspired them with rumors, threats, and his ferocious hatred of subservience.

Enlisting Black Support

It is difficult to estimate how many people may have been involved in the plot, but within Charleston itself, well over one hundred probably figured into the scheme by its latter stages. Vesey enlisted teamsters and stablers who had access to large numbers of horses, blacksmiths who could make knives and swords, and others who worked in shops from which powder, shot, and guns could be stolen. A select few, including Vesey and "Gullah" Jack, recruited far into the countryside, where Jack claimed he had spoken to more than six thousand slaves. The date originally set for the uprising was the moonless night of Monday, July 15, by which time many whites had left town for summer homes on Sullivan's Island or in the cooler piedmont to the west. The date was moved forward to Sunday, June 16, by early June, after Vesey realized a slave had revealed the plot. Sunday was also selected because hundreds of slaves from the countryside routinely came into Charleston on that day to sell in the marketplace, and the conspirators thus would not create suspicion by concentrating themselves in the city.

Phalanxes of slaves—many from rural parishes—led by Vesey and his closest associates were to mass at various points around the city and attack it, some seizing strategic bridges, some setting fires, and others taking poorly guarded arsenals. Banking on surprise, the rebels planned to kill many whites as they emerged confused from their houses to battle fires. No whites were to be spared. The rebels believed that as they realized initial successes, many more blacks would take heart and assist them. Vesey also claimed that President Jean-Pierre Boyer of Haiti would send boats and troops to help the rebels and to evacuate them by sea if necessary. By early June, Vesey's plan was neatly in place and, if executed correctly, would have devastated Charleston.

Despite initial doubts about the rumored plot, however, white officials resumed suspicion after securing the confession of a lesser conspirator on June 8; the local militia was thus out in force on the planned evening of at-

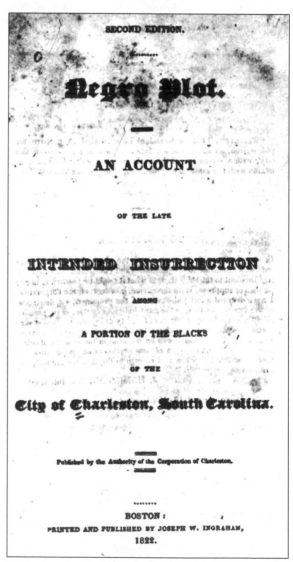

Title of a book published shortly after Denmark Vesey's planned rebellion failed. *(Arkent Archive)*

tack. Vesey had to cancel the attack, and within days, he and his closest allies were arrested. They were summarily tried and were hanged on July 2. Among them, only Monday Gell confessed; the balance died without saying anything of the plan. A proposed raid to rescue Vesey and the others from the gallows never occurred, but black mourners throughout Charleston risked wearing sackcloth and black crepe to show sympathy for the executed. Arrests, trials, and hangings extended into August and kept the town anxious for weeks. By the end, of the 131 suspected conspirators arrested and tried, thirty-five were executed, forty-three deported, and fifty-three acquitted.

Repercussions

The effects of the extensive conspiracy reverberated through Charleston and southern society for years to come. A rewritten slave code placed new restrictions on blacks, and the plot was used to justify razing the African Church. Many whites, especially artisans, unsuccessfully demanded the removal or reduction of the free black population and their confinement to the most menial labor. The most foreboding action, however, was the passage in December, 1822, by the South Carolina legislature of the Negro Seamen's Act. The act was intended to prevent potentially subversive contact between local blacks and alien ones by requiring all ship captains entering Charleston's harbor to place any black mariners onboard in the local jail until the ship's departure. As many vessels, especially American and British, employed large numbers of black sailors, the act sparked an immediate controversy. Although the law violated Congress's right to regulate trade and was found unconstitutional in 1823, the act continued to be enforced by the state and became South Carolina's first act of nullification, setting it on its course toward civil war. The fear Denmark Vesey generated thus helped fuel the conflict between the states that led to the elimination of the slavery he detested so deeply.

—*Peter P. Hinks*

Suggested Readings:

Freehling, William W. "Denmark Vesey's Peculiar Reality." In *New Perspectives on Race and Slavery in America: Essays in Honor of Kenneth M. Stampp*, edited by Robert H. Abzug and Stephen e. Maizlish. Lexington: University of Kentucky Press, 1986.

_____. *Prelude to Civil War: The Nullification Controversy in South Carolina, 1818-1836*. New York: Harper & Row, 1966.

Lofton, John. *Insurrection in South Carolina: The Turbulent World of Denmark Vesey*. Yellow Springs, Ohio: Antioch Press, 1964.

Pearson, Edward A., ed. *Designs Against Charleston: The Trial Record of the Denmark Vesey Slave Conspiracy of 1822*. Chapel Hill: University of North Carolina Press, 1999.

Robertson, David. *Black Rebellion: A Life of Denmark Vesey*. New York: Alfred A. Knopf, 1999.

Starobin, Robert S., ed. *Denmark Vesey: The Slave Conspiracy of 1822*. Englewood Cliffs, N.J.: Prentice-Hall, 1970.

Wade, Richard C. "The Vesey Plot: A Reconsideration." *Journal of Southern History* 30 (May, 1964): 148-161.

Wikramanayake, Marina. *A World in Shadow: The Free Black in Antebellum South Carolina*. Columbia: University of South Carolina Press, 1973.

Vietnam War: American military involvement in Vietnam officially began in August, 1964, and rapidly developed into extensive ground fighting with Viet Cong guerrillas, a contest that the U.S. forces and their South Vietnamese allies would eventually lose. During this period of heightened U.S. involvement in Southeast Asia, one out of seven U.S. troops stationed in the region was an African American.

Ultimately, Vietnam became the most unpopular war in U.S. history. Polls indicated that the majority of African Americans came to oppose the war by 1969, significantly earlier than the white majority.

Racism in the Vietnam-Era Military

African Americans serving in Vietnam worked under a military command structure that was disproportionately white and southern. African Americans were overrepresented in numbers among both enlisted and drafted soldiers, yet only 3 percent of the Army's officers were black. In 1967 blacks made up almost 10 percent of U.S. Marines but constituted less than 1 percent of Marine Corps officers. It was clear that, despite the official desegregation of the U.S. armed forces ordered in 1948, discriminatory structures remained. In Vietnam, this eventually produced destructive racial conflicts as well as profound changes in African American perceptions of the military.

In mid-1966, the Defense Department devised "Project 100,000" to decrease the high rejection rate of African American enlistment applicants. Declaring that increased black enlistment would "rehabilitate" poor urban blacks and return them to society with socially useful skills, the military lowered induction standards and initiated special training programs.

This recruitment strategy, which coincided with the escalation of ground hostilities against the Vietnamese, succeeded in swelling the pool of recruits by approximately 340,000 during the 1966-1968 period. More than 40 percent of these recruits were African Americans. Many of the training programs envisioned by Project 100,000 subsequently folded under fiscal pressures, while the program's recruits became stigmatized as inferior, and many were given extensive combat duties.

By all accounts, black troops stationed in Southeast Asia achieved an extraordinary degree of racial consciousness. Some even formed underground organizations within the military dedicated to the defense of black troops against racist white officers.

Open Hostility

Open racial conflict was not uncommon in Vietnam, and many white officers accused blacks of disloyalty. By 1968 senior military officers were describing racial tensions as a serious and explosive problem. Field commanders frequently sought to restrict all symbols associated with black nationalism. Predictably, this only elevated tensions further, and by the late 1960's, virtual race riots were occurring in the Army. By 1972 the Navy experienced similar conditions.

At its worst, a fear developed among white officers that blacks would shoot at them instead of the enemy. The specter of "fragging"—attacks on officers in the field by their own troops, usually by grenades—took on ominous racial overtones by 1972. Some 788 fully documented cases of fragging occurred during the war, a substantial percentage of which were suspected to be racially motivated. Official sources conceded that the actual number was probably much higher.

Discriminatory Practices

White officers, in turn, responded with behaviors ranging from verbal harassment and discrimination in military housing to unfair assignment in dangerous military missions. When ensuing disputes resulted in court martials, the military justice system mirrored its civilian counterpart by inflicting identifiable patterns of discrimination upon African Americans. An internal Defense Department study in 1972 concluded that blacks convicted of offenses during active service were receiving substantially harsher sentences than white offenders convicted of similar crimes.

A 1971 CONGRESSIONAL BLACK CAUCUS investigation found that more than half of those

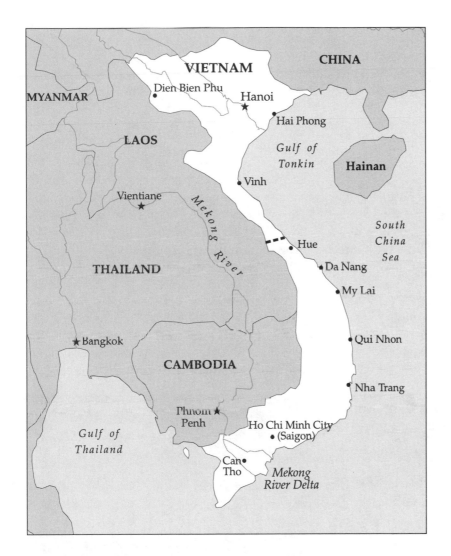

clusive on this point that by 1973 the EQUAL EMPLOYMENT OPPORTUNITY COMMISSION ruled that employers who required Vietnam veterans to have honorable discharges were engaging in racial discrimination.

Race and Casualties

In Vietnam, blacks died in numbers significantly higher than the black percentage of the U.S. population would have predicted. According to independent analyses of government sources, the BLACK BELT of the old PLANTATION South and the coastal Carolinas stood among the areas with the highest relative percentages of black losses. Some analysts concluded that blacks constituted nearly one-quarter of all U.S. casualties in 1965; the percentage dropped after the disproportionate victimization of black troops became widely publicized.

Defense Department reporting procedures presented significant problems for constructing a precise racial analysis of Vietnam casualties. It has been established, however, that measures were eventually taken by the Pentagon to reduce combat exposure of black troops and to avert the potentially explosive implications of a high black casualty rate.

Far from ending with the war, this controversy became part of the "Vietnam syndrome" and returned to haunt the Defense Department during the subsequent 1991 Gulf War. As troops were sent to the Persian Gulf combat

in military detention were African Americans. A NATIONAL ASSOCIATION FOR THE ADVANCEMENT OF COLORED PEOPLE (NAACP) report concluded that whites were twice as likely as blacks to be released without punishment for a first offense and that blacks received almost half of all dishonorable Army discharges. A separate study conducted by the NATIONAL URBAN LEAGUE uncovered similar discriminatory discharge patterns in the Air Force.

Many dishonorable discharges of African Americans were based on inconclusive evidence and yet went uncontested because of black distrust of white military lawyers and lack of legal awareness. The data was so con-

theater, blacks accounted for about one-fourth of the total forces. This produced a determined African American opposition to involvement in a bloody ground war like the fighting in Vietnam.

Black Opposition to the Vietnam War

Most African Americans initially supported the war, as did the majority of U.S. citizens as a whole. It was not until 1969 that a national poll appeared in *Newsweek* magazine indicating that 56 percent of African Americans opposed the war in Vietnam. A later Gallup Poll in the spring of 1971 showed that 83 percent of African Americans (compared with 67 percent of whites) believed that U.S. intervention in Vietnam was a mistake from the beginning.

As late as 1966, however, polls showed that only 35 percent of African Americans opposed U.S. involvement in Vietnam. While this total represented a substantial opposition relative to the larger population, it nevertheless created controversy within the African American community. The community's strong support for the war effort during the early years revealed the established tendency to see military participation as beneficial to career mobility. A 1965 survey indicated that approximately 40 percent of African Americans in the armed services had enlisted to increase their career opportunities, roughly twice the figure reported for whites. The growth of antiwar sentiment within the Civil Rights movement, however, eventually helped to build a critical awareness toward U.S. interventionism.

By mid-1965, activists of the STUDENT NON-VIOLENT COORDINATING COMMITTEE (SNCC) began vigorously opposing the "white man's war" in Vietnam, and in January, 1966, SNCC

One of the most controversial aspects of the Vietnam War was the public perception that the draft discriminated against African Americans. *(Library of Congress)*

became the first civil rights organization to denounce the war officially. Later the same year, the Georgia legislature attempted to deny Julian BOND his elected seat as a state representative after he publicly declared his opposition to the war. Bond was later ordered seated by the courts.

Influential Pacifists

Martin Luther KING, Jr., a committed pacifist, opposed U.S. military involvement in Vietnam on moral grounds. Throughout 1965, King attempted to convince the leadership of the CIVIL RIGHTS movement to take a strong antiwar stand. Many movement leaders remained reluctant, however, believing that such a stand would seem unpatriotic and result in an uncontrollable backlash.

In January, 1966, King could no longer hold back his views, and he issued a scathing attack on the war, denouncing it as disastrous for the African American community. Although King was forced to declare his position strictly as an individual, his influence had a dramatic impact, and the SOUTHERN CHRISTIAN LEADERSHIP CONFERENCE issued its formal endorsement of King's antiwar stand later that spring. King made his most famous antiwar speech at New York's Riverside Church on April 4, 1967, just days before he led a massive antiwar rally in New York City. His principled stand against military destruction in Vietnam had profound echoes throughout the African American community.

Also influential as a voice of African American dissent was heavyweight boxer Muhammad ALI, a member of the NATION OF ISLAM. Ali openly opposed the Vietnam War in 1966 and asserted that he "had no quarrel" with the Viet Cong. Following his public antiwar statements, Ali's draft status was reclassified, and he was ordered to report for active service.

Ali steadfastly refused induction, claiming exemption from the draft based on his Muslim

---

"Blood"

During the Vietnam War, many African American soldiers began referring to one another as "bloods." The term was exclusive to those serving in combat infantry and as helicopter door gunners. It was not applied to noncommissioned officers or the few black officers serving in Vietnam. Black soldiers wanted to establish their own identity as "grunts" separate from their white counterparts. The term reflected the divisive nature of the war on the battlefront and at home. Wallace Terry popularized the term in his book *Bloods: An Oral History of the Vietnam War by Black Veterans* (1984).

---

beliefs. The courts rejected his case, and he was convicted of draft evasion, stripped of his championship title, and sentenced to five years' imprisonment (his conviction was later overturned by the U.S. SUPREME COURT). Ali's principled refusal to serve in the armed forces dramatically affected the African American community, and Ali emerged a hero to dissenting youth of all races who opposed the draft.

—*Richard A. Dello Buono*

Suggested Readings:

Baskir, Lawrence M., and William A. Strauss. *Chance and Circumstances: The Draft, the War, and the Vietnam Generation*. New York: Alfred A. Knopf, 1978.

Harris, Norman. *Connecting Times: The Sixties in Afro-American Fiction*. Jackson: University Press of Mississippi, 1988.

Kolko, Gabriel. *Anatomy of a War: Vietnam, the United States, and the Modern Historical Experience*. New York: Pantheon Books, 1985.

Schuyler, Philippa. *Good Men Die*. New York: Twin Circle, 1969.

Taylor, Clyde, comp. *Vietnam and Black America: An Anthology of Protest and Resistance*. Garden City, N.Y.: Anchor Press, 1973.

Westheider, James E. *Fighting on Two Fronts: African Americans and the Vietnam War*. New York: New York University Press, 1997.

Vincent, Edward (b. June 23, 1934, Stubenville, Ohio): CALIFORNIA politician. Vincent received a B.A. in politics and government from the California State University at Los Angeles. His long-standing interest in civic and political affairs led to work with community organizations on a variety of issues. He entered local politics as a member of the school board and the city council of Inglewood, California, and was elected Inglewood MAYOR in 1986. In the 1990's he went on to serve as a California state assemblyman.

Virginia: Virginia was the home of the first African Americans, Nat TURNER's rebellion, and the nation's first black governor. According to estimates by the CENSUS OF THE UNITED STATES, the Virginia population stood at about 6.7 million in 1997; the state's African American population of a little over 1.3 million represented 20 percent of the state's population.

In 1619, three months before the Pilgrims arrived at Plymouth Rock, twenty indentured servants from Africa landed at Jamestown. Over the next hundred years, INDENTURED SERVITUDE of both whites and blacks gradually gave way to a system of black SLAVERY. Despite brutal living conditions for slaves, by 1720 the Virginia colony's slave population was increasing chiefly by reproduction rather than importation of Africans. It had multiplied sevenfold, to some 190,000—more than 40 percent of all Virginians—fifty years later. The "natural rights" principles of the AMERICAN REVOLUTION were in obvious conflict with slavery, but slaveholders, who included many government leaders (including President Thomas Jefferson), took no steps to resolve the contradiction.

By the eve of the CIVIL WAR in 1861, Virginia's black population had grown to 550,000, of whom more than a tenth were free. Those still enslaved were subject to being sold away, as Virginia increasingly exported slaves to other states. Resistance to slavery took many forms, including famous rebellions led by GABRIEL near Richmond in 1800 and by Nat Turner in Southampton County in 1831.

During the Civil War, more than thirty thousand slaves escaped to Union positions in eastern or northern Virginia; more than five thousand joined the Union army. Following the war, economic conditions in the state were bleak and the federal "radical Reconstruction" program was exceptionally short-lived there. Though twenty-seven African Americans were elected to the state legislature in 1869, the increasingly reactionary majority moved steadily to disfranchise blacks, effectively completing this task with the state's constitutional revision of 1902.

In the twenty years before WORLD WAR I, JIM CROW segregation prevailed; economic conditions were grim for most blacks, whether tenant farmers or city dwellers. One unin-

After Virginia closed its public schools in June, 1959, black students attended classes in make-shift facilities. *(Library of Congress)*

tended consequence of these conditions was the development of African American institutions, from fraternal organizations and Maggie L. WALKER's Richmond businesses to outspoken newspapers such as the Richmond *Planet* and the Norfolk *Journal and Guide*. Many black Virginians escaped injustices in Virginia by migrating northward; there were fewer African Americans in the state in 1930 than in 1900.

In 1951 African Americans in rural Prince Edward County launched a court case that eventually became part

Meanwhile, white children were bused to supposedly private schools financed by private and government contributions. *(Library of Congress)*

of the U.S. SUPREME COURT's BROWN V. BOARD OF EDUCATION decision of 1954, striking down racially segregated public schools. In the most extreme instance of the state's "massive resis-

tance" to desegregation, the county closed its public schools from 1959 to 1964. The civil rights struggle in Virginia took place largely in the courts, but there were also scores of SIT-INS

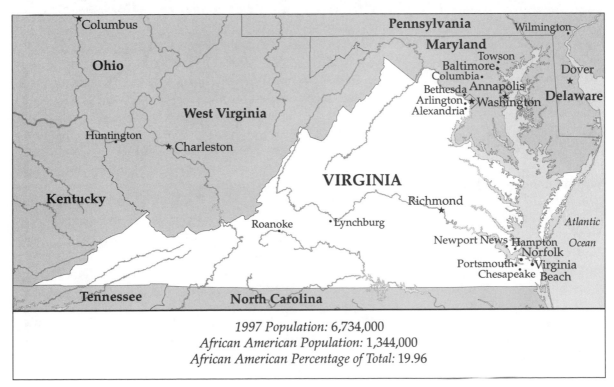

1997 Population: 6,734,000
African American Population: 1,344,000
African American Percentage of Total: 19.96

and other direct actions throughout the state. One such protest, in Danville in 1963, resulted in police violence reminiscent of that in BIRMINGHAM, ALABAMA.

Between 1970 and 1995, partly because of a re-migration of African Americans from the North, the black population in the state grew by nearly 50 percent, to more than 1.2 million. Public schools, universities, and other institutions were successfully if belatedly desegregated. In 1989 L. Douglas WILDER, the grandson of slaves, was elected the first black governor in the nation.

Virginia is the birthplace of numerous distinguished African Americans, including educator and congressman John Mercer LANGSTON, Booker T. WASHINGTON, poet Anne Spencer, civil rights forerunner Vernon JOHNS, blood-bank pioneer Charles R. DREW, "father of black history" Carter G. WOODSON, historian Luther P. Jackson, and sociologist Charles S. JOHNSON.

—George F. Bagby

Virgin Islands: The Virgin Islands are a group of about 110 WEST INDIES islands, many of them tiny and uninhabited, located east of PUERTO RICO between the Caribbean Sea and the Atlantic Ocean.

The Virgin Islands are divided into two territories, the U.S. Virgin Islands (which belonged to Denmark until 1917) and the British Virgin Islands. The U.S. Virgin Islands consist of three large islands, St. Croix, St. John, and St. Thomas, and more than fifty other smaller islands. The U.S. Virgin Islands had an esti-

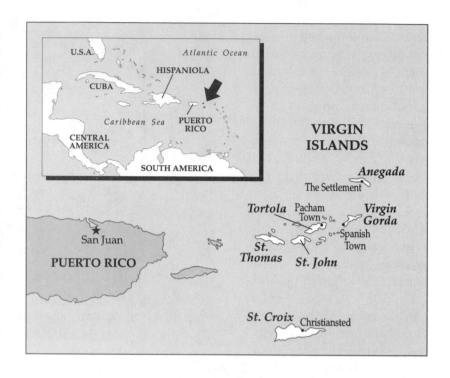

mated 1999 African American population of 87,000, or 80 percent of the total number of residents. The primary British Virgin Islands are Tortola, Anegada, Virgin Gorda, and Jost Van Dyke.

St. Thomas was first occupied by Danes in 1666. After 1673 the Danes brought in slaves to work on sugar cane PLANTATIONS; both cotton and sugar plantations operated on the Virgin Islands. By 1715 there were some three thousand slaves on St. Thomas. In 1684 the Danes claimed St. John, colonizing the island with planters in 1717. All the islands became part of the notorious "triangle of trade." Slaves would be transported from Africa to the islands. Rum and molasses would be shipped to Europe, from whence manufactured goods would be shipped to the islands. Charlotte Amalie, on St. Croix, in particular became a major center in the SLAVE TRADE. The system of SLAVERY that existed on the islands was harsh and repressive, and brutal punishments were routinely handed down.

In 1733 the slaves revolted on St. John, holding the island for six months until an international force broke the siege. Many slaves then committed SUICIDE rather than return to slavery. The Danes abandoned St. John to purchase St. Croix. By 1742 there were 1,900 slaves on St. Croix. In 1848 another slave uprising occurred, and slavery was abolished that same year. A number of slave rebellions also occurred on the British islands in the early nineteenth century.

In 1917, after many years of periodic negotiations, the United States purchased the Danish Virgin Islands, assigning a naval government. Public schools and modernized hospitals were built, and the native African Americans were trained and hired to fill the new white-collar positions. The U.S. Navy also established two all-African American naval bands, with the highest-ranking African American officer at the time, Alton A. Adams, Sr., as the bandmaster of the St. Thomas Naval Band.

The British islands gained their own elected government in 1967, and the U.S. islands followed in 1970. Both declined to agitate significantly for full independence, as both gained economic benefits from their links with the powerful countries that kept them as territories. By the late twentieth century, the Virgin Islands had thriving tourist economies and, compared with many Caribbean countries, a high standard of living. A devastating hurricane in 1995 caused considerable damage, but within a few years the tourist industry was back on its feet.

—Rose Secrest

Visual arts: African Americans have made significant contributions to visual arts in areas such as painting, illustration, sculpture, photography, film direction and cinematography, and FASHION design. The long histories of African Americans in the various visual arts share some common attributes, including an Afrocentric orientation in black folk culture creations, use of motifs and themes from an AFRICAN HERITAGE in modern styles, and adaptations of Eurocentric artistic ideals. A special relationship to ANCESTORS, community, and nature as well as an affinity for decoration and design are some of the recurrent themes in African American visual arts.

During the slave years and into the postcolonial period, African Americans gave their personal signatures to a wide variety of utilitarian arts and crafts. In the eighteenth and nineteenth centuries, black people in the Americas established themselves in the more Eurocentric genres of portraiture and landscape painting. The HARLEM RENAISSANCE years and the 1960's showed a return to an Afrocentric emphasis amid social and political concerns. Achievements in the visual arts of film direction and cinematography began in the early part of the

Children in an impoverished area of Charlotte Amalie on St. Thomas Island in 1941. *(Library of Congress)*

twentieth century, resurfaced strongly in the 1960's and 1970's, and exploded into mainstream prominence in the 1980's and 1990's, exposing African American culture and themes to a wider audience.

Retentions from Africa

Africans were first brought to the New World in the early sixteenth century. The artistic creations of the first black people in the Americas expressed both a private and a public aspect. Retentions from AFRICA can be seen in the hoodoo fetishes, quilts, canes and staffs, dolls, pottery, shells, beads, bone carvings, and gravestones of the early colonial period. The use of woven and painted material in clothing and house decorations suggests West and Central African motifs as well as establishing a unique fashion in adaptations of black dress that survived through the twentieth century world of fashion.

In the public sphere, African Americans were known to be excellent gold- and silversmiths, stoneware crafters, cabinetmakers, printers, engravers, and ironworkers who often incorporated aspects of African architectural and decorative techniques into their creations. The grotesque "monkey pots," or water jugs, created by slaves serve as one example. Many old buildings in LOUISIANA, SOUTH CAROLINA, and GEORGIA contain elements of African design. The African House (1750) on the Metoyer Estate in Louisiana, for example, reflects the architectural design found in a West African village. Thomas Day, a free black slaveholder, was a noted cabinetmaker during the early 1800's who utilized African designs in his work. A slave named Henry Gudgell carved a number of walking sticks in the 1800's that boast designs closely linked to African creations.

Early Painters

The first professional African American artists, both free and slave, were portrait painters. Scipio MOORHEAD was a slave painter active in BOSTON, MASSACHUSETTS, in the 1770's. None of his work survives. Phillis WHEATLEY, America's first black poet, dedicated a poem "to S.M., an African painter," probably referring to Moorhead. Neptune Thurston of Rhode Island was a slave known to have painted portraits around 1775. He may have influenced Gilbert Stuart, the famous painter of George Washington. The Reverend G. W. Hobbs, a former slave living in BALTIMORE, MARYLAND, painted the first known portrait pastel of another African American, in 1785.

The first authenticated African American artist was Joshua JOHNSTON. Born a slave in Baltimore, he is listed in that city's directories between 1796 and 1824 as a free householder who painted white society portraits such as *Young Lady on a Red Sofa* (c. 1810) in the style of Charles Peale. His *Portrait of a Cleric* (1805) depicts a black man. Julien Hudson was a free black portraitist active in the 1830's and 1840's whose *Self Portrait* (1839) is one of the first known self portraits by an African American.

Throughout the early and mid-1800's, a number of free black artists associated themselves with the ABOLITIONIST MOVEMENT. Robert Douglas, Jr. (1809-1887) was the first black person to attend the Pennsylvania Academy of Fine Arts, America's oldest art school. He created a lithographic portrait of William Lloyd GARRISON and was one of the first black artists to choose European exile. Patrick Henry Reason was a PHILADELPHIA engraver who created the emblem of the British antislavery movement, depicting a chained slave in *Am I Not a Man and a Brother?* His companion piece, *Am I Not a Woman and a Sister?*, shows his concern for the denial of rights of black women. His *Portrait of Henry Bibb* (1840) suggests a familiarity with photography, which had been brought to the United States from Europe only recently.

One of the first Americans to use photography was Jules Lion, a mulatto artist who introduced the daguerreotype to NEW ORLEANS, LOUISIANA, in 1840 or earlier. Lion is noted for his portrait of the famous mulatto naturalist and artist John James Audubon, who was one of the greatest American painters of the natural world. Other painters of this era included David Bostill Bowser, who painted a portrait of Abraham Lincoln as well as marine landscapes that focus on personal impressions. A. B. Wilson was a self-taught painter who lived in Philadelphia and created a lithographic portrait of the Reverend John Cornish in 1840. William Simpson was listed in the BOSTON, MASSACHUSETTS, directories (1860-1866) as a portrait painter. He is known for his Loguen portraits (1835) of Bishop Loguen and his wife Caroline, a fugitive slave.

Robert DUNCANSON was the first African American landscape painter to receive widespread recognition in the United States and abroad. Influenced by Thomas Cole and Asher B. Durand of the Hudson River school, Duncanson was a master of atmospheric and pastoral elements. Listed in the Cincinnati, Ohio, directory as a daguerreotypist, Duncanson was associated with J. P. Ball, a black PHOTOGRAPHER who started taking pictures in 1845. The wide aerial perspective Duncanson used in *View of Cincinnati* (c. 1852) suggests a camera angle and is one of the few surviving examples of an early American cityscape. Duncanson traveled to Europe a number of times and rendered several classical versions of the ruins of Pompeii. His painting *Uncle Tom and Little Eva* (1853) was inspired by the antislavery novel UNCLE TOM'S CABIN (1852) and suggests his social conscience. Duncanson helped dispel the myth of black intellectual inferiority in the fine arts. His late landscapes combined elements of naturalism with romantic fantasy, resulting in a unique style.

Edward Mitchell BANNISTER studied under noted sculptor William Rimmer. Considered to be the first black American regionalist painter, Bannister produced his first commis-sioned work, *The Ship Outward Bound*, in 1855. He won the bronze medal for painting at the Philadelphia Centennial Exposition (1876) for *Under the Oaks* (now lost) but was refused entry into the exhibit because of his color. Bannister painted atmospheric landscapes reminiscent of the Dutch masters and the Barbizon school, witnessed in such paintings as *Driving Home the Cows* (1881) and *Approaching Storm* (1886). It is reputed that Bannister painted to disprove a statement published in the *New York Herald* in 1867 that said "the Negro seems to have an appreciation for art, while being manifestly unable to produce it." Bannister was founder of the Providence Art Club, which later became the Rhode Island School of Design.

Early Sculptors

Eugene Warbourg was a SCULPTOR from New Orleans who departed to Europe in the 1850's. His only existing sculpture is a portrait bust of John Young Mason (c. 1853). Edmonia LEWIS was one of the few women and the only black woman represented at the Philadelphia Centennial Exposition. *The Dying Cleopatra* (c. 1876), a marble work in the neoclassical tradition, depicted the beauty of African people and won an award. As the first major African American woman sculptor, Lewis was also one of the first black women to attend OBERLIN COLLEGE. She strongly expressed African American and humanistic themes in her work. *Forever Free* (1867) shows two slave figures on the day of emancipation. Lewis, who was part Native American, was a visionary artist who foreshadowed many of the themes of racial injustice and black pride that were to reemerge in the 1920's, 1930's, and 1960's.

Painters of the Late 1800's

Grafton Tyler Brown was a lithographer, painter, and itinerant artist who probably was the first black artist to work in CALIFORNIA, where he created many early views of San

Francisco. As a member of a geological survey party in the West, Brown witnessed many natural wonders that he later depicted in paintings such as *Grand Canyon of the Yellowstone* (1891).

Henry Ossawa TANNER was the second black person to study at the Pennsylvania Academy of Fine Arts, where he worked under Thomas Eakins. Tanner taught at Clark College in Atlanta and worked as a photographer in that city. In 1891 Tanner studied with Benjamin Constant in Paris, painting landscapes before returning to the United States in 1892. His *The Banjo Lesson* (1893) is one of the most famous early African American genre paintings. Depicting an old man with a young boy on his knee strumming a banjo, the painting expresses a sense of continuity and tradition in African American culture. Tanner returned to Paris, where he painted a series of religious subjects such as *Two Disciples at the Tomb* (1906), *The Three Marys* (1910), and *Daniel in the Lions' Den* (c. 1916) that secured his reputation as a master of modern religious painting. Recognized both in the United States and abroad, Tanner was elected to the French National Academy. He remained an expatriate because of racial prejudice. His romantic religious paintings, while extending an academic style, rejected modernism and failed to develop black themes in a distinctive African American way.

Other important artists of the period include William A. Harper, a pupil of Tanner who died at the age of thirty-seven while traveling in Mexico. He was primarily a landscape painter rooted in the Barbizon school, as witnessed in such paintings as *Autumn Landscape* (c. 1900-1910) and *Early Afternoon at Montigny* (1905). James V. Herring founded the art department at HOWARD UNIVERSITY in 1930 and organized the first major black-run art gallery. His work, for example *Campus Landscape* (1924), shows the influence of French Impressionism in line and color.

Sculptors of the Late 1800's and Early 1900's
Meta Vaux Warrick FULLER and May Howard Jackson were two black female sculptors who initiated black themes that pointed the way to the HARLEM RENAISSANCE. Fuller studied in Paris and was influenced by Rodin. Sculptures such as *The Wretched* (1903), *Waterboy* (1914), and *The Awakening of Ethiopia* (1914) were neoclassical in origin yet influenced by an emotional impressionism. Jackson rejected European themes and stressed in all of her work a deep concern with African American social problems. Her *Head of a Negro Child* (1916) is a fine example of her work, infused with dignity and hope.

Harlem Renaissance
During the 1920's in HARLEM, New York, a new awareness of black culture developed into an artistic movement known as the Harlem Renaissance. Critics such as Alain LOCKE in his *The New Negro: An Interpretation* (1925), publishers and collectors such as James L. Coady and Albert C. Barnes, and organizations such as the Harmon Foundation stressed the positive attributes of African American cultural achievements. The first major exhibition of art by black Americans was held at the International House in NEW YORK CITY in 1928. The exhibition was one way of expressing those attributes to a wider audience. A sense of self-reliance, respect, and pride in African ancestry fostered the movement. White music critic, photographer, and novelist Carl Van Vechten helped popularize Harlem, and black photographers such as James VAN DER ZEE, Morgan and Marvin Smith, and Gordon PARKS, Sr., recorded the lively scene. Black female photographers such as Elise Forrest Harleston and Jennie Louise Welcome, the sister of James Van Der Zee, also were active at this time.

The popularity of African American cultural expression in MUSIC, DANCE, and fashion led to an international awareness of black

American creativity during the Jazz Age. Although a black American, Elizabeth Keckley, had once designed a ball dress for Mary Todd Lincoln, it was stars such as the black performer Josephine BAKER who helped transform the Parisian fashion world. Eventually the clothes, dances, and speaking styles of black musicians, and actors would influence large segments of the American fashion and social worlds.

At the same time, African American interest in cinema generated an independent FILM movement, establishing a tradition that continued through the twentieth century. The first black film, *Darktown Jubilee*, starring Bert WILLIAMS, was made in 1914. Oscar MICHEAUX is the best-known early black director. He made his first film, *The Homesteader*, in 1918. His *Within Our Gates* (1920) and *Body and Soul* (1925), the latter starring Paul ROBESON, were silent films influenced by Hollywood productions but with black actors. Micheaux's *The Exile* (1931) was the first black talking picture, and *God's Step Children* (1937) tackles black social issues such as passing. Micheaux made more than thirty films between 1918 and 1948.

Emmett J. Scott, in collaboration with the NATIONAL ASSOCIATION FOR THE ADVANCEMENT OF COLORED PEOPLE (NAACP), made a film called *The Birth of a Race* (1918) that stands as a counterstatement to D. W. Griffith's racist THE BIRTH OF A NATION (1915). The Ebony Film Company's *Spyin' the Spy* (1915) and the LINCOLN MOTION PICTURE COMPANY'S *The Realization of a Negro's Ambition* (1916) are other early silent films. The Colored Players Film Corporation was responsible for *Ten Nights in a Barroom* (1926), with Charles Gilpin, and *Scar of Shame* (1927). Folklore inspired films such as *Georgia Rose* (1930), *Absent* (1928), a black western titled *Bronze Buckaroo* (1938), a black horror film titled *Son of Ingagi* (1940), and straightforward folktales such as *The Blood of Jesus* (1941) and *Go Down Death* (1944). WORLD WAR II inspired Carlton Moss's *The Negro Soldier* (1943), made for the Department of the Army.

Painters of the Harlem Renaissance and 1930's
As a painter, illustrator, and muralist in the forefront of the Harlem Renaissance, Aaron DOUGLAS studied with Winold Reiss in New York and Othon Frieze in Paris (1931). Douglas illustrated James Weldon Johnson's *God's Trombones: Seven Negro Sermons in Verse* (1927) and painted a series of murals that combined an inspirational vision of African American nobility with proletarian themes. His angular silhouettes offset by jagged intrusions, wavy lines, and pastel circles transformed Art Deco conventions with African art motifs and African American themes. His murals entitled *Aspects of Negro Life* (1934) are displayed at the SCHOMBURG CENTER FOR RESEARCH IN BLACK CULTURE in the New York Public Library. In them, he traces the course of African Americans from Africa through SLAVERY to an en-

Hale Woodruff has been acclaimed as a master of modernist painting. *(Library of Congress)*

Malvin Gray Johnson's *Thinnin' Corn. (National Archives)*

lightened future. Douglas depicted the dignity, courage, and hope of African Americans on an epic scale.

Archibald J. MOTLEY, Jr., and Palmer C. HAYDEN brought new attention to black genre painting. Motley did a series of canvases between 1933 and 1936 that includes *The Barbecue*, *Saturday Night*, and *The Chicken Shack*. The paintings render in vivid detail the raucous nightlife of Harlem. Hayden combined African sculpture with a modern setting in his still life *Fetiche et Fleurs* (1926) and depicted street life in Harlem in pictures such as *Midsummer Night in Harlem* (c. 1934). Both artists based their art on black life in the United States. Many other artists, including Hale Woodruff, Charles Alston, Dox Thrash, Eldzier Cortor, and Joseph Delaney, participated in or were influenced by the Harlem Renaissance and went on to work for the Federal Art Project, a Depression-era government program for artists.

Artists such as Charles Sebree, Charles White, John Wilson, and John Biggers developed their own variations on the social realist style. Many artists worked in a social-protest style. Hale Woodruff visited with Henry

Ossawa Tanner in 1927 and soon after painted the *Card Players* (1930), which shows the influence of cubism. His *Amistad* (1939) murals are large works commemorating the AMISTAD SLAVE REVOLT (1839). Malvin Gray Johnson also experimented with American cubism and African themes in such paintings as *Negro Masks* (1932).

William Edouard Scott was a painter and muralist who attended the Art Institute of Chicago and who helped define a new African American tradition in painting. Traveling to HAITI in 1931 on a Rosenwald Grant, Scott executed a series of paintings on folk themes. *Haitian Fisherman* (c. 1931) and *When the Tide is Out* (c. 1931) are examples of rich coloring and expressive brush stroke applied to indigenous motifs. Ellis Wilson is another black artist who traveled to Haiti and painted local subjects, in *Funeral Procession* (1940) and *Field Workers* (1941), using an expressionistic style. Laura Wheeler Waring and Edwin A. Harleston are best known for their realistic figure portraits. In Waring's *Frankie, Portrait of a Child* (1937) and Harleston's *The Old Servant* (1930), genre scenes are executed with impressionistic coloring that contributed much to the tradition of American portraiture.

Sculptors and Photographers

A stonemason named William Edmunson started sculpting in stone when he was fifty years old. His direct yet unique figures (among them the undated *Eve* and *Nude Woman Seated on a Stool*) show a distinctive style reminiscent of African totem sculpture. Selma Burke also stylized sculptures, as in

Temptation (1938). Two other sculptors, Sargent JOHNSON and Richmond BARTHÉ, were concerned with African American themes in their work. Johnson's *Forever Free* (1933) and Barthé's *Blackberry Woman* (1932) and *African Dancer* (1933) depict black subjects with Afrocentric stylizations. Many photographers were working in the early part of the century, including Addison Scurlock, P. H. Polk, and Ellis L. Weems, who was active in the early 1920's.

Primitive Painters

Artists including Bill Traylor, Clementine Hunter, Horace PIPPIN, Minnie Evans, and Edward Webster can be grouped together as "primitives." Their approach relies in part on intuition and an independent, nonacademic attitude that results in unique work combining naïve experimentation with folk elements. Pippin in some ways exemplifies this group. His style suggests the limners of early Americana, but his content depicts African American culture. His devastating experiences fighting in the trenches during WORLD WAR I are expressed in his painting *The End of the War: Starting Home* (c. 1931). Pippin painted genre scenes such as *Domino Players* (1943) and *Cabin in the Cotton III* (1944) as well as still-life interiors such as *Victorian Interior* (1946). Near the end of his life, he turned to spiritual themes, as in *The Holy Mountain II* (1945).

Traylor and Hunter were self-taught artists who concentrated on American scenes handled with a naïve folk quality. Hunter's *The Funeral on Cane River (1948)* and *Cotton Ginning* (1975) are good examples of her art. Evans was born in a log cabin in North Carolina. Her paintings, many influenced by the Book of Revelations, are filled with designs and arcane imagery. *Design Made at Airlie Garden* (1967) expresses her style well. Edward Webster, who worked as a postal carrier, also shows the influence of religion in his paintings. A good example is *The Nativity* (1957).

Black Modernists

A connection might be made in the use of color, perspective, and design between the "primitive" African American painters and the black modernists, who were influenced by European movements such as fauvism, expressionism, and cubism as well as by African art. Artists such as William H. Johnson, Romare Bearden, Thomas Sills, Jacob Lawrence, Claude Clark, and Beauford Delaney heightened their colors and utilized abstract design qualities to produce high emotion in their work. Hughie Lee Smith retained elements of Surrealism in his work. James Porter, the author of *Modern Negro Art* (1943), Margaret Burroughs, Augusta Savage, and James Lewis were educators as well as artists successful in the modernist tradition.

Artists in other areas also developed along modernist lines. Sculptors in this style include William Artis, Marion Perkins, Elizabeth CATLETT, John Rhoden, Ed Wilson, Earl

A Decorative Head by sculptor William E. Artis. *(National Archives)*

Hooks, and William Taylor. Allan Rohan CRITE, Wilmer Jennings, Walter WILLIAMS, Richard Mayhew, George Ridley, Jr., and Sam Middleton were successful illustrators, printmakers, and painters. Photographers such as Austin Hansen and Roy DeCARAVA were active in Harlem during and after World War II. Female photographers working in this period included Louise Martin, and Wilhelmina Pearl Selena Roberts.

William H. JOHNSON worked his way through the National Academy of Design in New York. In 1924 he traveled to Europe, where he lived and painted for twenty years. Influenced by African art as well as by German expressionism, Johnson returned to the United States. In paintings such as *Harbour Under the Midnight Sun* (c. 1935-1938) and *Mt. Calvary* (1939), he produced work that expressed his personal vision of the world.

Jacob LAWRENCE is perhaps the best-known African American postwar painter and illustrator. He used African American themes of history and culture in a number of series of paintings, such as the Frederick DOUGLASS series (1937-1938). These series may have been influenced by the historical an-

tecedents of Egyptian wall painting and Mexican murals. Lawrence was a master craftsman able to merge narration, figuration, and abstract design into striking statements. He illustrated poet Langston HUGHES's *One-Way Ticket* (1948). Concerned with African American history, culture, and social injustice, Lawrence depicts historical figures and black communal life with harsh angular movement and explosive colors. His distorted but highly intuitive paintings combine elements of expressionism and cubism with African American themes. In paintings such as *Street Scene #1* (1936) and *3 Family Toilet* (1943), Lawrence affirmed his commitment to the bitter struggle of black people for personal dignity and freedom.

Romare BEARDEN was a member of the American Academy of Arts and Letters and received the President's National Medal of Arts in 1987. As a painter, scholar, and curator, Bearden added to, as well as preserved, the traditions of African American art. Bearden studied with the German social satirist painter George Grosz. He is recognized as one of America's finest collagists. He sometimes used the *dechirage* technique, in which paper is torn away to reveal underlying areas. He juxtaposed dynamic colors and distorted images to create a unified iconography that was particularly American but influenced by the Dada and Surrealist movements. *Conjur Woman* (1964) suggests a fascination with African American religious traditions. He used photomontage images of masks and textiles from Africa in combination with black vernacular themes and

Part of a series on the Great Migration painted by Jacob Lawrence in 1941. *(National Archives)*

Romare Bearden's *After Church*. *(National Archives)*

saw a connection between his methods and JAZZ improvisation. Bearden organized "Contemporary Art of the American Negro" (1966) as the first major show in Harlem since the 1930's. He wrote *The Painters Mind: The Relations of Structure and Space in Painting* (1969) with Carl Holty. Bearden was working on a history of African American artists with Harry Henderson when he died in New York City in 1988, at the age of seventy-six.

The Black Arts Movement

The Black Arts movement of the 1960's and 1970's demanded that art and politics be interconnected and that African American arts be given public access and recognition. Numerous museums and galleries were founded in response to the movement, and others began showing a greater interest in African American art. The Studio Museum of Harlem had a long history of presenting black artists. Com-

munity workshops and galleries sprang up in many major cities, such as the Cinque gallery in Manhattan and the Black Man's Art Gallery in San Francisco. Benny Andrews and Cliff Joseph were cofounders of the Black Emergency Cultural Coalition, which supported black artists. After the 1963 MARCH ON WASHINGTON, Alvin Hollingsworth and Norman Lewis founded Spiral, a group of black artists organized around the black aesthetic.

In 1968 Jeff Donaldson and Frederic Jon Eversley, among others, founded AFRICOBRA, or the African Commune of Bad Relevant Artists. Weusi ("black" in Swahili) was founded in Harlem in 1965. In 1971 Kay Brown and Faith RINGGOLD helped found a group of black women artists called Where We At. The Black Arts movement also resulted in a return to public art, as witnessed by the many politically inspired murals collectively painted on buildings in major cities. Among them is the

Wall of Respect (1967) in Chicago. During the late 1960's and 1970's, street art in mural form was created by artists such as William Walker and Mitchell Caton in Chicago and Dana Chandler in Boston.

Paintings with themes encompassing civil rights and the VIETNAM WAR, many of which depicted the American flag, were produced by Reginald Gammon, Herman "Kofi" Bailey, David Braford, Bertrand Phillips, Manuel Hughes, Phillip Lindsay Mason, William Henderson, and David Hammon, among many others. A number of artists were inspired by visits to Africa. Among them were Ademola Olugebefola, Raymond Saunders, Lucile Malkia Roberts, Floyd Coleman, and David Driskell. Other artists, such as Paul Keene, Arthur Carraway, and Mikelle Fletcher, were influenced by VOODOO and a synthesis of pan-African and American themes.

Painters such as Thomas Sills, Richard Mayhew, Daniel Johnson, Xenobia Smith, Milton Young, Emilio Cruz, and Bernie Casey worked in abstract and geometric symbolist styles. Charles Young, Teixeira Nash, Edward Sowells, and particularly Robert Thompson extended the expressionist experimentation in figurative paintings.

Artists Using Other Forms

Assemblage and painted constructions offered other avenues of expression for black artists such as Noah Purifoy, Sam Gilliam, Christopher Shelton, Joe Overstreet, Alvin Loving, Bing Davis, Ron Griffin, Marie Johnson, Edward Bural, and Betye Saar. Contemporary sculptors made important contributions in the post-World War II years. Among them are Juan Logan, John Riddle, Mel Edwards, Houston Conwill, and particularly Richard Hunt, whose welded steel forms pushed sculpture in a new direction.

Tom Lloyd, who edited *Black Art Notes*, Ed Love, Mel Edwards, Walter Johnson, Evangeline Montgomery, and P'lla Mills also were known for steel and welding construction. Earl Hooks, Mahler Ryder, Daniel Johnson, Walter Jackson, Larry Urbina, and Ben Hazard used plastics and resins to create sculptures. Barbara CHASE-RIBOUD used the lost-wax technique and fiber-wrapped art that recalled weaving, whereas Allen Fannin used yarns, and Maven Hassinger and Napoleon Jones Henderson used pottery and carvings. Ruth Waddy, Margo Humphrey, Carol Ward, Devoice Berry, Marion Epting, and Cleveland Bellow worked in silkscreen and lithography. Mikki Ferrill and Phillda Ragland-Njau are two of the better-known female photographers from this civil rights period.

The Fashion Industry and Crafts

African Americans also were active in the fashion industry in the 1960's and 1970's, designing clothes and influencing the international market. Among them were Willi Smith, Patrick Kelley, Jay Smith, and Ann Lowe, who designed dresses for film stars as well as making Jacqueline Kennedy's wedding dress. Lois Alexander had her own boutique in Washington, D.C., for more than thirty years, and in 1979 she opened the Black Fashion Museum in Harlem.

Many black artists of this period turned to traditional crafts. Bill Maxwell, Camille Billops, and Doyle Lane worked in clay and ceramics. Art Smith, Bob Jefferson, Joanne Lee, and Margaret Collins used jewelry and beads. Douglass Phillips used stained glass. Other artists, recalling an Afrocentric tradition of tree and yard decoration, used found objects and other devices to create provocative sculptures and constructions. Among these artists were Sultan Rogers, Bessie Harvey, Ibibio Fundi, Derek Webster, Mr. Imagination, and John Outerbridge. Ben Jones and Lovett Thompson used African sculpture forms to create modern sculpture in *The Junkie* (1970). Robert Reid and Makam Bailey combined elements of street art, GRAFFITI, and other black iconographies into their works. Finally, a number of artists used nature and animal symbology combined with the traditions of Surrealism to express African American themes. These include Irene Clark, Norma Morgan, Gary Rickson, Suzanne Jackson, and Leslie Price.

Black Filmmaking
A second important phase of filmmaking occurred during this period. Black FILM DIRECTORS worked with limited budgets on films starring black actors and featuring African American themes. Melvin VAN PEEBLES directed *Watermelon Man* (1970) and *Sweet Sweetback's Baadasssss Song* (1971) and wrote the screenplay for *The Sophisticated Gents* (1981). Ossie DAVIS directed *Cotton Comes to Harlem* (1970). Gordon Parks, Sr., made *The Learning Tree* (1969) and *Shaft* (1971), and his son, Gordon Parks, Jr., directed *Super Fly* (1972). These last two films were part of the BLAXPLOITATION trend in filmmaking, which used themes of black militancy and urban unrest in urban crime dramas. Sexual themes were common in blaxploitation films. Other notable directors and films from this period are Hugh A. Robertson's *Melinda* (1972); Robert Downey's satiric comedy about a black takeover of an advertising agency, titled *Putney Swope* (1969); Charles Burnett's *Killer of Sheep* (1977); Larry Clark's *Passing Through* (1977); and Haile Gerima's *Bush Mama* (1977).

The 1980's and 1990's
The 1980's and 1990's witnessed the blossoming of a new interest in African American culture and its influence on mainstream American culture as a whole. Black fashion designers such as Carl Jones, Thomas Walker, C. D. Greene, Eric Gaskins, and Bryon Lars created distinctive styles influenced by urban street fashion as well as by old films. Others, such as Arthur McGee, had been creating original clothes since the 1950's. Once again, as in

the 1920's and 1930's, celebrities from sports and films, as well as from television, created new fashion styles.

Black directors created films with black actors and black themes that have been seen by culturally diverse audiences. Among these directors is Spike LEE, with *She's Gotta Have It* (1986), *School Daze* (1988), *Do The Right Thing* (1989), *Mo' Better Blues* (1990), *Jungle Fever* (1991), and *Malcolm X* (1992). Other directors contributing to this movement are Robert Townsend with *Hollywood Shuffle* (1987), Reginald and Warrington Hudlin with *House Party* (1990), Mario Van Peebles with *New Jack City* (1991), and John Singleton with *Boyz 'N the Hood* (1991). Julie DASH's *Daughters of the Dust* (1992) concerns a South Sea Island Gullah family and resonates with the themes of community, ancestor worship, and African retentions in clothing, food, and language.

African Americans continued to use the visual arts to redefine their culture through a revitalization of spirit that draws from African and African American sources. Some artists, such as Alma Thomas and Lois Mailou Jones, created important art for much of the twentieth century. Other female artists, such as Bessie Harvey, Betye Saar, Jean Lacy, Varnette Honeywood, and Renee Stout, used painting and various types of assemblage to express Afrocentric themes of community and religion in new ways. During 1998-1999, a traveling exhibition, "Elizabeth Catlett Sculpture: Fifty-Year Retrospective," was shown in various U.S. museums. The exhibition paid homage to one of the great black women sculptors.

Women contributed strongly to the tradition of African American photography. Among them are Coreen Simpson, Marilyn Nance, Lorna Simpson, and Carrie Mae WEEMS. A number of photographers, such as Anthony Barboza, Billy (Fundi) Abernathy, Dawoud Bey, Todd Gray, and Wendell White, used African American figures and themes in their pictures. Moneta SLEET, Jr., was the first black photographer to win the Pulitzer Prize, in 1969. Chuck Stewart took photographs of jazz stars, and Dick Saunders was a well-known photojournalist. In 1995 Don Camp became only the second African American photographer to receive a Guggenheim Fellowship.

Multicultural awareness has influenced such painters as Emma Amos, Howardena Pindell, Vernell DeSilva, Larry Rivers, and Jean Michel Basquiat. Ancestral arts and trips to Africa affected other painters, such as Roosevelt "Rip" Woods, Jr., Charles Searles, Leon Refro, Jack Whitten, Vusumuzi Maduna, William T. Williams, Matthew Thomas, Kofi Kayiga, James Phillips, and Marion Brown. They express, through their use of design, color, and geometries, a renewed interest in Afrocentric music and movement. They and other artists continued to express the essential spirit of African American culture.

—*Stephen Soitos*
—*Updated by Jeffry Jensen*

See also: Fashion; Painters and illustrators.

Suggested Readings:

Dallas Museum of Art. *Black Art Ancestral Legacy: The African Impulse in African-American Art*. New York: Harry N. Abrams, 1989.

Driskell, David C., ed. *African American Visual Aesthetics: A Postmodernist View*. Washington, D.C.: Smithsonian Institution Press, 1995

Fine, Elsa H. *The Afro-American Artist: A Search for Identity*. New York: Hacker Art Books, 1982.

Lewis, Samella S. *African American Art and Artists*. 2d ed. Berkeley: University of California Press, 1994.

Moutoussamy-Ashe, Jeanne. *Viewfinders: Black Women Photographers*. New York: Dodd, Mead, 1986.

Patton, Sharon F. *African-American Art*. New York: Oxford University Press, 1998.

Robinson, Joyntyle T., and Maya Angelou, eds. *Bearing Witness: Contemporary Works by African American Women Artists*. New York: Spelman College and Rizzoli International, 1996.

Stuckey, Sterling. *Going Through the Storm: The Influence of African-American Art in History*. New York: Oxford University Press, 1994.

Thompson, Robert F. *Flash of the Spirit: African and Afro-American Art and Philosophy*. New York: Vintage, 1984.

White, Jack E. "The Beauty of Black Art." *Time* (October 10, 1994): 66-73.

Willis-Thomas, Deborah. *Black Photographers, 1940-1988: An Illustrated Bio-Bibliography*. New York: Garland, 1989.

Voodoo: Religion that originated in AFRICA and was brought to HAITI by slaves. It is also known as Voudoun, Vodou, Vadu, and Vodun. The roots of Voodoo practice are credited to the West African Yoruba people and their beliefs. The word "Voudoun" and its variations are probably French or African in origin, while the word "Voodoo" derives from Louisiana Creole terminology. Translated from the Yoruba language, "Voudoun" means god, creator, or great spirit. Worshipers communicate with the god through numerous spirits or deities called loa and perform ceremonies to honor the loa in return for help in their personal lives.

Practitioners offer sacrifices to the loa in the form of vegetables, fruits, and sometimes animal meat such as chicken, goat, or dog. Each loa has a preferred sacrifice, which is believed to nourish and invigorate them. Worshipers also believe that a loa can possess their bodies in order to further communicate their wishes.

Ceremonies are led by a priest (a houngan) or a priestess (a mambo). The priest or priestess conducts ceremonies for events such as births, marriages, and deaths. Ceremonies are also performed to prevent or end bad fortune and to heal. Candles, rattles, drums, and elaborately decorated flags are items commonly used in the rituals. Anyone may participate regardless of race, gender, or nationality. African slaves in Haiti could not openly practice Voodoo. Doing so often resulted in imprisonment or even execution. In most instances, French colonists insisted that slaves practice Roman Catholicism. Many slaves, believing that Voodoo provided a connection between them, continued to worship in secret. As a result, ROMAN CATHOLIC tenets became meshed with Voodoo beliefs. Voodoo was transported via the slave trade from Haiti to other Caribbean islands such as Jamaica and CUBA; it evolved into Obeah in JAMAICA and SANTERÍA in Cuba.

Voodoo is practiced in the United States in New Orleans, New York, Chicago, and major cities with large concentrations of Haitian immigrants. Worldwide, Voodoo has an estimated fifty to sixty million followers. Voodoo worshipers have pointed out that the film industry and broadcast media have exaggerated aspects of Voodoo and incorrectly portrayed the religion as demonic. Followers maintain that black magic, "Voodoo dolls," and such fantastic creatures as zombies falsely depict the religion. While some practitioners may include black magic and dolls in their worship, these are not common practices. Another misconception of Voodoo is the belief that Hoodoo and Voodoo are the same. Although the two resemble each other in many aspects, Hoodoo focuses on folk magic and the use of herbs, charms, and minerals.

—*Sandra Walton Gillespie*

Suggested Readings:

Davis, Rod. *American Voudou: Journey into a Hidden World.* Denton: University of North Texas Press, 1998.

Metraux, Alfred. *Voodoo in Haiti.* Reissued edition. Translated by Hugo Charteris. New York: Schocken Books, 1989.

Olmos, Margarite Fernandez, and Lizabeth Paravisini-Gerbert, eds. *Sacred Possessions: Voudou, Santeria, Obeah, and the Caribbean.* New Brunswick, N.J.: Rutgers University Press, 1997.

Voter Education Project: Attempt to register African American voters in the South. The Voter Education Project (VEP) was started by the Southern Regional Council (SRC) in March of 1962. The idea for the VEP evolved from discussions started by officials of the Justice Department and SRC leaders after the CONGRESS OF RACIAL EQUALITY (CORE) had sponsored its FREEDOM RIDES through the South. The VEP was conceived as a nonpartisan voter registration drive and provided financial support for voter registration campaigns throughout the South. The VEP at first was financed by the Taconic Foundation, the Field Foundation, the Edgar Stern Family Fund, and the National Association of Intergroup Relations Officers.

The VEP voter registration activities were executed through the leading civil rights organizations, including the NATIONAL ASSOCIATION FOR THE ADVANCEMENT OF COLORED PEOPLE (NAACP), STUDENT NONVIOLENT COORDINATING COMMITTEE (SNCC), and SOUTHERN CHRISTIAN LEADERSHIP CONFERENCE (SCLC). In MISSISSIPPI, an umbrella organization known as the Council of Federated Organizations (COFO) was the conduit for the VEP voter registration efforts. In the mid-1960's through a part of the 1970's, the VEP provided leadership and assistance to the MISSISSIPPI FREEDOM DEMOCRATIC PARTY.

The VEP registered approximately 688,000 African Americans as voters in eleven southern states between April, 1962, and November, 1964. The VEP registration drive resulted in one of the largest and most significant increases in African American voters since the U.S. SUPREME COURT had outlawed all-white primaries in *Smith v. Alwright* in 1944.

The VEP provided strategy and administration. Its first executive directors were Wiley A. Branton (1962-1965), Vernon E. JORDAN, Jr. (1965-1970), and John Robert LEWIS (1970-1977). After the main burst of voter registration, the SRC conformed to a 1969 tax reform law which stated that any tax-exempt organi-

Birmingham women participating in a May, 1963, voter education meeting. *(Library of Congress)*

zation engaged in voter-registration activities was not allowed to receive more than 25 percent of its financial support from one source. To comply, the SRC decided in 1970 to separate from the VEP, and the VEP organized itself as an independent body. The VEP was granted a charter and tax-exempt status as an independent voter-registration organization. It also began a program of informing black office-holders about issues and about techniques of achieving the goals held by black voters.

Voters: African Americans have long recognized that the ballot box is one of the most effective instruments that can be used to achieve equality. With the right to vote comes political power, and with political power comes the ability to effect real and lasting changes within American society and to allow the voices of minority groups to be heard.

History

Although some blacks were permitted to vote in each of the original thirteen North American colonies, African American suffrage was not established as a national policy until the ratification of the FIFTEENTH AMENDMENT in 1870. Before that time, the U.S. Constitution left the question of electoral qualifications up to the states. Since slaves were not recognized as American citizens, they were not given the right to vote, and only a few states permitted free blacks to vote. For purposes of congressional representation, however, which is determined by a state's population, the U.S. CONSTITUTION stated that "all other persons" (for example, black slaves) were to be counted as three-fifths of a person. Thus, those states with large slave populations procured a relatively large number of representatives in Congress on the basis of possessing a large body of slaves who could not vote.

Even before the AMERICAN REVOLUTION began, several states began restricting the black vote: SOUTH CAROLINA in 1716, VIRGINIA in 1723, and GEORGIA in 1761. As the slave population grew, and with it the fear of SLAVE RESISTANCE, state after state began restricting suffrage to white men. DELAWARE prohibited black voting in 1792, KENTUCKY in 1799, OHIO in 1803, NEW JERSEY in 1807, MARYLAND in 1810, LOUISIANA in 1812, CONNECTICUT in 1814, TENNESSEE in 1834, NORTH CAROLINA in 1835, PENNSYLVANIA in 1838, and FLORIDA in 1845. NEW YORK allowed only those blacks who owned property to vote, a qualification not required of white voters, and the new states coming into the Union all banned black voting. Thus, in the pre-CIVIL WAR United States, free blacks were permitted to vote without restriction only in five New England states.

The Fifteenth Amendment

Resistance to black suffrage continued throughout the Civil War and into RECONSTRUCTION. Even after slavery was formally abolished by the THIRTEENTH AMENDMENT in 1865, the defeated southern states continued to oppose the recognition of the free status of African Americans. Blacks legally received the right to vote in 1867 with the passage of the first RECONSTRUCTION ACT, which granted African Americans voting rights as part of the price paid by rebellious southern states for readmission to the Union. Yet in the lower North, where most northern blacks lived, white voters in referendum after referendum rejected black suffrage. In 1869 black men could vote in only twenty states.

During this time, congressional Republicans pressed for a constitutional amendment to secure the right of blacks to vote in every state, thus avoiding the risk of possible rejection by state referenda. The Fifteenth Amendment finally became law on March 30, 1870, after thirteen months of debate and a number of compromises. To ensure passage, its sponsors were forced to omit a clause outlawing literacy tests and another banning racial discrimination in determining qualifications for holding political office. Nevertheless, most African Americans celebrated its ratification, believing it to be a solemn written pledge by the U.S. government that their right to vote was now guaranteed. Subsequent events would make a mockery of the law, however, as blacks would continue to be denied full voting rights for almost a century thereafter.

At first, the white South did not challenge the legality of black suffrage. Instead, southern racists resorted to terror, intimidation, and economic pressure. Polling places were mysteriously moved the night before elections, blacks were required to produce registration certificates, and those accused of even minor crimes based on flimsy evidence were stripped of their voting privileges. These and other devious tactics succeeded in drastically reducing the number of black voters. By 1900 the African American vote had practically disappeared in the South.

Attempts at Reform

On May 31, 1870, the Enforcement Act was passed, which directed that all citizens otherwise qualified to vote in any election should not be denied that privilege because of race. States were allowed to establish certain qualifications for voter eligibility but were prohibited from obstructing any person from casting a vote. The act was amended in 1871 to eliminate fraudulent voter-registration practices. The U.S. circuit courts could, upon petition, commission election supervisors to oversee both registration and voting in any state.

Poll Taxes and Literacy Tests

In direct defiance of the Enforcement Act, many states, especially in the South, continued to frustrate African Americans' attempts at voting as the twentieth century dawned.

Newly enfranchised African Americans line up to vote shortly after the ratification of the Fifteenth Amendment. *(Associated Publishers, Inc.)*

voters. The results were equally devastating in other states.

The Civil Rights Years

In the 1950's, many Americans believed that the problems of racism and discrimination would not be solved until blacks had secured the right to vote; however, a majority of African Americans of voting age in the South had yet to cast a single ballot in an election. Although poll taxes had been outlawed in most state and local elections, southern whites continued to utilize comprehension and literacy tests, as well as intimidation, to keep blacks from voting.

In 1957, after much pressure by civil rights advocates, Congress passed the first civil rights act since 1875, which also provided for the creation of a Commission on Civil Rights that empowered the government, through the federal courts, to file lawsuits on behalf of any person who was denied the right to vote. Unfortunately, the new law contained many loopholes, and proved to be largely ineffective in guaranteeing voting rights. As a result, a new civil rights act was passed in 1960 that required that all registration and voting records be made available for public inspection. The act required state election officials to preserve records for at least twenty-two months for inspection by the U.S. attorney general and made it a federal crime to obstruct or ignore any federal court order pertaining to voting rights.

The Civil Rights Act of 1964 contained a section that served to strengthen the provisions of the two previous acts, and guaranteed protection against the use of different stan-

The most effective weapon used against black voters was the poll tax. Payment of the tax was required several months before the election, at which time a tax receipt had to be presented. In addition, only property owners were allowed to vote, and voters were required to read, understand, and interpret the state or federal constitution to the satisfaction of election officials. In addition, some states, such as Oklahoma, exempted any voters whose ancestors had been registered to vote in 1866, which in effect meant that only black registrants were required to take literacy tests. In states such as Louisiana, these tactics were almost 100 percent effective in keeping blacks away from the polls, even though the state contained more than 130,000 eligible black

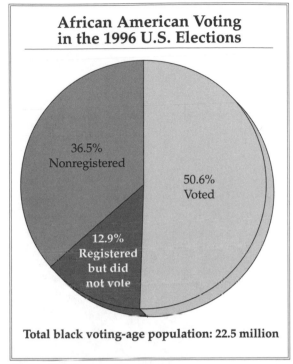

African American Voting in the 1996 U.S. Elections

36.5% Nonregistered

50.6% Voted

12.9% Registered but did not vote

Total black voting-age population: 22.5 million

Source: U.S. Bureau of the Census.

Note: The 50.6% of blacks who reported voting in 1996 may be compared with the 56.0% of whites who reported voting and with a 54.2 % figure for all races and ethnicities. The black voting-age population was estimated at about 22.5 million.

crease dramatically. By 1968 more than 50 percent of the black voting-age population in the South was registered, a development that greatly increased the numbers of African Americans elected to public office. In 1966 there were ninety-seven black members of state legislatures and nine members of Congress; by 1973, there were more than two hundred blacks serving in thirty-seven state legislatures and sixteen black members of Congress. Soon, African Americans would also be elected to serve as MAYORS of several large American cities, including Chicago, Los Angeles, Newark, New Orleans, and New York.

The large numbers of registered African American voters began to show their influence among the major political parties as well. In the 1960 presidential election, one of the closest in American history, black voters in several key states delivered decisive votes to John F. Kennedy. In the 1968 presidential election, 20 percent of the Democratic vote came from African Americans. Such large and influential numbers prompted black leaders to demand a greater voice in party affairs. In 1984

dards for black voters. Following the passage of this act, the Twenty-fourth Amendment to the Constitution was ratified, abolishing the poll tax as a prerequisite for voting in federal elections

The most important and far-reaching piece of voting-rights legislation was the VOTING RIGHTS ACT OF 1965, which provided for direct federal examination of voter registration. The act outlawed all knowledge, character, and literacy tests and greatly strengthened the existing laws. As a result, the percentage of registered black voters began to in-

Voter education class conducted in Mississippi shortly after passage of the Civil Rights Act of 1957. *(Library of Congress)*

Among the most enduring images of the struggle for voting rights were those of people who marched from Selma to Montgomery, Alabama, shortly before President Lyndon Johnson signed the Voting Rights Act of 1965. *(AP/ Wide World Photos)*

the Reverend Jesse JACKSON, during the announcement of his candidacy for the Democratic presidential nomination, made it clear that his main goal was to induce more African Americans and other disfranchised people to vote. The surge of black registration and voting in the 1980's was largely the result of Jackson's strong showing in the 1984 presidential primary.

The newly found strength of the African American voter has come as a result of the changes within the Civil Rights movement. The coalitions that were formed to push for the passage of civil rights legislation in the 1960's have been replaced by ever-increasing numbers of black elected officials in local, state, and federal government and by the increased participation of black American citizens in the political process. Thus, the large number of actively participating black voters

has become the new mechanism for future social, political, and economic change.

—*Raymond Frey*

Suggested Readings:

Davidson, Chandler, and Bernard Grofman. *Quiet Revolution in the South: The Impact of the Voting Rights Act, 1965-1990*. Princeton, N.J.: Princeton University Press, 1994.

Finkelman, Paul, ed. *African-Americans and the Right to Vote*. New York: Garland, 1992.

Gordon, Ann D. and Bettye Collier-Thomas. *African American Women and the Vote, 1837-1965*. Amherst: University of Massachusetts Press, 1997.

Guinier, Lani. *The Tyranny of the Majority: Fundamental Fairness in Representative Democracy*. New York: Free Press, 1994.

Keech, William R. *The Impact of Negro Voting: The Role of the Vote in the Quest for Equality*. Chicago: Rand McNally, 1968.

Kousser, J. Morgan. *Colorblind Injustice: Minority Voting Rights and the Undoing of the Second Reconstruction.* Chapel Hill: The University of North Carolina Press, 1999.

Lusane, Clarence. *No Easy Victories: Black Americans and the Vote.* New York: Franklin Watts, 1996.

Moon, Henry L. *Balance of Power: The Negro Vote.* Westport, Conn.: Greenwood Press, 1977.

Reeves, Keith. *Voting Hopes or Fears? White Voters, Black Candidates and Racial Politics in America.* New York: Oxford University Press, 1997.

Tate, Katherine. *From Protest to Politics: The New Black Voters in American Elections.* Rev. ed. Cambridge, Mass.: Harvard University Press, 1994.

Walton, Hanes Jr. *Invisible Politics: Black Political Behavior.* Albany: State University of New York Press, 1985.

Voting Rights Act of 1965: Legislation signed on August 6, intended to eliminate discriminatory voting restrictions and expand registration of black voters. The act mobilized the most significant change in the politics of the South since the RECONSTRUCTION ACT OF 1867. This law made voting booths and polling stations that effectively had been closed for nearly one hundred years accessible to more than 2.5 million African Americans. The potential impact of this act lies in the fact that there were numerous counties in the South where the African American vote could carry elections. For

In March, 1965—five months before President Lyndon Johnson signed the Voting Rights Act—Birmingham, Alabama, police used physical force against college students demonstrating for voting rights. *(AP/Wide World Photos)*

example, the act effectively removed all-white city councils from southern cities with African American majorities. The impact of this legislation was such that white southerners tried to prevent the law from taking effect. Massive voter-registration projects, confrontations between African Americans and local officials, and federal assistance were necessary before any actual headway was made.

The Voting Rights Act abolished poll taxes, GRANDFATHER CLAUSES, literacy tests, and other rules that were employed to disqualify African American voters. The act also empowered the U.S. attorney general to send federal registrars into counties where evidence of discrimination was present. The signing of the Voting Rights Act by President Lyndon Johnson followed demonstrations in Selma, Alabama. Selma exemplified many southern cities, in that half of its population was African American, but only 2 percent of eligible African American voters were registered.

The Voting Rights Act had an immediate impact. Through the efforts of the SOUTHERN CHRISTIAN LEADERSHIP CONFERENCE, the STUDENT NONVIOLENT COORDINATING COMMITTEE, the federal government, and grassroots organizations, more than three hundred thousand African Americans were registered in the South for the first time. Most southern states registered more than half of their eligible African American voters. Four African Americans were elected to county and state legislative offices. White candidates such as moderate Wilson Baker, who defeated Jim Clark, a staunch foe of civil rights activists and integration, for sheriff, also benefited from African American votes. Over the subsequent months and years, African American voters helped elect African American officials to numerous positions at the local, state, and federal levels, as well as electing white and other officials who were sympathetic and responsive to their needs.

W

WAAC and WAVES: Female members of the armed forces. Women Accepted for Volunteer Emergency Service (WAVES) was authorized on a trial basis during WORLD WAR II by a congressional bill signed by President Franklin D. Roosevelt on July 30, 1942. The WAVES were to be a temporary auxiliary to the U.S. Naval Reserve, with members having no permanent military status. African American women were not admitted until December, 1944, and then only under public pressure. Among the first black WAVES were Harriet Ida Pickens, Francis Ellis, and Francis Eliza Willis. During all of World War II, only seventy-two black women were enlisted and only two more became officers. In contrast, by August of 1945 there were more than eighty thousand WAVES serving in their noncombat positions. Most WAVES were discharged at the end of World War II, but their numbers increased during the 1950's and 1960's. By 1970 black representation had improved considerably, and about

African Americans were not admitted in the Navy's WAVES program until World War II was nearing its end. *(National Archives)*

fifty out of a total of about two thousand officers were black. The WAVES no longer exist. Their members and functions were integrated into the regular Navy.

The Women's Auxiliary Army Corps (WAAC) was created by congressional legislation signed by Roosevelt on May 14, 1942. Black women were among those eager to volunteer, but just as for black men in the military, their participation was limited to 10 percent of the total. Also, as was the case for black men, various black organizations and the black press objected to this limit. The actual percentage of black WAACs did not rise above 6 percent, however, between 1943 and 1946. Of the first 440 women to report to Fort Des Moines, Iowa, for training, 40 were black.

The WAAC organization, renamed the Women's Army Corps (WAC), became an official part of the Army in July, 1943. Members still had only temporary status in the military. During World War II, black WAC officers trained and commanded black units and performed other noncombat tasks. As was the case for WAVES, all WAACs (and later WACs) were volunteers. About one hundred black women served as WAAC or WAC officers during World War II, and about three hundred had been officers by 1970.

In July, 1943, black WAC recruiting officers were withdrawn from the field. This withdrawal, along with charges that the War Department was failing to give technical training to black women,

During World War II much of the work done by members of the WAAC and WAVES was designed to foster public support of the war effort. *(National Archives)*

led to complaints in the black press. Eventually, black WACs found themselves assigned to more technical tasks.

Political pressure from the black community also led to the creation of the 6888th Central Postal Battalion, the only black WAC battalion to serve overseas. Its eight hundred members, all black, were commanded by Major Charity Adams. The battalion's mission was to establish a central postal directory in Europe. The battalion arrived in England in February, 1945, and shortly thereafter moved to France.

In June, 1948, the Women's Armed Forces Integration Act gave women permanent status in the regular and reserve components of the armed forces. The minimum age and educational requirements for enlistment, however, were higher for women then for men. With the creation of an all-volunteer military

in the 1970's, more positions opened to women. Women were allowed to hold positions in 90 percent of all occupational specialties. The WAC was disestablished in April, 1978, with its members reassigned to regular Army or other positions.

Waddles, Mother (Charleszetta Lina; b. October 7, 1913, St. Louis, Missouri): Mission director and charity leader. Mrs. Payton "Mother" Waddles, an ordained PENTECOSTAL minister, has been called "DETROIT's black angel" in recognition of her charity work in that city. Along with being the biological mother of ten children, she served as mission director and founder of the nonprofit, nondenominational, charitable organization Waddles' Perpetual Mission for Saving Souls of All Nations, Inc., which began operation in 1956. The mission's Emergency Service Program was established to provide food, clothing, shelter, medicine, and transportation to the needy and to maintain kitchens on Detroit's skid row.

Mother Waddles had her own radio and television programs and was named a life member of the National Association for the Advancement of Colored People (NAACP). She served on the Mayor's Task Force Committees and was honorary chair of the Women's Conference of Concern. Over the

Mother Waddles in 1975. *(AP/Wide World Photos)*

course of her career, she received more than 150 awards, including the 1988 Humanitarian Award from the National Urban League. She was featured in the traveling Smithsonian exhibit, "Black Women of Courage."

Waddy, Joseph (b. 1911, Louisa, Virginia): Judge. Waddy received his LL.B. degree from Howard University in 1938. He pursued his legal career mainly in the District of Columbia. Between 1939 and 1962, he practiced for a law firm before being appointed as an associate judge of the domestic relations municipal court. In 1967 he became a judge on the U.S. District Court for the District of Columbia.

Wade-Davis bill: Legislation sponsored by Senator Benjamin F. Wade and Representative Henry W. Davis. The bill, introduced in 1864, unsuccessfully attempted to set RECONSTRUCTION policy. President Abraham Lincoln allowed the bill to expire at the end of the congressional session without signing it. The battle over the bill presaged the struggles to set Reconstruction policy at the conclusion of the war.

Waldon, Alton Ronald, Jr. (b. December 31, 1936, Lakeland, Florida): U.S. representative from NEW YORK STATE. Waldon served in the U.S. Army from 1956 to 1959 and was discharged at the rank of specialist fourth class. He graduated from John Jay College with his bachelor of science degree in 1968. He attended law school at New York University and earned his J.D. degree in 1973. From 1962 to 1975, Waldon was a captain with the New York City Housing Authority Police Department. In 1975 he became deputy commissioner of the New York State Division of Human Rights, serving until 1981. In that year, Waldon became an assistant counsel to the

County Service Group of the New York State Office of Mental Retardation and Developmental Disabilities. In 1982 he was elected to the New York State House of Representatives as a representative from the Thirty-third Assembly District. He served as an assemblyman until 1986.

When Congressman Joseph Addabbo died in 1986, the DEMOCRATIC PARTY leaders of New York's Sixth Congressional District were authorized to select a candidate to fill the remainder of Addabbo's term. In May of 1986, they nominated Waldon to run in the special election. Absentee ballots gave Waldon a narrow victory over Floyd H. Flake for the congressional seat. Waldon took office on July 29, 1986, and was appointed to serve on the House Committee on Education and Labor and the House Committee on Small Business.

During his term on Capitol Hill, Waldon supported legislation to halt the illegal traffic in crack cocaine and sponsored a resolution to create a national task force to address the problem of functional illiteracy. He also called on the House to override President Ronald Reagan's veto of legislative sanctions against South Africa and introduced a resolution proposing that the president attend a summit with African leaders whose countries bordered on South Africa. Waldon opposed the U.S. government's covert aid to rebel forces in Angola who were supported by South Africa's white minority government.

Waldon ran for reelection as the Democratic candidate for the Sixth Congressional District but lost the primary in September of 1986 to Floyd H. Flake, who went on to win in the general election. Waldon completed his congressional term and returned to New York, where he was appointed to serve as a commissioner on the New York State Investigation Committee from 1987 to 1990. In 1991 he was elected to the New York State Senate from the Tenth Senate District. He served in the state senate through the 1990's.

Walker, Alice (b. February 9, 1944, Eatonton, Georgia): Novelist, essayist, and poet. Alice Malsenior Walker was born the eighth of eight children to SHARECROPPER parents in Eatonton, GEORGIA. Her research into her family history led her to believe that the family name belonged to the white man who owned and fathered a child by her then eleven-year-old great-great-grandmother. She kept her maiden name for quite another reason: Her great-great-great-grandmother, a slave with two babies, had walked from Virginia to Eatonton, Georgia. Allied to her pride in her family was the excitement she felt upon the realization that she shared her name with her spiritual ancestor, Sojourner TRUTH ("Sojourner" being equivalent to "Walker, and "Alice," in old Greek, meaning "truth"). Walker also often expressed pride in her mother's Cherokee grandmother.

Youth and Education
Because her mother could no longer carry Alice to the fields where she worked alongside her husband, Alice entered first grade at the early age of four. Always precocious, Alice was successful and happy in school until an accident (a brother shot her with a BB gun) blinded her in one eye and made her feel ugly. Her family moved shortly after the accident, and Alice entered a school that had formerly been a penitentiary. She was unhappy; the building frightened her, and the children tormented her. Alice was sent back to live with her grandparents and to her old school. Her grades and disposition were not to return to near their former heights, however, until she was fourteen, when her brother Bill and his wife took her to their local Boston hospital, where the "glob" on her eye was removed. Soon her self-confidence and grades improved, and she eventually graduated as valedictorian of her class.

Walker left for SPELMAN COLLEGE in ATLANTA, GEORGIA, when she was seventeen. She remained at Spelman for two and one-half years; she found the school opposed to change, however, and left to attend Sarah Lawrence College in New York. During her final college year, she wrote her first book, *Once: Poems* (1968), and published her first short story, "To Hell with Dying."

Activism and Teaching Career
Walker went to the South in the mid-1960's with her husband, Mel Leventhal, a civil rights activist, to educate and assist prospective voters. Her trips during her college years provided the impetus for what was to become her life's work. She deliberately sat in the front section of a Greyhound bus on her way to Atlanta. When asked to move to the back, she vowed to change the social order that had humiliated her. It was Martin Luther KING, Jr., who first gave her the hope that such change was possible. When Walker realized that even in a college course in southern writers she had not been presented with the works of African American writers, Walker vowed to correct her "miseducation." In researching a story on VOODOO, she discovered the work of Zora Neale HURSTON, the writer of what she came to consider one of the greatest American novels, *Their Eyes Were Watching God* (1937).

Once Walker herself began teaching, she included Hurston's work in her course (which she believed to be the first of its kind) on black women writers. She taught the course first at Wellesley College and later at the University of Massachusetts. Walker's devotion to Hurston did not stop with her courses or with Walker's essays, in which Hurston's influence is often evident. Walker sought out her spiritual aunt's burial site in Florida. The search was difficult; Hurston was not remembered in her own town, and her grave, in the middle of an overgrown field, was not marked. Walker scouted and found what she believed to be the burial site. She purchased a marker to be placed there in honor of the writer.

Essays

Walker's conscience would not allow her to participate in violent or armed struggle, so she applied her activist energies to the mental, the literary, and the oral: She studied the peoples of the world and took her ideas to them. She became both a prolific writer and a much-sought-after speaker. Her ideas are spelled out in her collections of essays *In Search of Our Mothers' Gardens: Womanist Prose* (1983) and *Living by the Word: Selected Writings, 1973-1987* (1988). The idea of change became the constant focus of her work.

In the 1990's Walker published two books of essays, *The Same River Twice; Honoring the Difficult* (1996) and *Anything We Love Can Be Saved: A Writer's Activism* (1997). The former included reflections on the issues and controversies surrounding the film version of her novel *The Color Purple*, and the latter explicitly explored her social and political activism.

Alice Walker in 1991. *(Jeff Reinking/Picture Group)*

"I am preoccupied," she once said, "with the spiritual survival, the survival *whole* of my people. But beyond that, I am committed to exploring the oppressions, the insanities, the loyalties, and the triumphs of black women." Her work further shows her commitment to the "survival *whole*" of the earth and its creatures.

Novels

Walker's novels illustrate the ideas of her essays. *The Third Life of Grange Copeland* (1970) explores conditions in the South that contribute to the mistreatment of women. Grange Copeland's struggle to survive as a sharecropper for a white man who degrades him causes him to turn his own abuse upon his wife, who commits SUICIDE. His son Brownfield's life is a repetition and a magnification of his own: Brownfield serves and hates his servitude, and he finally fires a gun into the face of his wife. Grange, however, finds redemption through Brownfield's daughter, Ruth. He allows his unhappy life to inform hers, but he bestows upon her all the love he would like to have given his own wife and children. Grange dies saving Ruth.

Meridian (1976) begins where *The Third Life of Grange Copeland* ends, in the turbulent 1960's. In college, the title character becomes a part of a radical group that her pacifist beliefs force her to abandon. She does not, however, abandon their common goals: She goes South to help oppressed blacks to vote and to achieve their everyday rights peacefully.

Celie in *The Color Purple* (1982) undergoes physical and mental abuse from her stepfather and husband, but she is saved by a woman who teaches and loves her. Whereas Grange teaches Ruth the caution necessary to the young black girl's survival in a world that does not see her as significant, Shug teaches the mature

Celie to surrender herself to the earth, to its creatures, and to their informing spiritual force, all of which are ready to serve and to love her. Learning that God is everything and that she is a part of everything frees Celie from her hatred of her abusive husband and brings, finally, all of what has troubled her life to happy resolution.

Lissie, the informing spirit of *The Temple of My Familiar* (1989), remembers as her earliest incarnation one of the earliest humans, who learned her lessons from the beasts. The peaceful lesson that Lissie teaches the novel's other principals brings them from their bestiality to a perfect union with the earth, with their loved ones, and with their own no-longer-abused bodies.

Walker's 1990's novels both explore the conflicts between individual sexual identity and society. In *Possessing the Secret of Joy* (1992), an African woman named Tashi undergoes the tribal rite of genital mutilation (female circumcision). The trauma of the event eventually leads her to madness after she has married and moved to the United States. With the help of therapists, she comes to understand her conflicts and become stronger. In *By the Light of My Father's Smile* (1998), the two daughters of parents studying the tribal Mundo people of Mexico discover their desires and sexual identities. All four members of the family struggle to find love and happiness, which they attain only after passing into the spiritual world after death.

Walker is best known for her Pulitzer Prize-winning novel *The Color Purple*, which was made into a successful motion picture. Her poetry, collected in *Once, Revolutionary Petunias and Other Poems* (1973), *Goodnight, Willie Lee, I'll See You in the Morning: Poems* (1979), *Horses Make a Landscape Look More Beautiful* (1984), and *Her Blue Body Everything We Know: Earthling Poems, 1965-1990 Complete* (1991), and her short stories, collected in *In Love and in Trouble: Stories of Black Women* (1973) and *You Can't Keep a Good Woman Down* (1981), contain unique pieces of writing, most of which offer some aspect of the corrective vision for humankind set forth in her essays and in her novels. Her children's biography *Langston Hughes: American Poet* (1974) and her edition of Hurston's works, *I Love Myself When I Am Laughing . . . And Then Again When I Am Looking Mean and Impressive: A Zora Neale Hurston Reader* (1979), afford this same view.

—*Judith K. Taylor*

See also: Literature.

Suggested Readings:

Christian, Barbara. "Novel for Everyday Use: The Novels of Alice Walker." In *Black Women Novelists: The Development of a Tradition, 1896-1976*. Westport, Conn.: Greenwood Press, 1980.

De Veaux, Alice. "Alice Walker." *Essence* (September, 1989): 56-62.

De Weever, Jacqueline. *Mythmaking and Metaphor in Black Women's Fiction*. New York: St. Martin's Press, 1992.

Howard, Lillie P., ed. *Alice Walker and Zora Neale Hurston: The Common Bond*. Westport, Conn.: Greenwood Press, 1993.

Johnson, Yvonne. *The Voices of African American Women: The Use of Narrative and Authorial Voice in the Works of Harriet Jacobs, Zora Neale Hurston, and Alice Walker*. New York: Peter Lang, 1998.

Parker-Smith, Bettye J. "Alice Walker's Women: In Search of Some Peace of Mind." In *Black Women Writers (1950-1980): A Critical Evaluation*, edited by Mari Evans. Garden City, N.Y.: Anchor, 1984.

Walker, Alice. *Anything We Love Can Be Saved: A Writer's Activism*. New York: Random House, 1997.

_____. *The Same River Twice: Honoring the Difficult, a Meditation on Life, Spirit, Art, and the Making of the Film "The Color Purple" Ten Years Later*. New York: Charles Scribner's Sons, 1996.

Winchell, Donna H. *Alice Walker*. New York: Twayne, 1992.

Walker, David (September 28, 1785, Wilmington, North Carolina—1830, Boston, Massachusetts): Abolitionist author. In 1829 Walker wrote one of the most significant documents in African American history, a pamphlet called *Walker's Appeal, in Four Articles: Together with a Preamble to the Colored Citizens of the World*. A stinging indictment of slavery, Walker's pamphlet called for free northern blacks to make common cause with southern slaves in a violent overthrow of slavery. Condemning slavery as a violation of God's and nature's laws, Walker's *Appeal* fired the first shot in the ABOLITIONIST MOVEMENT's war against slavery.

Walker himself was a runaway slave who escaped to PENNSYLVANIA. A tailor by trade, Walker operated a used-clothing shop in PHILADELPHIA and sold clothing and cloth door-to-door. Although prosperous, Walker burned with bitter memories of his slave experience and vowed to fight the institution of slavery in any way he could. His pamphlet raised a storm of controversy throughout the United States, especially in the South, where attempts were made to ban its circulation. Walker's advocacy of violent revolution to overthrow slavery touched a nerve in a nation fearful of its slaves. His violent prophecies almost came true two years later, with the bloody Nat Turner rebellion in Southhampton County, Virginia. Walker himself died in suspicious circumstances, perhaps the victim of a backlash against his pamphlet, shortly after the *Appeal*'s publication.

Walker, George (1873, Lawrence, Kansas—1911, Lawrence, Kansas): Singer and comedian. Walker was attracted to show business at an early age. He left Lawrence High School to follow a MINSTREL group of African Americans. From performing in minstrel shows, he graduated to performing in circuses and musical shows. In 1893 he met Bert WILLIAMS in California. Williams was a singer, an instrumental musician, and a comedian whose parents had migrated from Nassau, in the BAHAMAS of the WEST INDIES, to California. By 1895 Walker and Williams had put together their talents to form a team that would make a great impact on American show business.

Success did not come until Walker and Williams advertised themselves in theaters as "Two Real Coons," an idea that came to them after observing white performers in blackface billing themselves as "coons." Walker and Williams began to enjoy popularity in Californian theaters. In 1896 they started performing in New York City, appearing first in *The Gold Bug*. It was during their stay in New York that they brought into vogue the cakewalk, a type of dance invented by African Americans for competitions in which a cake traditionally was awarded as prize.

Walker and Williams made history when, in 1902, they teamed up with Jesse Shipp (director) and Will Marion Cook (playwright) to produce a musical play, *In Dahomey*. It was the first African American production ever to open on Broadway, in 1903. Its success attained international proportions when Walker and Williams performed it at the Shaftesbury Theatre and at a command performance at Buckingham Palace in London in 1903. It was followed by another successful production, *Abyssinia*, at the Majestic Theatre in New York City in 1906. These two plays are important in the annals of African American theater history because they boldly introduced African settings, characters, and songs into American show business. Walker last teamed with Williams in 1908, when they produced *Bandana Land* with much success. Walker fell ill while the production was still running in 1909.
See also: Comedy and humor.

Walker, Madam C. J. (Sarah Breedlove; December 23, 1867, Delta, Louisiana—May 25, 1919, Irvington, New York): Entrepreneur. Born to former slaves and sharecroppers Owen and Minerva Breedlove, Madam C. J. Walker became the first African American woman millionaire and a pioneer in the cosmetics industry. She was one of the best-known African American women of the early twentieth century.

Early Years

Walker was orphaned by age seven and was reared by Louvenia, her married sister, in Vicksburg, Mississippi. She married a man named McWilliams at age fourteen in order to escape the cruelties of Louvenia's husband; however, McWilliams was killed when Walker was twenty, leaving her alone to rear Lelia (later known as A'Lelia), their two-year-old daughter. Shortly thereafter, Walker moved to St. Louis, Missouri, where she worked as a washerwoman for eighteen years; she put Lelia through public schools and Knoxville College, a private black school in Tennessee.

Founding a Manufacturing Company

Suffering from thinning hair, Walker began experimenting with patent medicines and hair-care products. In 1905 she dreamed that a black man appeared to her with a formula for a new hair preparation. She mixed these ingredients and, pleased with the results, began selling the preparation to friends and neighbors. In July she moved to Denver to be with her brother's wife, who had been recently widowed, but she continued to peddle her product to local African American women.

Six months later, she married Charles J. Walker, a newspaperman who brought his understanding of advertising and mail-order operations to the business. The relationship was of short duration, however, because Charles Walker was satisfied with only a local market. Madam C. J. Walker had larger plans.

In 1906 she put twenty-one-year-old Lelia in charge of her company, while she traveled throughout the country, giving demonstrations in homes, churches, and clubs. Two years later, they moved to Pittsburgh, where Lelia ran both the manufacturing operation and Lelia College, which trained African American women to be cosmetologists. Walker continued to travel.

Impressed with the transportation facilities in Indianapolis, INDIANA, in 1910, she decided to build a plant and relocate her headquarters there, and she placed both under the leadership of Freeman B. Ransom. She had met Ransom when he was working as a train porter during his vacations from Columbia University Law School. This arrangement freed Walker and her daughter to move to New York in 1913; there, she established a second Lelia College in her expensively furnished HARLEM

Madam C. J. Walker in 1905. *(National Archives)*

brownstone. Walker continued her travels, often using Lelia's adopted daughter, Mae, as a model to demonstrate the Walker System.

The Walker System

"Kinky" and "nappy" hair, rather than being simply descriptive terms, were considered to be badges of slavery. Walker developed a system—consisting of a shampoo, the application of a pomade "hair grower," vigorous brushing, and the use of hot-iron combs—that resulted in a shiny, smooth coiffure. She called her beauticians "hair culturists," "scalp specialists," or "beauty culturists" to distinguish them from "hair straighteners." Walker insisted that her purpose was not to straighten hair but to encourage hair growth and cures for common scalp problems.

The Walker System offended some preachers who objected to attempts by black women to make themselves "look white," but popular songs sung by black men praised "long-haired babes." The Walker System's popularity rested on its ability to provide the versatility in styling African American women desired. Even the internationally renowned entertainer Josephine Baker used the Walker System, and the French developed their own pomade called the "Baker-Fix."

Walker's method differed from earlier hair-care practices, which often involved dividing hair into sections that were tightly wrapped with string and twisted. This process left the hair straighter when it was brushed out, but the strain could lead to balding. Walker's early efforts were an attempt to stimulate hair growth to overcome this problem.

She also used her "miracle ingredient," sulphur, to address common scalp infections caused by poor nutrition and other problems associated with a low standard of living. In addition, she developed a steel comb with wide teeth to accommodate thicker hair.

Walker advertised her products widely in African American newspapers and magazines. Her primary competition came from Annie M. Turnbo Malone's "Poro System"; "Poro Colleges" were located in St. Louis and Chicago. Other African American-owned beauty-product companies of the time included Madame Sarah Spencer Washington's "Apex System" of Atlantic City and the Boston company of W. A. Johnson and his wife, M. L. Johnson. Some white-owned companies, such as Ozono and Kinkilla, also competed in the black hair-care market.

Madam C. J. Walker's Hair Grower, a pomade sold in tins embellished with her portrait, remained her best-selling product. Despite the argument over "looking white," Walker emphasized the view that being well groomed instilled pride. More important than her success in the cosmetics industry, however, was the opportunity she afforded to African American women. Few had the education to succeed in most professions, but Walker offered many the opportunity of leaving domestic service to become economically independent entrepreneurs.

Walker Agents

On her travels, Walker recruited agents who signed contracts to sell her products exclusively and to follow her hygienic system, which was a regimen antedating similar practices later put into law by most states. A 1919 editorial in THE CRISIS magazine suggested that Walker had revolutionized the personal habits of millions of women. Walker agents, dressed in white shirts and long black skirts and carrying black satchels of hair-care products, were a common sight making house calls throughout the United States and in the Caribbean. Walker's assistants taught women how to set up beauty parlors in their homes, keep business records, and become financially independent. Speaking before Booker T. WASHINGTON's NATIONAL NEGRO BUSINESS LEAGUE in 1913, Walker presented herself as a role model to other women. Starting with only one dollar and fifty cents eight years earlier, she had come to own her own factory and employ more than one thousand women.

Madam C. J. Walker Hair Culturists' Union of America

About the time Mary Kay Ash of Mary Kay Cosmetics was born, Walker organized local and state clubs of women selling her hair-care products. In 1917 members of more than two hundred clubs met in Philadelphia for their first convention. They learned new techniques, shared business experiences, and heard Walker address them on "Women's Duty to Women." In addition to showing others how to be independent, Walker encouraged philanthropy by giving prizes to the clubs with the best charitable records. She also encouraged political and social involvement. For example, at her suggestion, the convention wired President Woodrow Wilson to urge passage of legislation making LYNCHING a federal crime.

Club Women and Philanthropies

Walker compensated for her lack of formal education by hiring tutors and becoming an avid reader. She joined the National Association of Colored Women (NACW), the organization of the nation's most educated and progressive African American women, and was introduced to the membership along with Mary McLeod BETHUNE at the group's 1912 convention. Through the NACW, she associated with Bethune, Ida B. WELLS, Mary Talbert, and others. At the NACW's 1918 convention, she was given the honor of burning the mortgage to Frederick DOUGLASS's Washington home, having made the largest contribution to pay off the loan and refurbish the house as a memorial and museum.

Her interest in women's education was strong. She contributed women's scholarships to TUSKEGEE INSTITUTE and to Charlotte Hawkins' Palmer Memorial Institute and be-

queathed five thousand dollars each to Bethune's Daytona Normal and Industrial Institute for Negro Girls and Lucy Laney's Haynes Institute in Augusta, Georgia. She also contributed to homes for the aged in St. Louis and Indianapolis and to the Young Women's Christian Association, and she was a strong supporter of the NATIONAL ASSOCIATION FOR THE ADVANCEMENT OF COLORED PEOPLE (NAACP).

Final Years

Walker remained president and sole owner of the business and continued to travel throughout her life, despite problems with HYPERTENSION. She found time to enjoy an electric car. Her mansion in Harlem became famous as "Dark Tower" when her daughter, by then known as A'Lelia, presided over a salon of talented African Americans. Called the "joy goddess" of the HARLEM RENAISSANCE by poet Langston HUGHES, A'Lelia introduced authors, artists, and musicians to white publishers, critics, and patrons of the arts.

Walker also built a thirty-four-room mansion designed by African American architect Vertner Tandy, at Irvington, New York. Internationally renowned tenor Enrico Caruso named the estate "Villa Lewaro" by combining the initial syllables of Walker's daughter's name, which had become A'Lelia Walker Robinson.

Walker died in 1919 at Villa Lewaro of chronic nephritis. Funeral services were conducted there, with interment in Woodlawn Cemetery in the Bronx. She left her company to her daughter, stipulating that the presidency always be held by a woman.

A'Lelia was succeeded as the company president by her own daughter, Mae Walker Perry; Perry was followed in turn by her daughter, A'Lelia Mae Perry Bundles. The manufacturing plant planned by Walker was completed in 1927 and renovated in the 1980's. Known as the Madam Walker Urban Life Center, it serves as a cultural center in downtown Indianapolis.

—*Christie Farnham*

Suggested Readings:

Bundles, A'Lelia P. *Madam C. J. Walker.* New York: Chelsea House, 1991.

_____. "Madam C. J. Walker: Cosmetics Tycoon." *Ms.* (July, 1983): 91-94.

Davis, Marianna W., ed. *The Arts, Media, Business, Law, Sports.* Vol. 1 of *Contributions of Black Women to America.* Columbia, S.C.: Kenday Press, 1982.

Gates, Henry Louis, Jr. "Madam's Crusade: A Black Woman's Hair-Care Empire Set a Style and Smashed Barriers." *Time* (December 7, 1998): 165.

Giddings, Paula. *When and Where I Enter: The Impact of Black Women on Race and Sex in America.* New York: William Morrow, 1984.

Haskins, Jim. *One More River to Cross: The Stories of Twelve Black Americans.* New York: Scholastic, 1992.

James, Edward T. et al., eds. *Notable American Women, 1607-1950: A Biographical Dictionary.* Vol. 3. Cambridge, Mass.: Belknap Press, 1971.

Walker, Maggie (July 15, 1867, Richmond, Virginia—December 15, 1934, Richmond, Virginia): Banker and organizer. After her father's death, Maggie Lena Draper Walker helped her mother support the family, working as a washerwoman while she attended school in VIRIGNIA. She graduated from Richmond's Colored Normal School in 1883, and she taught until her marriage to Armstead Walker in 1886.

At the age of fourteen, Walker joined the Independent Order of St. Luke. She became its Right Worthy Grand Secretary in 1899 and served until her death, as the order grew from one thousand to more than eighty thousand members in twenty-three states. Walker founded youth branches, published a weekly newspaper, the *St. Luke Herald*, created an educational loan fund, and ran a department store. The order was a mutual benefit society, providing insurance, economic, social, and political services for its members.

The Saint Luke Penny Savings Bank, which Walker established in 1903, was her best-known achievement. Walker was the first female bank president in the United States. She ran the bank, reorganizing it as the Consolidated Bank and Trust Company in 1934. By the 1990's, it was the oldest continually black-owned and black-run bank in the nation. The bank was an outgrowth of the Independent Order of St. Luke.

Walker also founded and led other organizations to benefit African Americans. Believing that education and employment of black women would benefit the whole race, Walker was active in the Richmond Council of Colored Women, Virginia State Federation

Maggie Walker, the first woman bank president in U.S. history. *(Associated Publishers, Inc.)*

of Colored Women, National Association of Wage Earners, International Council of Women of the Darker Races, National Training School for Girls, and Virginia Industrial School for Colored Girls. She worked in the NATIONAL ASSOCIATION FOR THE ADVANCEMENT OF COLORED PEOPLE, Richmond Urban League, Negro Organization Society of Virginia, and Virginia Interracial Commission. Supporting women's suffrage, she worked for voter registration and belonged to the Virginia Lily Black Republican Party, running on its ticket for state superintendent of schools. She also managed the finances of the National League of Republican Colored Women.

Maggie and Armstead Walker had two sons, Russell and Melvin. In 1904 the family moved into the home in Richmond's Jackson Ward that was later purchased and operated by the National Park Service as the Maggie Lena Walker National Historic Site. After her husband's death in 1915, Walker expanded her household to include her mother, her sons, and their wives and children. By 1928 health problems had confined her to a wheelchair. Walker died of diabetic gangrene at her home.

Walker, Margaret Abigail (b. July 7, 1915, Birmingham, Alabama): Author and educator. Walker received a B.A. from Northwestern University in 1935, an M.A. from the University of Iowa in 1940, and a Ph.D. from Iowa in 1965. She also was granted several honorary doctorates. She was born the daughter of a Jamaican-born METHODIST minister and a music teacher.

Walker's academic career was multifaceted. She taught at Livingstone College in NORTH CAROLINA and at West Virginia State College before joining the faculty at Jackson State University in 1949. She taught there until her retirement in 1979. She was the recipient of many awards, including a Yale Younger Poets Award, a Rosenwald Fellowship, a Ford Fellowship, and a Houghton Mifflin literary fellowship.

Walker's literary career soared with the publication of a collection of poetry, *For My People*, in 1942. She received a Yale Younger Poets Series Award for that volume. She did not publish another volume of poetry for more than twenty years. In 1966 Walker's acclaimed novel of the African American experiences of the CIVIL WAR, *Jubilee*, was published. The Houghton Mifflin Award-winning novel was written as her doctoral dissertation. *Jubilee* is noted for its historical accuracy and its authenticity of folk material. It spans the antebellum period through RECONSTRUCTION. The central character is Vyry, one of the most complex and admirable examples of an African American heroine to appear in an American novel. Vyry is intelligent, brave, daring, loyal, persistent, and indefatigable. *Jubilee* often is compared favorably with *The Autobiography of Miss Jane Pittman* (1971) by Ernest J. GAINES.

After receiving critical acclaim for *Jubilee*, Walker returned to writing poetry, conducting research, teaching, and promoting the causes of African Americans. An excellent example of generational views is available in Nikki Giovanni's *A Poetic Equation: Conversations Between Nikki Giovanni and Margaret Walker* (1974). A biography by Walker, *Richard Wright, Daemonic Genius: A Portrait of the Man, a Critical Look at His Work*, appeared in 1988.

Walker, T-Bone (May 28, 1910, Linden, Texas—March 16, 1975, Los Angeles, California): BLUES singer and guitarist. Aaron Thibeaux "T-Bone" Walker was the only son of Movelia Jimerson and Rance Walker, both musicians. The Walker family moved to DALLAS, TEXAS, in 1912, where Aaron was soon imbued with his parents' passion for music. He sang with his stepfather, Marco Washington, at local drive-ins and, at age ten, was lead-boy for the legendary bluesman Blind Lemon JEFFERson, a family friend. By 1923 Walker had taught himself to play guitar and had begun to play at private parties in the Dallas area. In the late 1920's, Walker traveled throughout the South with a road show headed by Ida Cox. Walker also made his first recordings on the Columbia label and achieved some local celebrity by winning first prize at Cab CALLOWAY's Amateur Show in Dallas.

Walker moved to LOS ANGELES in 1934. He spent the next several years working at the Little Harlem Club in Los Angeles and the Trocadero in Hollywood. He is credited with being the first blues guitarist to use electric amplification. In the late 1930's and early 1940's, Walker toured and recorded with the Les Hite Orchestra. During the war years, he toured army bases throughout the United States but also continued to play clubs in the Los Angeles area. From 1946 until the early 1950's, Walker toured the country with his own band and recorded on the Capitol and Imperial record labels. He then solidified his West Coast reputation with an extended engagement at the Blue Mirror Club in San Francisco and frequent appearances on local television shows.

In the 1960's, blues music enjoyed a dramatic rise in popularity, in part as a result of its acknowledged formative influence on rock music. Consequently, T-Bone Walker became something of an international celebrity. Having first played in England and Europe in 1962 with a package tour called Rhythm & Blues USA, he criss-crossed North America and Europe in the late 1960's and early 1970's, appearing at dozens of folk, blues, and jazz festivals, including the 1967 Monterey Jazz Festival and the 1972 Montreux Jazz Festival. In 1970 Walker won a Grammy Award for an album on the Polydor label entitled *Good Feelin'*. Walker is generally acknowledged to have been one of the great modern blues guitarists. Billed as "Daddy of the Blues," he influenced such diverse talents as Chuck Berry, Eric Clapton, Jimi Hendrix, Albert Collins, and B. B. King.

Wallace, Michele (b. January 4, 1952, New York, New York): Journalist, cultural critic, and feminist. Wallace's chief subject is the lack of respect black women have received in American society. Wallace once described her Harlem childhood as sheltered and middle-class. Her mother, Faith Ringgold Wallace, was an artist. Her father, Robert Earl Wallace, was a JAZZ pianist who died of a heroin overdose when she was thirteen.

Wallace attended the City University of New York, from which she received a B.A. in 1974. She was a book review researcher for *Newsweek* in 1974 and 1975 and was an instructor in journalism at New York University beginning in 1976. Her most influential work, *Black Macho and the Myth of the Superwoman*, was published in 1979. She taught in the black studies department at the University of Oklahoma and, in 1987, took a position at the State University of New York at Buffalo. A collection of her essays entitled *Invisibility Blues: From Pop to Theory* was published in 1990, and *Black Popular Culture: A Project by Michele Wallace* was published in 1992.

Wallace achieved notoriety with *Black Macho and the Myth of the Superwoman*, her probing analysis of the sexism and racism that relegated black women to second-class citizenship in American society and, more particularly, in the CIVIL RIGHTS and BLACK POWER movements of the 1960's. She notes that black women were denied a voice because of two misconceptions: the belief that the black woman was a "superwoman" who emasculated the black man and took over his role as head of the household and as chief breadwinner, and the idea that the black man, in order to be liberated, had to prove that he was "macho" by suppressing the black woman to gain his own self-respect. In support of her position, Wallace cites, among other sources, the MOYNIHAN REPORT on the black family, which deplored black female dominance, and Stokely CARMICHAEL's infamous remark that the proper position of the black woman in the Black Power movement was "prone."

Wallace's essays are often commentaries on those works she feels have the greatest potential influence on popular attitudes toward race and gender. She wrote essays, for example, about Alice WALKER's novel *The Color Purple* (1982), Ntozake SHANGE's choreopoem *for colored girls who have considered suicide/ when the rainbow is enuf* (1976), and the films of Spike LEE.

Wallace, Sippie (November 11, 1898, Houston, Texas—November 1, 1986, Detroit, Michigan): BLUES singer and musician. Beulah "Sippie" Wallace (born Beulah Belle Thomas) traveled with a number of tent shows during World War I, then migrated to CHICAGO, ILLINOIS. She cut a number of sides with OKeh Records. She is most remembered as a blues singer with strong ties to GOSPEL MUSIC, having served as director of the National Convention of Gospel Choirs and Choruses for most of the 1930's. Wallace influenced many later singers. In 1976 she recorded a duet of her own classic "Women Be Wise" with Bonnie Raitt.

Waller, Fats (May 21, 1904, Waverley, New York—December 15, 1937, Kansas City, Missouri): Composer and pianist. A legendary performer of New York stride piano, Thomas Wright "Fats" Waller was active in night-

clubs, theaters, and recording studios. Known for such solo recordings of his own works as "Handful of Keys" (1929), Waller was heard on so-called "race records" during the 1920's. Born to Edward Waller, a BAPTIST clergyman, and his wife, Adeline, young Fats Waller played organ for church services. Waller received his training from the equally legendary James P. JOHNSON.

In the early 1920's, Waller began to be heard on recordings, and sheet music publications of his compositions were released. His 1922 recordings of "Birmingham Blues" and "Muscle Shoals Blues," both for OKeh Records, were followed by the publication of "Wild Cat Blues" and "Squeeze Me." Waller also made an impact in the broadcasting field; he could be heard as both pianist and singer on WHN in NEW YORK CITY. In New York, Waller performed on organ and piano at the Lafayette and Lincoln theaters in HARLEM. He coauthored, with Andy Razaf, the music for *Keep Shufflin'* (1928) and *Hot Chocolates* (1929), both of which were Broadway productions. With Razaf, he also composed the music for *Load of*

Pianist Fats Waller performing at New York City's Carnegie Hall. *(Archive Photos)*

Coal. As a recording artist, Waller performed in the late 1920's with McKinney's Cotton Pickers, Morris's Hot Babes, and Fats Waller's Buddies, an early integrated ensemble.

By the 1930's, Waller's recording career had expanded, and the formation of the sextet Fats Waller and his Rhythm resulted in numerous recordings. Waller ventured to the West Coast in the mid-1930's to work with Les Hite's band. He also made Hollywood film appearances, which included *King of Burlesque* and *Hooray for Love!*, both in 1935. In 1943 Waller appeared in *Stormy Weather* with Lena Horne. Waller's international reputation was launched with two European tours, in 1938 and in 1939. "London Suite" (1939), an extended work, displayed Waller's solo piano skills. Waller died of pneumonia after an arduous touring schedule.

Walrond, Eric (1898, Georgetown, British Guiana—1966, London, England): Author. Walrond was one of the most important figures associated with the HARLEM RENAISSANCE. He became a journalist upon arrival in New York, writing for *Opportunity*, the publication of the NATIONAL URBAN LEAGUE. His short stories discuss discrimination and racial prejudice; his collection of ten stories, *Tropic Death* (1926), has a tropical setting (the Barbados, Panama, and British Guiana) and deals with poverty, famine, racial prejudice, and imperialism. His work is noted for its experimental, impressionistic qualities.

Walters, Alexander (August 1, 1858, Bardstown, Kentucky—February 2, 1917, New York, New York): Religious leader and civil rights activist. Both of Walters's parents, Henry Walters and Harriet Mathers Walters, were slaves. He was the sixth of eight children, four of whom died as infants. He studied at private schools and was educated for the ministry in the AFRICAN METHODIST EPISCOPAL ZION (AMEZ) CHURCH. He graduated in 1875 as class valedictorian, ending his formal education.

In 1876 he and his brother Isaac took jobs as waiters in Indianapolis, INDIANA. He was licensed to preach by the Quarterly Conference of the AMEZ Church in March, 1977, and was appointed pastor of a newly organized church in Indianapolis. On August 28, 1877, he married Kate Knox, with whom he had five children.

Walters was ordained a deacon on July 8, 1879. In 1881 he was elected assistant secretary of the Kentucky Conference, beginning a rapid rise within his church. He held pastorates in Louisville, Kentucky, San Francisco, California, and Portland, Oregon, between 1881 and 1886. He was elected to represent California at the General Conference held in May, 1884. The conference elected him as first assistant secretary.

Between 1886 and 1888, Walters pastored in Chattanooga and Knoxville, Tennessee. He then became pastor at the historic Mother Zion Church in New York, New York. On May 4, 1892, he was elected bishop of the Seventh District by the General Conference of the AMEZ Church.

Walters joined with the publisher T. Thomas FORTUNE in the National Afro-American League, which disbanded after two years because of a lack of interest. Walters noted how the U.S. Congress had retreated from its commitment to civil rights, how state legislatures had begun barring African Americans from the polls, and how the U.S. SUPREME COURT had legitimated the policy of "separate but equal" in the 1896 case of *Plessy v. Ferguson*. He asked Fortune to call a meeting of black leaders. On September 15, 1898, the National Afro-American Council was formed in Rochester, New York, with Walters as president. He would be elected to the office of president seven times.

On December 29, 1898, at its second meeting, the council drew up what was probably the most comprehensive program to date to address the problems of African Americans. Walters addressed the council, opposing Booker T. WASHINGTON's policy of separation. At the August 18, 1899, national meeting in Chicago, Illinois, he opposed the idea of emigration to LIBERIA and presented a defense of equal rights for black people in the United States. He also was elected president of the Pan-African Association at the Pan-African Congress held July 23-25, 1900, in London.

Washington gained control of the National Afro-American Council, which became a forerunner of the NIAGARA MOVEMENT. Walters joined the District of Columbia branch of the Niagara movement in 1908. He also joined the NATIONAL ASSOCIATION FOR THE ADVANCEMENT OF COLORED PEOPLE soon after its founding. In 1909 he and other black leaders including W. E. B. DU BOIS signed a document calling for a national conference on the "race problem," in the wake of the Springfield race riot, in which white people killed and wounded scores of African Americans and drove hundreds of others from that Illinois city.

Walters traveled to West Africa in 1910 to reorganize the Cape Coast, West Gold Coast, and Liberian conferences of the AMEZ Church. He thought that the church's priority should be to lay the basis for education and let churches be natural outgrowths of schools. He was offered the post of minister to Liberia by President Woodrow Wilson in 1915, but he declined because of his duties in the United States. His autobiography, *My Life and Work*, was published in 1917.

Wanderer: American ship involved in the illegal SLAVE TRADE to the United States in 1858. Although the institution of SLAVERY was legal in the South in the 1850's, several forms of legislation had outlawed the importation and sale of slaves from outside the United States. The most powerful prohibition was the Act of 1820. This act declared that any citizen of the United States who participated in the slave trade, either by owning a ship or being a member of a ship's crew involved in the international slave trade, was a pirate whose acts were consequently punishable with death. Despite this strong decree, the illegal transportation of slaves to the United States grew during the 1850's. The *Wanderer* was a typical case of the period.

Owned ostensibly by its captain, William C. Corrie, the *Wanderer* actually belonged to Charles A. L. Lamar, a strong advocate of legalizing the slave trade and a leader of a syndicate involved in the illegal trade. The ship left New York after escaping slave-trade charges. From Charleston, SOUTH CAROLINA, it was supposed to go to TRINIDAD but turned to AFRICA instead. The ship loaded slaves at Ambrizete Bay before heading back to the United States. The U.S.S. *Vincennes* spotted the *Wanderer* off the coast of West Africa and tried to approach it. Commanded by Benjamin J. Totten, the *Vincennes* was patrolling the African coast in search of slave ships. Despite its efforts, the *Vincennes* was not able to catch up to the *Wanderer* and lost sight of it.

The *Wanderer* reached St. Andrews Sound on the GEORGIA coast on November 28, and some three hundred to four hundred Africans were taken off the ship. These slaves were transported to the Dubignon plantation nearby. They were later sold throughout the South. (Their experiences were recorded by anthropologist Charles Montgomery, who conducted interviews with many of the survivors in the early twentieth century.)

Captain Corrie imprudently took the *Wanderer* to Brunswick, Georgia, to buy supplies. Although slaves were no longer present in the ship, customs collector Woodford Mabry saw that the ship had been used to transport slaves. Unlike regular cargo ships, slave ships had to carry special equipment such as water containers, food, shackles, and other items necessary for the survival of human beings.

Mabry confiscated the *Wanderer* and arrested three of its crew members, Nicholas A. Brown, Miguel Arguin, and Juan de Bajesta. J. Egbert Farnham, the supercargo (or commercial officer) of the *Wanderer*, was arrested in New York. All of these men were indicted in Georgia district court under the Act of 1820. This was a difficult case to prosecute, however, because the slaves had disappeared into the general slave population of the South. Without that major piece of evidence, it was difficult to convict the slavers. In Farnham's trial, the jury was deadlocked, and he was not retried. Nicholas A. Brown was tried and acquitted, which led to the dismissal of charges against the other two crew members. The state of Georgia sold the *Wanderer* at a third of its cost, to Lamar himself.

The case of the *Wanderer* illustrates the difficulties encountered by the legal system in the 1850's with illegal trade. Although legislation prohibited the trade in slaves, this form of commerce flourished because insufficient ships patrolled the waters, prosecutors were not vigorous enough in these cases, and many Southerners sympathized with the trade.

Ward, Clara (April 21, 1924, Philadelphia, Pennsylvania—January 16, 1973, Los Angeles, California): GOSPEL MUSIC singer and composer. Ward began her career as a gospel singer and pianist at the age of six. In 1934 she was an accompanist for the Ward Trio, a family group that included her mother, Gertrude, and her sister, Willa. The group received national recognition in 1943 when it sang at the NATIONAL BAPTIST CONVENTION. After this appearance, the group began touring throughout the United States.

In 1949 the group joined with composer W. Herbert Brewsters. Their association lasted

fifteen years and produced "Surely God Is Able," the song that made the group one of the most popular female gospel groups of the time.

Gospel singer Clara Ward in 1959. *(AP/Wide World Photos)*

Ward was highly regarded for her ability to express drama in slow gospel ballads and nonmetrical hymns such as Thomas DORSEY's "When I've Done the Best I Can." Later, Ward improved on her style by incorporating techniques such as shrieks and growls, turning her style to what is known as "hard" gospel. An example of this is her 1957 release "Packing Up."

During the 1960's, Ward turned increasingly toward secular music, even though her gospel music had attracted wide audiences. The move to secular music cost her much of her gospel following. In 1963 she performed in the first gospel musical written by Langston HUGHES, entitled *Tambourines to Glory*. She made several successful tours abroad and appeared at major U.S. venues, including the Newport Jazz Festival.

Ward, Samuel Ringgold (October 17, 1817, eastern shore of Maryland—1866, St. George Parish, Jamaica): Congregational minister, orator, and abolitionist. Ward served two pastorates, neither a black congregation. He was cofounder of the Liberty Party and helped to organize the Free Soil Party in New York State. He was a friend of abolitionist Frederick Douglass. In 1851 Ward left the United States for Canada. The bulk of his 1855 *Autobiography of a Fugitive Negro: His Anti-Slavery Labours in the United States, Canada, and England* is devoted to his experiences in Canada and the British Isles (1853-1855). Ward spent his final years farming in Jamaica.

Warfield, William (b. January 22, 1920, West Helena, Arkansas): Singer. Warfield trained at the Eastman School, with his study interrupted by service in the Army. He made his recital debut in New York City in 1950. Warfield's debut was followed by numerous recordings and tours of the United States, Europe, Africa, the Middle East, and Central and South America, performing with major orchestras. He is highly regarded for his interpretations of spirituals and for his performances of Porgy in George Gershwin's *Porgy and Bess*. Warfield joined the faculty of the University of Illinois in 1974. He also served as president of the National Association of Negro Musicians.

War of 1812: Conflict fought between the United States and Great Britain from June, 1812, through the spring of 1815. In part a continuation of hostilities and resentments between the two nations in the aftermath of the American Revolution, the War of 1812 began with a declaration of war by the U.S. Congress on June 18, 1812, and officially closed with the signing of the Treaty of Ghent on December 14, 1814. However, as word of the treaty was slow to reach battlefronts, fighting continued into 1815—an unavoidable circumstance acknowledged under the terms of the agreement.

Historical Background
As a fledgling nation, the United States profited considerably during the first thirty years of its existence from the European wars in which Great Britain and France were primary antagonists. These were the French Revolutionary Wars (1792-1802) and the Napoleonic Wars (1803-1815). The British navy drove French and Spanish ships from major trade routes, allowing American shippers the opportunity to carry merchandise between France and Spain and between French and Spanish Caribbean colonies. Despite America's previously paltry shipping power, U.S. businessmen looked to a newly robust shipping industry to expand trade and fill a gap left by the preoccupation of France and England. Between the early 1790's and 1807, the American merchant marine was able to increase its number of vessels by 300 percent.

Increasingly, though, Great Britain, a legendary maritime power, sought to cripple American commerce and shipping. By 1805 the British sought to block American ships from the North Sea coast of France. The resentment expressed in response by the United States, a neutral power, was exacerbated by other long-standing grievances against the British, who had a history of refusing to sign trade agreements favorable to the United States. The British had neglected to withdraw from American territory along the Great Lakes, and on American frontiers, British support for Native Americans in conflicts with European-American settlers had consistently rankled the U.S. government.

In 1807 the British government attempted to channel all neutral trade through Great Britain, where a duty would be charged. British naval officers also claimed the right to come aboard American merchant ships and to take into custody any personnel whom they considered British sailors. On certain occasions, British officers claimed that U.S. citizens were British and removed them from American ships. This practice, known as impressment, allowed American resentment of the British to come to a focus over specific incidents in which citizenship rights were flagrantly violated.

The Prelude to War

Of the many confrontations and conflicts between the United States and Great Britain during the several years prior to war, the most notorious incident involved three African American sailors. On June 22, 1807, the American frigate *Chesapeake*, commanded by Commodore James Barron, was approached by the British ship *Leopard* and requested to stop. When Barron refused, the *Leopard* fired several broadsides into the *Chesapeake*. Barron then stopped, allowing his ship to be boarded and four sailors to be removed, of whom only one proved to be a British subject. The other three—William Ware, Daniel Martin, and John Strachan—were African Americans with full U.S. citizenship. The incident was widely publicized in the United States, arousing considerable indignation against the British. Shortly thereafter, President Thomas Jefferson interdicted all American harbors and waters to vessels of the British navy. The United States, however, lacked sufficient naval power to declare immediate war.

Serving in the U.S. Navy

African Americans fought in every sea engagement of the War of 1812. During the war, free African Americans of the northern states enlisted in the Navy in great numbers, while in the South, many slaves were offered their freedom in exchange for service in the Navy. It is estimated that one-sixth of the U.S. Navy servicemen during the war were African Americans.

The most memorable naval battle of the war was fought on Lake Erie. Captain Oliver Hazard Perry, in anticipation of the battle, had sent word from Lake Erie requesting that his superior, Commodore Isaac Chauncey, send reinforcements. When Chauncey sent a company of African Americans, Perry sent back a message complaining bitterly about the prospect of leading "inferior" men into battle. Chauncey replied with a scathing letter that rebuked the captain's prejudice: "I have yet to learn that the color of the skin . . . can affect a man's qualifications or usefulness. I have fifty blacks on board this ship and many of them are my best men." Between fifty and one hundred of Perry's 432 men at Lake Erie were African Americans. By the time the battle was won, Perry had amended his views; he was known to have marveled over the bravery of the black sailors.

At the Battle of Lake Champlain, as well, many of the gunners who contributed to the American victory were African Americans, including John Day, who served on board the *Viper*, and Charles Black, whose father had fought at Bunker Hill. Nathaniel Shaler, the captain of the privateer *Governor Tompkins*, reported on the bravery of John Johnson and John Davis, African Americans who, though mortally wounded, implored their shipmates to fight.

The Battle of New Orleans

Late in 1814, the British turned their attention to the South, seeking to gain control of the logistically crucial port of New Orleans, through which nearly half of U.S. produce passed en route to various markets. The British began assembling an armada in the Caribbean, intercepting merchant ships and bringing trade in the South to a standstill. Major General Andrew Jackson, charged with defending the Gulf Coast and the southern states, issued a proclamation calling upon free African Americans to join the fight against the

Contemporary engraving of the Battle of New Orleans, in which approximately six hundred African Americans fought under Andrew Jackson. *(National Portrait Gallery, Smithsonian Institution)*

British. While African American participation in the Navy was widespread, the U.S. government had refused African Americans enlistment in the Army until that point.

Jackson's opinion of African Americans had been influenced in 1813 at the Battle of Fort Boyer near Mobile, Alabama. An African American named Jeffrey had mounted a horse and rallied American troops to fight off a British charge. The rally had succeeded, and Jackson had given Jeffrey the rank of major. Jackson's proclamation addressed African Americans as citizens of the nation; its first words were:

> Through a mistaken policy, you have heretofore been deprived of a participation in the glorious struggle for national rights, in which *our* country is engaged. This no longer shall exist.

The Battle of New Orleans was the greatest land battle of the war. Two battalions made up of approximately six hundred African Americans, with African American line officers, fought under Jackson. On December 23, 1814, Jackson and his men met a British army on the Gulf Coast near the mouth of the Mississippi. For more than two weeks, they skirmished to within a few miles of New Orleans. The fighting came to a climax in a ferocious struggle on January 8, 1815. Within twenty-five minutes, more than two thousand British soldiers were killed, wounded, or taken prisoner; American losses were tiny in comparison. The Treaty of Ghent had been signed several weeks previously, but the Battle of New Orleans, along with other impressive American victories during the final six months of the war, established the United States in the popular mind as having triumphed.

Richard Seavers

Throughout the war, the British used their naval might to enforce blockades off the coasts of the United States and to capture American prisoners of war in large numbers. More than five thousand of these men were kept at Dartmoor prison in the west of England. American sailors who had entered the British Navy but who refused to fight against the United States were also confined there; one such was Richard Seavers, an African American from Massachusetts.

Seavers, reportedly the largest and strongest man in the prison, stood six feet five inches and carried himself with a regal bearing. He demonstrated a natural leadership in prison block four, to which all black prisoners were assigned. A former teacher of boxing, Seavers was known to stride imperially through the prison, carrying a large club, attended by two white boys, and wearing a great bearskin cap. He came to be known as "King Dick," a renowned figure who is described in various memoirs of life at Dartmoor prison. King Dick zealously governed block four, dispensing beatings if prisoners were caught stealing. Yet his rule was accepted by the majority of the inmates, and he presided over organized gambling, boxing and fencing events, musical performances, and productions of William Shakespeare. The more respectable prisoners in other blocks requested transfers to block four because of its superior order.

Results of the War

The War of 1812 established American rights as a neutral nation and won recognition of the United States from the maritime powers of the world. As has been the case with nearly all wars in U.S. history, the participation and sacrifices of African Americans raised hopes that racist practices would be considerably diminished at war's end. The Treaty of Ghent, however, declared that all slaves captured by the British during the war would be returned to American slavery. In 1820 the U.S. Army adjutant general's office ordered that African Americans were not to be received as recruits in the Army.

—James Knippling

Suggested Readings:

Altoff, Gerard T. *Amongst My Best Men: African-Americans and the War of 1812*. Put-in-Bay, Ohio: Perry Group, 1996.

Carter, Samuel. *Blaze of Glory: The Fight for New Orleans.* New York: St. Martin's Press, 1971.

Hickey, Donald R. *The War of 1812: A Forgotten Conflict*. Urbana: University of Illinois Press, 1989.

Horsman, Reginald. *The War of 1812*. New York: Alfred A. Knopf, 1969.

Nell, William C. *Services of Colored Americans in the Wars of 1776 and 1812*. Boston: Prentiss & Sawyer, 1851. Reprint. New York: AMS Press, 1976.

Wilson, Joseph T. *The Black Phalanx: A History of Negro Soldiers of the U.S. in the Wars of 1775-1812 and 1861-1865*. Hartford, Conn.: American, 1888. Reprint. New York: Arno Press, 1968.

War on Poverty: Government programs for the poor initiated in the 1960's. By 1961 several forces had created a need for programs to reduce poverty in the United States. One was the paradox of extreme poverty in the midst of a wealthy nation. In these pockets of poverty there was starvation, poor sanitation, joblessness, poor health, and illiteracy. A second force was the limited effectiveness of earlier welfare programs, focused on health, nutrition, and income maintenance, in meeting the needs of the poor. A third force was the organized protests of African Americans during the Civil Rights movement for jobs and new programs to lift them out of poverty.

The principal programs in the War on Poverty focused on employment and education, food and nutrition, and health care. In the areas of job training and employment, the following initiatives were developed or expanded: the Neighborhood Youth Corps, the Job Corps, the 1964 Economic Opportunity Act, and the Manpower Development and Training Act. Educational initiatives included HEAD START, the UPWARD BOUND PROGRAM, Follow Through, and Title I of the Aid to Education Act. The food stamp program, Emergency Food Aid, and the school lunch program were expanded during this period. Finally, the Neighborhood Health Centers program and the Medicaid program were implemented as part of the War on Poverty.

These programs were supplemented by the implementation of a community action program (a political action program that attempted to empower the poor) and a legal services program that was geared toward improving the access of the poor to affordable legal representation. Although cash assistance programs originated before the War on Poverty, between 1965 and 1975 they were expanded significantly. The AID TO FAMILIES WITH DEPENDENT CHILDREN (AFDC) and the Aid to the Aged, Blind, and Disabled were the primary targets of expansion in cash assistance programs. As a result of these programs, there was a significant decrease in the percentage of poor Americans between 1965 and 1975, to less than 10 percent of all families but still more than 25 percent of African American families. The community action programs also helped to increase the level of participation of African Americans in the political process.

Warwick, Dionne (b. December 12, 1941, East Orange, New Jersey): Singer. Warwick's parents valued music, especially GOSPEL MUSIC singing, and saw to it that their daughter received musical training at an early age. At the age of six, she began singing gospel music in her church choir. Later, as a college student at the Hartt College of Music in Hartford, CONNECTICUT, she was able to supplement tuition costs by singing in a trio, the Gospelaires, comprising herself, her sister Dee Dee, and her cousin Cissy Houston, who later became the mother of singer Whitney HOUSTON.

Dionne Warwick (left) with Cissy Houston and Whitney Houston in 1987. *(AP/Wide World Photos)*

It was through the songs of composer Burt Bacharach and lyricist Hal David that Warwick became well known. Recordings of his songs, many of which reached the top ten, led to greater public exposure. In 1963 she went on an international tour that culminated in Paris, where she was received ecstatically. Critic Jean Monteaux endowed her with the name, "Paris's Black Pearl," a symbolic assessment of her tremendous audience appeal. Warwicks's first number one-hit, "Then Came You" (1974), was recorded with the Spinners.

Eventually, antagonism within the Bacharach team and dissension among associates created a rift that caused Warwick to dissociate herself as collaborator. The conflicts were not resolved until 1986. Warwick had a number of successful albums in the late 1970's and early 1980's, and recorded the hit "I'll Never Love This Way Again" in 1979. As an active participant in the USA for Africa project, Warwick joined with forty-four other singers to record "We Are the World," a smash hit worldwide whose proceeds were donated for African relief.

Washington, Booker T. (April 5, 1856, near Hale's Ford, Virginia—November 14, 1915, Tuskegee, Alabama): Social reformer. Booker Taliaferro Washington was born a slave on a VIRGINIA farm. His father was said to be white, but his mother Jane apparently never told Booker or his older brother John anything about their paternity. By 1860 Jane had married a slave named Washington from a nearby farm and had borne a daughter named Amanda by him.

Youth and Education
After emancipation in 1865, Jane and her three children followed her husband to Malden, WEST VIRGINIA. There, Booker joined his stepfather working in the town's salt furnaces, but after much begging, the boy was also allowed to attend school. Known only by his first name until he began going to school, he told his teacher his full name was Booker Washington. Sometime later, he added the middle name Taliaferro.

Never happy with his stepfather, Washington moved out of the family cabin sometime within his first two years in Malden. He became the houseboy of General Lewis Ruffner and his wife Viola. Viola Ruffner took a motherly interest in Washington and encouraged his education. She also taught him the virtues of rigorous cleanliness and hard work.

In 1872 Washington decided to further his education by traveling to HAMPTON INSTITUTE in Virginia. He arrived dirty and practically penniless. There, he met two more whites who

Booker T. Washington was widely perceived as the leading spokesperson for African Americans during his time. *(Library of Congress)*

played important roles in the development of his personality. Mary F. Mackie admitted Washington and hired him as a janitor after an entrance exam that consisted of his sweeping a room. The head of the school, General Samuel Chapman Armstrong, was a New Englander who became a father figure to Washington. At Hampton, Washington was taught the dignity of labor and the benefits of discipline and self-improvement.

After graduating from Hampton in 1875, Washington returned to Malden to teach. Three years later, he entered Wayland Seminary in Washington, D.C. In 1879 Washington returned to Hampton to teach night school. During the 1880-1881 school year, he became supervisor of the dormitory for Native American students. In May, 1881, Armstrong received a letter from Tuskegee, Alabama, asking him to recommend a white man to head a new school for African Americans. Instead, Armstrong recommended Washington.

The Tuskegee Institute

When Washington arrived in Tuskegee on June 24, 1881, he expected to find a school to head. All that existed, however, was an uncertain two-thousand-dollar appropriation from the state legislature. Utilizing the industrial education format of Hampton and currying the favor of prominent whites, he was able to create Tuskegee Normal and Industrial Institute. All students were required to work, and they made bricks, built buildings, and raised food for the school. They were taught a trade as well as academic subjects. Soon, Washington reached out to surrounding farmers through yearly conferences and educational outreach programs. By 1915 Tuskegee had an endowment of nearly two million dollars.

To raise money for his school, Washington embarked on many speaking tours and became well known. In 1895 he was asked to speak at the Cotton States and International Exposition in ATLANTA, GEORGIA, in the mid-

dle of a decade of bloody racial violence. Washington had the difficult task of addressing an audience composed of white and black northerners and southerners without offending anyone. Incredibly, he succeeded.

His speech became known as the ATLANTA COMPROMISE and spelled out a basis for interracial cooperation. From whites, Washington asked for economic and educational opportunities for African Americans. Appealing to white self-interest, he noted that black southerners made up one-third of the region's population. Kept ignorant and poor, they would drag the South down; through industrial education, they could help to bring the dawning of a richer "New South." In return for educational and economic opportunity, Washington asked black southerners to forego temporarily agitation for civil and political rights. He argued that if African Americans made themselves indispensable to the South, they would soon be granted all the rights they desired.

One reason his speech was so popular was that almost everyone who heard it interpreted the speech differently. When it became apparent that white southerners interpreted Washington's comments as an endorsement of segregation, black support for the Atlanta Compromise began to erode. Washington's popularity, however, remained high among whites. Prominent Americans such as Andrew Carnegie and John D. Rockefeller supported Tuskegee, and in 1901 Washington dined with President Theodore Roosevelt at the White House. The publication of Washington's immensely popular *Up from Slavery: An Autobiography* (1901) further enhanced his status.

National Prominence

Washington belittled the importance of politics and civil rights in speeches but became one of the most powerful men in the South. Presidents consulted him on political appointments, philanthropists sought his advice on charitable contributions, and much of the BLACK PRESS became financially dependent on his support. He sought to control such organizations as the National Afro-American Council to increase the power of his "Tuskegee Machine." He also practiced in secret what he preached against in public. Behind the scenes, he challenged segregation and disfranchisement through quiet diplomacy and secret financial contributions. Nevertheless, conditions continued to deteriorate for African Americans.

Rights that had been won for blacks during RECONSTRUCTION were being increasingly denied, and some black leaders challenged both the conciliatory nature of Washington's accommodationism and his emphasis on industrial education at the expense of higher education. Under the leadership of William Monroe TROTTER and W. E. B. DU BOIS, several dozen black intellectuals founded the NIAGARA MOVEMENT in 1905 as an alternative to Washington's leadership. The movement was largely unsuccessful, but a number of its members joined with white liberals four years later to organize the NATIONAL ASSOCIATION FOR THE ADVANCEMENT OF COLORED PEOPLE (NAACP). Probably because of the group's links with Du Bois, Washington continued to have a strained relationship with the organization until his death.

Last Years

During his last two decades at Tuskegee Institute, Washington gave many speeches, published books and articles, received numerous honors, and was asked to serve on boards of trustees and to join dozens of organizations. He retained the support of prominent white politicians in the north and the south as well of the majority of African Americans. At the same time, he expanded the influence of Tuskegee by founding the NATIONAL NEGRO BUSINESS LEAGUE in 1900 and beginning National Negro Health Week in 1914. When

Bust of Booker T. Washington by sculptor Richmond Barthó. *(National Archives)*

Washington died on November 14, 1915, he was survived by his wife Margaret and three children. He had been predeceased by two wives, Fanny and Olivia.

Historical Assessment

Few African American leaders have been more controversial than Booker T. Washington. Some scholars have depicted him as a power-hungry politician who bartered away the rights of his people. Others have denounced his bourgeois capitalism and deification of white middle-class values. A few assert that Washington was a dedicated, practical realist who accomplished as much as was possible in an age of escalating racism. Still others have seen seeds of black nationalism in his self-help ideology and his organization of all-black institutions. Many believe Washington was a complex man who played so many different roles that the real Washington is virtually impossible to know. All agree that his legacy was mixed, with both positive and negative consequences.

—Linda O. McMurry

See also: Black capitalism; Business and commerce; Conservatives; Garvey, Marcus.

Suggested Readings:

Denton, Virginia L. *Booker T. Washington and the Adult Education Movement*. Gainesville: University Press of Florida, 1993.

Du Bois, W. E. B. *The Souls of Black Folk*. Chicago: A. C. McClurg, 1903.

Harris, Thomas E. *Analysis of the Clash over the Issues Between Booker T. Washington and W. E. B. Du Bois*. New York: Garland, 1993.

Harlan, Louis R. *Booker T. Washington: The Making of a Black Leader, 1856-1901*. New York: Oxford University Press, 1972.

_____. *Booker T. Washington: The Wizard of Tuskegee, 1901-1915*. New York: Oxford University Press, 1983.

_____. *Booker T. Washington in Perspective: Essays of Louis R. Harlan*. Edited by Raymond W. Smock. Jackson: University Press of Mississippi, 1986.

Hill, Roy L. *Booker T's Child: The Life and Times of Portia Marshall Washington Pittman*. 2d ed. Washington, D.C.: Three Continents Press, 1993.

Washington, Booker T. *The Booker T. Washington Papers*. 13 vols. Edited by Louis R. Harlan et al. Urbana: University of Illinois Press, 1972-1984.

Wintz, Cary D., ed. *African American Political Thought, 1890-1930: Washington, Du Bois, Garvey, and Randolph*. Armonk, N.Y.: M. E. Sharpe, 1996.

Washington, Denzel, Jr. (b. December 28, 1954, Mt. Vernon, New York): Stage and FILM actor. Denzel Washington's work runs a gamut of styles from romance to serious drama, from action-adventure to comedy. Some critics have credited him with helping to redefine the portrayal of African Americans in the film industry.

Family Life

Washington was born the son of a PENTECOSTAL minister, for whom he was named, and a beautician who had been a gospel singer prior to her marriage. Reared in a strict, religious household, neither he nor his two siblings were allowed to watch much television or go to many films. They spent much of their time at church or in one of the beauty parlors their mother owned. His parents worked several jobs in order to give their children a decent home. Washington's parents separated when he was twelve, however, finally getting a divorce when he was fourteen. After Washington's mother received custody of the children, she removed Washington from public school and enrolled him in Oakland Academy in upstate New York, a private school primarily attended by white children of wealthy families.

Collegiate Years

In 1972, after graduating from Oakland, Washington entered Fordham University with aspirations of becoming a medical student. While still an undergraduate, Washington received his first exposure to acting while working as a camp counselor one summer in Lakeville, Connecticut. Persuaded to participate in a talent show by the other staff members, Washington found himself quite comfortable on stage, where he enjoyed the audience response. In his junior year, he signed up for an acting workshop with film actor and professor Robinson Stone, whom Washington credits as being directly responsible for his success. Stone recognized talent in Washington and encouraged him to audition for university productions. After winning the title role in productions of Eugene O'Neill's *The Emperor Jones* and William Shakespeare's *Othello* from several theater majors, Washington decided to commit himself to the acting profession.

First Professional Roles

Prior to his graduation from Fordham in 1977 with a bachelor's degree in journalism, Washington acquired an agent. Washington obtained a role in the NBC television film *Wilma*, based on the life of track star Wilma Rudolph. On the last day of filming, Washington was introduced to his future wife, Pauletta Pearson, a singer and pianist.

With the exception of the television film *Flesh and Blood* in 1978 and a few theater roles, Washington found the early part of his new career to be financially frustrating. He entered a three-year acting program at the American Conservatory Theater in San Francisco with the assistance of Stone, but he left after the first year and returned to New York. Unable to find work, he reluctantly accepted a position in a New York recreation center. Prompted by Pauletta to continue auditioning, Washington tried out for the role of MALCOLM X in *When the Chickens Come Home to Roost* (1980) at the New Federal Theater. Upon being cast as the legendary Black Muslim leader, Washington resigned the recreation center job. In addition to dying his hair red to match that of the slain activist, Washington studied Malcolm's life in an attempt to understand his motivations. Critics and audiences alike were stunned at how Washington seemed to become Malcolm X. His performance garnered him an AUDELCO Recognition Award. Within the next two years, his career would take several major turns.

Washington received his first film role in *Carbon Copy* (1981), playing a jive-talking black teenager. Although the role secured him financially for a period, critics were unappreciative.

Major Stage Roles

Returning to the stage, Washington drew the interest of prominent Off-Broadway theater companies, including the New York Shakespeare Festival and the National Black Touring Circuit. He appeared in productions of *Ceremonies in Dark Old Men*, *Coriolanus*, *Every Goodbye Ain't Gone*, *Spell #7*, and *The Mighty Gents*. In 1981 Washington won the role that would be his major break. Hired by the Negro Ensemble Company as a last-minute replacement, he originated the role of Private Melvin Peterson in Charles Fuller's Pulitzer-Prize winning drama *A Soldier's Play*. His performance garnered him that year's Obie Award as best supporting actor.

Fame in Television and Film

While performing in *A Soldier's Play* in Los Angeles, Washington landed the part of Dr. Phillip Chandler on the television series *St. Elsewhere*. Although he remained on the show for five seasons, his first two years were frustrating. Little was done to make his character anything more than a token black doctor. To remedy this dilemma, he was given sabbaticals to do other projects, and the show's writers began to give him more interesting stories. After marrying Pauletta Pearson in 1983, Washington appeared in the television film *License to Kill* (1983) and reprised the character of Peterson in *A Soldier's Story* (1984), the film version of Fuller's play.

Wanting to work with Gene Hackman and director Sidney Lumet, Washington petitioned and won the role of a media lobbyist—a part originally written as a white character—in the film *Power* (1986). After starring in the title role of the television film *The George McKenna Story* (1986), Washington was asked to play martyred South African leader Steven Biko in Richard Attenborough's film *Cry Freedom* (1987). Although critics hailed his performance, and he received an Academy Award nomination, *Cry Freedom* was a bittersweet experience for Washington. He felt that the story of Biko's struggle against South Africa's apartheid system was compromised by Attenborough's decision to focus the film on Donald Woods, Biko's white friend and the author of the book upon which the film was based.

After receiving numerous film offers, Washington left *St. Elsewhere* in 1987. Immediately, he found himself involved in several projects at once. After playing a former paratrooper returning home to Thatcherite England from the Falklands War in *For Queen and Country* (1988), he returned to the stage with his first Broadway role as Sylvester Cooper in the Ron Milner comedy *Checkmates*. Directly after the close of *Checkmates* in New York, Washington went to the Caribbean to shoot *The Mighty Quinn* (1989). He then journeyed to Georgia to film *Glory* (1989), in which he portrayed a CIVIL WAR soldier and former slave named Trip. Always an avid researcher, Washington immersed himself in historical records and slave diaries to bring authenticity to the film. Again, critics praised his performance for its intensity. Washington won an Academy Award as best supporting actor.

Denzel Washington with the Oscar he won in 1990 for his role in *Glory*. (AP/Wide World Photos)

Work in the 1990's

In 1990 Washington switched from serious drama to comedy with the film *Heart Condition*, playing a hip black lawyer who dies and haunts a bigoted white cop (Bob Hoskins) after the attorney's heart is transplanted into the officer's body. The film reminded many critics of *Carbon Copy*, another ill-fated comedy about black-white relationships.

Washington then returned to drama, starring in Spike LEE's jazz film *Mo' Better Blues* (1990) as trumpeter Bleek Gilliam. Lee stated that he wanted Washington for the role after seeing the effect he had on women during a performance of *Checkmates*. Washington reported that Lee's improvisational style of directing made the film one of his most enjoyable working experiences. Afterward, Washington performed the title role in Shakespeare's *Richard III* for the New York Shakespeare Festival.

In the 1991 action-adventure film *Ricochet*, he played framed police officer Nick Styles. In 1992 Washington appeared as the romantic lead in *Mississippi Masala*, a film about interracial love and prejudice. He also reprised the role of Malcolm X, this time in Spike Lee's controversial film biography, *Malcolm X*. His work in this film again earned him recognition by the Motion Picture Academy, which nominated him for best actor. Other film work in the 1990's included roles in *Philadelphia* (1993), *The Preacher's Wife* (1996, with Whitney Houston), *Courage Under Fire* (1996), *He Got Game* (1998), and *The Bone Collector* (1999). In early 2000 he was nominated for an Academy Award for his portrayal of boxer "Hurricane" Carter in *The Hurricane* (1999).

—*Gary Anderson*

Suggested Readings:

Bogle, Donald. *Blacks in American Films and Television: An Illustrated Encyclopedia*. New York: Garland, 1988.

Brode, Douglas. *Denzel Washington: His Films and Career*. New York: Carol, 1996.

Davis, Thulani. "Denzel in the Swing." *American Film* (August, 1990): 26-31.

Hoban, Phoebe. "Days of Glory: Denzel Washington—From Spike Lee's Blues to Richard III." *New York Magazine* (August 13, 1990): 34-38.

Randolph, Laura B. "The Glory Days of Denzel Washington." *Ebony* (September, 1990): 80-82.

Shah, Diane K. "Soldier, Healer, Seller of Rye." *GQ* (October, 1988): 312-317.

Washington, Fredi (b. December 23, 1903, Savannah, Georgia): Stage and FILM actor. Fredricka Carolyn "Fredi" Washington began her career as a dancer, performing in nightclubs and in the touring production of *Shuffle Along* (1922-1926). In her first dramatic stage role, she appeared opposite Paul ROBESON in the play *Black Boy* (1926). Her most notable performance came in the role of Peola in the popular film *Imitation of Life* (1934). In 1937 she cofounded the Negro Actors Guild and served as its executive secretary.

Washington, George (1817, Frederick County, Virginia—1905): Pioneer. The son of a white mother and a slave father, Washington was given to a white family that he accompanied to OHIO and later to MISSOURI. He ran businesses as a sawmill operator and a tailor but moved to what is now WASHINGTON STATE to escape discriminatory laws. He bought land and established the town now known as Centralia by offering free lots to people willing to settle there, along the Northern Pacific Railroad.

Washington, Harold (April 15, 1922, Chicago, Illinois—November 25, 1987, Chicago, Illinois): ILLINOIS politician and MAYOR of CHICAGO. Harold Washington's father, Roy, was a practicing attorney and an AFRICAN METHODIST EPISCOPAL minister; his mother was a homemaker. As a child, Washington was known for his slender build, his interest in sports, and his appetite for books. For example, while playing for his neighborhood baseball team, he was often found with a glove in one hand and a book in his pocket. Washington read a wide range of books and magazines, but he found himself particularly drawn to his father's large collection of books on power and self-determination. His reading was diverse; from books, he taught himself how to run the hurdles as part of his stint as a track runner in high school.

Washington's early development was also supplemented by open discussions of politics and religion, conducted by his father at the dinner table almost every night. Washington wrote that "before I reached my teens, I was aware of presidents, mayors, governors, aldermen, and people of that nature." When Washington turned seventeen, he dropped out of high school to enter the Civilian Conservation Corps, for which he planted trees and quarried limestone in Bitely, Michigan. Once he returned to Chicago, he married his childhood sweetheart, Nancy Dorothy Finch.

Between the completion of high school in 1939 and his 1942 enlistment in the armed forces in WORLD WAR II, Washington was employed in a variety of jobs that ranged from selling snacks at a bus station in Chicago to working as a laborer in the Chicago stockyards and operating data-processing machines in the Chicago Merchandise Mart. While serving in the Pacific between 1942 and 1946, Washington completed his high school training by taking correspondence courses in history, literature, chemistry, and English literature. After World War II, Washington took advantage of the G.I. Bill to complete his undergraduate studies as a political science major at Roosevelt University. After his graduation from Roosevelt, he studied law at Northwestern

University's law school, where he was the only African American admitted among an incoming freshman class of 185.

In 1952 Washington received his law degree from Northwestern, and in 1953 he was admitted to the Illinois bar. In 1954 he became active in local politics, succeeding his late father as the Chicago DEMOCRATIC PARTY's Third Ward precinct captain. In 1954, too, he joined the Chicago city corporation counsel's office as an assistant prosecutor, a post he occupied until 1958. In 1960 he began a four-year term as an arbitrator for the Illinois State Industrial Commission.

Entry into Politics
In 1964 Washington ran for and won election to the Illinois House of Representatives. From the start of his legislative career in 1965, he was a persuasive speaker and a fighter for the concerns of his constituents. In 1965 he was at the forefront of a fight to reform consumer credit. In 1969 Washington organized an African American caucus in the Illinois House of Representatives. He was also responsible for helping make Martin Luther King, Jr.'s birthday a commemorative day in Illinois. Although Washington was seen as an initiator at the legislature in Springfield, Illinois, he ran his precinct as an integral part of the Democratic machine in Chicago. During his tenure in the state legislature, Washington was involved in legislation ranging from the Fair Employment Practices Act to saving Provident Hospital, a beleaguered African American hospital on Chicago's South Side.

First Race for Mayor
Pressure for the election of an African American mayor in the city of Chicago escalated in the 1970's. Washington's first attempt to pursue candidacy for the mayor's office came in 1977, in a special election that occurred after the death of Mayor Richard J. Daley in December, 1976. Although Washington was picked as a potential candidate for mayor by two separate committees, he withdrew his candidacy after Congressman Ralph Metcalfe stated that he would not support Washington because of Washington's early 1970's troubles with the Internal Revenue Service; he had been convicted of having failed to file income-tax returns for four years and had served a month in jail. Washington nevertheless was unofficially submitted as a candidate in the 1978 race, but he lost. Yet even though Washington lost the 1978 race, the effort helped bring more African American representatives to the city council and helped Washington to become a U.S. Congressman in 1980 following Metcalfe's death.

Second Campaign for Mayor
Several forces led Washington to again seek the mayor's office in 1982. First, Chicago's African American community was disappointed with the lack of concern that Mayor Jane Byrne had shown for their needs. Second, several grass-roots coalitions developed to raise the consciousness of African American Chicagoans regarding the possibility of the election of an African American mayor in 1983. These organizations contributed to the movement to elect Washington by placing welfare recipients, the poor, the ELDERLY, African Americans, and Hispanics on the voting rolls as well as by coordinating fund-raisers across the city. Third, the African American business community provided financial support for his campaign. Fourth, more than 250 African American ministers showed their support for Washington's candidacy by urging their congregations to register to vote. In the wake of this overwhelming current of mobilization in the African American community, Washington again entered the race for mayor.

While it was the activity of the coalitions that solidified Washington's support in the African American and Hispanic communities, it was a series of debates and public speaking events in January, 1983, that broadened his appeal to the rest of the city. Washington captured the votes of the masses in a televised debate with incumbent Jane Byrne and candidate Richard M. Daley (son of the late mayor, Richard J. Daley) as well as through public appearances with prominent supporters. As a result of these efforts, Washington narrowly defeated Byrne and Daley in the Democratic primary and captured the party's nomination.

Following Washington's primary victory, the REPUBLICAN PARTY primary winner, Bernard Epton, attempted to use Washington's earlier tax conviction and conducted a campaign of race-based politics in an effort to win the general election. In spite of such tactics, Washington became Chicago's first African American mayor, receiving 640,738 votes to Epton's 599,144 votes.

Chicago mayor Harold Washington speaking on the night of his reelection in February, 1987. *(AP/Wide World Photos)*

Washington the Mayor

Washington was elected mayor on a reform platform; he promised to eliminate patronage jobs, increase the ethnic diversity of city government, and promote the growth of industry in Chicago. His main obstacle to these objectives was a bloc of twenty-nine city councilmen organized to oppose Washington's programs. The coalition attempted to stop Washington's appointments of agency officials, the passage of the city budget, and the funding of capital improvements for the city. They also used the media in an attempt to draw Washington into conflict with Hispanics, Jews, and the gay community to dilute his political base. Washington's opponents hoped that, as a result of these efforts, Washington would be seen as an ineffective mayor and would lose in the 1987 election.

In spite of such opposition, Washington was able to oversee a number of important changes. He reduced the number of discretionary (patronage) jobs in Chicago from more than forty thousand to fewer than a thousand; he used affirmative action policies to boost the percentage of city contracts for minority- and women-owned businesses; and he obtained bonds for sorely needed capital improvements to the infrastructure of the city of Chicago. Furthermore, following twenty years of decline in industry and employment, the number of jobs in Chicago increased. Retail sales and manufacturing investment also increased during the same period.

Washington's battles with the twenty-nine councilmen ended after a court ruling ordered the reconfiguration of council wards drawn by Mayor Jane Byrne in 1981. The reconfiguration created seven new wards and changed the power balance between the mayor and his enemies on the council. After special elections were held in 1986 to fill the new seats, an even balance was achieved between Washington's supporters and his foes, leaving the final vote to the mayor on issues affecting his political agenda.

Final Campaign

In the 1987 election Washington faced and beat Byrne in the primary and won the general election by a wide margin. In his second term, Washington moved his fights from the local to the national level, fighting the attempted takeover of the Chicago Housing Authority by the U.S. Department of Housing and Urban Development and by supporting Jesse Jackson in his candidacy for president. On November 25, 1987, however, not long after his reelection, Washington died of a heart attack.

—*Llewellyn Cornelius*

Suggested Readings:

Bennett, Larry. "Harold Washington and the Black Urban Regime." *Urban Affairs Quarterly* 28 (March, 1993): 423-440.

Brasfield, Curtis G. *The Ancestry of Mayor Harold Washington (1922-1987)*. Bowie, Md.: Heritage Books, 1993.

Clavel, Pierre, and Wim Wiewel, eds. *Harold Washington and the Neighborhoods: Progressive City Government in Chicago, 1983-1987*. New Brunswick, N.J.: Rutgers University Press, 1991.

Holli, Melvin G., and Paul M. Green, eds. *The Making of the Mayor, Chicago, 1983*. Grand Rapids, Mich.: Wm. B. Eerdmans, 1984.

Levinsohn, Florence H. *Harold Washington: A Political Biography*. Chicago: Chicago Review Press, 1983.

Miller, Alton. *Harold Washington: The Mayor, the Man*. Chicago: Bonus Books, 1989.

Rivlin, Gary. *Fire on the Prairie: Chicago's Harold Washington and the Politics of Race*. New York: Henry Holt, 1992.

Travis, Dempsey. *An Autobiography of Black Politics*. Chicago: Urban Research Institute, 1987.

_____. *"Harold": The People's Mayor, an Authorized Biography of Mayor Harold Washington*. Chicago: Urban Research Press, 1989.

Young, Henry J., ed. *The Black Church and the Harold Washington Story: The Man, the Message, the Movement*. Bristol, Ind.: Wyndham Hall Press, 1988.

Washington, Mary Helen (b. January 21, 1941, Cleveland, Ohio): Educator. Washington taught English in Cleveland's public schools (1962-1964) before becoming an instructor in English at St. John College in that city. She moved to the University of Detroit in 1972, becoming director of its BLACK STUDIES program in 1975. She won the Richard Wright Award for Literary Criticism in 1974. She taught at the University of Massachusetts at Boston in the 1980's and at the University of Maryland in the 1990's

Between 1975 and 1991, Washington edited and wrote introductions for four respected collections of black writing: *Black-Eyed Susans: Classic Stories by and About Black Women* (1975), *Midnight Birds: Stories by Contemporary Black Women Writers* (1980), *Invented Lives: Narratives of Black Women, 1860-1960* (1987), and *Memory of Kin: Stories of Family by Black Writers* (1991). *Invented Lives* is noteworthy for having brought attention to the history of black women writers.

Washington, D.C.: Capital of the United States. Washington, D.C. (for District of Columbia), officially became the seat of the U.S. government in 1800. A federal district, it straddles the border between MARYLAND and VIRGINIA but is not a part of either state. Because Washington is the home of the federal government, events that occur there carry both political and symbolic importance. Hundreds of nongovernmental organizations have their headquarters there in order to be close to the national center of power. The U.S. Bureau of the Census estimated that Washington's population in 1997 was about 529,000, of which 333,000, or 63 percent, were African American.

The U.S. CONSTITUTION stipulated that the District of Columbia would not be a part of any state and would be overseen by the U.S. government. The city was planned largely by a French architect, Pierre L'Enfant, in the

1790's and was surveyed by a team that included a self-taught African American mathematician and astronomer named Benjamin BANNEKER. In 1800 the population of the city was about 10,000 whites, 3,200 black slaves, and 800 free blacks. Washington, D.C., was located between a free state (Maryland) and a slave state (Virginia), and it was in many ways a southern city. It is an ironic historical fact that the capital city of the "land of the free" contained a large slave population until 1862 and maintained southern-style policies of segregation until the 1940's.

However, Washington was also home to abolitionist activity in the early nineteenth century, and many FREE BLACKS established businesses and schools there. By the 1820's and 1930's it was a destination for free blacks from other parts of the country. The growing African American population made many whites—both civic leaders and working-class people—somewhat uneasy. In 1935 and 1836 there were racial disturbances when whites violently opposed abolitionists and free blacks.

Slavery was abolished in the district in 1862, during the CIVIL WAR, and Washington became a refuge for runaway slaves fleeing the CONFEDERACY. African Americans established charitable organizations to help them. In the years after the war, a number of notable African Americans, including Alexander CRUMMEL and Frederick DOUGLASS, moved to

After slavery was abolished in Washington in 1862, the city became a refuge for runaway slaves. When the Thirteenth Amendment abolished slavery throughout the nation after the Civil War, thousands of the city's African Americans turned out to celebrate.

the city. Crummel established the American Negro Academy, and HOWARD UNIVERSITY was founded in 1867. The black population tripled in the 1860's, and by 1868 blacks were serving on the city's Common Council and Board of Aldermen. (Washington, D.C., had home rule until 1870, when Congress severely limited it.) By 1880 about a third of the population of Washington, D.C., was African American.

Race riots erupted again in the early twentieth century; in 1919 inflammatory newspaper stories led to two days of rioting in which whites attacked blacks, blacks retaliated, and four people were killed before order was returned. By the 1930's, the early stirrings of the Civil Rights movement were being felt in the capital. Such figures as Ralph BUNCHE, E. Franklin FRAZIER, and Charles Hamilton HOUSTON, teachers at the increasingly important Howard University, were raising African American awareness, and protests were becoming more common.

A widely publicized event in the nation's capital was the 1939 refusal of the Daughters of the American Revolution (DAR) to allow black opera singer Marian ANDERSON to appear at their Constitution Hall. First Lady

Eleanor Roosevelt was appalled, and she arranged for Anderson to perform outdoors in front of the Lincoln Memorial. The triumphant event drew about seventy-five thousand people. Two years later, labor leader A. Philip RANDOLPH threatened President Franklin D. Roosevelt with a major protest march on Washington if he would not act to integrate the industries making military equipment for WORLD WAR II. The threat convinced Roosevelt to issue EXECUTIVE ORDER 8802 mandating equal rights in hiring in defense industries.

Washington's black population continued to grow after WORLD WAR II, and by 1960 African Americans made up a slight majority of Washington's population. In 1961 a constitutional amendment was ratified that gave the district's residents the right to vote in presidential elections. The single most famous event in the history of the Civil Rights movement occurred in Washington, D.C., in 1963: the culmination of the MARCH ON WASHINGTON led by Martin Luther KING, Jr. On August 23, King delivered his "I have a dream" speech to a crowd of 250,000 at the Lincoln Memorial.

Five years later, in the wake of King's assassination in April, 1968, riots rocked the capital. Before his death, King had been planning a 1968 march on Washington by the POOR PEOPLE'S CAMPAIGN. Less than two months after King's death, Ralph ABERNATHY led the march, which proved a major disappointment. As the highly visible triumph of the 1963 march had symbolized the hope and promise of the movement (to some extent realized by major civil rights legislation in 1964 and 1965), so the disarray of the 1968 event seemed to signal the movement's passing.

Since 1870 Washington, D.C., had been governed by a three-member commission appointed by Congress, a situation that long caused resentment in the district. In 1974 residents could, for the first time, elect a city council and a mayor. Washington's first mayor was Walter Washington. Marion BARRY was

Walter E. Washington, the first person to hold the office of mayor of Washington, D.C. *(Library of Congress)*

In 1994 and 1995, the district's financial woes had become a crisis, and Washington was on the verge of bankruptcy. In response, the federal government established the D.C. Control Board to oversee the city's finances. In the fall of 1995 Washington was in the media spotlight again when Louis FARRAKHAN and Benjamin CHAVIS led the MILLION MAN MARCH there; the event stressed African American unity.

Barry did not seek reelection in 1998, and Anthony Williams was elected mayor. By the late 1990's the crime rate had subsided significantly, new businesses were locating in the district, and under federal scrutiny the district's finances were, if not quite healthy, at least not worsening.

—*McCrea Adams*

See also: Civil rights and congressional legislation; Electoral politics; Politics and government; Supreme Court, U.S.

Suggested Readings:

Barras, Jonetta R. *The Last of the Black Emperors: The Hollow Comeback of Marion Barry in the New Age of Black Leaders.* Baltimore: Bancroft Press, 1998.

Edmonds, Thomas N., and Raymond J. Keating. *D.C. by the Numbers: A State of Failure.* Lanham, Md.: University Press of America, 1995.

Fletcher, Michael A. "For Black Migrants, D.C. Liberated Lives." *Washington Post* (May 24, 1999): A01.

Jaffe, Harry S., and Tom Sherwood. *Dream City: Race, Power, and the Decline of Washington, D.C.* New York: Simon & Schuster, 1994.

Muhammad, Tariq K. "Tech Boom in the Beltway." *Black Enterprise* (June, 1999): 243-248.

Washington State: The state of Washington had a 1997 population of about 5.6 million, according to the CENSUS OF THE UNITED STATES. The state's approximately 196,000 African

elected in 1978, and he served three consecutive terms, becoming increasingly controversial. Barry was convicted of using crack cocaine in August, 1990, and served a six-month prison term.

The district also had other problems; by the end of the 1980's, the violent crime rate had skyrocketed to the point that Washington was widely considered the murder capital of the United States. Moreover, Washington was operating with a large and growing budget deficit. These problems were exacerbated by the fact that, since the mid-1960's, the district's population had been shrinking. By the mid-1990's it had decreased by nearly 200,000 as middle-class African American and white families left the city for the suburbs of Maryland and Virginia. Sharon Pratt KELLY was elected mayor in 1990; despite initial promise, her inexperience doomed her mayoral term to failure. Washington voters reelected Barry in 1994.

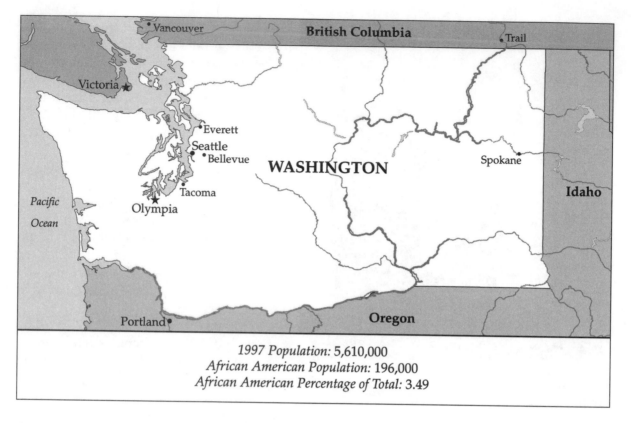

1997 Population: 5,610,000
African American Population: 196,000
African American Percentage of Total: 3.49

Americans composed 3.5 percent of the total.

In 1845 George Washington Bush, the first African American to settle in the Washington Territory, bought farmland near Olympia with his family. The territory's provisional government had declared its opposition to African American settlers, and it later passed the 1850 Land Grant Act to withhold Donation Land claims from persons of African descent. Despite this opposition, Bush's farm thrived, and his son William Owen represented Washington Territory at the 1876 Centennial Exhibition in Philadelphia.

Owen won prizes for grain specimens, and in 1889 he became the first African American to serve in the state legislature. Other notable early African American residents include John Conna, who as assistant sergeant-at-arms at the first state senate session was instrumental in ratifying a public accommodations clause in the state's new constitution. George WASHINGTON platted the town of Centralia in 1873.

Horace Cayton founded Seattle's first African American newspaper, the Seattle Republican, in 1891.

During a coal miners' strike in the late 1880's, mine owners brought hundreds of African American miners in to break the strike. The Klondike gold rush of the late 1890's and WORLD WAR I attracted more African Americans to the region, but it was not until WORLD WAR II, with the accelerated building of ships and aircraft in Washington, that the African American population boomed. During the war years, the population of African Americans grew from eight thousand to thirty-two thousand. In 1989 Norm Rice became Seattle's first African American mayor.

—Rose Secrest

Waters, Ethel (October 31, 1900, Chester, Pennsylvania—September 1, 1977, Chatsworth, California): Singer and actor. Waters grew up very interested in theatrical activities such as singing, dancing, and acting. Because of her POVERTY, she could not obtain formal training in the performing arts. She compensated for this by watching people perform and imitating them in the privacy of her home. At any opportunity, she would sing, dance, and perform before an audience.

Her career in VAUDEVILLE began when, during one of her performances at a party in 1917, some vaudeville performers noticed her theatrical ability and gave her a singing and dancing role in their company. That year, she toured with the Braxton and Nugent circuit. She was particularly successful in her singing of the St. Louis blues. Waters was engaged to perform at a New York City club called Edmond Johnson's Cellar until 1925, when she got a better opportunity at the famous Plantation Club.

Waters debuted as a Broadway star after successfully performing in *Africana*, a revue she put together with the assistance of Donald Hayward and Earl Dancer. Broadway roles in *Blackbirds* and *Rhapsody in Blue* followed in quick succession, but the shows were more successful on tour than on Broadway. In a production of *As Thousands Cheer*, Waters became the first African American since Egbert (Bert) WILLIAMS to star in an otherwise all-white performance on Broadway. Waters was in demand for radio performances and on Broadway, where she performed in the musical *At Home Abroad* in 1935.

During the Federal Theatre Project era, Waters took a

break from singing to give an excellent performance of Shaw's *Androcles and the Lion*. She also played successfully the difficult role of Hagar in DuBose and Dorothy Heyward's *Mamba's Daughters*. With that performance she established herself as a full-range actor. In 1950 she put on a brilliant performance of the character Berenice Sadie Brown in Carson McCullers's play *The Member of the Wedding*, at the Empire Theatre. Her unforgettable performance helped the play win the Drama Critics Circle Award for best American play of the year (1950). Waters also starred in Hollywood films such as *Pinky* (1949), *Tales of Manhattan* (1942), and *Cabin in the Sky* (1943) and in the television show *Beulah*.

Ethel Waters performing in 1935. *(AP/Wide World Photos)*

Waters, Maxine (b. August 15, 1938, St. Louis, Missouri): CALIFORNIA politician. During her service in the U.S. Congress, Waters demonstrated her skills as a community organizer and advocate for human rights, and she won approval and funding for a number of important initiatives for underprivileged Americans.

Waters graduated from California State University, Los Angeles, with a bachelor's degree in sociology. She was elected to the California State Assembly in 1976 and reelected six additional times. During those years, she rose to the powerful position of Democratic Caucus chair and was responsible for some of the boldest legislation ever passed in California. Her legislative accomplishments include the nation's first statewide child abuse prevention training program.

Waters was first elected to the U.S. House of Representatives from California in 1990 and was reelected for her fifth consecutive term in 1998. During that time, she gained a reputation as an outspoken advocate for women, children, people of various ethnic backgrounds, and poor people. Serving on the Banking, Finance and Urban Affairs Committee and the Committee on Veterans' Affairs, she was often in the forefront of issues dealing with economic development, police brutality, concerns of veterans, and international affairs. Following the LOS ANGELES RIOTS in 1992, Waters defined the hopelessness and despair that prevails in cities throughout the United States and vowed to improve conditions. She worked at the grass-roots level to change the lives of gang members and unemployed African American and Latino youth. In 1993 President Bill Clinton signed into law a $50 million appropriation for Waters's Youth Fair Chance program, which established an intensive job and life skills training program for unskilled, unemployed youth.

From 1997 to 1998, Waters served as the chair of the CONGRESSIONAL BLACK CAUCUS and formulated the comprehensive Agenda for Black America, outlining action for justice, equality, and fairness. She also effectively advocated expanded U.S. debt relief for developing nations in Africa and elsewhere. During the 1998 House impeachment proceedings for President Clinton, Waters was critical of the process. In 1998 she was appointed to the influential position of chief deputy whip of the DEMOCRATIC PARTY.

—*Alvin K. Benson*
See also: Congress members; Politics and government.

Representative Maxine Waters calling for protection for Haitians in proposed legislation on immigration in late 1997. *(AP/Wide World Photos)*

Waters, Muddy (McKinley Morganfield; April 4, 1915, Rolling Fork, Mississippi—April 30, 1983, Westmont, Illinois): CHICAGO BLUES singer. Waters worked and lived as a teenager and young man on Stovall's plantation in Clarksdale, MISSISSIPPI, where he also played guitar. Waters often watched and listened to accomplished blues players, including Son House and Robert Johnson, the influence of whom can be heard on Waters's 1941-1942 recordings for Alan Lomax and the Library of Congress.

In 1943 Waters moved to CHICAGO. Along with Willie DIXON, Elmore James, and HOWLIN' WOLF, he helped create the highly amplified, rhythmically intense style known as the Chicago blues. Waters was known both for his voice, which was deep and loudly resonant, and for his guitar playing, which often exhibited a startling electric slide technique. He began to record for Chess Records in the late 1940's, and by 1950 he had settled on a combo of musicians that would accompany him on most of his records of the 1950's: Little Walter on harmonica, Otis Spann on piano, Jimmie Rodgers on second guitar, and Dixon (who wrote many of Waters's more famous songs) on bass. With this band, Waters recorded "I'm Your Hootchie Cootchie Man" in 1954 and "Mannish Boy" (Waters's version of Bo Diddley's "I'm a Man") in 1955.

Waters recorded dozens of songs that are considered standards of the Chicago blues, including "Baby Please Don't Go," "Forty Days and Forty Nights," and "Got My Mojo Working." Although recorded in Chicago, many of these songs reflect Waters's rural Southern roots, with lyrical references to farming and Southern black folk religion. Although his most influential work was recorded in the 1950's, Waters enjoyed considerable success throughout the 1960's, in part as a result of the attention paid to him by popular white rock artists such as the Rolling Stones and Eric Clapton. Waters continued to perform and occasionally record throughout the 1970's. In 1987 the band ZZ Top, among others, raised funds for a Muddy Waters exhibit at the Delta Blues Museum in Clarksdale, Mississippi.

Wattleton, Faye (b. July 8, 1943, St. Louis, Missouri): Reproductive rights advocate. Having observed the results of "back alley" abortions during her career as a nurse, Alyce Faye Wattleton vicariously experienced the hardship, and sometimes death, of women who tried to terminate unwanted pregnancies. Appointed president of the Planned Parenthood Federation of America (PPFA) in 1978, she managed the nation's oldest and largest voluntary reproductive health organization in its crusade to safeguard individual rights concerning pregnancy and pregnancy termination. As president of Planned Parenthood, she played a major role in defining the national debate over reproductive rights and the shaping of family planning policies of governments worldwide. Her unprecedented vision and courage projected the PPFA into the forefront of the battle to preserve women's fundamental rights.

Attacks by antichoice, or prolife, factions in the White House, U.S. SUPREME COURT, Congress, and state legislatures seriously jeopardized Americans' reproductive rights and threatened federally funded family planning programs that served millions of low-income families in the United States and in the developing world. Articulate leadership, endless energy, and high visibility have characterized Wattleton's strategies for bolstering an uncompromising prochoice position.

Wattleton obtained a bachelor's degree from Ohio State University and a master's degree in maternal and infant care, with certification as a nurse-midwife, from Columbia University. In 1970 she became executive director of Planned Parenthood in Dayton, Ohio. Wattleton also served as chairwoman of the National Executive Directors' Council of PPFA.

Faye Wattleton at a press conference in 1983. *(Library of Congress)*

Wattleton received the 1989 American Public Health Association Award of Excellence, the Better World Society 1989 Population Medal, the 1989 Congressional Black Caucus Foundation Humanitarian Award, and numerous other citations and several honorary degrees. In 1992 she resigned from the presidency of the PPFA, but she continued to fight for reproductive rights and to fight reproduction victimization. Among her activities in the 1990's was hosting a Chicago talk show.

Watts: District in the southern portion of Los ANGELES, CALIFORNIA. Originally a middle-class district of white-collar workers, Watts was transformed by WORLD WAR II into a community with a preponderance of African American residents. Those who had migrated to Los Angeles during the war years, usually from the rural South, to work in shipyards and other government-related industries experienced great difficulty in finding housing. Blatant discrimination, as well as more subtle economic forms of discrimination, kept black residents out of most of Los Angeles. Prohibitively high rents, along with then-legal RESTRICTIVE COVENANTS, effectively served to retain the whites-only composition of most of the districts in the city. Thus it was economic necessity that precipitated the enormous increase of population, especially of African Americans, in Watts during the immediate postwar years.

The newly arrived residents were by no means assured of jobs, nor of job security once they had found employment. Unstable employment was perhaps the most important factor in maintaining poverty and deprivation in Watts. Critical community services, such as decent schools, transportation, and medical care, as well as adequate housing, became severely deficient. Even for those people who found jobs in defense-related industries, work was low-paying and often seasonal. Because of the lack of public transportation, expensive commutes often were involved.

The WATTS RIOTS that began on August 11, 1965, called attention, on a nationwide scale, to the deplorable GHETTO conditions and provided the public graphic illustrations of the horrors of life for Watts's approximately ninety thousand residents. Six days of rioting left thirty-four people dead and more than a thousand wounded. Out of the horrors of the riots emerged a new identity, one that stressed black pride and emphasized a sense of community and solidarity. Groups and projects formed, sponsored both by the government and by the community. Theater projects were spawned, and day-care and HEAD START educational programs were developed. More attention was paid to job training and procurement, and housing conditions were improved through new projects. Residents achieved political representation, and through the legislative process sought employment and contracts for minority-owned and -operated businesses.

As a community Watts possessed a unique work of outdoor art as an emblem: towers built by an Italian immigrant, Sebastiano Rodia, known more commonly as Simon. Created between 1921 and 1954 out of discarded materials—bottles and bottle caps, broken tiles and pottery, seashells, and old shoes, to name a few—and rising some fifty-five, ninety-seven, and ninety-nine feet, the three Watts Towers served as reminders that art can reside in environments normally considered unsympathetic and that creativity can occur despite appalling circumstances.

By the late 1990's, Watts had undergone a major demographic shift, as Mexican and Central American immigrants had increasingly moved to the area in the 1980's and 1990's. By the end of the 1990's, Spanish was spoken by as many Watts residents as was English. There were both tensions and cooperation between blacks and Latinos. Watts in the 1990's contained both signs of progress, such as a new civic center and library, and many reminders that it was still a poor area without enough jobs. The average per-capita income in Watts was roughly $5,000 in 1996, compared with a Los Angeles County average of about $18,000.

Watts, J. C., Jr. (b. November 18, 1957, Eufaula, Oklahoma): Professional FOOTBALL player and politician. Named the most valuable player of the Orange Bowl in 1980 and 1981, Watts received his bachelor's degree in journalism from the University of Oklahoma in 1981. He was drafted by the Canadian Football League and played as a quarterback for the Ottawa Roughriders from 1981 to 1985 before joining the Toronto Argonauts in 1986.

After retiring from football, Watts returned to OKLAHOMA and served as president and owner of Watts Energy Corporation between 1981 and 1989. He became active in various community and government organizations, serving on the Environmental Protection Agency Board on National Drinking Water, as commissioner on the Oklahoma State Corporation Commission, as honorary chairman of the March of Dimes in 1991, and as a youth director for Sunnylane Baptist Church. In 1994 Watts campaigned for Congress as a Republican candidate. With his victory over Democrat David Perryman in Oklahoma's Fourth Congressional District, Watts became only the second black member of the REPUBLICAN PARTY to serve in the House of Representatives since the election of Gary A. FRANKS of Connecticut in 1990. After Watts took office in 1995, House Speaker Newt Gingrich selected him to head a task force responsible for encouraging more African Americans to register to vote as Republicans. Watts was reelected in 1996 and 1998.

J. C. Watts, Jr., speaking at the National Press Club in early 1995. *(AP/Wide World Photos)*

Watts, Rolanda (b. July 12, 1959, Winston-Salem, North Carolina): Broadcast journalist and talk show host. Rolanda Watts began her broadcasting career at a local television station in her hometown of Winston-Salem, NORTH CAROLINA. A magna cum laude graduate of Spelman College in Atlanta, Georgia, Watts received her master's degree in journalism from New York's Columbia University. Before finding a niche as a nationally syndicated talk show host, Watts worked as a reporter and news anchor at television station WNBC in New York City.

When King World Productions hired Watts to host a new talk show, *Rolanda* was launched into the highly competitive syndicated television talk show market in 1992. The show's producers altered the format in February of 1995, switching the focus from news-oriented topics to issues with a more youthful, commercial appeal. This change was credited with helping the show become one of the most widely distributed programs in syndication.

Frye swerved across adjacent lanes on a busy street. Area residents, including the suspect's relatives, began gathering at the scene to observe the arrest.

At first, the incident was void of tension and anger, and observers joked with the police officer. The suspect's mother even scolded her son publicly for his behavior and urged him to cooperate with the officer. When Frye became angry and resisted the arrest, while shouting obscenities at the police officer, the mood of the crowd gradually changed to one of anger.

An altercation developed between the officer, Frye, and members of the crowd. As it intensified, a second officer arrived, carrying his riot baton to assist the arresting officer. When the second officer began hitting bystanders with his baton in an attempt to disperse them, the scene became more chaotic, resulting in several arrests.

Rumors later abounded regarding the incident, replete with embellished details of the arrests and police brutality. This incident fur-

Watts riots: Widespread disturbance in the WATTS district of LOS ANGELES, CALIFORNIA, in August, 1965. The Watts district was an overcrowded GHETTO area whose residents predominantly were African American. The riots brought the poverty-stricken area to the attention of the American public.

The riots stemmed from an incident on August 11 involving a Los Angeles police officer and an intoxicated African American driver, Marquette Frye. The officer stopped the twenty-one-year-old man for reckless driving in a Watts neighborhood after

Youths looting lampshades in the midst of the Watts rioting. *(AP/Wide World Photos)*

ther increased the already existing tensions between the African American Watts community and the Los Angeles police force. The Watts area exploded into violence the next day, following a meeting intended to ease tensions.

Rioting, rock throwing, looting, sniper shooting, and arson occurred in the midst of tension, bitterness, and anger. Approximately five thousand African Americans rioted, targeting white-owned businesses to loot and destroy. More than twelve thousand National Guards and several thousand local police officers were called into Watts.

Order eventually was restored on August 16, after six days of rioting that resulted in more than thirty deaths, about one thousand injuries, and nearly four thousand arrests. Hundreds of families were left homeless. Property damage was estimated by various observers at $40 million to more than $200 million.

Weaver, Robert Clipton (b. December 29, 1907, Washington, D.C.—July 17, 1997, New York, New York): Government official. Weaver was the first African American to be named as a cabinet member when Lyndon Johnson made him the secretary of housing and urban development in 1966. Previously, Weaver had served in several high-ranking federal posts and was a member of Franklin D. Roosevelt's "black cabinet." Weaver earned a Ph.D. in economics at Harvard University and wrote several books analyzing the plight of African American workers. He was also an adviser to several fellowship funds and served as a director of the John Hay Whitney Foundation.

Webb, Chick (February 10, 1909, Baltimore, Maryland—June 16, 1939, Baltimore, Maryland): Drummer, bandleader, and composer. William Henry "Chick" Webb was forced to endure and overcome a physical deformity caused by TUBERCULOSIS of the spine. Webb began playing the drums when he was three years old. Six years later, he was performing on pleasure steamers in Sheepshead Bay. As a teenager, Webb played with the Jazzola Orchestra and began his long association with guitarist John Trueheart. In 1926 he formed his own band in New York. The band performed at such clubs as the Black Bottom and the Paddock. Eventually, Webb became the resident bandleader, with his Harlem Stompers, at the SAVOY BALLROOM in Harlem. He would remain at the Savoy for approximately ten years.

Although his deformity could be very painful, Webb was a dynamic drummer. According to most jazz experts, he is considered to be one of the great drummers of his time. As a bandleader, Webb was competitive. He always wanted to have the best possible band in town. During this time, he heard the teenage Ella FITZGERALD sing, and he instantly knew that she would be a major talent. In 1935 she became part of his band, and it was not long before the band's show was built around Fitzgerald's singing. Webb continued to play the drums as forcefully as ever, even though playing was becoming increasingly painful. His drum equipment always had to be specially constructed in order for him to perform.

Webb was admired greatly by his fellow drummers for his swing style and his solid technique. The legendary drummer Gene Krupa referred to Webb as "the little giant of the drums." In 1938 Fitzgerald sang the hit song "A-tisket, A-tasket." Both Fitzgerald and Webb became immensely popular because of the song. During the summer of 1938, Webb's band broke a number of attendance records at various ballrooms and theaters. Webb's health was not very good, yet he continued to perform as often as he could. In late 1938, he had to be hospitalized because of pleurisy. Webb remained in the hospital until January of 1939. He went back to leading his band until he was forced to return to the hospital. He finally died shortly after undergoing major urological surgery.

In addition to his spectacular drumming and impressive bandleading, Webb cowrote several memorable songs, including "Stompin' at the Savoy," "Lonesome Moments," "Holiday in Harlem," and "Heart of Mine." In 1947 a recreation center in memory of Webb was opened in BALTIMORE, the city of his birth.

Webster, Ben (March 27, 1909, Kansas City, Missouri—September 20, 1973, Amsterdam, The Netherlands): JAZZ tenor saxophonist. By the time he joined pianist Duke ELLINGTON's band on a permanent basis in 1939, Webster was a veteran musician who, although he had not led a recording session, had played and recorded with such significant musicians as singer Billie HOLIDAY, trumpeter Roy ELDRIDGE, saxophonist Benny CARTER, and pianist Teddy WILSON. Webster had an accomplished career highlighted by his four years with Ellington, probably the best years of the Ellington band. Webster was part of the reason why the band was so good. His solos on "Cotton Tail" (1940) and "All too Soon" (1940) demonstrated his fiery potential and his more rhapsodic side, respectively.

Webster made some of his greatest recordings in the 1950's, particularly on an album with pianist Art TATUM (1956), on his own *Soulville* (1957), and on singer Jimmy Witherspoon's *At the Renaissance* (1959). In the mid-1960's, he moved permanently to Europe, where he performed frequently with his own groups.

Always a master ballad player, late in his life Webster turned to ballads with increased frequency and with added poignancy. His playing became more intimate. Occasionally, he concluded performances by emitting a barely audible breath through his saxophone, as if to blur the boundary between sound and silence. This practice can be heard on "Deep River" (1970) and "The Man I Love" (1972), to cite but two examples. Originally influenced by saxophonist Coleman HAWKINS, Webster developed his own breathy style, perfectly suited to the material he played.

Weems, Carrie Mae (b. April 20, 1953, Portland, Oregon): PHOTOGRAPHER and folklorist. Weems earned a master of arts degree in photography from the University of California at San Diego in 1984.

She once called herself an "image-maker," and Weems's work explores and comments on racial, gender, and class issues as it shows African American culture from an insider's perspective. It sometimes incorporates stereotypical cultural imagery such as watermelons and fried chicken. It also sometimes includes narrative text as well as photographs. Her *Sea Islands Series* explores history and folklore as it depicts the SEA ISLANDS off the coast of Georgia.

Weems was a Smithsonian Fellow, and in addition to her own work in the 1980's and 1990's she organized various group exhibitions and conferences related to photography, black photographers, and women photographers. The first retrospective of Weems's photography was held at the National Museum of Women in the Arts in Washington, D.C., in 1993.

Wells, Ida B. (married name Ida B. Wells Barnett; July 16, 1862, Holly Springs, Mississippi—March 25, 1931, Chicago, Illinois): Journalist and CIVIL RIGHTS activist. Ida Bell Wells was one of the nation's leading equal rights crusaders around the beginning of the twentieth century. This African American woman journalist, whose career spanned more than forty years, was a pioneer in the area of investigative reporting, specializing in cases where civil rights of black Americans had been violated in the most extreme way—by LYNCHING. Her investigations entailed using records from the white press to uncover the reasons underlying large-scale mob executions of blacks during the turbulent years following the CIVIL WAR. What Wells uncovered corroborated her theory that race hatred, and not the common cry of "rape," was the real motivation behind the rising menace to African Americans of her day.

Study on Lynching

In 1895 she published *The Red Record*, which contained her findings. Wells's seminal report covered a three-year period, 1892-1894. It sacrificed breadth in order to achieve more depth than the *Chicago Tribune's* 1892 report, which had revealed that, in 728 cases in which blacks had been lynched over an eight-year period, rape or attempted rape was mentioned in only one-third of the cases. In her study, Wells analyzed the evidence for the relatively small number of lynchings ostensibly carried out to punish rapists. She found that many of the so-called rapists were not guilty of any crime for a variety of reasons, a common one being that the sex act had been consensual. Wells also reported that in the vast majority of lynchings, the reasons advanced by lynching perpetrators in justification of their crimes ranged from charges of sassiness or drunkenness to thievery and murderous assault by blacks.

Not only did Wells use her journalistic talent to get across her antilynching message, but she also utilized other platforms. As an orator, she was commanding and convincing; as the organizer of a powerful crusade against lynching in the United States and in England, she was dynamic and effective.

Early Life and Education

Wells was born in Holly Springs, MISSISSIPPI, the first of eight children born to Jim and Lizzie Wells. Jim Wells, the son of his white master and a slave woman, had been favored

Ida B. Wells was one of the greatest equal rights crusaders of the early twentieth century. *(Arkent Archive)*

by his father, who had him apprenticed in his youth to a carpenter. Later, the consummate skill Jim Wells acquired in carpentry allowed him to support his wife and children after the Civil War ended in 1865.

From the ruins of the postwar South, Jim Wells carved out a relatively comfortable living for himself and his family. Choosing to stay close to his roots after the emancipation of the slaves, Jim Wells left his master's farm and settled his family closer to the center of town. In those days, Holly Springs was a beautiful town of rolling hills, cotton plantations, and stately architecture. Although little actual fighting had occurred in the town, it had been hit in the war's scathing aftermath when Union soldiers had passed through, destroying the main street and many beautiful homes. In helping to restore the town, Jim Wells had all the work he could handle. His skill and ambition gave him and his family status in the larger community among both whites and blacks.

While she was growing up, Ida, like all the Wells children, attended school. Mother Lizzie joined the children in the classroom and learned how to read. Ida B. Wells first attended Tiny Schools and later Rust University, both in Holly Springs. From the beginning, she distinguished herself as an apt student.

The peaceful quality of Ida's world was abruptly shattered the year she turned sixteen. In 1878 a terrible yellow-fever epidemic claimed the lives of both her parents on the same day. Her ten-month-old brother also died of the fever.

Supporting Her Family

Calling upon a reserve of inner strength and fortified by the Christian foundation her parents had given her, Ida steeled herself to become head of a household of six. (Another brother had died before the epidemic.) Ida quit school and began teaching six miles from home to support the family. Several years later, when her two brothers could fend for themselves, Ida moved to Tennessee with her two sisters to secure a higher-paying teaching position. (One sister who was paralyzed was taken in by an aunt.)

In May, 1884, while on her way to her job in Woodstock, TENNESSEE, Wells boarded the Chesapeake and Ohio Railroad in MEMPHIS. Having a first-class ticket, she sat in a first-class car and refused to move to the dingy smoking car, where blacks were expected to sit. She stubbornly defied the conductor, who had to enlist the assistance of two other white men to throw her from the train. Afterward, Wells sued for justice. Justice came in 1885, when a federal court judge ruled in her favor and awarded her five hundred dollars in dam-

ages. After the judgment, which was widely reported across the country, the state of Tennessee petitioned to have the trial moved to the state's supreme court. The state's appeal was granted. In the second trial, Wells lost her claim and was assessed a two-hundred-dollar fine.

When the second railroad verdict was handed down, Wells had already started to teach in Memphis. She had also joined a literary group; by 1887, she was regularly contributing to a church newspaper. That same year, she purchased a part interest in the local black newspaper, the *Free Speech and Headlight*.

Journalism Career

As an independent journalist, Wells placed in her paper several articles critical of the Memphis school board. Finally, one article pointing to an illicit affair between a prominent white man and a black female teacher got her into serious trouble. The exposé cost Wells her teaching job in 1891.

Theretofore, journalism had been something of a hobby for Wells; but with the turn of events, journalism became the only available professional work to which she could turn. Wells vigorously took on the challenge of making her newspaper profitable enough to provide her with a livelihood. She set about increasing the *Free Speech and Headlight*'s circulation, recruiting new subscribers across the state. She was so successful in her efforts that soon her income from the newspaper surpassed the salary she had received as a teacher.

Fight Against Lynching

Wells's journalistic battle against lynch mobs began on March 9, 1892, when her friend Thomas Moss, a young black entrepreneur, and two of his partners were brutally murdered for protecting their store against a band of white men. Their store, located just outside Memphis city limits in a section popularly called the Curve, sat in a spot unprotected by city law. Therefore, when a group of strange white men who were rumored to be raiders sent to close down the successful black business approached the store, the black men took an armed stand. In a quick volley of fire, several of the whites were injured. Although the black grocers surrendered and submitted to arrest immediately after the whites identified themselves as agents of the law, a lynch mob formed. In the middle of the night, the mob mutilated and killed the blacks.

After the black store owners were lynched, Wells set aside the official version of events reported in the white press and made her own analysis. She connected the grocers' case to others that had been explained by what she now believed were lies told by whites to justify crimes against blacks. Her startling reinterpretation of the facts greatly alarmed the white community. On March 21, 1892, *The Free Speech and Headlight* published an editorial that stated:

> Nobody in this section of the country believes the old threadbare lie that Negro men rape white women. If the Southern white men are not careful, they will over-reach themselves and public sentiment will have a reaction; a conclusion will then be reached which will be very damaging to the moral reputation of their women.

Several days later, Wells's entire editorial, along with castigations of it, was reprinted in a leading white Memphis paper. The white paper flayed Wells's column and ended its criticism with a call for group revenge on the black person who had written the offending piece. Luckily, while a mob gathered, Wells (who then owned 50 percent of the *Free Speech and Headlight*) was in PHILADELPHIA; fortunately, too, her partner in the business was forewarned of the impending mob attack and managed to escape. Consequently, when the would-be lynchers finally descended upon

the office of the black newspaper, they found the building empty. They vented their anger by destroying the entire operation. They then sent forth the warning that if Wells reappeared in the city within the next twenty years, she, too, would be lynched.

Wells was convinced by her friends to stay in the North for her own safety. T. Thomas FORTUNE gave her a one-fourth interest in his paper, the NEW YORK AGE, in exchange for her subscription lists and her promise to write a weekly column covering news from the black South.

Public Lectures and Lobbying Efforts
Soon after Wells resigned herself to her exile status in 1892, she embarked upon an antilynching campaign that remained in high gear for the next three years. She started the movement by lecturing in northeastern cities, sharing her opinions about the underlying causes of lynching. She journeyed to England in 1893 and again in 1894, staying for several months each time, arousing the sympathies of the English and pushing them to exert pressure on American lawmakers to do something about lynching. During her antilynching campaign, Wells stirred people and electrified audiences wherever she went. Although white American legislators expressed disdain for Wells and her work, they realized she was placing them under national and world scrutiny. By the end of her campaign in 1895, some southern governors and legislative bodies were issuing antilynching proclamations and trying to adopt measures to stop lynch mobs.

In 1895 Wells decided to retire from the public stage and leave the fight for justice for others ready to take up the banner. On June 27 of that year, she married Ferdinand Lee Barnett, the founder of the *Conservator*, the first black-owned newspaper in CHICAGO. Although Wells stuck to her plan of rearing a family, she found it impossible to turn her back on the black struggle for civil rights.

Whenever she felt she was needed in a difficult case, she sallied forth to do battle; with her fiery pen, she continued to expose the flaws in whites' accounts of alleged crimes committed by blacks for which lynchings were ostensibly carried out as punishments.

Later Years

After settling in Chicago in 1895, Wells became greatly concerned about the plight of urban blacks. Her concern led her into the field of social work. Over the next thirty-five years, she worked as a probation officer, a women's club organizer, and the founder and director of the Negro Fellowship League, which provided assistance to homeless young black men. After many years of service, following a brief illness, Wells died on March 25, 1931. For her work on behalf of Chicago's most downtrodden citizens, in 1940 a Chicago housing project was dedicated to her memory; in 1950, the city of Chicago honored her as one of its most illustrious women.

More than any other person of her day, Ida B. Wells opened the eyes of many people, black and white, who had believed the old propaganda supporting lynching; more than anyone else, she helped to undermine the spirit of vigilantism in the United States. Her crusade for justice helped to awaken Americans to the need for social change.

—*Sarah Smith Ducksworth*

Suggested Readings:

Adams, Samuel L. "Ida B. Wells: A Founder Who Never Knew Her Place." *The Crisis* (January, 1994): 43-46.

Boyd, Melba J. "Canon Configuration for Ida B. Wells-Barnett." *The Black Scholar* 24 (Winter, 1994): 8-13.

DeCosta-Willis, Miriam, ed. *The Memphis Diary of Ida B. Wells*. Boston: Beacon Press, 1995.

Duster, Alfreda M., ed. *Crusade for Justice: The Autobiography of Ida B. Wells*. Chicago: University of Chicago Press, 1970.

Giddens, Paula. *When and Where I Enter: The Impact of Black Women on Race and Sex in America*. New York: William Morrow, 1984.

Harris, Trudier, comp. *The Selected Works of Ida B. Wells-Barnett*. New York: Oxford University Press, 1991.

McMurry, Linda O. *To Keep the Waters Troubled: The Life of Ida B. Wells*. New York: Oxford University Press, 1999.

Sterling, Dorothy. *Black Foremothers: Three Lives*. Old Westbury, N.Y.: Feminist Press, 1979.

Thompson, Mildred I. *Ida B. Wells-Barnett: Exploratory Study of an American Black Woman, 1893-1930*. Vol. 15 in *Black Women in American History*. Washington, D.C.: George Washington University Press, 1979.

WERD radio: The first African American-owned radio station in the United States. The 900-watt AM station in ATLANTA, GEORGIA, was purchased by a businessman, J. B. Blayton, on October 4, 1949, and was owned by Blayton and his son until the late 1950's. Jack Gibson, the station's first black program director, developed a programming format oriented toward African Americans that included a daily newscast based on the city's black newspaper, *The Daily World*, a fifteen-minute daily news commentary, a discussion program on race relations, music shows showcasing groups and songs popular in the black community, and a children's program. The station remained profitable during the Blaytons' ownership.

Wesberry v. Sanders: U.S. SUPREME COURT ruling in 1964 that extended the principle of "one person, one vote" to apportioning congressional voting districts. Chief Justice Earl Warren declared that *Wesberry v. Sanders* set down the principle that representative government meant equal representation for equal numbers of people. Several months later, the Court extended the principle to apply to all branches of state legislatures in REYNOLDS V. SIMS. An important effect of these apportionment decisions was to make it more difficult to dilute African American voting power through GERRYMANDERING.

—*Christopher E. Kent*

Wesley, Charles Harris (December 2, 1891, Louisville, Kentucky—August 16, 1987, Washington, D.C.): Historian, educator, and author. Known as a fine teacher of history, Wesley was influential in writing a more complete history of African Americans and in promoting HIGHER EDUCATION.

After graduating from FISK UNIVERSITY, Wesley taught history and modern languages in the Teachers College at HOWARD UNIVERSITY from 1913 to 1920. In 1921 he was appointed professor of history and head of the

Historian Charles Harris Wesley. *(Associated Publishers, Inc.)*

department. He attended Harvard University as an Austin scholar and received his Ph.D. in history in 1925, becoming only the fourth African American to receive a doctorate from Harvard.

From 1931 to 1940, Wesley served as the general president of the Alpha Phi Alpha fraternity. In 1942 he was appointed president of Wilberforce University. He served as the president of Central State University from 1947 to 1965 and developed it into a full-fledged institution of higher education. From 1965 to 1972, he was executive director of the Association for the Study of Afro-American Life and History. He was named the director of the Afro-American Historical and Cultural Museum in PHILADELPHIA in 1976.

Wesley wrote more than twelve books dealing with African American history, including *The History of Alpha Phi Alpha: A Development in Negro College Life* (1929), *The Story of the Negro Retold* (1959), and *The Negro in Our History* (1962, with Carter G. Woodson); he also edited a ten-volume set entitled *The International Library of Negro Life and History* (1968).

—*Alvin K. Benson*

See also: Historiography; Intellectuals and scholars; Professors.

West, Cornel (b. June 2, 1953, Tulsa, Oklahoma): Educator and philosopher. The author of numerous books, papers, and essays, West is known as an educator, philosopher, and social activist. The topics of his writings and lectures range from race and politics to religion and Marxism.

Cornel West's parents met at FISK UNIVERSITY and reared their family on the various Air Force bases at which West's father was employed as a civilian administrator. The family eventually settled in a black neighborhood in Sacramento, California. West was a bright child who excelled in school despite bouts with asthma. At the age of eight, he became determined to enroll at Harvard University after reading a juvenile biography of Theodore Roosevelt. His family attended a BAPTIST church in Sacramento that was next door to the local office of the BLACK PANTHER PARTY. West's contact with the Black Panthers shaped his political views about the second-class status of African Americans, and he refused to participate in the flag salute at school in protest. After striking a teacher who forced him to salute the flag, West was suspended from elementary school for six months and eventually was transferred to an accelerated school across town.

West was accepted at Harvard when he was seventeen years old, and he took odd jobs as a dishwasher and janitor to earn money to pay his tuition. He took eight courses per semester during his junior year in order to graduate early. He graduated magna cum laude

Cornel West. *(Jon Chase/Harvard News Office)*

with a bachelor's degree in Near Eastern languages and was accepted into a doctoral program in philosophy at Princeton University. After receiving his Ph.D. from Princeton, West returned to Harvard as a W. E. B. Du Bois Fellow. West next took an academic post at Union Theological Seminary, teaching there until 1984. In 1980 he also began serving as a visiting professor of religion at several institutions, including such prestigious universities as Yale University School and the University of Paris.

In 1984 he was appointed to teach at Yale Divinity School. The Yale appointment eventually became a joint professorship with the American Studies Department. While at Yale, West was active in the campus movement to force the university to divest itself of its South African investments, and he was arrested during a protest. The university administration expressed its disapproval of West's actions by canceling his scheduled leave to teach at the University of Paris and requiring him to teach a full course load at Yale. Although West managed to meet both teaching commitments by commuting between Paris and New Haven, Connecticut, he left Yale at the end of the academic year to resume teaching at Union Theological Seminary. Princeton then hired West to revive its struggling program in African American studies. Joined by novelist Toni MORRISON, historian Nell PAINTER, and biographer Arnold RAMPERSAD, West began to serve as director of Afro-American studies at Princeton in 1986.

In 1982 West published the book *Prophesy Deliverance!: An Afro-American Revolutionary Christianity*, which was based on a series of lectures he gave at a black church in Brooklyn, New York. *Prophetic Fragments* (1988) and *The American Evasion of Philosophy: A Genealogy of Pragmatism* (1989) followed. In 1991 he returned to his interests in political philosophy and published *The Ethical Dimensions of Marxist Thought*. In 1992 West published *Breaking Bread: Insurgent Black Intellectual Life*, a series of conversations he had with black feminist and social critic bell HOOKS.

After joining the faculty of Harvard University in 1993, West relocated to the Boston area with his wife Elleni, an Ethiopian-born social worker, and family. West's book *Race Matters* (1993) brought him to the attention of a broader audience in mainstream society. Published on the one-year anniversary of the 1992 Los Angeles riots, the book discussed the conditions and crisis that precipitated the rage. West then, with Michael Lerner, coauthored a book entitled *Jews and Blacks*, which was published in the spring of 1995. Later that year, West participated in the MILLION MAN MARCH, a historic march made by African American men to the Capitol in Washington, D.C. West and George E. Curry edited a collection entitled *The Affirmative Action Debate*, published in 1996.

—*Updated by Kimberly Battle-Walters*

West, Dorothy (June 2, 1907, Boston, Massachusetts—August 16, 1998, Boston, Massachusetts): Novelist, editor, and short-story writer. West came to the attention of the literary world in 1926 when she placed second to Zora Neale HURSTON in a writing contest sponsored by *Opportunity* magazine. As a member of the literary elite of the HARLEM RENAISSANCE, she served as founder and editor of the literary magazines *Challenge* and *New Challenge* during the 1930's. West wrote extensively about the obsessive color consciousness that exists within the black middle class and about the middle class's loss of moral and spiritual values in its process of emulating white ideals. Her novels *The Living Is Easy* (1948) and *The Wedding* (1995) satirize the pretensions of the black bourgeoisie of Boston and the resort community of OAK BLUFFS on Martha's Vineyard. West published numerous short stories, many of which first appeared in *Opportunity*, the *Messenger*, the *Saturday Evening Quill*, and

Dorothy West, one of the last surviving figures of the Harlem Renaissance, in 1995. *(AP/Wide World Photos)*

The New York Daily News. These stories were collected in the book *The Richer, the Poorer* (1995).

Westerfield, Samuel Z. (b. 1919, Chicago, Illinois): Political appointee and economist. Westerfield graduated from HOWARD UNIVERSITY in 1939 with his A.B. in economics and political science. He later earned his M.A. and Ph.D. degrees from Harvard University in economics. Westerfield continued in academia as a professor and research associate from 1940 to 1961 and served as a faculty member at Howard University, West Virginia State University, LINCOLN UNIVERSITY, and ATLANTA UNIVERSITY. In 1961 he was appointed to serve in the Department of the Treasury as associate director of the debt analysis staff. His expertise in the areas of African and Latin American economics led him to serve as senior adviser to the Treasury Department's Office of International Affairs. In 1964 President Lyndon Johnson appointed Westerfield to serve on the staff of the Bureau of African Affairs of the U.S. Department of State as deputy assistant secretary for economic affairs. Westerfield was appointed to serve as U.S. ambassador to LIBERIA in 1969.

See also: Diplomats.

West Indian heritage: Immigration to the United States from the WEST INDIES began in the early nineteenth century and increased somewhat after the Civil War. However, the major waves of Caribbean immigration did not occur until the twentieth century. Caribbean natives sought to leave the West Indies to escape overcrowding, an unequal distribution of wealth and land, limited educational opportunities, and poor economic conditions. The Caribbean is often spoken of as having a "culture of migration" because of the continued flight of its residents from economic and political problems. The United States (along with Canada and Great Britain) has been one of the key destinations of West Indian immigrants.

Because West Indian people who have emigrated generally maintain a strong identification with their Caribbean heritage, and because they have other outward similarities, they sometimes give the impression of being a unified West Indian community. Actually, the West Indian community in the United States represents a broad spectrum of customs and attitudes that reflect the diversity of West Indians' origins on a string of islands in the Caribbean Sea.

Waves of Immigration
Between 1911 and 1920, the United States experienced the first wave of immigration by West Indians, most of whom settled in NEW YORK CITY. During the HARLEM RENAISSANCE of the 1920's, 25 percent of the population of HARLEM, New York consisted of foreign-born blacks, the majority of whom were from the Caribbean islands. In the 1930's, West Indian immigrants encountered resentment and hostility, because their arrival coincided with the northward migration of southern African Americans, and the two groups were frequently in competition for the same jobs. Nevertheless, there was a steady trickle of immigration from the West Indies until the late 1960's, when a large jump in the number of immigrants occurred once more. This increase resulted partly because of the 1965 amendments to the Immigration Act of 1921 and a similar act in 1924 that had set ethnic quotas on immigration, and partly because of Great Britain's concurrent ban on West Indian immigration.

The primary areas of settlement by West Indian immigrants in the United States are New York and NEW JERSEY, particularly New York City. In 1977 West Indians made up about 20 percent of New York City's black population. Smaller numbers of West Indian immigrants, but larger numbers of part-time migrant laborers, also reside in FLORIDA. The loss of skilled professional and technical workers from the West Indies to the United States has been termed a "brain drain" by West Indian governments, but many unskilled workers have also immigrated to the United States to work as domestic workers or farm laborers.

West Indian African Americans
The SLAVE TRADE linked Africa, the West Indies, and the United States in a triangle of oppression. Their peoples thus share a common history, but they do not necessarily share the same culture. African Americans and West In-

dians have much in common: their African ancestry, their slave pasts, and the racism and segregation that both groups suffered after the emancipation of slaves. Yet the relations between West Indian immigrants and native black Americans have not always been harmonious.

Whether they are skilled or unskilled immigrants, West Indians in the United States tend to place great emphasis on a few key goals: education for themselves and their children, social and economic betterment, family unity, and home ownership. This strong desire for upward mobility, sometimes at the cost of racial solidarity, has tended to alienate the West Indian community from other African Americans. This factor, together with the perception, strongest during the GREAT DEPRESSION of the 1930's, that West Indians were taking jobs from American-born blacks, has caused some friction between West Indian Americans and other American blacks.

In contrast to African Americans, many British West Indians have tended to identify with Great Britain as their "mother" country rather than with Africa. This British perspective has often alienated these immigrants from other African Americans. Many West Indian immigrants and their descendants celebrate British holidays and ceremonial events, play cricket and soccer, and place British culture and customs above their American counterparts. A large number of West Indian immigrants also speak nostalgically of the islands, intending to return there to retire. This identification with a Caribbean heritage has led to tightly knit (and often closed) community structures evident in the many nationalistic West Indian benevolent societies. These differences have naturally tended to estrange the West Indians from native African Americans and sometimes have led to antagonism and misunderstandings between the groups.

There are also many West Indians who have immersed themselves in African American culture and taken on the causes of their fellows. These immigrants, many of whom have been attracted to the United States by its democratic ideals, have united with other African Americans in the fight for equality and against racism. Brooklyn, which has the largest concentration of Caribbean people outside the Caribbean, has hosted the West Indian-American Day Parade on Labor Day for more than thirty years. This massive carnival celebrates the best aspects of West Indian and African American unity with music, dance, and food of the West Indies drawing everyone into celebration and harmony.

Prominent Individuals

Many West Indian immigrants and their descendants have played important roles in the development and diversity of African American culture. African Americans of West Indian descent have been leaders in a variety of spheres, including politics, education, art, and literature. John Brown RUSSWURM, a former slave from JAMAICA, was one of the first African Americans to graduate from a college and went on to coedit the first African American newspaper, FREEDOM'S JOURNAL. Sidney POITIER, who was educated in the West Indies, in 1963 became the first African American to be awarded an Academy Award for best actor. Shirley CHISHOLM, a well-known feminist and political activist, was born in Brooklyn as a second-generation Barbadian American. She was the first African American woman to serve in Congress.

Claude MCKAY, a prominent poet and novelist, was born in Jamaica and moved to the United States in 1912 to further his studies. After a few years, he gave up studying to live in New York City and pursue a writing career. He lived in England and elsewhere from 1922 to 1934, during which time he published three novels, among them *Home to Harlem* (1928), based on Harlem life in the 1920's. McKay returned to live and write in the United States until he died in 1948. His interest in African American culture and Harlem in particular is clear in some of his later writings: articles on the Harlem labor movement and a journalistic work entitled *Harlem: Negro Metropolis* (1940). McKay is perhaps best remembered for his poetry; his ironic protest poems are characteristic of much of the writing of the Harlem Renaissance. He believed that black folk culture could become a central, energizing factor in the revitalization of a degenerate Western civilization.

Marcus GARVEY, a powerful political organizer and supporter of black nationalism, was also born in Jamaica. In 1912 he studied in England, where he met several African nationalists and read Booker T. WASHINGTON's *Up from Slavery* (1901). These new influences inspired Garvey to return to Jamaica and form a self-help organization to foster racial pride, education, and Afrocentrism as a philosophy. In 1916 Garvey went to the United States to gain support for his organization, the UNIVERSAL NEGRO IMPROVEMENT ASSOCIATION (UNIA), and he founded many branches of the group in New York City and elsewhere. Initially, support for Garvey came from the West Indian immigrant community, but gradually Garvey won African Americans over to his black nationalist ideals.

In 1918 Garvey founded a newspaper, the NEGRO WORLD, which helped to spread his message worldwide. By 1919 Garvey had formed two African American companies, the BLACK STAR LINE, which operated a steamship line to Africa, and the Negro Factories Corporation, which provided loans and advice to African Americans starting small businesses. Garvey also negotiated with the government of Liberia to start a UNIA-led back-to-Africa project. However, the collapse of the Black Star Line brought Garvey into legal trouble, and he was imprisoned for mail fraud. In 1927 he was deported to Jamaica, where his political career was short-lived. He died in 1940 in England.

Despite his failings, Marcus Garvey was one of the forefathers of the black pride and black nationalist movements, and he demonstrated that African Americans of all backgrounds could be united in a mass movement built on worldwide black solidarity.

Paule MARSHALL, a novelist originally from BARBADOS, has written many powerful novels about the West Indian experience and particularly about the acculturation experiences of African Americans of West Indian descent. Her most celebrated novel, *Brown Girl, Brownstones* (1959), tells the story of Selina Boyce, a second-generation Barbadian growing up in Brooklyn. Selina's struggle to live between two cultures and two lands is powerfully portrayed by Marshall, and the novel stresses the value of community, but it offers no easy answers to the issues it raises about assimilation and biculturalism.

—*Fiona R. Barnes*

Suggested Readings:

Diaz-Briquets, Sergio, and Sidney Weintraub, eds. *Determinants of Emigration from Mexico, Central America, and the Caribbean*. Boulder, Colo.: Westview Press, 1991.

Kasinitz, Philip. *Caribbean New York: Black Immigrants and the Politics of Race*. Ithaca: Cornell University Press, 1992.

Laguerre, Michel S. *American Odyssey: Haitians in New York City*. Ithaca, N.Y.: Cornell University Press, 1984.

Model, Suzanne. "Caribbean Immigrants: A Black Success Story?" *International Migration Review* 25 (Summer, 1991): 248-276.

Palmer, Ransford W. *Pilgrims From the Sun: West Indian Migration to America*. New York: Twayne, 1995.

Parrillo, Vincent N. *Strangers to These Shores: Race and Ethnic Relations in the U.S.* Boston: Houghton-Mifflin, 1980.

Samuels, Wilfred D. *Five Afro-Caribbean Voices in American Culture: 1917-1929*. Ann Arbor, Mich.: University Microfilm International, 1977.

Stengel, Richard. "Resentment Tinged with Envy." *Time* (July 8, 1985): 56-57.

Vickerman, Milton. *Crosscurrents: West Indian Immigrants and Race.* New York: Oxford University Press, 1999.

West Indies: The islands of the West Indies stretch in an arc of almost 2,500 miles from the BAHAMAS, which are east of Florida, to the Netherlands Antilles (Bonaire, Curaçao, and, until 1986, Aruba) off the coast of Venezuela. The arc is never more than 160 miles wide. The islands range in size from tiny uninhabited rocks to CUBA, which is among the world's largest islands.

The four larger islands in the north, Cuba, JAMAICA, Hispaniola (on which are located HAITI and the DOMINICAN REPUBLIC), and PUERTO RICO, are the Greater Antilles. The Lesser Antilles extend from the VIRGIN IS-LANDS to Grenada. The inner arc is composed of mountainous, volcanic islands. The smaller outer arc is flatter and drier. Trinidad, Tobago, and the Netherlands Antilles are an extension of the South American continent.

Except for the Bahamas, most of the islands are volcanic mountain peaks that are heavily forested on the windward (the northern and eastern) side. On the leeward side the islands are drier; the natural harbors are located on the leeward side. The trade winds blowing from the northeast make the climate pleasant even though all the islands except the Bahamas are located in the tropics.

Beginning of Colonization

At the time Christopher Columbus discovered the West Indies, Indians inhabited the area. The Ciboney lived in the north, the Arawak in the middle, and the Caribs in the south. Except for a small number of Caribs living on the

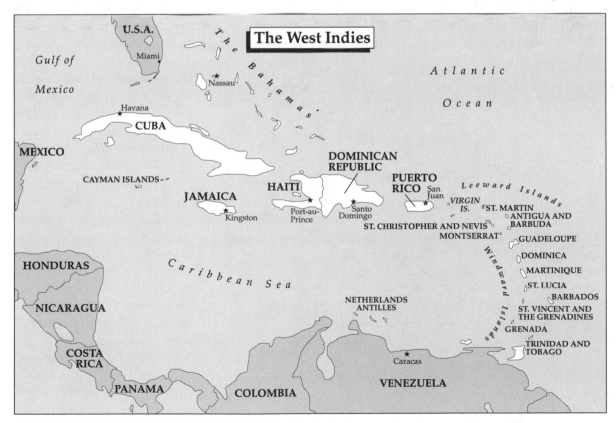

southern islands, the Indians were killed off by European diseases introduced with discovery.

The Spanish largely neglected the West Indies in favor of silver-rich Mexico and Peru. They settled only the islands of the Greater Antilles. When England, France, and the Netherlands moved overseas, however, all three established colonies in the West Indies and began to develop valuable sugar PLANTATIONS on the islands. The islands were admirably suited for growing sugar.

Importation of Slaves

To provide the labor necessary for the plantations, slaves were imported from AFRICA. More than four million Africans were brought to the islands between the introduction of slaves by the Dutch in the 1640's and the abolition of the SLAVE TRADE in the first half of the nineteenth century. By the 1750's, nine out of ten people on the sugar islands were slaves. Because of the high death rate and low birthrate, the slave trade was necessary to maintain the slave labor force.

Bahamian family living on a sugar plantation in the early twentieth century. *(Library of Congress)*

Slavery in the West Indies

Shortly after their introduction, slaves were performing all types of jobs, but most slaves were field hands on the sugar estates. The master had total control. Working conditions were harsh, and living conditions bad. The average life span of a field hand, once put to work, was only ten years. Slaves on the non-sugar-producing islands and in the towns were fewer and fared better.

Except in the Spanish areas, SLAVE CODES treated slaves as property, permitting their masters to do as they pleased. Slave codes on the British, French, Spanish, and Dutch islands sought to protect the whites and control the blacks. The courts handed down savage punishments, including lashing, torture, mutilation, and death. Slave codes were harshest on the islands where blacks far outnumbered whites.

Laws of MANUMISSION in the French and Spanish colonies were more generous than those in the British colonies, where the law required the consent of the master for manumission. British law also denied FREE BLACKS all legal rights except trial by jury. Free blacks could not carry weapons, enter certain trades, travel without identification, or dress in luxury clothes. In the Spanish and French colonies, free blacks did have legal rights.

Owners and managers of plantations demonstrated no interest in slaves except as labor. Slaves were expected to feed, clothe, and house themselves. Slaves built their own small, thatched-roof huts of mud and straw; the huts had no windows or closable doors. Most slaves had no furniture, only a few cooking pots. Although laws required owners to clothe their slaves, most masters paid little attention. Many handed out bolts of cloth for the female slaves to make into clothing. As late as 1800, travelers remarked that slaves wore little and that some worked naked. On Sundays and holidays, slaves dressed in better clothes they bought or made.

Overwork and serious malnourishment accounted for the high death rate and low birthrate among slaves. Masters used two methods to feed their slaves. On islands where land was more plentiful, slaves were allotted provision grounds on which they grew food. On

Contemporary drawing depicting the harsh conditions under which slaves labored in the West Indies during the early nineteenth century. *(Library of Congress)*

the more crowded islands, food was imported. In both cases the diet was monotonous and inadequate. Most slaves lived on gruels or stews made of cornmeal, rice, millet, and kidney beans. Yams, sweet potatoes, cassava, and potatoes might be added. The diet contained little protein or fat.

Urban slaves lived better and longer, had greater liberty, and could more easily purchase freedom than field slaves. Many were craftsmen or peddlers who acquired liquid cash that could be used to buy freedom and, after emancipation, land. Urban freedmen supported themselves in the same ways as urban slaves. The distinction between urban slaves and freedmen had become blurred before emancipation.

SLAVE RESISTANCE was always present. Slaves pretended to be sick, broke tools, worked slowly, and stole food. At times slaves attacked whites, but they were caught and suffered savage deaths. Whites feared poisoning by slaves, especially on the French islands, but

organized slave rebellions were the masters' greatest fear. Strong measures were taken to prevent slaves from congregating in large numbers or communicating with slaves from neighboring estates.

During the series of eighteenth century wars for empire between England and France, the West Indian colonies of both nations suffered blockades, conquests, and shortages that resulted in the loss of markets, crops, and slaves. Food imports were disrupted for as long as a year, and slaves starved to death.

Haiti

In 1788 events leading to revolution in France stimulated revolutionary activity in Haiti that ended with the creation in 1804 of the black republic of Haiti. Until 1791, during the first stage of the revolution, the white elite population fought among themselves and with the "coloreds" (people of mixed race). In August, 1791, black slaves rose up and within two months killed two thousand masters and destroyed 280 plantations. A two-year struggle between whites, coloreds, and blacks ended in 1793 with emancipation, the first large-scale emancipation of black slaves in the world. The remaining whites fled to neighboring islands or the United States. In 1794 Napoleon legalized slavery and attempted unsuccessfully to restore slavery on Haiti. His forces were forced to withdraw two years later, and the victorious Haitians declared independence on January 1, 1804.

Abolition of the Slave Trade

On the British islands, slavery lasted longer. The abolition of the slave trade, the first goal of reformers in England, was accomplished in 1808. Denmark and France had already abolished the slave trade. With prodding from the English, it was abolished by Holland, Spain, Sweden, and the United States within sixteen years. However, an illegal slave trade continued in the French West Indies until 1831 and delivered 80,000 slaves to Guadeloupe and Martinique. The illegal trade continued to Spanish Cuba until 1865 and brought in more than 500,000 slaves.

Emancipation on the British Islands

The British empire was the first to end slavery itself, in 1833. Abolition was demanded by reformers in England and forced upon the islands' colonial assemblies by Parliament. Before abolition, colonial assemblies had removed restrictions on coloreds in the 1820's, allowing them to vote and hold office. They also called for registration of slaves and for improving slave conditions. These measures did not satisfy any group—slaves, masters, or reformers.

After 1815 slave rebellions increased significantly on the British islands. It had been usual for planters to hear about plots in time to arrest the leaders, but after 1815 planters were able to stop only one of fourteen major revolts. The planters' position was becoming untenable.

Slave unrest and the discontent of reformers with the slow progress of reform hastened complete emancipation in the British West Indies. A slave revolt on Jamaica in 1831 had a major impact. Over 60,000 slaves took part and devastated more than 750 square miles. The brutal repression and execution of 540 slaves caused a violent reaction in England. The Emancipation Act of 1833 followed; it provided for emancipation in August, 1834, but with a subsequent period of apprenticeship. Agricultural workers were required to work for their former masters for six years, and domestics for four years. Parliament voted a compensation of about twenty-five pounds per slave. Dissatisfaction both in England and on the islands forced Parliament to end apprenticeship two years early.

The British West Indies were totally unprepared for emancipation. A new political, social, and economic system had to be created. The adjustment was not easy and took many years. The island governments did not establish the justice, education, and medical care systems that the masters had formerly provided. Blacks and coloreds were not granted full legal or voting rights. Discriminatory laws continued to exist until the third decade of the twentieth century.

Almost everywhere blacks abandoned the sugar estates, and sugar production fell, sometimes as much as 50 percent. Planters sold or simply abandoned their lands. Blacks purchased small holdings or squatted on vacant land, creating free villages. The movement to free villages was greatest in Jamaica, where two-thirds of the laborers left the estates and in Trinidad, where half did. Trinidad maintained sugar production by importing indentured labor from India. In BARBADOS, almost all the land was held in estates, and there were no free villages. The freedmen there had to continue to work on the estates, and sugar production did not fall.

The British government believed that

blacks were not able to govern themselves. Direct rule from England was imposed on all the islands. The economies of the islands continued to decline as sugar produced more cheaply in Cuba and other areas of the world provided competition that the islands could not match. Attempts to substitute other crops failed.

After Emancipation

Emancipation on the other islands came later than emancipation on the British islands and, except in the case of Cuba, was easier. The two larger French islands of Guadeloupe and Martinique, which also imported indentured labor, continued to produce sugar. Sugar production flourished in Cuba, where the use of black slaves increased as the result of the development of sugar estates.

On the French islands, blacks enjoyed greater legal protection and had more economic opportunities than on the Spanish or British islands. The white population declined, and the blacks became a larger proportion of the total population.

By the end of the nineteenth century, the United States had become the main economic and political force in the Caribbean. After almost a century of economic decline, American capital and technology rebuilt the sugar, coffee, and banana industries. Large U.S. corporations dominated production and controlled the market price. U.S. capital and technology improved the infrastructure and developed industry, mining, and banking, but the major portion of the economy remained agriculture.

Political Changes, Economic Struggles

In the twentieth century, the political status of the islands changed. The French islands became overseas departments of France in 1946. In 1952 Puerto Rico became a commonwealth associated with the United States, and in 1954 the Dutch possessions became an autonomous part of the Kingdom of the Netherlands. The U.S. VIRGIN ISLANDS became a territory with self-government in 1968. An attempt in 1958 to unite the British colonies under a single administrative authority failed. The Federation of the West Indies did not survive the withdrawal of Jamaica and TRINIDAD AND TOBAGO in 1962, and all except the smallest British islands had become independent by 1983.

By the year 2000, the greatest problem facing the independent Caribbean nations was no longer discrimination or lack of rights but economic troubles. Sugar production continued but was less and less able to compete worldwide. Industries are limited, resources other than agriculture are scarce, and capital and technology are lacking. Agriculture and the tourism industry that developed after WORLD WAR II are the main economic pursuits. Unemployment is high, and migration to other islands or to the mainland is large. The United States remains the dominant economic influence. Attempts at economic development sponsored by the Caribbean nations and the United States have been only partially successful.

—*Robert D. Talbott*

See also: Jamaica and Jamaican Americans.

Suggested Readings:

Georges, Eugenia. *The Making of a Transnational Community: Migration, Development, and Cultural Change in the Dominican Republic.* New York: Columbia University Press, 1990.

Knight, Franklin W. *The Caribbean: The Genesis of a Fragmented Nation.* New York: Oxford University Press, 1978.

Parry, J. H., P. M. Sherlock, and A. P. Maingot. *A Short History of the West Indies.* 4th ed. New York: St. Martin's Press, 1987.

Rogozinski, Jan. *A Brief History of the Caribbean from the Arawak and the Carib to the Present.* New York: Meridian, 1992.

Rout, Leslie. *The African Experience in Spanish*

America. New York: Cambridge University Press, 1976.

Sherlock, Philip. *West Indian Nations: A New History.* New York: St. Martin's Press. 1973.

West Virginia: According to a 1997 estimate of the CENSUS OF THE UNITED STATES, about 1.8 million people lived in West Virginia, with the state's approximately 58,000 African Americans representing about 3.2 percent of the total.

Through the years, the number of African Americans in the state has fluctuated. In 1870 there were about 17,000. By 1910 about 64,000 African Americans called West Virginia home; the increase was attributable primarily to people coming to mine coal. By 1930 the state's African American population had grown to 115,000. However, by the end of the twentieth century, following the mechanization of min- ing in the 1960's and the decline of mining jobs in the 1970's and 1980's, the black population had decreased by about half.

The history of African Americans in West Virginia actually began in VIRGINIA, of which West Virginia was a part until June, 1863. In 1775 the colonial governor of Virginia allowed free Africans to be recruited into the British army. Some of those recruited soldiers fought in skirmishes with Native Americans west of the Alleghenies in what is now West Virginia.

Prior to the CIVIL WAR there was anti-slavery sentiment in the mountainous western part of Virginia. During the prewar period, a number of whites in western Virginia were arrested for teaching African Americans to read. In 1859 radical abolitionist John BROWN and his followers seized the federal arsenal at HARPERS FERRY in an effort to start a slave rebellion and establish a colony for runaway slaves in neighboring MARYLAND. When the South, including Virginia, seceded from the union and the Civil War began in 1861, the residents of western Virginia voted not to secede, then voted to create a new state. Leaders drafted a constitution, and West Virginia was admitted to the union in 1863.

In the 1860's and 1870's many African Americans moved into West Virginia to work in railroad construction. The JOHN HENRY MYTH grew out of this West Virginia construction work; the legendary John Henry could drive steel faster than a machine called the steam drill could.

In 1891 the West Virginia Colored Institute (later West Virginia State College) was

1997 Population: 1,816,000
African American Population: 58,000
African American Percentage of Total: 3.19

opened at Institute. The establishment of this college was quickly followed by the Bluefield Colored Institute, which later became Bluefield State College.

West Virginians were involved early in the CIVIL RIGHTS MOVEMENT. In 1958 the state's first chapter of the CONGRESS ON RACIAL EQUALITY (CORE) boycotted segregated five-and-dime store lunch counters. Restaurants, department stores, and theaters integrated in West Virginia during the early 1960's. A number of West Virginians of African American heritage have become leaders in their fields. They include civil rights leader Leon SULLI-VAN, educator Booker T. WASHINGTON, scholar Henry Louis GATES, Jr., and Basketball Hall of Fame member Hal Greer.

—*Annita Marie Ward*

Wharton, Clifton Reginald, Jr. (b. September 13, 1926, Boston, Massachusetts): Educator. Wharton worked as an economic researcher, beginning in 1948, for various university and private groups. He was elected as the president of Michigan State University in 1969, the first African American to lead a major, predominantly white university. He was appointed chancellor of the State University of New York in Albany in 1978 and was appointed to the President's Commission on World Hunger by Jimmy Carter in 1975. In 1992 President-elect Bill Clinton chose Wharton to serve in his cabinet as deputy secretary of state; Wharton served only from January to November of 1993.

Wharton, Clifton Reginald, Sr. (May 11, 1899, Baltimore, Maryland—April 23, 1990, Phoenix, Arizona): DIPLOMAT. Before beginning his career with the U.S. government, Wharton earned an advanced law degree from Boston University. He entered the U.S. foreign service in 1925 and served in several countries, in-cluding LIBERIA, Madagascar, and Portugal. In 1958 he became the first black diplomat to head a U.S. delegation to a European country when he was named ambassador to Romania. Wharton was named ambassador to Norway in 1961; he resigned from that post and retired from the foreign service in 1964.

Wheatley, Phillis (1753?, West Africa—December 5, 1784, Boston, Massachusetts): Poet. An African-born slave, Phillis Wheatley became famous as a child-prodigy poet and model of early African American achievement during the eighteenth century.

Early Life

In 1761 an African girl who was estimated to be about seven years old (because she was then just losing her baby teeth) was taken, probably from somewhere in the West African regions later known as Gambia and Senegal. She was transported to BOSTON, where she was bought by a rich tailor, John Wheatley, probably with the intention of providing some company for his wife, Susanna. The girl's owners renamed her Phillis Wheatley.

Phillis was comparatively lucky in that, unlike most slaves, she was bought for relatively light housework, rather than for grueling fieldwork; she was even more unusual in that, unlike virtually all house slaves, she was taught to read and to write. However, she was not educated primarily to raise her status or to cultivate her personal gifts—which were evidently extraordinary—but to help save her immortal soul. To eighteenth-century New Englanders, literacy and Christianity were closely interconnected, and the single text that was most widely used to teach reading and writing was the Bible.

Thus, a primary way in which Wheatley's precocity was measured during her childhood was the rapidity with which she managed to learn to parse complicated verses from the

Bible. Many of her most popular published poems, which began appearing in New England newspapers when she was only about thirteen years old (her earliest known published poem appeared in the *Rhode Island Mercury* on December 21, 1767), were conventional eighteenth-century Christian elegies.

Literary Fame

The publication that made Wheatley famous was her elegy "On the Death of the Rev. Mr. George Whitefield, 1770," a broadside commemorating a famous itinerant Christian preacher who had helped to inspire the mass Christian revivals of the eighteenth century that came to be known as the Great Awakening. After having been celebrated in the Colonies as America's "sooty prodigy," Phillis Wheatley was taken to England to meet many dignitaries, including the Countess of Huntington, the Lord Mayor of London, and America's colonial agent in Britain, Benjamin Franklin. A major condition of her fame under the new, English, and somewhat less demeaning sobriquet of "the Sable Muse" was her Christian piety; among the sponsors of her visit to England was a Christian missionary group, and the title of the volume of her poetry that was published in London during the year of her visit was *Poems on Various Subjects, Religious and Moral* (1773).

Later Years

News of the illness of her mistress called Phillis Wheatley back early from London—to which she had gone in part because of her own ill health. Susanna Wheatley died, John Wheatley died, the Wheatley family circle broke up, and the slave Phillis Wheatley, at around the same time that the British colonies of North America were beginning to rebel against the colonial power of Great Britain, was granted her freedom. In 1778 she married John Peters, an African American freedman about whom little is known other than the fact

Engraving of Phillis Wheatley used as a frontispiece in a collection of her poems published in 1773. *(Library of Congress)*

that Phillis's former owners had disapproved of him, that he had to change jobs often and was once imprisoned for debt, and that he might have been an early proponent of African American rights. With him, Phillis bore three children. The first two died in infancy; the third shared a deathbed with its mother, whose life ended when she was about thirty, alone—her husband may have been in prison for debt at the time—poor, and in a cheap boardinghouse where she had been forced to work during the final months of her life. Phillis Wheatley, the first African American known to have published a volume of poetry, was buried together with her dead baby in an unmarked grave someplace in Boston in 1784.

Literary Reputation

That Phillis Wheatley was largely forgotten soon after she died in obscurity suggests that she functioned in eighteenth-century literary and religious culture largely as a curiosity, and that interest in her then was condescending at best. When interest in her was revived by abolitionist culture in the 1830's, she was cited primarily as evidence of the humanity of African American slaves, in particular to help prove that eloquence and righteousness could survive even the brutal inhumanities of slavery.

Wheatley's poetry did not begin to be read for its strictly literary merits, as well as for its African American characteristics, until interest in the African American cultural heritage became widespread in the twentieth century. Such aesthetic and ethnic appreciations of Wheatley's verse have little use for its Christian religiosity, which had been deemed the prime condition of its excellence while it was being written. Modern readers have accordingly searched Wheatley's life and work for secular and humanist elements.

It has been noted that the prodigiousness of her literary gifts included knowledge not only of English and the Bible but also of Latin and the pagan lyric poets of Roman antiquity; such knowledge suggests the possibility that Wheatley was influenced also by pre- and non-Christian traditions. It has been noted also that she was called upon, both before and during the revolution, to write poems on American patriotic subjects and occasions: on the repeal of the Stamp Act, on the pardoning of a deserter, on "America," "On the Arrival of the Ships of War, and Landing of the Troops," and "On the Affray in King-Street"—an early name for what would later be known as the Boston Massacre. Moreover, in several of her letters, Wheatley emphatically and explicitly states her opposition to the institution of slavery.

Criticism of Her Work

Demands that Wheatley's poetry reflect modern aesthetic standards and modern ethnic and feminist pride seem to have yielded to more widespread, and more forceful, criticism. Scholars continue to try to find evidence of abolitionist sentiment in her poetry, and to find in it also some subtle indications of Afrocentrism, feminism, and resentment over her forced conversion to dominant European cultural norms, but these efforts still seem weak. In contrast, critics have noted how often in her poems Wheatley passes over opportunities to champion herself, her race, or her gender, and how often she expressly substitutes transcendent, theist values for immediate, humanist ones. Wheatley's work is often included in modern anthologies of American literature, but always with the same kinds of reservations: "Phillis Wheatley was the first important Afro-American poet, but only rarely does her poetry reveal an awareness of the problems of blackness"; "The only hint of injustice found in her poetry is in the line 'Some view our sable race with scornful eye'"; "Hers was a thoroughly conventional poetic talent, tied too strongly to Miltonic cadences and the balanced couplets of Alexander Pope."

Modern aesthetic and ethnic standards would seem in their own ways to have condescended to Phillis Wheatley as much as did eighteenth-century literary and religious ones. Perhaps a better way to kindle continuing interest in her writing would be to encourage wonder at its incredible lack of emphasis on the personal, especially given the painful facts of her life.

—*R. C. De Prospo*

Suggested Readings:

Bassard, Katherine C. *Spiritual Interrogations: Culture, Gender, and Community in Early African American Women's Writing*. Princeton, N.J.: Princeton University Press, 1999.

Foster, Frances S. *Written by Herself: Literary Production by African American Women, 1746-1892*. Bloomington: Indiana University Press, 1993.

Kendrick, Robert. "Remembering America: Phyllis Wheatley's Intertextual Epic." *African American Review 30 (Spring, 1996): 71-88.

Richmond, Merle A. *Bid the Vassal Soar: Interpretive Essays on the Life and Poetry of Phillis Wheatley and George Moses Horton*. Washington, D.C.: Howard University Press, 1974.

_____. *Phillis Wheatley*. New York: Chelsea House, 1988.

Robinson, William H. *Phillis Wheatley: A Bio-bibliography*. Boston: G. K. Hall, 1981.

_____. *Phillis Wheatley and Her Writings*. New York: Garland, 1984.

_____. *Phillis Wheatley in the Black American Beginnings*. Detroit: Broadside Press, 1975.

Shields, John C. "Phillis Wheatley's Subversive Pastoral." *Eighteenth-Century Studies* 27 (Summer, 1994): 631-647.

The grave of Prince Whipple is one of forty sites on Portsmouth, New Hampshire's Black Heritage Trail. *(AP/Wide World Photos)*

Whipple, Prince: Revolutionary War soldier. Whipple's original name and date of birth are unknown. He is believed to have been born in Amabou, Africa. Legend says that his parents sent him to America to obtain an education.

Like most Africans in the Colonies, Whipple became a slave. During the AMERICAN REVOLUTION he was enlisted into the Continental Army either by Maryland or by his owner, to fill MARYLAND's quota for soldiers. Whipple served as an aid to a General Whipple from New Hampshire, and from him obtained his American name. He was with George Washington at the general's famous crossing of the Delaware River, and he is depicted in Emanuel Leutze's painting of that famous event. Whipple died at the age of thirty-two in Portsmouth, New Hampshire.

White, Bill (b. January 28, 1934, Lakewood, Florida): BASEBALL player and president of the National League. William DeKova "Bill" White became the first African American to serve as president of one of the major leagues, in 1989. He began his baseball career in the New York Giants system in 1953, playing for Danville in the Carolina League.

White first reached the majors in 1956, but then lost most of the next two seasons to military service. When he returned late in the 1958 season, the Giants had moved to San Francisco.

He did not hit well in his late-season return and was traded to the St. Louis Cardinals in March, 1959. The trade proved a great success for St. Louis, as White established himself as one of baseball's premier first basemen, starring with St. Louis through the 1965 season.

An exceptional defensive player, White also hit consistently and for power. He four times batted above .300 for the Cardinals, five times hit twenty or more home runs, and for three straight years batted in more than one hundred runners. He also helped St. Louis win the World Series in 1964. A quietly consistent player, White was somewhat overshadowed by more famous teammates such as the aging Stan Musial, third baseman Ken Boyer, center fielder Curt Flood, and pitcher Bob Gibson.

White, George Henry (December 18, 1852, Rosindale, North Carolina—December 28, 1918, Philadelphia, Pennsylvania): Politician and U.S. representative from NORTH CARO-LINA. White was born into slavery, but after emancipation he attended public schools in North Carolina. He entered Howard University in 1873 to pursue the study of medicine but soon switched to the study of law and returned to North Carolina. After his graduation in 1877, White began to teach and, in 1879, he was admitted to the North Carolina bar.

White was elected as a state representative in 1880 and lobbied for legislation to establish normal schools to train black teachers. He became the principal of the normal school that was established in New Bern, North Carolina. White was elected to the state senate in 1884 and then became prosecuting attorney and solicitor for North Carolina's second judicial district in 1886. His first venture into congressional politics occurred in 1894, when he ran for the REPUBLICAN PARTY nomination for North Carolina's Second Congressional District. He lost the nomination to Henry P. Cheatham, his brother-in-law and a former congressman.

Reconstruction-era politician George Henry White. *(Associated Publishers, Inc.)*

White defeated Cheatham for the nomination in 1896 and won the election against a Democrat and a Populist candidate.

White took office on March 15, 1897, and was the only black representative to serve during the Fifty-fifth Congress. He was a member of the House Committee on Agriculture and introduced legislation to make LYNCHING a federal crime. Although the bill did not succeed, it was the first such legislation to be brought before Congress. White was reelected in 1898, but editorial attacks in North Carolina papers and the intimidation tactics of white supremacy groups convinced him that running for a third term would be grueling and dangerous. In his final speech before Congress, he noted that his departure would leave no black representatives in the House or the Senate. He predicted that black exclusion from Congress would not continue indefinitely.

After his term ended, White opened a law

office in WASHINGTON, D.C., and began development of a black township on land that he and five partners had acquired in NEW JERSEY. The town, named Whitesboro in honor of its organizer, had a population of more than eight hundred black residents by 1906. White moved from Washington to PHILADELPHIA in 1905 and began a new legal practice. In addition, he founded People's Savings Bank, a financial institution dedicated to assisting black home buyers and business entrepreneurs. White also worked with numerous black organizations, including the Frederick Douglass Hospital and the NATIONAL ASSOCIATION FOR THE ADVANCEMENT OF COLORED PEOPLE. White's poor health forced him to close the People's Savings Bank shortly before his death.

See also: Black towns.

White, Walter Francis (July 1, 1893, Atlanta, Georgia—March 21, 1955, New York, New York): Writer and activist. As a writer and as executive secretary of the NATIONAL ASSOCIATION FOR THE ADVANCEMENT OF COLORED PEOPLE (NAACP), White led in the crusade for African American rights. By his tireless efforts, he won the affection of African Americans and the respect of leaders both in the United States and throughout the world.

White dedicated his life to working for the betterment of African Americans. In his publications, he dramatized their mistreatment; as executive secretary of the NAACP, he sought legal remedies for the evils he described. Because he was equally skilled in changing the views of ordinary Americans and in persuading their leaders to risk action, White played an important part in the early stages of the CIVIL RIGHTS movement.

Though Walter Francis White was fair-skinned enough to have "passed" for white, when a white mob rampaged through his neighborhood during the ATLANTA riot of

Walter Francis White could easily have "passed" as a white person but he not only chose to live as an African American, he also championed civil rights for black people. *(Schomburg Center for Research in Black Culture, New York Public Library)*

1906, he chose to live as an African American. After graduating from ATLANTA UNIVERSITY in 1916, White took a job with an insurance company. He also became involved in organizing a protest against a discriminatory school-funding plan and in establishing an Atlanta branch of the NAACP. His efforts were so successful that in 1908 he was asked to become assistant secretary of the NAACP, based in New York.

White began traveling throughout the South, pretending that he was a white reporter from New York or Chicago. He used the information he collected as a basis for articles in newspapers and magazines and for two novels, *The Fire in the Flint* (1924), which focused on LYNCHING, and *Flight* (1926), which was about blacks who "passed" as whites. Although he was awarded a Guggenheim Fellowship to write a third novel, instead White produced a well-documented history of lynching, *Rope and Faggot: A Biography of Judge Lynch* (1929).

After two years as acting secretary of the NAACP, in 1931 White was named executive secretary. During the next twenty-four years, he lobbied for antilynching legislation and against white primaries, poll taxes, unequal education, and job discrimination. His investigations into the treatment of black soldiers during WORLD WAR II, described in *A Rising Wind* (1945), provided one of the bases for President Harry S Truman's EXECUTIVE ORDER 9981 desegregating the armed forces. White's activities on the international scene included advising U.S. delegations to the United Nations and working for better race relations in the West Indies and in India.

In 1949 long-standing resentments within the NAACP, aggravated by the fact that White had divorced his African American wife and married a white woman, resulted in his being deprived of most of his power. However, he remained executive secretary until his death in 1955. Whatever his flaws, White was a courageous and effective leader in the struggle for civil rights.

—*Rosemary M. Canfield Reisman*

Suggested Readings:

Cannon, Poppy. *A Gentle Knight: My Husband Walter White*. New York: Rinehart, 1956.

McGuire, William, and Leslie Wheeler. *American Social Leaders*. Santa Barbara, Calif.: ABC-Clio, 1993.

Waldron, Edward E. *Walter White and the Harlem Renaissance*. Port Washington, N.Y.: Kennikat, 1978.

White backlash: Negative response of some white people to gains made by African Americans. These opponents of equality or of what they perceived as unfair special dispensations for African Americans acted out their hostilities in a variety of ways, from direct violence to voting for politicians who shared their views. An example of white backlash occurred in 1964, when Senator Barry Goldwater's campaign for the presidency attracted many white people opposed to the Civil Rights movement.

White Citizens Council: White segregationist group centered in MONTGOMERY, ALABAMA. The council became very active in attempts to weaken the MONTGOMERY BUS BOYCOTT of 1955. As African American resistance to segregation on buses grew, the council increased its membership to counter that resistance. It became the largest organized white group in Montgomery.

The council held large rallies to express racist propaganda. The council often held meetings in union halls and became allied with the labor movement in the South. The group vowed to fight desegregation efforts at all costs. It went after anybody or any group, black or white, that supported the bus boycott or desegregation. The members' tactics included violence. Several bombings and bomb threats were made against the organizers of the bus boycott, including Martin Luther King, Jr.

White flight: As most commonly used, migration of white people from an area into which African Americans are moving. White flight occurs as a result of direct or indirect prejudice. Some white people are unwilling to have African American neighbors. Others believe that migration of African Americans into an area will reduce property values, so they move out as a precaution.

This type of behavior is not confined to whites. The same scenario can occur when any group that is perceived to be from a lower social or economic level tries to move into a new area. The term "white flight" therefore can be misleading. African Americans also have been known to leave a neighborhood when other ethnic groups move in. During the nineteenth century, African Americans fled from a number of New York City neighborhoods when Italian immigrants moved in. They also left Detroit neighborhoods when Polish immigrants moved in. In more recent years, African Americans have left some Southern California neighborhoods in response to an increasing presence of Central American and Asian immigrants.

White supremacy: Attitude, ideology, or policy that claims superiority of Euro-American peoples over "nonwhite" populations. White supremacy is a conscious effort to make "race" a qualification for membership in civil society. The perceived inferiority of a particular skin pigmentation, ancestry, religion, or physical characteristic can be the foundation of white supremacist views. White supremacist views are the foundation of organizations such as the KU KLUX KLAN.

The philosophy of groups such as the Ku Klux Klan rests on belief in white supremacy. *(James L. Shaffer)*

Whitfield, James Monroe (April 10, 1822, Exeter, New Hampshire—April 23, 1871, San Francisco): Poet, abolitionist, and barber. Whitfield was recognized as one of America's most powerful antislavery poets. An outspoken proponent of black independence and racial justice, Whitfield effectively combined his poetic craftsmanship and his anger. He believed that the African American problem could be solved by emigration and colonization, and he was active in the COLONIZATION MOVEMENT.

Little is known about Whitfield's early life; however, records show that he did not have a formal education. From 1839 to 1859, he lived in Buffalo, NEW YORK, and earned a living as a barber. After apparently spending two years in CENTRAL AMERICA and focusing on the feasibility of colonization, he lived in San Francisco, California, from 1861 to 1871. He also spent short periods of time in Oregon, Idaho, and Nevada.

In 1850 Whitfield met Frederick DOUGLASS. Subsequently, Whitfield became a frequent contributor of protest poetry and letters to Douglass's newspapers, the *North Star* and *Frederick Douglass' Paper*. Douglass commended Whitfield for his leadership capability.

In 1853 Whitfield published *America and Other Poems*, for which he is widely known. His poetry explores such subjects as slavery, love, religion, and death. In 1854 and 1856, Whitfield devoted his energies to the National Emigration Convention in Cleveland and received national recognition for his work. Whitfield resumed his trade as a barber in San Francisco until he succumbed to heart disease in 1871; he was buried in the Masonic Cemetery of San Francisco.

—*Nila M. Bowden*

Whitman Sisters: Dancers. As one of the leading family acts of African American vaudeville, these four sisters ran their own musical revue and maintained a successful touring company for more than forty years. The four Whitman sisters—Mabel, Essie, Alberta ("Bert"), and Alice—were daughters of a southern METHODIST minister. Mabel and Essie first performed as harmony singers to raise money for their father's church. In 1904 they teamed with Alberta in NEW ORLEANS to become the Whitman Sisters' New Orleans Troubadours, traveling and sharing business responsibilities. Mabel handled bookings, Essie made costumes, and Alberta composed music and served as financial secretary. In 1909 Alice joined the troupe and became a favorite with audiences.

Mabel left the company for a while to tour abroad with her own show. When she returned, the original, four-person act was renamed the Whitman Sisters and subsequently landed top billing with the THEATRE OWNERS BOOKING ASSOCIATION, a black VAUDEVILLE circuit stretching from New York to Florida and from Chicago to New Orleans.

Mabel eventually retired from the stage to become the troupe's full-time manager. The remaining Whitman sisters developed special stage talents. Essie was featured as a comedienne with a drunk act, Alberta did a male impersonation, and Alice was billed as "the queen of the taps." With a JAZZ ensemble and a cast of some thirty singers, dancers, and comedians, the show included novelty acts, production numbers with a chorus line, and a boy-girl song and dance. When silent films became popular, the Whitman Sisters shortened their act to fit between

screenings, and business continued to thrive.

Alice's son Albert, who performed at the age of four, was the last family member to join the show. Mabel died in 1942, and the show closed the following year. The Whitman Sisters provided an enduring example of success for other African American performers. They gave hundreds of dancers their first break in show business and launched the careers of many who later became notable entertainers. The Whitman Sisters helped black dancers shed slave dance stereotypes and earn respect for their talents.

Wideman, John Edgar (b. June 14, 1941, Washington, D.C.): Novelist, short-story writer, essayist, and scholar. Wideman spent most of his early childhood and youth in Homewood, Pennsylvania, a predominantly African American section of Pittsburgh, and in Shadyside, Pennsylvania, which was predominantly white. Wideman was a gifted athlete and secured an athletic grant to attend the University of Pennsylvania as a member of the basketball team. He excelled both on the court and in the classroom. He graduated Phi Beta Kappa in 1963, with a B.A. in English. He won a prestigious Rhodes Scholarship, the second African American to win that honor, after Alain Locke. Wideman was awarded a bachelor's degree in philosophy from Oxford University in 1966.

Wideman continued his education by attending the famed Creative Writing Workshop at the University of Iowa during the 1966-1967 academic year. It was there that he began to expand his literary talent. With these solid academic credentials, he returned to the University of Pennsylvania, where he began a distinguished career as an educator, lecturer, and author.

Homewood and Philadelphia
Among Wideman's many books are *A Glance Away* (1967), written when he was twenty-six

years old, and *Philadelphia Fire* (1990). In between these novels, Wideman's most acclaimed works were *Sent for You Yesterday* (1983), which won the 1984 PEN/Faulkner Award for Fiction, and *Fever* (1989), a collection of twelve loosely related short stories.

The novel *Hiding Place* (1981) is the first book of the Homewood trilogy, followed by *Damballah* (1981), which is a collection, and *Sent for You Yesterday*. *Hiding Place* features the relationship of Sybela Owens and Charles Bell, both early settlers of Homewood. Their lineage proceeds downward to Tommy, a child of the 1940's facing false charges of armed robbery and murder. He hides with Mother Bess Owens, herself a recluse since the death of her husband and son. The bulk of the novel is devoted to the efforts of Bess and Tommy to end their different forms of hiding.

Wideman's acclaimed novel *Philadelphia Fire* is based on the 1985 police firebombing of a West PHILADELPHIA row house that housed the radical Afrocentric cult known as the MOVE ORGANIZATION. Narrated from the point of view of Cudjoe, a gifted but tortured African American writer, the novel explores race relations in the 1980's and examines the role of authority society.

Wideman's 1990's Work

In the late 1980's and 1990's, Wideman taught at the University of Massachusetts. He continued to publish both fiction and nonfiction, and to win awards and critical acclaim. In 1990 he won his second PEN/Faulkner Award (the first American writer to win more than one) for his novel/meditation *Philadelphia Fire*. Two years later, he published *All Stories Are True*, a third collection of tales and narratives which for the most part leave behind Wideman's fictionalized Homewood—a black section of Pittsburgh—to explore personal memories, family pain, and various manifestations of the racial struggle.

Also in 1992 Wideman published two retrospective collections, *The Stories of John Edgar Wideman* and *The Homewood Books*. The former volume brings together all three of Wideman's volumes of tales, in reverse chronological order: *All Stories Are True*, *Fever* from 1989, and *Damballah* from 1981. *The Homewood Books* combines *Damballah* with the two novels *Hiding Place* and *Sent for You Yesterday*, which won the PEN/Faulkner Award in 1984. These two collections, encompassing much of Wideman's career as a writer of fiction, led to a critical reassessment and increased appreciation of the body of his work, particularly the Homewood stories. Several critics compared Wideman to William Faulkner, both in his linking of many generations within a family and in his creation of a vivid fictional locale. In addition, several critics concluded that Wideman had established himself as the country's leading black male writer.

In 1994 Wideman returned to the autobiographical and meditative mode of his earlier, acclaimed *Brothers and Keepers* in *Fatheralong: A Meditation on Fathers and Sons, Race and Society*. The six interlinked sections of the book shift from meditative narrative to meditative essay. The center of the narrative portions is a trip Wideman made with his father in October of 1992 to Greenwood, SOUTH CAROLINA—a trip back to the South to explore family origins and learn about his paternal grandfather and great-grandfather. Near the end of the book, Wideman's father visits him in Massachusetts to attend (actually, to miss) the wedding of Wideman's son Daniel; again, the narrative brings together several generations of African American men. Throughout, Wideman interweaves memories of growing up with and without his father and thoughts of his brother and his other son, both in prison.

The meditative portions of *Fatheralong* focus on "the paradigm of race," the basic European American conception of "white," "black," superior, and inferior. Wideman looks at the destructive effects of that racist view on black men and the ties between them. He also explores the work of memory and stories in attempting to restore some of those links in "Great Time," an African realm that transcends European, linear conceptions of time. In 1996 Wideman published *The Cattle Killing*, a novel set in Philadelphia during an outbreak of yellow fever in the eighteenth century. This novel and *Two Cities* (1998) explore both the destructive aspects of racism and the redemptive power of love—communal love, intimate love, love of self, and love of life. The two cities of the title are Pittsburgh and Philadelphia.

—*Updated by George F. Bagby*

Wilder, L. Douglas (b. January 17, 1931, Richmond, Virginia): VIRGINIA politician. Lawrence Douglas Wilder grew up in an era of widespread segregation and discrimination, yet by the 1990's he had attained the status of a major national Democratic Party spokesman. After receiving his early education in the segregated schools of his hometown, he enrolled at Virginia Union University, where he took his bachelor's degree in 1951.

After graduation, he served in the KOREAN WAR and became a bona fide hero. He fought in the battle for Pork Chop Hill, an epic struggle that became the topic of a 1950's Hollywood film. In that battle, Wilder won a Bronze Star for carrying injured comrades off the field while enemy fire peppered the entire hill. Once behind the lines, he did not rest; he made return trips until he had carried most of the

wounded to safety. By the time he was in Korea, Wilder apparently already had a nose for politics. Using the leverage that a Bronze Star gave him, he complained to his white commanders that many African Americans had been passed over for promotions. The command listened, and blacks began, belatedly, receiving their due.

Early Career
After his return to the United States, Wilder decided to attend HOWARD UNIVERSITY Law School in Washington, D.C., and received his J.D. in 1959. He was soon admitted to the Virginia bar. In time, he became one of the best trial lawyers in the South. The son of an insurance agent and a domestic worker, Wilder disappointed his parents with his career choice. They did not believe that he could buck the Virginia establishment of white judges and white juries; they wanted him in a "safe" occupation in which he could develop an African American clientele within the black community, a trade that would insulate him from the discrimination of the white world. Neverthe-

L. Douglas Wilder takes the oath of office as governor of Virginia on January 13, 1990, as his daughter, Loren, holds a Bible for him. *(AP/Wide World Photos)*

less, as Wilder began to achieve career goals, his parents realized that they had a special son, even if he was occasionally something of a fun-loving free spirit.

He enjoyed the once-thriving U Street clubs of Washington, D.C., places where he could listen to jazz and absorb generous doses of alcohol. At one club, however, he had his comeuppance. One of his professors saw him and gave him a strongly worded lecture that had a decided effect. Wilder settled down, studied hard, and pulled his grades up.

In the 1950's and 1960's, Wilder participated in the CIVIL RIGHTS movement, always acting as a pacifist and as a believer in nonviolence. He joined the Richmond branch of the NATIONAL URBAN LEAGUE, eventually becoming a director of the board. A member of the NATIONAL ASSOCIATION FOR THE ADVANCEMENT OF COLORED PEOPLE (NAACP), he volunteered his time to the association's legal defense fund, handling test cases without demanding a fee. He joined other civic groups, including the Red Shield Boys Club, for which he eventually became chairman of the board, the Masons, and the Shriners.

Entry into Politics

Riding the crest of the Civil Rights movement, Wilder sought political office in 1969. He wanted a seat in the state senate. He was unorthodox in his first campaign; he believed that he had to be, since whites held the majority in his district. He ran as a healer who could bring the races together. He located his headquarters in the white section of town, but he did not cater to whites on most issues. In one campaign speech, for example, delivered on the steps of the state capitol, he criticized the state song, "Carry Me Back to Old Virginny," because it glorified slave times and the master-slave relationship.

Wilder won his 1969 race and became the first African American elected to the Virginia senate since the RECONSTRUCTION era. In the following years, he became a consummate legislative leader as a compromiser and healer. He was a staunch fiscal conservative, and he took other positions that pleased the conservative leaders within the DEMOCRATIC PARTY and the conservative voters around the state. Yet Wilder could play hardball with conservatives; he proved that in 1982, when he threatened to run for the U.S. Senate, thus dooming his party's chances for success, unless an archconservative dropped out of the race. The conservative candidate complied with Wilder's demand. Wilder achieved another political first in 1985, when he sought and won the lieutenant governorship. Four years later, he was elected Virginia's governor.

Record as Governor

Wilder's governorship drew mixed responses, and he had many critics. Some leaders labeled him an opportunist, citing his shifting record on at least two major issues. First, critics noted that Wilder had reversed his stand against capital punishment. For years its strongest foe in Virginia, Wilder embraced it once he had to appeal to the state's entire constituency. Second, although for years he had been a strong believer in privacy rights, in the late 1980's he advocated mandatory drug tests for college students. That reversal came after a major drug scandal at the University of Virginia.

Others criticized his management of the state's $2.2 billion shortfall. He closed that gap without increasing taxes, but his methods displeased many people. His methods included applying state lottery money—cash that was once spent on roads—to the shortfalls. Further, with his budget slashing, he doomed some programs while consolidating others. For example, former governor Gerald Baliles had created a department of world trade to spur the state's economic development. As Baliles left office, the Corporation for Enterprise Development, a think tank, ranked Virginia as the eighth state in international marketing;

under Wilder, Virginia fell to twenty-second.

Wilder also upset some among his African American constituency. For example, he publicly stated that poor, ghetto-dwelling urban African Americans had caused many of their own problems. He argued that many had a great aversion to honest hard work but had no aversion to having illegitimate babies. On the other hand, he suggested that Virginia restrict its college tuition-aid program to those in poverty. He also argued that the affluent in the United States should be excluded from such federal programs as Medicare and agricultural subsidies. Such money, he argued, should be spent on the truly needy, not on the middle and upper classes.

Presidential Campaign

In 1991 Wilder began a campaign for the presidency. In his strategic planning, he sought to have the electorate perceive him as a new kind of Democrat. According to Wilder, whereas traditional Democrats believed in taxing and spending, he did not; whereas other Democrats were soft on military spending, he was not; and whereas traditional Democrats were also soft on crime, he was not. Further, he promised to lower the national deficit without raising taxes by pursuing policies similar to those he had developed in Virginia. He argued that he could reduce military spending by $10 billion without weakening the American military machine. He said that he could trim $25 billion out of the federal bureaucracy alone. Further, he promised to give more federal money to states and cities for education, for roads, and for a war on crime.

Although Wilder withdrew from the presidential race, his campaign—indeed, his political career as a whole—may have benefited the country. The white electorate in the 1980's had proved largely unwilling to support national African American leader Jesse JACKSON. Many whites perceived him as too radical, even though he fit the liberal Democratic mold.

Wilder appeared more moderate than Jackson. Wilder appealed to more white voters than Jackson; his career in Virginia alone proved that. After the efforts of Jackson and Wilder, it was no longer farfetched to believe that an African American could one day win nomination for the presidency or the vice presidency from one of the major American political parties. Wilder's term as governor ended in 1994, and he subsequently began teaching at Virginia Commonwealth University.

—*James Smallwood*

Suggested Readings:

Baker, Donald P. *Wilder: Hold Fast to Dreams: A Biography of L. Douglas Wilder.* Cabin John, Md.: Seven Locks Press, 1989.

Barnes, Frank. "The Wilder Side." *The New Republic* 201 (November 13, 1989): 9-10.

Barone, Michael, and Gloria Borger. "The End of the Civil War." *U.S. News & World Report* (November 20, 1989): 45-48.

Bennett, Lerone. "Inaugurating the Future." *Ebony* 45 (April, 1990): 8-12.

Dingle, D. T. "Governor Wilder: Champion of the 'New Mainstream.'" *Black Enterprise* 20 (March, 1990): 17.

Haywood, R. L. "Inside Look as First Black Governor of Virginia Takes Charge." *Jet* 77 (February 5, 1990): 8-11.

Jones, David R. *Racism as a Factor in the 1989 Gubernatorial Election of Doug Wilder.* Lewiston, N.Y.: Edwin Mellen Press, 1991.

Williams, Michael. "Putting a New Face on Virginia's Future." *Black Enterprise* 21 (June, 1991): 284-294.

Yancey, Dwayne. *When Hell Froze Over: The Untold Story of Doug Wilder: A Black Politician's Rise to Power in the South.* Dallas, Tex.: Taylor, 1988.

Wiley, George (February 26, 1931, Bayonne, New Jersey—August 9, 1973, off Chesapeake Beach, Maryland): Welfare rights activist. Wiley, a soft-spoken organic chemistry profes-

Welfare rights leader George Wiley during the 1960's. *(Library of Congress)*

sor from Syracuse University, gave up an academic career to become a social activist. He left Syracuse University to serve as associate director of the Congress of Racial Equality (CORE) from 1964 to 1966, when he resigned to establish the NATIONAL WELFARE RIGHTS ORGANIZATION (NWRO). Created to "provide for bread, justice, dignity, and democracy of welfare recipients," the NWRO consisted at its greatest strength of some eight hundred local groups of welfare recipients and low-income people across the United States. As leader of the organization, Wiley led marches and filed lawsuits on behalf of increased rights and respect for those on welfare. In founding the NWRO, Wiley provided the first forum for welfare recipients to speak out on their own behalf, and he encouraged local chapters to develop spokespeople and become skilled at organizing.

During the 1960's, much of Wiley's work with the NWRO involved lobbying and demonstrations. In 1969 he and other NWRO members met with Robert Finch, then secretary of health, education and welfare, to discuss the needs of welfare mothers and lobby for increased public assistance to the poor. In an attempt to secure emergency aid for an American hunger crisis, he tried to stage a sit-in at President Richard Nixon's 1969 conference on food, nutrition, and health. At a VIETNAM WAR moratorium in Washington, D.C., in the late 1960's, Wiley gave an urgent speech describing the enormous toll the war was taking on the poor and on African Americans in particular.

Wiley approved rent strikes to protest low welfare allowances and demonstrations against retail stores that denied credit to welfare recipients. Wiley's crusade has been credited with quadrupling family assistance for the poor in the United States, increasing welfare eligibility by eliminating residency requirements, and ensuring welfare recipients' right to privacy. After a rift developed between Wiley and other members of the NWRO, he resigned early in 1973. That same year, he founded a new organization, the Movement for Economic Justice, just before his death in a boating accident on Chesapeake Bay. The NWRO closed its national office in 1975, but several local chapters remained active.

Wiley, Ralph (b. April 12, 1952, Memphis, Tennessee): Author, lecturer, and screenwriter. A prolific writer of social commentary, Wiley is known as a provocative thinker in the area of social discourse.

Through a critical examination of concepts and ideals that most Americans have come to accept as fact or as natural truths, Wiley makes Americans think, even if he enrages or provokes them. In his writings and lectures, he picks, prods, and chides others in an effort to expose actualities that may be long-lost or largely ignored truths. As an author, satirist, journalist, lecturer, playwright, film critic, and sports commentator, Wiley appeared as a frequent guest on many television programs. He authored a number of books, including *Why Black People Tend to Shout* (1992), *What Black People Should Do Now* (1993), *By Any Means Necessary: The Trials and Tribulations of the Making of "Malcolm X"* (1992), coauthored with Spike LEE, and *Dark Witness* (1996).

Wiley's career in journalism began in 1972 and culminated in a nine-year stint with *Sports Illustrated* between 1982 and 1990. In 1986 Wiley was named a senior writer for *Sports Illustrated*; he wrote more than two hundred articles for the magazine. Among them were twenty-eight cover stories on professional and collegiate athletes, including Muhammad ALI, Bo Jackson, Dwight Gooden, Patrick Ewing, Jerry Rice, and Joe Montana. *Best Seat in the House* (1998) is a collaborative venture with Spike Lee that was the basis for the 1998 Disney/Touchstone film *He Got Game*. In the 1990's Wiley became the chairman and chief executive officer of Heygood Images Productions, Inc., a multimedia concept and consulting firm based in Washington, D.C.

—*Alvin K. Benson*

Wilkins, Roger Wood (b. March 25, 1932, Kansas City, Missouri): Journalist, government official, and educator. Roger Wilkins's father was Earl William Wilkins, a journalist with the black *Kansas City Call*; his mother, Helen Jackson Wilkins, was an organizer for the Young Women's Christian Association (YWCA). Roger spent his youth in both segregated and integrated neighborhoods, in both middle- and working-class settings. His family, however, was always conscious of racial issues. His mother was the first African American to serve on the national board of the YWCA and

his uncle Roy served for several decades as executive secretary of the NAACP.

Wilkins earned his bachelor's degree from the University of Michigan at Ann Arbor in 1953, and completed his law degree in 1956. He was hired by the law firm of Delson, Levin and Gordon in New York City, where he specialized in international law. In 1960 Wilkins moved to WASHINGTON, D.C., to serve as special assistant to the administrator of the U.S. Agency for International Development (AID). After two years, he took a job with the Community Relations Service (CRS), then housed in the Department of Commerce. Created under the Civil Rights Act of 1964, the CRS was responsible for sending out race relations specialists to defuse community crises. Wilkins headed the Community Action division, a section that examined the impact of federal programs on selected cities with the intention of preventing racial violence.

In 1966 President Lyndon B. Johnson named Wilkins director of the CRS and moved

Author Roger Wilkins in 1982. *(AP/Wide World Photos)*

the program under the auspices of the Department of Justice. In his new appointment, Wilkins also served as assistant attorney general of the United States, the first black to achieve that position. During three years in that capacity, Wilkins argued that federal policy should be directed toward eliminating the root causes of racial injustice rather than responding to incidents of urban unrest when they occurred.

After President Richard Nixon took office in 1969, Wilkins left the federal government to accept a position at the Ford Foundation. There, he directed funding of programs for job training, education, and drug rehabilitation within poor communities. When he left the foundation in 1971, Wilkins read a memo to the board of trustees that criticized the organization for preserving its homogenous character as a group of "rich, thrusting, white men over forty-five" who could not understand the experience of the minority citizens of a different gender or racial background. At the Ford Foundation, as in a number of his other positions, Wilkins felt the conflict of working with white men on behalf of African Americans and questioned whether his efforts might be more effective through working directly with African Americans.

Determined to effect social change through journalism, Wilkins next became an editorial writer with *The Washington Post*. In his new job, he shared in the paper's Pulitzer Prize for its coverage of the Watergate scandal. Wilkins subsequently worked as a COLUMNIST and member of the editorial board of *The New York Times* and as an editor at *The Washington Star*. In 1982 he became a senior fellow at the Institute for Policy Studies. Next, he joined the faculty of George Mason University and was named Clarence J. Robinson Professor of History and American Culture in 1987.

Among Wilkins's publications include *A Man's Life: An Autobiography* (1982) and *Quiet Riots: Race and Poverty in the United States* *(1988, with Fred Harris). He wrote scripts for two documentaries that were aired on PBS television: Keeping the Faith (1987) and Throwaway People (1990).*

Wilkins, Roy (August 30, 1901, St. Louis, Missouri—September 8, 1981, New York, New York): Civil rights leader. Sometimes called "Mr. Civil Rights," Roy Wilkins played a major role in the CIVIL RIGHTS movement of the 1950's and 1960's, working with other activists including Martin Luther KING, Jr., Whitney YOUNG, and A. Philip RANDOLPH. Wilkins, who spent his life working to improve conditions for African Americans, was best known for his work with the NATIONAL ASSOCIATION FOR THE ADVANCEMENT OF COLORED PEOPLE (NAACP).

Early Life

Roy Wilkins's parents, who were originally from Mississippi, fled to St. Louis for safety in 1900 after Wilkins's father defended himself from a white man who had attempted to order him out of the road. He left to escape being beaten and lynched, a practice commonly used to punish African Americans who were considered disrespectful toward whites.

Wilkins's mother died in 1906, leaving behind three young children. Their father eventually took them to St. Paul, MINNESOTA, to be reared by an aunt. Even though Wilkins lived in poverty, life in St. Paul provided him his first experience of living in a racially integrated community and attending integrated schools. Although he experienced bouts with racial prejudice, it was this experience that shaped his later belief that racial integration was an achievable and necessary goal.

During Wilkins's teenage years, he worked various jobs to earn money for college. He worked as a caddy, a red cap, a slaughterhouse worker, and eventually as a waiter on a dining car for the Northern Pacific Railroad.

In 1920, when an African American man was accused of raping a white girl, three African American men were lynched by a mob of five thousand whites in Duluth, Minnesota. The incident had a profound effect on the eighteen-year-old Wilkins, making him more aware of the strength of racial hatred. As a result, Wilkins became more interested in learning about the goals and work of the NAACP. He later won a prize of twenty-five dollars in a college oratorical contest; Wilkins's entry, entitled "Democracy or Demoncracy?," focused on the Duluth LYNCHING.

Wilkins attended the University of Minnesota in St. Paul, where he joined the NAACP. His love for journalism led to his working on the campus newspaper, *The Minnesota Daily*; he eventually became the paper's night editor. Wilkins also worked on the staff of two African American newspapers in the St. Paul community. He graduated in 1923 with a degree in sociology and a minor in journalism.

Early Career

Despite Wilkins's journalistic talent and experience, upon his graduation the white-owned newspapers of St. Paul were not interested in hiring him. He found his first job in Kansas City, MISSOURI, working for the *Kansas City Call*, an African American weekly newspaper. While living in Kansas City for eight years, Wilkins observed and experienced the blatant racial prejudice of the city's JIM CROW policies.

In Kansas City, for example, African Americans were not allowed to try on clothing in white-owned stores. Schools, parks, theaters, and other public facilities were either off-limits to African Americans or segregated. Wilkins's lifelong fight for civil rights began when he organized a boycott of the segregated theaters and campaigned for voters to reject bonds that upheld segregation. While in Kansas, Wilkins married Aminda (Minnie) Badeau on September 15, 1929.

W. E. B. Du Bois, the editor of the NAACP's *The Crisis*, offered Wilkins a position as the magazine's business manager, but Wilkins declined; he was more interested in the journalism and writing of *The Crisis* than in its business aspects. In 1931 Walter WHITE, the acting executive secretary of the NAACP, invited Wilkins to serve as the organization's assistant secretary. Impressed by White's leadership and his work for civil rights, Wilkins accepted the position. His work as a journalist continued during his early career in the NAACP; he investigated discriminatory pay practices directed against African American workers involved in dam and levee construction projects in the Mississippi Delta.

In 1934 Wilkins was arrested for the first time when he demonstrated to protest the refusal of Attorney General Homer Cummings to include the issue of lynching on the agenda of a major conference on crime. That same year, he was appointed editor of *The Crisis* when Du Bois resigned. Wilkins also continued to serve as an assistant secretary and administrator in the NAACP. In 1949 he was appointed the NAACP's acting executive secretary when White took a leave of absence.

Leading the NAACP

Following the death of Walter White in 1955, Wilkins was named the NAACP's executive secretary; in 1964 his title was officially changed to executive director. Under his leadership, the NAACP undertook the legal battle of school desegregation; court cases were necessary to ensure that states implemented and enforced the landmark U.S. SUPREME COURT decision of *Brown v. Board of Education*, which had outlawed school segregation in 1954. Wilkins's administration also fought to integrate the Army, planned and sponsored events to end discrimination, and pressured presidents to implement civil rights legislation. Wilkins and Clarence Mitchell, an NAACP lobbyist, worked relentlessly to-

In August, 1963, Roy Wilkins (center), singer Marian Anderson, and actor Paul Newman joined the thousands of Americans marching on Washington, D.C. *(AP/Wide World Photos)*

gether to secure the passage of much of the civil rights legislation of the 1950's.

In the 1960's, during Wilkins's leadership of the NAACP, the Civil Rights movement reached its pinnacle: the era of SIT-INS, FREE-DOM RIDES, protest marches, and emergence of radical organizations. In 1963, while Congress debated civil rights legislation, the MARCH ON WASHINGTON for jobs and freedom occurred on August 23. Roy Wilkins was one of the key speakers, along with other civil rights giants such as A. Philip Randolph and Martin Luther King, Jr. After the March on Washington, President John Kennedy met with King, Wilkins, and other leaders to pledge his support for black efforts to achieve equality.

Division Within the Movement

With the emergence of the BLACK POWER MOVEMENT, radical activists increasingly criti-

cized Wilkins and the NAACP for being too old-fashioned and conservative. Young radicals argued that the social climate of the Civil Rights movement had changed to a more volatile one, and that the advocacy of nonviolence and integration had become anachronistic. Wilkins responded by denouncing the Black Power movement as fanatical.

In 1972 the first National Black Political Convention was held in Gary, Indiana. The leaders from the convention met later to draft a document, referred to as the National Black Political Agenda, that voiced their platforms on social, economic, and political issues pertaining to African Americans, U.S. foreign policy, school busing, and other issues. Because the positions outlined in the document were not a consensus of views, Roy Wilkins withdrew the NAACP's support from the paper. Again, he was criticized for his conservative views by various other leaders, including Mayor Richard Hatcher of Gary.

Despite growing criticism of his leadership, however, Wilkins remained widely respected as a civil rights leader. He continued to serve as the executive director of the NAACP until his retirement in 1977.

Achievements

Wilkins received numerous awards, including the prestigious SPINGARN MEDAL in 1964. While he was primarily active in the Civil Rights movement, he was appointed to other positions in which he was influential in working to achieve equality for all. He served as the chairman of the Leadership Conference on Civil Rights, and he was appointed to serve as a trustee member of the Eleanor Roosevelt Foundation, the Kennedy Memorial Library Foundation, and the Estes Kefauver Memorial Foundation. Wilkins was also a member of the board of directors of the Riverdale Children's Association, the John LaFarge Institute, the Stockbridge School, and the Peace with Freedom organization.

Declining health in the last years of his life forced Wilkins to cut back on his busy schedule. He died in New York City in 1981 at the age of eighty.

—*Kibibi Mack-Williams*

Suggested Readings:

Bennett, Lerone, Jr. *Before the Mayflower: A History of Black America*. 6th ed. Chicago: Johnson, 1987.

Franklin, John Hope, and Alfred A. Moss, Jr. *From Slavery to Freedom: A History of African Americans*. 7th ed. New York: Alfred A. Knopf, 1994.

Kellogg, Charles F. *NAACP: A History of the National Association of the Advancement of Colored People*. Baltimore, Md: Johns Hopkins University Press, 1967.

Weisbrot, Robert. *Freedom Bound: A History of America's Civil Rights Movement*. New York: Plume, 1991.

Wilkins, Roy. *Standing Fast: The Autobiography of Roy Wilkins*. New York: Viking Press, 1982.

Wilson, Sondra K., ed. *In Search of Democracy: The NAACP Writings of James Weldon Johnson, Walter White, and Roy Wilkins (1920-1977)*. New York: Oxford University, 1999.

Wilkinson, Frederick D., Jr. (b. January 25, 1921, Washington, D.C.): Business executive. After being graduated from HOWARD UNIVERSITY with an A.B. degree earned magna cum laude, Wilkinson entered the U.S. Army. He earned a certificate in business law and accounting from the Army University Center of Oahu in 1946. In 1948 he earned his M.B.A. from Harvard University.

Wilkinson began working for Macy's department store in NEW YORK CITY in 1949, as a junior assistant buyer. He became senior assistant buyer in 1950 and buyer in 1952. He stayed in that position until 1968, when he was named as a company vice president. The New York City Transit Authority hired Wilkinson in 1974 as its executive officer for passenger service. He held that position until 1976, then was executive officer for surface transit. American Express Company made Wilkinson its vice president for travel in 1977. He became vice president for consumer cards in 1979 and senior vice president in 1985. Wilkinson also served as trustee of Jamaica Hospital in New York State and of the NATIONAL URBAN LEAGUE, for which he was national treasurer at one time. He also was on the board of directors of the Jamaica Chamber of Commerce and of Freedom National Bank.

Williams, Albert P. (b. Savannah, Georgia): JUDGE. Williams graduated from Lincoln University with his A.B. degree in 1940. After serving in WORLD WAR II, he attended Brooklyn Law School and earned his J.D. degree in 1952. Williams passed the New York State bar examination and entered private practice as an attorney.

Williams's public legal career began in 1962, when he served as chief trial attorney in the torts division of the Queens County Civil Court in New York. He continued in this post until 1969, then served as assistant corporate counsel for the City of New York. Williams accepted his first judicial appointment in 1970, when he became a judge of the civil court of New York City. He was selected to serve as an associate justice on the New York State supreme court in 1978.

Williams, Ann Claire (b. August 16, 1949, Detroit, Michigan): Federal JUDGE. Williams grew up in Detroit and graduated with her B.A. in education from Wayne State University in 1970. She worked as an elementary school music teacher and earned her M.A. in counseling from the University of Michigan in 1972. Williams then entered law school at the University of Notre Dame, earning her J.D. degree in 1975.

She worked as a judicial clerk for Judge Robert A. Sprecher in Chicago from 1975 to 1976. Williams then served as an assistant U.S. attorney in the U.S. attorney's office in Chicago, attaining the position of deputy chief attorney before serving as the chief attorney on the Organized Crime Drug Enforcement Task Force for the North Central Region from 1983 to 1985. In addition to her work as a U.S. attorney, Williams was an adjunct professor at Northwestern University and served on the faculty of the National Institute for Trial Advocacy beginning in 1979. President Ronald Reagan appointed Williams to a lifetime post as U.S. district judge for the Northern District of Illinois in June of 1985. Upon taking her post, Williams became the first African American woman appointed to the federal bench by Reagan.

Williams, Bert (November 12, 1874, Antigua, West Indies—March 4, 1922, New York, New York): VAUDEVILLE star. Egbert Austin "Bert" Williams is considered one of the finest comedians in the history of American show business. He appeared in two films, *Darktown Jubilee* (1914) and *A Natural Born Gambler* (1916), and recorded such hit songs as "It's Nobody's Business but My Own," "Oh Death Where Is Thy Sting," and "It's Getting So You Can't Trust Nobody." He is best known, however, for his partnership with song-and-dance man George WALKER and for his work with the Ziegfeld Follies.

Early Years
Born in the WEST INDIES as Egbert Austin Williams, he migrated as a young child with his family to Riverside, CALIFORNIA. His father, a railroad worker, wanted Williams to earn a degree at Stanford University; however, three of Williams's white friends persuaded him to join their theatrical troupe. Often, he could not stay in the same hotels or eat in the same restaurants as his white peers. When the group finally reached San Francisco, their clothes were so filled with lice that they had to be burned. The hardships led to the disbanding of the quartet, and only Williams decided to pursue a career as an entertainer. Musically gifted, he could play almost any instrument and had a fine singing voice. As a solo act, he first performed with Lew Johnson's Minstrels for two dollars a week and later played San Francisco vaudeville houses for seven dollars a week.

Partnership with Walker
Growing tired of working alone, Williams agreed to form a partnership with George Walker, a former MINSTREL and medicine-show entertainer from Lawrence, Kansas. Initially, Williams played a straight man to Walker's fool, but it was not long before the roles were reversed. During this early period in their career, the team was often unemployed, so they spent many nights watching other vaudevillians work their craft. After studying white comedians who performed in blackface, the team felt they had to conform to tradition and portray stereotypical black characters in order to achieve success. They billed themselves as the "Real Coons" and toured across the nation.

In 1896, while Williams and Walker were playing at a second-rate vaudeville house in Chicago, a Broadway theater manager named George Lederer heard of the team and sent for them to perk up a faltering Victor Herbert musical called *The Gold Bug*. Although they could not stop the ill-fated show from closing, the experience served to boost Williams and

Walker's career. For forty weeks, they played in first-rate vaudeville houses along the East Coast. Their act also popularized the cake-walk among New York's high society.

Enthused by their East Coast popularity, the team set sail for London, where they unexpectedly met with a cool reception. Back in New York, they garnered modest success in 1900 with the shows *The Policy Players* and *The Sons of Ham*. Like other musicals of the day, these shows featured improvised routines that were changed nightly. Music and dance were of utmost importance. Termed "coon shows" by contemporaries, these musicals did not differ greatly from minstrel entertainments. *The Sons of Ham* featured a song that would become one of Williams's trademark numbers, "I'm a Jonah Man."

Most Significant Productions
Williams and Walker might not be well remembered if it were not for their next three musical shows, created in collaboration with some of the era's most talented black artists: director Jesse Shipp, composer Will Marion Cook, lyricist-comedian Alex Rogers, and actor-singer-dancer Ada Overton Walker (George's wife). Williams and Walker had long wanted to perform in the first-rate Broadway houses that had traditionally prohibited black musicals. In contrast to their former musicals, the company sought to devise a show with an African setting and a more formal structure. The result was *In Dahomey* (1903), which featured two detectives from Boston, Shylock Homestead (Williams) and Rareback Pinkerton (Walker), who are hired to find a lost silver casket. The show did little to enlighten audiences about African culture, and actually spent only one of three acts in an African setting. The team's old vaudeville routines, humorous tunes, and popular cakewalk numbers were the real draws for the musical.

Following a successful Broadway run, the show sailed to England for a London engagement. *In Dahomey* was greeted by a lukewarm reception until the show gave a command performance in honor of the ninth birthday of the Prince of Wales. Afterward, ticket sales picked up considerably, and the musical initiated a cakewalk craze that swept England and France. Upon its return to the United States, the show had a successful tour in 1904 and 1905. The musical returned 400 percent profit to its producers and quelled the belief that all-black-cast shows lost money. Moreover, the team, especially Williams, became the talk of the entertainment world.

Stories circulated about Williams, who offstage was the antithesis of his onstage persona and who had married a demure former Chicago showgirl named Lottie. Williams was light skinned and broad shouldered, and his manners were correct and elegant; his library contained works by Charles Darwin, Thomas Paine, Arthur Schopenhauer, Oscar Wilde, Voltaire, Immanuel Kant, Johann von Goethe, and Mark Twain.

In 1906 the next Williams and Walker show, *Abyssinia*, followed the adventures of African Americans Rastus Johnson (Walker) and Jasmine Jenkins (Williams) on the African continent. Unlike its predecessor, the show strayed from minstrel stereotypes and depicted a more complimentary image of African life.

The production of *Bandana Land* (1908) marked the end of the partnership. In the play, Bud Jenkins (Walker) attempts to swindle a railway company in a land-speculation deal and tries to trick Skunkton Bowser (Williams) out of his inheritance. Like the two previous shows, *Bandana Land* proved to be a profitable investment for its producers. Walker's philandering, however, had made him susceptible to SYPHILIS, a debilitating disease that had no cure at that time. Early in the run of the show, Walker began to show symptoms of syphilitic infection: He lisped, stuttered, and forgot his lines. He continued his role as long as he was physically able, but by February, 1909, Walker

Vaudeville star Bert Williams in 1931. *(Library of Congress)*

had become bedridden. For the final weeks of the run, his wife Ada wore his costume to perform his role. Walker died two years later at the age of thirty-eight.

Ziegfeld Follies

Williams once again performed a solo act. In 1909 he starred in his last all-black-cast show, *Mr. Lode of Koal*. For the next ten years, he became a headliner with the famed previously all-white cast of the Ziegfeld Follies. Initially, other Follies entertainers threatened to strike if Williams was hired. The producer called their bluff, and predictably, the cast relented; some, however, insisted they would not appear on stage with a black man. This threat remained until Williams proved much too popular with audiences for other cast members to ignore. During this period, "Nobody" appropriately became Williams's theme song, as he endured racial slurs from his white colleagues and from society at large. He was also one of the few black entertainers of the decade given the opportunity to perform on Broadway. Follies comedian W. C. Fields would say of Williams, "He is the funniest man I ever saw and the saddest man I ever knew." Williams left the Follies in 1919 and signed to star in the revue *Broadway Brevities of 1920*. The show became his last; he was struck down by pneumonia and died at the age of forty-seven.

Career Assessment

The Williams and Walker team was not without its detractors. While the black press lauded their talents, it criticized the duo for playing in Jim Crow houses where ushers were the only blacks allowed on the main floor. Critics also accused them of not overtly challenging black stereotypes; their shows included demeaning material, and Williams donned a blackface mask throughout his career. Moreover, the financial and critical success of their shows had little lasting impact on encouraging managers to book black acts in first-rate Broadway houses.

Nevertheless, the team is remembered for its more praiseworthy accomplishments. They introduced many of the most popular songs of their era, such as "Dora Dean," "I Don't Like No Cheap Man," and "When It's All Goin' out and Nothin's Comin' In." Many of Williams's trademark songs—"Jonah Man," "I Must Be Crazy but I Ain't No Fool," "Nobody," and "Why Adam Sinned"—were written by the comedian in collaboration with lyricist Alex Rogers. The team's shows were written and staged by some of the era's most talented black artists. They employed numerous black actors, some of whom, such as Charles Gilpin and Abbie Mitchell, went on to star in dramatic roles on Broadway. The legacy of the team, especially of Williams, will continue to be acknowledged with admiration.

—*Gary Anderson*

Suggested Readings:

Charters, Ann. *Nobody: The Story of Bert Williams*. New York: Macmillan, 1970.

Haskins, James. *Black Theater in America*. New York: Thomas Y. Crowell, 1982.

Riis, Thomas L. *Just Before Jazz: Black Musical Theater in New York, 1890-1915*. Washington, D.C.: Smithsonian Institution Press, 1989.

Smith, Eric L. *Bert Williams: A Biography of the Pioneer Black Comedian*. Jefferson, N.C.: McFarland, 1992.

Stein, Charles W., ed. *American Vaudeville as Seen by Its Contemporaries*. New York: Alfred A. Knopf, 1984.

Woll, Allen L. *Black Musical Theatre*. Baton Rouge: Louisiana State University Press, 1989.

Williams, Chancellor (b. December 22, 1905, Bennettsville, South Carolina): Historian. Williams completed his elementary education at the Marlboro Academy in Bennettsville, SOUTH CAROLINA, before his family moved to Washington, D.C. He attended Dunbar High School and Armstrong High School in WASHINGTON, D.C. His B.A. in education and M.A. in history are from HOWARD UNIVERSITY. Williams did postgraduate nonresident studies at the University of Chicago and the University of Iowa, then earned his Ph.D. from The American University in 1949.

Williams spent a year as a visiting research scholar at Oxford University in England and at the University of London. He began direct field studies in African history in 1956, using University College (later called the University of Ghana) as a base. He attempted to determine the independent achievements of African people and the nature of civilization in Africa before Asian and European influence. His final field studies, covering twenty-six countries and more than one hundred language groups, were completed in 1964.

Williams was president of a baking company, editor of *The New Challenge*, organizer of a cooperative, an economist with the U.S. government, a high-school teacher, a school prin-cipal, a historical novelist, and a university professor in addition to his career as a historian. His *The Destruction of Black Civilization: Great Issues of a Race from 4500 B.C. to 2000 A.D.* (1971) won the 1971 Book Award from the Black Academy of Arts and Letters. It is an overview of the history of black nations and various black cultural ideas.

Williams, Daniel Hale (January 18, 1858, Hollidaysburg, Pennsylvania—August 4, 1931, Idlewild, Michigan): Surgeon. One of the best-known physicians of his day, Daniel Hale Williams was the fifth child of Daniel Williams, Jr., a barber, and Sara Price Williams. As a youngster, Williams moved to WISCONSIN, where in 1878 he graduated from Haire's Classical Academy in Janesville. Having decided to become a physician, he apprenticed himself to Henry Palmer, a prominent physician who had served as surgeon general of Wisconsin. Under Palmer's guidance, Williams prepared himself to enter the Chicago Medical College, an affiliate institution of Northwestern University, from which he received a medical degree in 1883.

Early Professional Career
After serving an internship at Mercy Hospital in Chicago, Williams established a private practice in an integrated Chicago neighborhood. Despite the restrictions and limitations that often affected black doctors, Williams, an ambitious, hardworking man, assumed many responsibilities. He became attending physician at the Protestant Orphan Asylum and a member of the surgical staff of the South Side Dispensary. In 1885, two years after having earned his medical degree, he became a demonstrator of anatomy at his alma mater. During the same period, he accepted a position as a surgeon with the City Railway Company. Williams's reputation as a physician also earned for him an appointment to the Illinois

State Board of Health. As one of the few black sanitarians of the era, he served on the board for four years and helped to draft public health legislation.

As a public health official, Williams was anxious to provide additional hospital facilities for residents of CHICAGO. Moreover, as a black surgeon, he was also aware of the dire need to establish an institution where African Americans could secure medical internships and nurse's training. His hopes were realized in 1891 with the opening of the Provident Hospital in Chicago, which had an interracial staff and which eventually opened a school for nurses. Beginning with practically no resources, this hospital, under Williams's guidance, made a significant contribution to training black health-care professionals. Its nurse's training program was the first of its kind for black women in the United States. Williams served on the surgical staff of Provident from its beginning until 1912, save for short periods of time he spent at Freedmen's Hospital in Washington, D.C., and at Meharry Medical College in Nashville, Tennessee.

Successful Heart Surgery

It was during Provident's early history that "Dr. Dan," as he came to be known, became the first surgeon to perform open-heart surgery. In July of 1893, James Cornish, a black expressman, was admitted to the hospital with a stab wound in the region of his heart. At first, the wound appeared superficial, but the patient's distress soon indicated that his condition was more serious than originally thought. Medical opinion of the day did not recommend surgery in cases of this type. Williams, however, was convinced that the patient would die if the wound was ignored. He entered the thoracic cavity and sutured Cornish's pericardial sac. The patient not only survived but also fully recovered. Williams, who was only thirty-seven at the time, had performed an astonishing operation. Claims were

made that a St. Louis surgeon had performed a successful heart operation in 1891, but the *New York Medical Record* reported in 1897 that Williams's surgical procedure was the first recorded case of suture of the pericardium.

Reorganizing Freedmen's Hospital

In February of 1894, Williams accepted an appointment at the Freedmen's Hospital in Washington, D.C. As surgeon-in-chief, he viewed this institution as having a special mission: to provide training for black interns and nurses who were denied access to other institutions and to provide decent health care for its patients, the majority of whom were black. Accordingly, Williams implemented a system in which young medical-school graduates could secure temporary residence within the hospital and could also perform practical work on the wards. This system, Williams argued, would cut expenses, as fewer practicing

Pioneering heart surgeon Daniel Hale Williams. *(National Library of Medicine)*

physicians would be hired; at the same time, the young graduates could take advantage of opportunities that many hospitals had denied them on the basis of race. In 1894 Williams implemented the nurse's training program at Freedmen's, thereby permitting black women to secure professional training.

In his 1897 annual report, Williams complained about the condition of the hospital buildings at Freedmen's, describing them as old frame buildings built on army barracks. In order to render better services to patients, he argued, the hospital needed new buildings with adequate heat, light, and ventilation. Although he did not realize all of his ambitions for Freedmen's, Williams was able to organize the hospital into seven departments: medical, surgical, gynecological, obstetrical, dermatological, genito-urinary, and throat and chest. He also established more internships and was able to acquire a serviceable horse-drawn ambulance. Williams resigned his position at Freedmen's in 1897, having become disgusted with the internal politics and other problems associated with the institution.

Williams returned to Chicago after he left Freedmen's, with plans of resuming his work at Provident. Things had changed at the hospital during his absence; Dr. George C. HALL had become a powerful force at Provident. An intense rivalry developed between the two men, with Hall emerging as the winner.

Eventually, Williams severed his ties with Provident. Throughout the painful ordeal, however, he continued to be a significant influence in the medical profession in Chicago and the nation. In 1899, for example, he became a professor of clinical surgery at Meharry Medical College. As one of the two successful medical colleges for blacks, Meharry had a unique mission, and Williams was determined to make it a first-rate institution; he was responsible for establishing the first surgical clinics at the college. Upon his return to Chicago, he served as a member of the surgical

staff of the Cook County Hospital, a white-administered institution.

Other Medical Appointments and Activities
In 1913 Williams became an associate attending surgeon at St. Luke's, a white Chicago hospital. For a black practitioner of the day, the appointment was an unusual honor, and it enabled Williams to become influential in running one of the largest gynecological services in the city. That same year, when the American College of Surgeons was organized, Williams was invited to become a charter member, the only African American so honored. For many years, he was the only black who held membership in the organization.

Despite his acceptance into the mainstream of American medicine—the white medical community—Williams continued his efforts to improve the status of and to promote professionalism among black physicians. In 1895, when a group of black doctors attending the Cotton States and International Exposition in Atlanta met to organize a medical association for black physicians, dentists, and pharmacists, Williams was present. He became a charter member of the body known as the National Medical Association, the black counterpart of the American Medical Association. At a meeting of the group held in New York City in 1908, Williams performed surgery at Lincoln Hospital as a part of "Negro Doctor's Clinic Day." At an evening session, he lectured on "Crushing Injuries to the Extremities." At another early National Medical Association meeting in St. Louis, he again demonstrated his surgical skills before fellow members.

Research
In addition to his commitment to improving the training of black health-care professionals, his involvement in medical and surgical societies, and his private practice, Williams was a researcher who contributed to medical journals and presented papers at professional

meetings. He was intent upon promoting sound surgical knowledge and correcting errors that had crept into medical thinking, including erroneous ideas about black health. American practitioners had long pointed to certain physiological differences between the races, many of which were unfounded. One such misconception, according to Williams, was that certain gynecological problems occurred only in whites. Accordingly, many physicians held that black women were not at risk for ovarian cysts, as this condition allegedly occurred only among whites.

In a paper entitled "Ovarian Cysts in Colored Women, with Notes on the Relative Frequency of Fibromata in Both Races," published in *The Chicago Medical Recorder,* he noted that, despite the literature and the information imparted in the best medical colleges regarding the incidence of ovarian cysts, the condition did affect blacks. As proof of his position, he stated that between 1886 and 1893 he had surgically removed ovarian cysts from blacks in Chicago; moreover, he had seen the condition among black women at the Washington, D.C., morgue and in the wards at Freedmen's Hospital. As further evidence, Williams cited the findings of the prominent New Orleans surgeon Rudolph Matas, who had also observed the condition in several blacks at that city's Charity Hospital. A longtime proponent of better health care for African Americans, Williams cautioned that generalizations regarding the absence or presence of certain conditions among blacks were likely to be incorrect, as many blacks received neither proper diagnosis nor treatment.

Final Years

In 1924 Williams's wife, the former Alice Johnson, died. Two years later, Williams suffered a stroke and went into semiretirement at his home in Michigan. He died there on August 4, 1931.

—*Betty L. Plummer*

Suggested Readings:

Buckler, Helen. *Daniel Hale Williams, Negro Surgeon.* New York: Pitman, 1968.

_____. *Doctor Dan, Pioneer in American Surgery.* Boston: Little, Brown, 1954.

Fenderson, Lewis R. *Daniel Hale Williams: Open-Heart Doctor.* New York: McGraw-Hill, 1971.

Jenkins, Edward S. *To Fathom More: African American Scientists and Inventors.* Lanham, Md.: University Press of America, 1996.

Patterson, Lillie. *Sure Hands, Strong Heart: The Life of Daniel Hale Williams.* Nashville: Abingdon Press, 1981.

Williams, David Welford (b. March 20, 1910, Atlanta, Georgia—May 6, 2000, Los Angeles, Calif.): Attorney and jurist. Williams received his education from Los Angeles Junior College, UCLA (A.B., 1934), and the University of Southern California Law School (LL.B., 1937). He became a JUDGE on the Los Angeles Municipal Court in 1956 and joined the Superior Court in 1962. In 1969 he was elevated to the federal bench, becoming the first black federal judge west of the Mississippi.

Williams, Eddie Nathan (b. August 18, 1932, Memphis, Tennessee): Political scientist. Williams became president of the Joint Center for Political Studies in 1972. The center, cosponsored by Howard University, tries to meet the information and technical needs of minority elected officials associated with the National Black Caucus. It provides information on voting patterns and on proposed legislation, among other data.

Williams holds a B.S. degree from the University of Illinois at Urbana (1954). He did postgraduate work at ATLANTA UNIVERSITY in 1957 and at Howard University in 1958. From 1955 to 1957, he was a radar officer in the U.S. Army. Following his discharge, he became a

Eddie Williams in 1990. *(AP/Wide World Photos)*

Children's Television Workshop and as chair of the National Coalition on Black Voter Participation.

reporter for the *Atlanta Daily World* newspaper. He was a fellow of the American Political Science Association in 1958, then became staff assistant for the U.S. Senate Committee on Foreign Relations. From 1961 to 1968, Williams was a foreign service officer with the State Department. He became vice president for public affairs at the University of Chicago in 1968 and served until 1972, when he joined the Joint Center for Political Studies.

Williams joined the Black Leadership Forum in 1977. He chaired an advisory commission on black population and advised the U.S. Census Bureau on the 1980 census. From 1970 to 1972, he was an editorial COLUMNIST for the *Chicago Sun-Times*. Williams also served as vice chair of the board of trustees of the National

Eric Williams at the time Trinidad was gaining its independence under his leadership. *(Library of Congress)*

Williams, Eric (September 25, 1911, Port of Spain, Trinidad—March 29, 1981, St. Anne, near Port of Spain, Trinidad): Political leader. Williams served as the leader of the modern nation of TRINIDAD AND TOBAGO for nearly twenty-five years.

In 1956 Eric Eustace Williams formed the first formal political party in Trinidad and Tobago. Known as the People's National Movement, the party won the national elections in September, 1956, with Williams being elected the chief minister of the country from 1956 to 1959, premier from 1959 to 1962, and prime minister from 1962 to 1981. Known as the "father" of his nation, Williams led Trinidad and Tobago into the Federation of the West Indies and to full independence from Britain in 1962.

Williams was educated at Queen's Royal College in England and won the Island Scholarship to Oxford University. At Oxford, he placed first in the first class of the History Honours School and earned his doctor of philosophy in 1938. Much of Williams's educational pursuits in England are documented in his book *Inward Hunger: The Education of a Prime Minister* (1969), one of more than thirty books that he wrote.

In 1939 Williams went to the United States and taught at HOWARD UNIVERSITY, serving as an assistant professor of social

2697

and political sciences. While at Howard, Williams began working as a consultant to the Anglo-American Caribbean Commission, a body established after World War II to study the future of the region. In 1948 he left Howard and served as head of the research branch of the Caribbean Commission until 1955. Returning to Trinidad and Tobago in 1955, Williams served as the country's political leader for nearly two and a half decades, dying in office in 1981.

—*Alvin K. Benson*

See also: Politics and government.

Williams, Franklin H. (b. October 22, 1917, Flushing, New York): Political appointee and association executive. Williams graduated from Lincoln University with his A.B. degree in 1941 and attended law school at Fordham University, earning his J.D. degree in 1945. Upon graduation, Williams served as assistant special counsel for the NATIONAL ASSOCIATION FOR THE ADVANCEMENT OF COLORED PEOPLE (NAACP) national office from 1945 to 1950. He was sent to CALIFORNIA to serve as the director of the NAACP's West Coast office from 1950 to 1959.

Williams's political career began in 1959, when he was appointed to serve as assistant attorney general for the state of California. He left that post in 1960 to become African regional director for the U.S. Peace Corps. In 1963 Williams was appointed to serve as U.S. representative to the United Nations Economic and Social Council. Williams left the U.N. in 1965 to accept an appointment as U.S. ambassador to Ghana, a post he held until 1968. While in the foreign service, Williams was chairman of the Association of Black Ambassadors and served as vice chairman of the Council of American Ambassadors.

He left public office to become director of Columbia University's Urban Center, also serving as president of the Phelps-Stokes Fund. In addition, Williams served as director on the boards of various corporations including Chemical Bank, Consolidated Edison of New York, and Borden, Inc.

See also: Diplomats.

Williams, George Washington (October 16, 1849, Bedford Springs, Pennsylvania—August 4, 1891, Blackpool, England): Historian, clergyman, lawyer, and legislator. Williams was probably the first professional African American historian. Although he had little opportunity for formal learning early in his life and pursued several occupations before beginning his principal career, he went on to become a noted historian.

The second child of mulatto parents, Williams trained to be a barber; then, at age fourteen, he falsified his name and age to join the Union army during the CIVIL WAR. After the war he joined the Mexican army and then re-

George Washington Williams, the first professional African American historian. *(Associated Publishers, Inc.)*

joined the U.S. Army. Following his military experience, Williams pursued a theological education and pastored for a time before resigning to found and become editor of a journal, *The Commoner*. His theological training would influence the style of all of his writing. In the 1870's, Williams began the study of law and supported himself by clerking in the Internal Revenue office and writing for the *Cincinnati Commercial* under the name Arisitides. In 1879 he was elected to the Ohio House of Representatives.

Williams said that his decision to become a full-time historian was based on the occasion of a Fourth of July speech he delivered at a centennial celebration. His foremost work, *History of the Negro Race in America from 1619 to 1880*, was published in 1883. The work's depth and scope marked a milestone in African American HISTORIOGRAPHY.

—*Victoria Price*

Williams, Hosea (b. January 5, 1926, Attapulgus, Georgia): Civil rights activist and clergyman. An ordained minister, businessman, politician, and lifetime civil rights crusader, Williams came to fame in the CIVIL RIGHTS movement of the 1960's. An integral part of the SOUTHERN CHRISTIAN LEADERSHIP CONFERENCE (SCLC), begun in ATLANTA, GEORGIA, under the direction of Martin Luther KING, Jr., Williams was a vigorous participant in the marches, demonstrations, boycotts, sit-ins, strikes, and other nonviolent direct action protects of the movement. He was arrested more than one hundred times for his involvement activities.

Williams became a unique voice and a contro-versial figure in national, state, and local politics, as well as in the religious ministry. Serving as pastor of the Martin Luther King, Jr., People's Church of Love, Incorporated, beginning in 1972, he simultaneously functioned as a successful businessman and holder of a number of organizational leadership positions and political offices in the state, city, and country. He began publishing the *Crusader Newspaper* in 1961 and kept it going for decades. He served as organizer and president of the Atlanta chapter of the SCLC from 1967 to 1969, as SCLC national executive director from 1969 to 1971, and as regional vice president from 1970 to 1971.

Williams's business experience includes the presidency of Kingwell Chemical Corporation (1975-1976) and the founding of Southeastern Chemical Manufacturing and Distribution Corporation in 1976. He was elected as representative to the Georgia state legislature in 1974. After his tenure as representative, he was elected to the Atlanta City Council. Later he was elected to the De Kalb County Commission. Williams claimed to be an independent but ran in elections as a Democrat because of African American preference for that party. In 1980 he served as an adviser to Ronald Reagan.

Hosea Williams instructing civil rights marchers in Selma, Alabama, in February, 1965. *(AP/Wide World Photos)*

Williams, John Alfred (b. December 5, 1925, Jackson, Mississippi): Novelist, journalist, social critic, and educator. In his early career, Williams wrote for several newspapers, including *The National Leader, Progressive Herald, The Age,* and *The Defender,* and worked for *Newsweek* magazine as a correspondent in Africa (1964-1965). Previously, he had written for EBONY and JET as a correspondent based in Spain (1958-1959). In 1961 Williams was awarded a fellowship by the American Academy of Arts and Letters, but the fellowship was rejected by the American Academy in Rome in what many observers at the time believed was an act of blatant racial discrimination. Williams later traveled extensively in AFRICA. In addition to his journalistic work there for *Newsweek,* he published a nonfiction book entitled *Africa: Her History, Lands, and People* (1962). Williams also wrote *The King God Didn't Save: Reflections on the Life and Death of Martin Luther King, Jr.* (1970). He served the Black Academy of Arts and Letters as director in the early 1970's. He taught English and creative writing at several prestigious American universities, including Rutgers, whose faculty he joined in 1979.

Williams is best known as a novelist and has several complex and highly regarded novels to his credit. Beginning with his first novel, *The Angry Ones* (1961), he followed with *Night Song* (1961), *Sissie* (1963), *The Man Who Cried I Am* (1967), *Sons of Darkness, Sons of Light* (1969), *Captain Blackman* (1972), *Mothersill and the Foxes* (1975), *The Junior Bachelor Society* (1976), *!Click Song* (1982), and *Jacob's Ladder* (1987).

His novels directly confront both racial and class tensions in American society. Williams, in several interviews, compared his style and artistic design to the patterns of jazz music. In his fiction, he experiments with the motions of time, multiple voices, and variations of form. Additionally, many of Williams's works deal with the challenges his African American characters face in reconciling the legacy of collective African American history with their own experience as individuals in American society. In this sense, his novels critique the dynamics of American culture as well as particular aspects of African American experience.

Williams, Maggie (b. December 25, 1954, Kansas City, Missouri): Political appointee. In 1993 Margaret Ann "Maggie" Williams was appointed to serve as chief of staff to First Lady Hillary Rodham Clinton. In this post, Williams handled scheduling, matters of protocol, and press contacts for the First Lady. As a member of the inner circle at the White House, Williams became one of the top-ranking African American officials in the Clinton administration.

In 1994 Williams and other high-level administrators were summoned to appear before a congressional hearing to answer questions about the involvement of the Clintons in the Whitewater investment partnership. Williams was questioned again in 1995 concerning her knowledge of events and activities at the White House that occurred in the wake of the 1993 suicide death of Clinton adviser Vincent Foster. This second round of questioning focused on Williams's role in the disposition of certain documents and files taken from Foster's office that pertained to the Clinton family's personal affairs.

Williams, Mary Lou (Mary Elfrieda Scruggs; May 8, 1910, Atlanta, Georgia—May 28, 1981, Durham, North Carolina): JAZZ pianist and composer. Williams was one of the first African American female jazz pianists, composers, and arrangers to achieve national recognition. In the later stages of her career, she composed and performed pieces which were inspired by her religious faith. Although she was born in the South, she was reared in Pittsburgh, PENNSYLVANIA, having been part of a family that in-

Jazz pianist Mary Lou Williams. *(AP/Wide World Photos)*

cluded her stepfather, whose last name, Burley, Williams assumed in her youth. Her professional career developed rapidly, and by 1925 she was performing with John Williams, whom she married.

Williams's recognition as a pianist during a time when most ensembles contained only male instrumentalists was highlighted by her joining, in 1930, the Andy Kirk ensemble, which became known as Andy Kirk and the Twelve Clouds of Joy. Williams eventually served as both arranger and pianist for the ensemble during the 1930's. Her skills as an arranger were also evident in her writing for the orchestras of Benny Goodman, Earl HINES, and Duke ELLINGTON. In 1942 Williams formed her own ensemble, which included Shorty Baker. As part of the emerging bop movement, Williams was associated with Dizzy GILLESPIE, for whom she also wrote arrangements. Her international reputation was furthered by a two-year European tour beginning in 1952.

A major transition occurred in Williams's professional career in the mid-1950's, when she embarked on religiously inspired activities. She reemerged in the 1970's, working in her later years as a soloist or in trio format, performing both ragtime and avant-garde music. One of the culminating recordings of her career was *The History of Jazz* (1970), which contained solo piano work as well as narrative history. She became artist-in-residence at Duke University in 1977. Among her noted recordings as a leader are "Zodiac Suite" (1945), "In London" (1953), "Black Christ of the Andes" (1963), and "My Mama Pinned a Rose on Me" (1977).

Williams, Ozzie (b. 1921): Aeronautical engineer. O. S. "Ozzie" Williams was the first African American to be employed as an aeronautical engineer by Republic Aviation, Inc. In the 1990's, he worked as vice president of Grumman International, where his projects included the application of solar and wind energy to Africa's needs. Williams received his baccalaureate and master's degrees in aeronautical engineering from New York University's College of Engineering. Upon receipt of his graduate degree, he joined Greer Hydraulics, Inc., where he served as a group project engineer and helped to develop the first airborne radar beacon for locating crashed aircraft.

As a specialist in small rocket engine design, Williams was also associated with the Reaction Motors Division of Thiokol Chemical Corporation. In 1961 he joined Grumman International to develop and produce the control rocket systems for the National Aeronautics and Space Administration (NASA) that guided lunar modules during moon landings. He also served as the engineer manager responsible for developing the lunar module's reaction control rocket system during the *Apollo* space program. These maneuvering engines on the lunar landing module were credited with helping to save the crew of the *Apollo 13* mission.

Williams, Robert Franklin (b. 1925): Political activist. Williams became one of the most notorious figures of the Civil Rights movement of the 1960's. Williams was the president of the NATIONAL ASSOCIATION FOR THE ADVANCEMENT OF COLORED PEOPLE (NAACP) chapter in Monroe, North Carolina, in the late 1950's. The NAACP was hated by southern white racists and was the target of numerous acts of racial harassment and terror. Williams's chapter was no exception; what he did about this harassment was exceptional, however. He organized a rifle club of fifty black men and drilled them in self-defense tactics. The group violently repelled a KU KLUX KLAN attack on the home of a local NAACP official. Williams then called on other southern NAACP chapters threatened by racial terrorists to emulate his chapter by forming gun clubs. Williams's actions disconcerted the national office of the NAACP, and at the annual convention of the NAACP in 1959, Williams and his chapter were expelled.

For the next few years, Williams spoke out in favor of armed resistance to southern racism. In 1962 he published *Negroes with Guns*, which outlined his strategy of using armed force to achieve racial equality. That year, he fled the country to escape prosecution on charges of kidnapping. Traveling to Cuba and then to China, Williams continued to advocate armed revolution as a way for African Americans to achieve freedom in the United States.

Williams, Vanessa (b. March 18, 1963, Millwood, New York): Singer, actor, and beauty pageant winner. On September 17, 1983, history was made in Atlantic City, New Jersey, when a twenty-year-old junior from Syracuse University named Vanessa Lynn Williams was selected to become the first African American woman to win the title of Miss America.

During her reign as Miss America in 1984, Williams received considerable media atten-

Vanessa Williams adjusting her Miss America crown during her 1984 coronation. *(AP/Wide World Photos)*

tion, made numerous talk show appearances, and was considered one of the most exemplary winners of the title. Her popularity and her title were threatened on July 20, 1984, when the Miss America headquarters received word that *Penthouse* magazine was planning to publish photographs of Williams posing nude with another woman in its September issue.

Upon hearing this, the pageant demanded that Williams relinquish her crown within seventy-two hours. Reluctantly but gracefully Williams resigned her title on July 24, 1984, during a televised press conference in New York City. First runner-up Suzette Charles of Mays Landing, New York, filled the remaining several weeks of the 1984 reign.

Controversy and Fallout
After the *Penthouse* controversy spilled over into the public arena, many Americans began

to express their opinions about Williams's loss of the pageant title. More than a few people chided the pageant for hypocrisy, arguing that the pageant promoted sex as well as sexist behavior by having young women in their late teens and early twenties parading on stage in swimsuits and evening gowns.

The African American community was divided on the issue. Some believed that Williams was an embarrassment; some were convinced that Williams was the victim of a racist conspiracy. Some African Americans believed that she was not representative of their community because of her light-skinned features, light hair, and green eyes. Williams also received hate mail from white racists who resented seeing an African American woman wearing the Miss America crown.

Beauty Pageant Winners

Aiken, Kimberly Clarice (b. 1975?, Columbia, S.C.). Miss America 1994. Representing South Carolina, Aiken was the first black Miss America from the South. During her reign, she worked with Habitat for Humanity and founded the Homeless Education and Resource Organization in her hometown of Columbia. Afterward, she worked as an accountant while pursuing a singing career.

Berry, Halle. Miss Ohio/U.S.A. and runner-up in Miss U.S.A. 1986. *See main text entry.*

Charles, Suzette (b. Mar. 2, 1963, N.J.). As the first runner-up in the 1984 Miss America pageant, Charles—who represented NEW JERSEY—succeeded Vanessa WILLIAMS as Miss America after the latter was stripped of her title during the end of her reign. As a child, Charles became an experienced show business entertainer; after completing Williams's reign, she began a career as a singer.

Gist, Carole (b. 1970, Detroit, Mich.). First African American to win the title of Miss U.S.A., in 1990. As a student at Northwood Institute, Gist entered the pageant as Miss MICHIGAN. At the end of her reign, she filed an $18 million lawsuit against the pageant, claiming discrimination, poor working conditions, and a failure to deliver all promised prizes.

Kennedy, Jayne (b. Nov. 27, 1951, Washington, D.C.). Miss Ohio/U.S.A. 1970. After completing her reign, Kennedy worked as a network television sportscaster and appeared in television shows through the 1970's. Her film appearances include *Let's Do It Again* (1975); *Body and Soul* (1981), in which she play opposite her then-husband, Leon Isaac Kennedy; and *Night Trap* (1993).

Moore, Kenya (b. c. 1971). Representing DETROIT, MICHIGAN, Moore became the second black Miss U.S.A. in 1993. After her reign she worked as a model and actress and appeared in many televison series and such films as *Waiting to Exhale* (1995). Her first leading role was in *Trois* (1999).

Turner, Debbye (b. 1965, Ark.). Miss America 1990. Turner was the second African American woman to win the title. While a veterinary science student at the University of Missouri, she represented the state of MISSOURI in the pageant. Turner created some controversy when she stated that "being black is the very least of who I am." After her reign she became a doctor of veterinary medicine. In the late 1990's she became the host of a daily television program in St. Louis.

AP/Wide World Photos

Vincent, Marjorie (b. Nov. 21, 1964, Chicago, Ill.). Miss America 1991. While a third-year law student at NORTH CAROLINA's Duke University, Vincent competed as Miss ILLINOIS. In addition to her academic achievements, Vincent was an accomplished classical pianist and was fluent in French and Creole. During her reign, she focussed on issues concerning battered women. During the late 1990's Vincent worked as a news anchor on a Peoria, Illinois, television station.

Winfrey, Oprah. Miss Black Tennessee. *See main text entry.*

Rebounding from Scandal

Gradually, Williams began to recover from what at first appeared to be a devastating blow to her aspirations for a career in show business. Her personal life also became more settled; in 1987 she married Ramon Hervey, a public relations executive who had become her manager; they soon had two daughters, Melanie and Jillian, and a son, Devin. She and Hervey divorced in 1997, and she later married professional basketball player Rick Fox.

Through Hervey's efforts, Williams was cast in a few film roles, but she and Hervey soon decided to concentrate on a singing career for her. Williams was quickly successful. In 1988 she was nominated for a Grammy Award as Best New Artist. By 1994 she had recorded three albums: *The Right Stuff* (1989), *The Comfort Zone* (1991), and *The Sweetest Days* (1994). The first two albums went gold and double platinum respectively. The single "Save the Best for Last" was a number one hit on the *Billboard* charts for almost two months and was nominated for several Grammys in 1992. In 1993 she reached number three on the pop music charts with "Love Is," a duet with Brian McKnight that was featured on the sound track of the Fox television series *Beverly Hills 90210*. Williams also appeared as a host on the VH-1 cable music program *The Soul of VH-1*.

Stage and Screen Career

In the 1990's Williams expanded her musical career to the Broadway stage and Hollywood. In 1994 she was chosen to replace Tony Award-winning actor Chita Rivera in the lead role of Aurora in the critically acclaimed Broadway production of *Kiss of the Spider Woman*. Williams's performance received positive reviews from critics. She was so well received that the play was extended through January of 1995, several months beyond its original closing date. Williams was also selected to record "Colors of the Wind," a song on the sound track of the Walt Disney animated film, *Pocahontas* (1995). In 1995 Williams appeared in a television remake of the musical *Bye Bye Birdie*, in which she performed the role of Rosie DeLeon.

The albums *Star Bright*, a Christmas album, and *Next*, a rhythm-and-blues album, were released in 1996 and 1997 respectively. Ready to give Hollywood another try, Williams was cast opposite Arnold Schwarzenegger in the film *Eraser* (1996). More films followed, including *Hoodlum* (1997, with Laurence FISHBURNE and Cicely TYSON) and *Dance with Me* (1998).

—*Elwood David Watson*

Former Miss America Vanessa Williams at the Grammy Awards ceremonies in 1989. *(AP/Wide World Photos)*